Migrating to Opportunity

Migrating to Opportunity

Overcoming Barriers to
Labor Mobility in Southeast Asia

Mauro Testaverde, Harry Moroz, Claire H. Hollweg,
and Achim Schmillen

WORLD BANK GROUP

Contents

Boxes

Figures

Tables

Foreword

Southeast Asia stands out globally on the movement of people across national borders. Among the countries of the Association of Southeast Asian Nations (ASEAN),
migration has continued to grow, while the share of intraregional movements in most
other regions has declined. Migrants from Cambodia, Lao PDR, and Myanmar head
to Thailand to work in agriculture, domestic work, construction, and manufacturing.
Indonesian migrants go to Malaysia for agricultural and domestic work. Malaysians
themselves work in Singapore, many of them commuting daily across the narrow Straits
of Johor. Malaysia and Thailand are among the few developing countries that have
already become major destinations for migrants. Singapore (another major destination) and the Philippines (among the largest origin countries) have highly sophisticated
migration systems. Migration within the region is expected to increase as the ASEAN
Economic Community, which was launched in 2015, aims to promote the free mobility
of professionals and skilled workers within the region.

These movements of people are a consequence of the region's rapid economic
growth and its diversity as well as a contributor to its continued vitality. The intra-
ASEAN differences are substantial: The region's wealthiest country is 25 times richer
than its poorest. The median age of the oldest ASEAN country is nearly twice that of
the youngest country. In some countries, labor shortages have already emerged while
others struggle to produce adequate employment for their still-growing and youthful
populations. Countries such as Singapore, Thailand, and Vietnam will be faced with a
shrinking labor force while Cambodia, Indonesia, Lao PDR, Myanmar, and the Philippines are expected to see their labor forces grow in the next two decades. The mismatch
in the supply and demand of labor will encourage people of working age to seek employment in different parts of the region. Migrants can already earn substantially more by

moving across borders. Average wages in high-income Singapore are at least five times those of any other ASEAN country, while a Cambodian migrant can earn three times more by moving for work in Thailand. Migrants' remittances benefit their households at home and help reduce poverty. And this diaspora helps bring back capital, knowledge, and skills when the migrants return home. In receiving countries, migrants help address labor market shortages, boosting production and stimulating competitiveness.

Yet, as *Migrating to Opportunity* shows, there is potential for even greater gain—to migrants and their families as well as the countries they leave and the ones in which they work. Within ASEAN, inappropriate policies and ineffective institutions to manage migration mean that there are missed opportunities. These arise from credit constraints faced by the poorest households, lack of information about available jobs, and high recruitment costs. Restrictive migration policies and weaknesses in the systems to manage migration are particular culprits. As a result, many potential migrants, often the poorest and most vulnerable, are unable to migrate while others seek out informal, often more dangerous, channels to avoid the expense of using formal, safer routes.

Migrating to Opportunity also suggests policy solutions to reduce these barriers that have benefits for both sending and receiving countries. These include providing information to migrants about employment opportunities, offering migration orientation programs to improve employment experiences abroad, and linking migration admissions systems to labor market demand. Overall, the book argues that destination countries should work toward migration systems that are responsive to their economic needs and consistent with domestic policies. Sending countries, on the other hand, should work to balance protections for migrant workers with the imperatives of sustaining growth.

The book shows that this is the time for the countries of Southeast Asia to ensure that their migration policies better match the region's evolving economic needs. The initiation of the ASEAN Economic Community in 2015 was a significant step toward deeper regional integration and included measures to promote mobility within the region. However, as *Migrating to Opportunity* shows, more ambitious action is needed to realize even greater benefits for the migrants themselves as well as for the countries they leave and the countries that receive them.

Sudhir Shetty
Chief Economist
East Asia and Pacific Region
The World Bank Group

Michal Rutkowski
Senior Director
Social Protection and Jobs Global Practice
The World Bank Group

Acknowledgments

This book was prepared by a team drawn from the Social Protection and Jobs Global Practice and the Trade and Competitiveness Global Practice of the World Bank. The team was led by Mauro Testaverde, and comprised Claire Hollweg, Harry Moroz, and Achim Schmillen. Jesse Doyle, Çağlar Özden, Farhan Samanani, Michele Tuccio, Soonhwa Yi, and Claudia Zambra provided inputs. Background papers for the book were written by Claire Hollweg, Harry Moroz, Farhan Samanani, Michele Tuccio, and Claudia Zambra, and an opinion survey was conducted and analyzed by a team managed by Carl Patrick Hanlon that included Mai Thi Hong Bo, Sharon Felzer, Livia Pontes Fialho, Diana Ya-Wai Chung, and Jane Zhang.

The team thanks Truman Packard for his guidance during the early stage of this work and Manolo Abella for his useful comments. The team also thanks Wendy Cunningham for her detailed comments and support. Ahsan Butt provided excellent research assistance. The book benefited from discussions with representatives from the ILO and IOM and from consultations with World Bank staff during a meeting held in Beijing in November 2015. The team would like to thank the World Bank country teams for their help in accessing the data necessary to conduct the study. Thanks also to Felix Schmieding (UN Development Programme) for the help in obtaining data for Myanmar.

During the preparation of the book, the team received insightful comments and useful material from Samik Adhikari, Andras Bodor, Laurent Bossavie, Yoonyoung Cho, Gabriel Demombynes, Anastasiya Denisova, Camilla Holmemo, Manjula Luthria, Mattia Makovec, Rafael Munoz Moreno, Darian Naidoo, Philip O'Keefe, Michael Packard, Ririn Purnamasari, Frederico Gil Sander, Rebekah Lee Smith, Nikola Spatafora, Brasukra Gumilang Sudjana, Mathis Wagner, Dewen Wang, and Maria Monica Wihardja.

The work was conducted under the general guidance of Sudhir Shetty and Jehan Arulpragasam. The team also thanks the staff of the ASEAN Secretariat for productive discussions during the concept stage of this work. The team is grateful for the excellent advice provided by two peer reviewers at the concept note stage (Ahmad Ahsan and Manjula Luthria), and by three peer reviewers at the decision review stage (Manjula Luthria, Saiyed Shabih Ali Mohib, and Elizabeth Ruppert Bulmer). We thank Maya Razat and Cecile Wodon for providing excellent administrative support.

The work conducted as part of this book was made possible through a grant from the World Bank's multidonor Trust Fund for Trade and Development.

About the Authors

Mauro Testaverde is an economist in the Social Protection and Jobs Global Practice of the East Asia and Pacific Region at the World Bank. He led the report team. Mauro's work focuses on labor mobility, human capital development, and the interaction of education, human resource management, and labor market policies. Mauro's research on these topics has been published in economic journals including the *Scandinavian Journal of Economics* and the *World Bank Economic Review*. Since 2012 Mauro has been part of World Bank teams providing technical and analytical assistance in the areas of labor policy and social protection systems. Before joining the World Bank, Mauro was part of the migration research team at the University of Southampton (U.K.) where he earned a PhD in Economics and an MA in Econometrics.

Harry Moroz is an economist in the Social Protection and Jobs Global Practice of the East Asia and Pacific Region at the World Bank. His work focuses on migration and migration systems, new approaches to labor market information, labor market programming, and risk management. Prior to joining the World Bank, Harry worked for the Chief Data Officer in the Mayor's Office of the City of Chicago and for the Drum Major Institute for Public Policy in New York City. He holds an MA in Public Policy from the University of Chicago.

Claire H. Hollweg is an economist in the Trade and Competitiveness Global Practice at the World Bank. She holds a PhD and an MA in Economics from the University of Adelaide. Prior to studying economics, she worked as a journalist and holds a BS in Journalism from the University of Colorado at Boulder. She also worked with the government of South Australia and the Pacific Economic Cooperation Council in Singapore.

Her research interests include development economics with a recent focus on the nexus of trade, labor markets, servicification of manufacturing, and upgrading in global value chains.

Achim Schmillen is an economist in the Social Protection and Jobs Global Practice of the East Asia and Pacific Region at the World Bank. He has 10 years of experience in research, analysis, policy advice, and technical assistance. His primary specialization is applied labor economics, and he has also worked extensively on social protection, education, and the economics of transition. Achim joined the World Bank in 2013 through the Young Professionals Program, and he initially worked as an economist for the South Asia Human Development Unit. His previous work experience includes time spent at the Institute for Employment Research (Nuremberg, Germany) and the Institute for East European Studies (Regensburg, Germany). Achim holds a PhD in economics from the University of Regensburg. He was a visiting researcher at the University of California, Berkeley, and a postdoc at the University of California, Los Angeles.

Abbreviations

AEC	ASEAN Economic Community
AQRF	ASEAN Qualifications Reference Framework
ASEAN	Association of Southeast Asian Nations
BNP2TKI	Badan Nasional Penempatan dan Perlindungan Tenaga Kerja Indonesia
CGE	Computable General Equilibrium
DIOC-E	Database on Immigrants in OECD and Non-OECD Countries (extended)
DOLAB	Department of Overseas Labor (Vietnam)
DOLISA	Department of Labour, Invalids and Social Affairs (Vietnam)
EAP	East Asia and Pacific
EPS	Employment Permit System (Republic of Korea)
EU	European Union
FDI	foreign direct investment
GDP	gross domestic product
ILMS	International Labor Migration Statistics Database in ASEAN
ILO	International Labour Organization
IOM	International Organization for Migration

ITS	Industrial Trainee Scheme (Republic of Korea)
KNOMAD	Global Knowledge Partnership on Migration and Development
MAC	Migration Advisory Committee (United Kingdom)
MLSW	Ministry of Labor and Social Welfare (Lao PDR)
MOHA	Ministry of Home Affairs (Malaysia)
MOLIP	Ministry of Labor, Immigration, and Population (Myanmar)
MOLVT	Ministry of Labor and Vocational Training (Cambodia)
MOM	Ministry of Manpower (Singapore)
MOU	memorandum of understanding
MRAs	mutual recognition arrangements
NAFTA	North American Free Trade Agreement
NQFs	national qualifications frameworks
OECD	Organisation for Economic Co-operation and Development
OWWA	Overseas Workers Welfare Administration (Philippines)
POEA	Philippine Overseas Employment Administration
POLO	Philippine Overseas Labor Office
QRF	qualification reference framework
RP-T	Resident Pass-Talent (Malaysia)
TVET	technical and vocational education and training
VP(TE)	Visitors Pass (Temporary Employment) (Malaysia)

Overview

Workers in Southeast Asia are on the move

The movement of people in Southeast Asia is an issue of increasing importance. Countries of the Association of Southeast Asian Nations (ASEAN) send migrants throughout the world but are also important destinations for migrants from the region. ASEAN countries now supply 8 percent of the world's migrants, up from 6 percent in 1995. They host only 4 percent of the world's migrants, but intraregional migration has grown strongly. ASEAN is one of the few global regions in which the share of intraregional migration increased between 1995 and 2015 (figure O.1). This has turned Malaysia, Singapore, and Thailand into regional migration hubs (figure O.2a). These three countries are now home to 6.5 million ASEAN migrants, 96 percent of the total. Cambodia, Indonesia, the Lao People's Democratic Republic, Malaysia, and Myanmar are the major regional senders of migrants (figure O.2b).

Workers move throughout Southeast Asia in search of economic opportunities. Most migration in the region consists of low-skilled, often undocumented, migrants looking for better-paying jobs. These opportunities manifest themselves in a variety of ways. Cambodia is a well-known sender of migrants, but Vietnam also sends migrants across the long border with Cambodia to work in fishing and construction (MMN and AMC 2013). The Philippines is not only a significant sender of migrants to the Middle East and the United States but also the origin of about a quarter of the world's ship crews (IOM 2013). Malaysian workers commute each day across the narrow Straits of Johor to work in Singapore. Even though most migration in the region is low-skilled, Malaysia and Singapore have special programs to attract global talent.

FIGURE O.1

Change in the share of intraregional migration,1995–2015

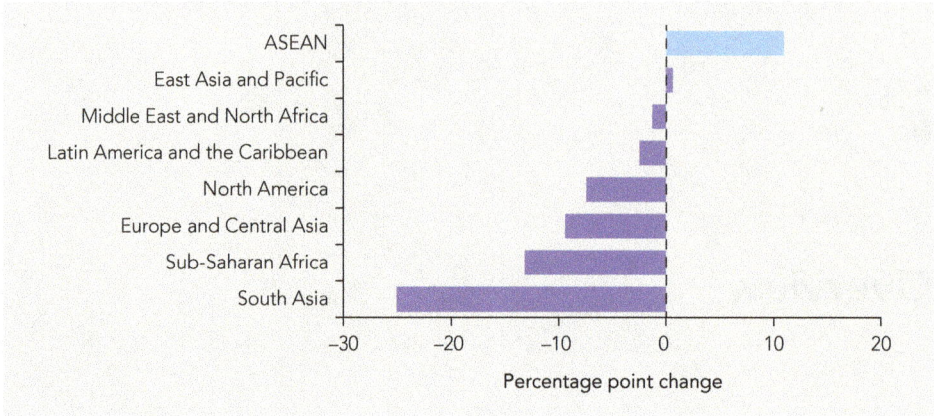

Source: UN 2015a.
Note: ASEAN = Association of Southeast Asian Nations.

FIGURE O.2

Intra-ASEAN migrant stock, 2015

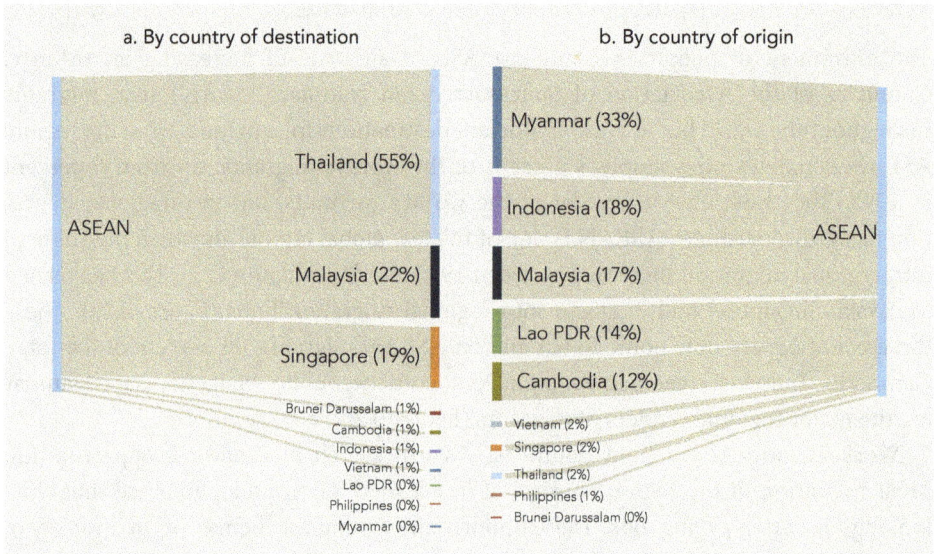

Source: UN 2015a.

This book highlights how mobility affects the well-being of workers, the constraints workers face when migrating for better opportunities, and the solutions to ease these constraints. The diversity of economic development in Southeast Asia means that there are ample opportunities for workers to seek out better jobs that pay higher wages. The book documents why workers are not always able to take advantage of these opportunities, what is lost when they are not able to take advantage of them, and potential policies that would expand their access to them.

Overarching themes of the book

1. ASEAN countries are significant senders of migrants globally, but also important destinations for migrants from the region.

2. Large intra-ASEAN migration flows are the result of significant diversity in economic development within the region.

3. Significant costs of international and domestic labor mobility in ASEAN limit the ability of workers to change firms, sectors, and locations.

4. The impacts of migration in the region are generally positive, although some groups lose out, and domestic policies play an important role in shaping these impacts.

5. Making movement between and within ASEAN countries less costly would improve the welfare of ASEAN workers.

6. Weaknesses in migration systems increase the costs of international labor mobility, but policy reforms can help to resolve these problems.

The rest of the overview is structured as follows. After discussing the steps that ASEAN member states have taken to facilitate labor mobility in the context of economic integration, the overview explains the benefits of increased labor mobility; explores the barriers to international migration; and presents the components of the migration system and the potential breakdowns within these components. The final section concludes with a discussion of strategies to reduce the barriers to international labor mobility.

The mobility of workers is an important part of economic integration in ASEAN

Through a series of agreements on subjects ranging from tariffs to harmonizing standards to the single regional market of the ASEAN Economic Community (AEC), the region has pursued an agenda of integration. In part as a result of these efforts, intraregional tariffs have declined significantly, and intraregional trade has increased from 17 percent of the region's world trade in 1990 to about 25 percent today (OECD 2016). However, regional integration is not complete. Nontariff barriers remain a significant issue, and ASEAN countries do not seem to be any more open to each other in the services trade than to countries outside the region (ASEAN Secretariat and World Bank 2015; OECD 2016). Indeed, according to recent research, incomplete integration is holding ASEAN back. Removing the remaining barriers to integration would significantly boost gross domestic product (GDP), exports, and total employment; and it would hasten structural change in several countries (ILO and ADB 2014).

Workers, too, can benefit from the opportunities created by further integration, but how much they do will depend in part on their freedom of movement. Workers must be able to move across jobs, sectors, and even countries in order to take advantage of new economic opportunities. However, barriers to labor mobility make such moves costly. These barriers include time-consuming job searches; skill mismatches that occur when a worker's skills are not perfectly transferable across firms, occupations, or sectors; rigid employment policies such as employment protection legislation; restrictive immigration systems; and high recruitment costs. In the absence of such barriers, workers would be free to switch jobs in pursuit of higher wages. Instead, they frequently forgo large wage gains because the gains fail to outweigh the associated barriers (Hollweg et al. 2014).

ASEAN member states have taken steps to reduce the barriers to labor mobility as part of their efforts to promote deeper regional integration (figure O.3). The 1995 ASEAN Framework Agreement on Services provided for the temporary movement of skilled professionals across borders. Mobility-related commitments were later collected in the ASEAN Agreement on Movement of Natural Persons. One of the five pillars of the AEC, which envisions a single regional market, is the free movement of skilled workers alongside the free movement of goods, services, and investment, and the freer flow of capital. In laying out the vision for the AEC in the Declaration of ASEAN Concord II in 2003, ASEAN member states pledged to "facilitate movement of business persons, skilled labor, and talents" in order to promote economic integration. The 2007 AEC Blueprint laid out specific actions to accomplish this, including facilitating the issuance

FIGURE O.3

ASEAN actions to facilitate labor mobility, 1995–2015

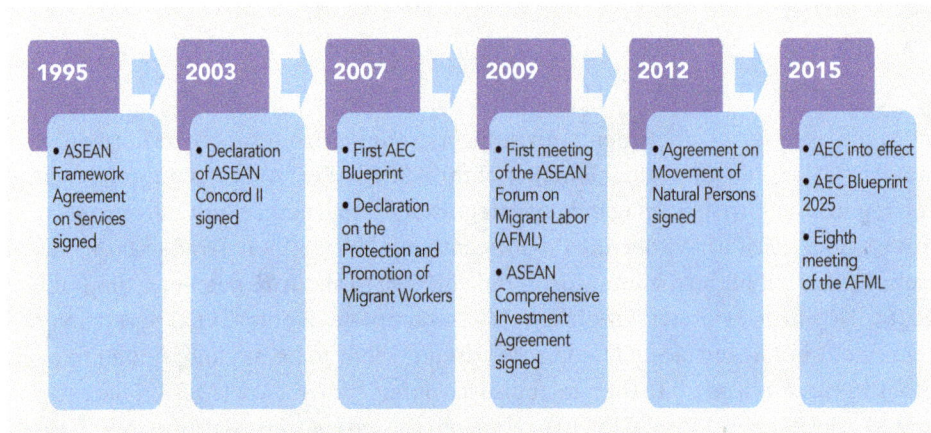

1995	2003	2007	2009	2012	2015
• ASEAN Framework Agreement on Services signed	• Declaration of ASEAN Concord II signed	• First AEC Blueprint • Declaration on the Protection and Promotion of Migrant Workers	• First meeting of the ASEAN Forum on Migrant Labor (AFML) • ASEAN Comprehensive Investment Agreement signed	• Agreement on Movement of Natural Persons signed	• AEC into effect • AEC Blueprint 2025 • Eighth meeting of the AFML

Note: ASEAN = Association of Southeast Asian Nations; AEC = ASEAN Economic Community.

of visas and employment passes and working to harmonize and standardize qualifications. The AEC Blueprint 2025 envisions reducing and standardizing documentation requirements and improving the mutual recognition of professional qualifications.

However, progress on implementing regional commitments related to labor mobility has been limited. Mutual recognition arrangements, in which multiple countries agree to recognize professional qualifications and facilitate the mobility of professionals in those fields, are the major steps the AEC has taken in this direction; but they are narrow in scope. These arrangements currently cover only doctors, dentists, nurses, engineers, architects, accountants, and tourism professionals, who account for about 5 percent of employment in ASEAN countries (Batalova, Shymonyak, and Sugiyarto 2017). Relatively onerous qualification and verification processes remain in place, even for the covered professions. Finally, and perhaps most important, each state's migration procedures remain paramount, meaning that the decision regarding how many and what type of work visas to grant and whether to accept or reject an application for a visa continues to rest with individual ASEAN member countries. For instance, Thailand bans migrants from working in 39 occupations, including engineering, accounting, and architecture—which are covered by mutual recognition arrangements.

Moreover, the AEC's focus on high-skilled migration ignores the majority of ASEAN migrants, who are low-skilled and often undocumented. The AEC does not have plans to facilitate the migration of low- or mid-skilled migrants, although some regional dialogue has taken place. In the 2007 Declaration on the Protection and Promotion of the Rights of Migrant Workers (Cebu Declaration on Migrant Workers), ASEAN member states agreed to promote the dignity of migrant workers, including those who are not documented, and to set forth the obligations of receiving and sending countries and of ASEAN itself. The ASEAN Forum on Migrant Labor was created to promote implementation of the declaration and has representatives from member states, employers, workers, and civil society (Asia-Pacific RCM Thematic Working Group 2015). However, the Cebu Declaration is nonbinding, and the instrument to protect migrant workers envisioned in it has not been adopted (Asia-Pacific RCM Thematic Working Group 2015; Martin and Abella 2014).

Lower barriers to mobility would make the region's workers better off

Lowering the barriers to mobility in ASEAN would increase the welfare gains workers receive from economic integration. Models of trade integration traditionally assume that workers are able to move seamlessly between jobs as integration creates new economic opportunities. However, workers' efforts to adjust to trade shocks can be disrupted by a wide range of barriers (Hollweg et al. 2014). Recognizing these barriers and incorporating them into models of trade integration can provide a more comprehensive picture of how workers are likely to be affected by integration. The economic modeling

FIGURE O.4
Estimated change in welfare under ASEAN trade integration

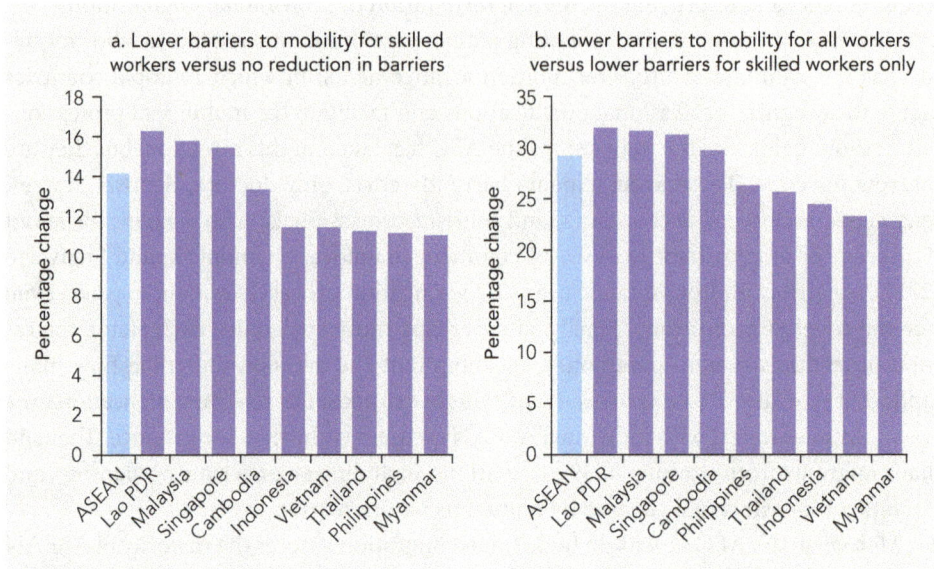

Source: Hollweg 2016.

in this book shows that trade integration has a substantially larger positive effect across all ASEAN countries when barriers to mobility are lowered for skilled workers, as the AEC currently envisions.[1] Regionwide, worker welfare would be 14 percent higher if these barriers were reduced (figure O.4a). With lower barriers to labor mobility, workers would be able to take advantage of higher wages, new employment opportunities, and more options to move to those employment opportunities. Worker welfare would improve even more across all ASEAN countries if barriers to mobility were lower for *all* workers. Regionwide, worker welfare would be 29 percent higher if barriers to mobility were reduced for all workers rather than only for skilled workers (figure O.4b).

Welfare gains manifest themselves in a variety of ways. The substantial literature on the impacts of migration on labor market outcomes provides concrete examples of how labor mobility affects the welfare of workers in migrant-destination countries, of workers in migrant-origin countries, and of migrant workers themselves.

First, migration can have positive impacts on the employment and wages of workers in destination countries, although these effects are generally small. Most evidence from high-income countries finds that migration has small impacts on the labor market outcomes of locals (Docquier, Özden, and Peri 2014; Longhi, Nijkamp, and Poot 2010). Results are generally small in East Asia as well, although larger impacts have been found in some cases. In Malaysia, for example, an additional 10 immigrants to a given state has been found to result in the employment of an additional 5 Malaysians who relocate to that state (Del Carpio et al. 2015). The impacts of immigration on wages are small and positive for local workers, but larger and negative for current migrants (Özden and Wagner 2016). In Malaysia, cheaper immigrant workers seem to lower production costs, which results in more output that, in turn, requires more employment.

However, certain groups of local workers in destination countries, particularly low-skilled ones, can be negatively affected by immigration, although these impacts are generally small and can be the result of rigid labor markets. Typically, low-skilled workers who have skills that are similar to those of migrant workers are at a greater risk of experiencing less positive or negative impacts. In Thailand, the impact of immigration on wages is modestly negative for local workers with less education, but positive for those with more education (figure O.5). Domestic labor market policies may be responsible for negative impacts on local workers. Rigid labor markets characterized by strong employment protection legislation—such as rules regarding firing, temporary employment, and collective dismissal—can make it more difficult for workers to switch jobs, firms, and geographic location in order to adjust to and benefit from the presence of immigrant workers (Angrist and Kugler 2003; D'Amuri and Peri 2014).

Second, nonmigrating workers benefit because out-migration tends to boost wages in sending countries. Significant out-migration can result in a contraction of the labor supply, which reduces competition and increases the wages of nonmigrant workers. In Mexico, a 10 percent decrease in workers in a given skill group as a result of out-migration was found to increase average wages by about 4 percent (Mishra 2007). Similar impacts have been found in Honduras, Moldova, Poland, and Puerto Rico (Mishra 2014).

Third, migrant workers themselves benefit from migration because of significant differences in wages across ASEAN countries, which create opportunities for workers

FIGURE O.5

Change in the wages of Thai workers due to the doubling of the size of the immigrant workforce in five immigration-intensive provinces

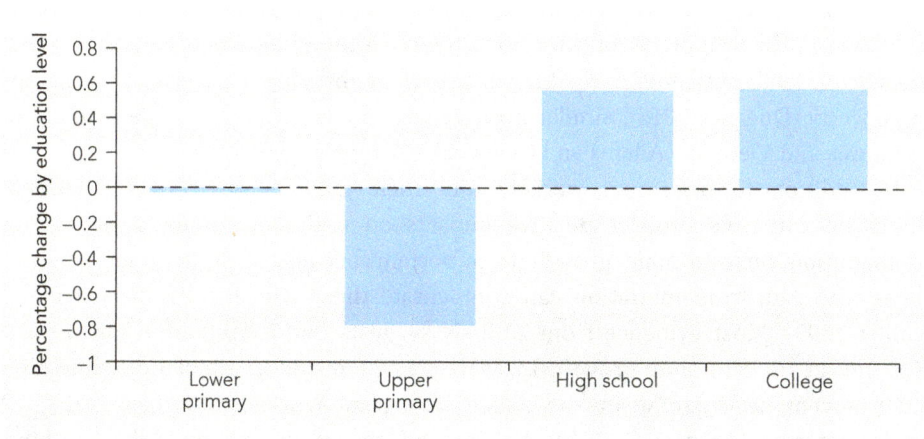

Source: Lathapipat 2014.

FIGURE O.6

Average monthly wages in ASEAN countries

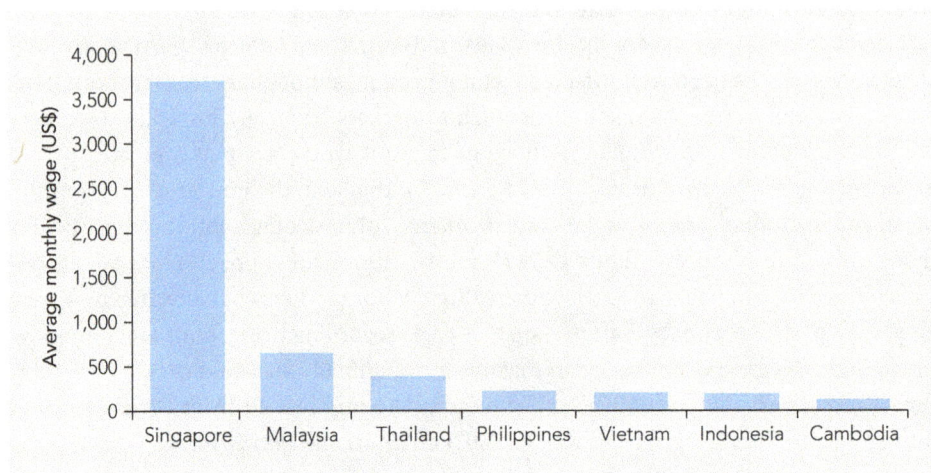

Source: ILO 2014.
Note: The year is 2013 for all countries except Cambodia, for which the year is 2012. ASEAN = Association of Southeast Asian Nations.

in countries with lower wages to gain significantly simply by moving across borders (figure O.6). Singapore's average monthly wage of US$3,694 in 2013 is more than 30 times that of Cambodia. Malaysia's average monthly wage is triple that of Indonesia, the Philippines, and Vietnam.

Even members of the household who do not migrate benefit from remittances that boost budgets and reduce poverty. Approximately US$62 billion in remittances were sent to ASEAN countries in 2015. Total remittances are 10 percent of GDP in the Philippines, 7 percent in Vietnam, 5 percent in Myanmar, and 3 percent in Cambodia (figure O.7). Studying 71 low- and middle-income countries, Adams and Page (2005) estimate that a 10 percent increase in remittances is associated with a 3.5 percent reduction in the proportion of poor households. In the Philippines, households that are able to send a member abroad have twofold or threefold greater odds of escaping poverty (Ducanes 2015). Similar positive impacts on poverty have been found in Indonesia and Vietnam (Adams and Cuecuecha 2014; Nguyen 2008).

In addition to benefiting workers and their families directly, international migration can have broader positive impacts on entire economies. The impact of migration on economic growth is important because it determines whether those who gain from migration can compensate those who lose (Felbermayr and Kohler 2009). Most evidence from ASEAN suggests that immigration has a positive impact on economic growth. In Malaysia, for instance, simulations find that a 10 percent net increase in low-skilled immigrant workers increases real GDP by 1.1 percent (Ahsan et al. 2014). In Thailand, recent analysis finds that, without migrants in the labor force, GDP would fall by 0.75 percent (Pholphirul, Kamlai, and

FIGURE O.7

Remittances received as a percentage of GDP in ASEAN countries, 2015

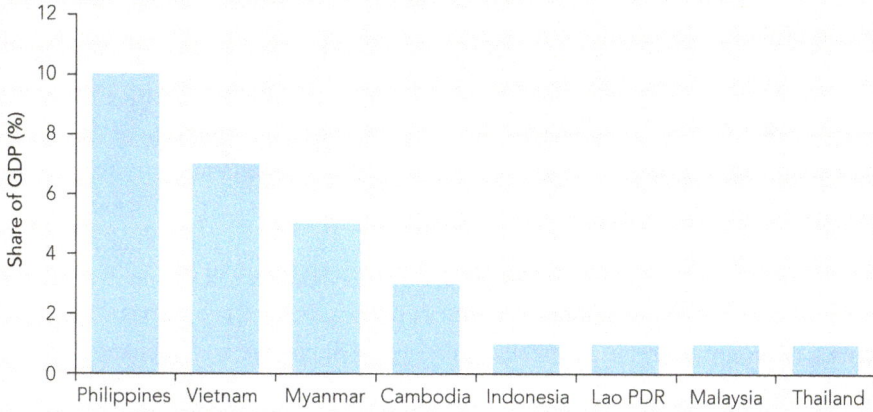

Source: World Bank Bilateral Remittance Matrix (database).

Rukumnuaykit 2010). Despite mixed evidence on the productivity impacts of immigration in ASEAN, there is no strong evidence that low-skilled migrants have a negative impact. In some cases, migrants seem to have facilitated the upgrading of local skills—for example, in Malaysia, significant immigration flows have coincided with rapidly increasing educational attainment.

While there is concern about the potential negative effects of "brain drain" in sending countries, these effects may be overstated and outweighed by "brain circulation." The emigration rates of high-skilled individuals in several ASEAN countries are quite high, at 15 percent in Cambodia and Lao PDR and around 10 percent in Singapore and Vietnam. Emigration of these highly skilled individuals is often perceived as costly because source countries pay for training that is used abroad and are depleted of the human capital necessary for economic growth. However, there are several reasons why the negative impacts of brain drain may be overstated and why brain circulation may be a more accurate description of high-skilled migration. First, high-skilled emigrants can have complex, nonlinear patterns of education, work experience, and migration in which training and work experience occur inside and outside of their country of birth (Özden and Phillips 2015). Second, high-skilled emigration can incentivize human capital formation in source countries by increasing the perceived returns to education, which are larger abroad, and encouraging nonmigrants to invest more in education. Research has found this to be the case for some, though not all, ASEAN countries (Beine, Docquier, and Rapoport 2008). Finally, migrants continue to engage with their source country in ways that can reduce the cost of transferring knowledge, ideas, and capital, leading to increased trade flows, larger foreign direct investment flows, and better institutions (Docquier and Rapoport 2012).

Workers still face significant costs to move

ASEAN's economic diversity means that there are significant opportunities to migrate for work. Many ASEAN countries have been part of the region's impressive growth, but large within-region disparities in income and population aging remain, making migration inside of ASEAN an attractive option. As noted, Singapore's average monthly wage is more than 30 times that of Cambodia (ILO 2014). Regional disparities in GDP per capita adjusted for purchasing power are similarly large: in all but one of ASEAN's 10 largest migration corridors, the GDP per capita of the destination country is at least twice that of the origin country (figure O.8). Different rates of population aging also affect the movement of people for employment in ASEAN. The working-age populations of Singapore, Thailand, and to a lesser extent, Malaysia will shrink in the coming decades, creating employment opportunities for migrants from countries with younger populations. For example, in 2015 the median age of Singapore and Thailand was higher than that of all of the main countries from which they received migrants (figure O.9).

However, barriers to labor mobility in the region limit the welfare gains from migration by preventing some people from moving for work and leading others to

FIGURE O.8

Ratio of destination- to origin-country GDP per capita in ASEAN's 10 largest migration corridors, 2015

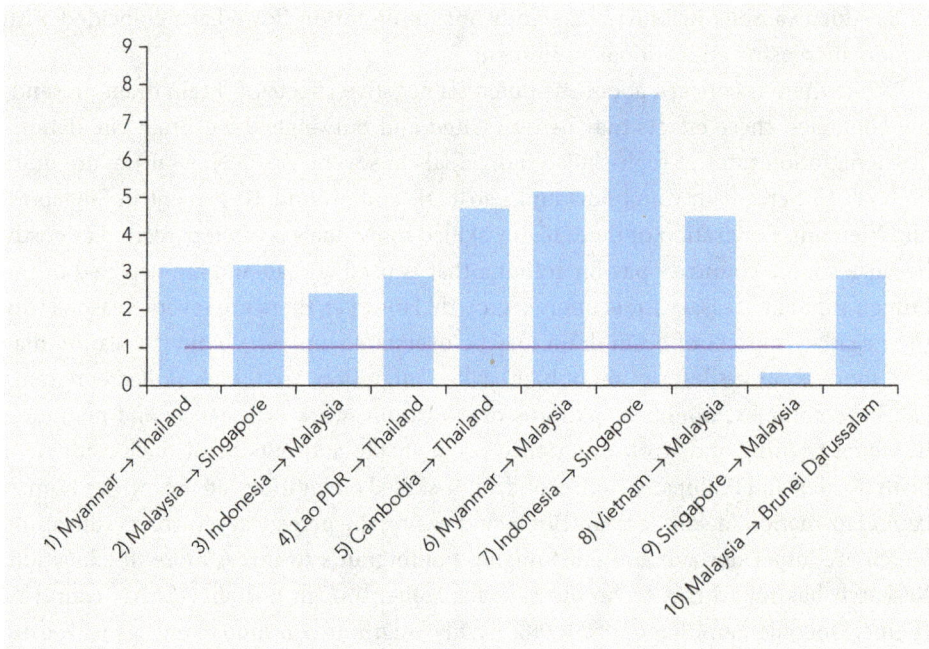

Sources: UN 2015a; World Development Indicators (database).
Note: The horizontal line indicates parity between destination- and origin-country GDP per capita, which is in purchasing power parity (constant 2011 international dollars).

FIGURE O.9

Median age in ASEAN's major migration corridors, 2015

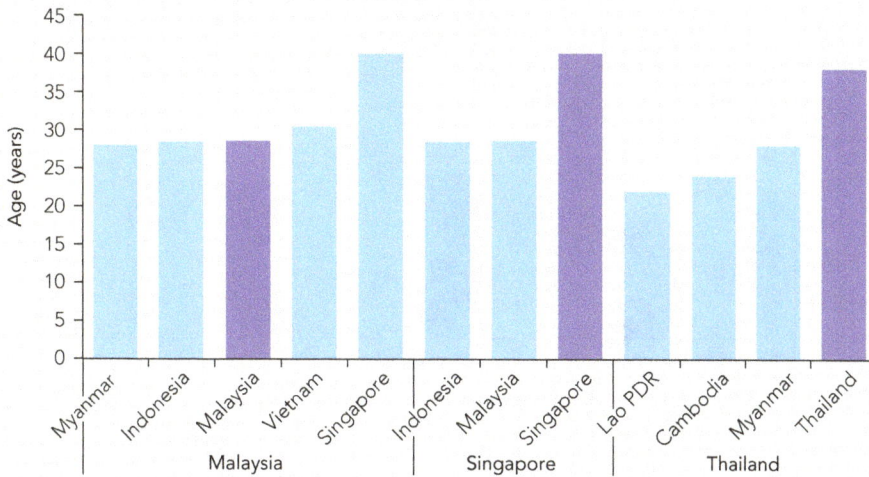

Source: UN 2015b.

migrate informally. The costliness of international migration can mean that the poorest households are unable to afford migration. Migration processes that are overly proce-dural and require significant time and resources can lead migrants to seek out informal channels. In these cases, migrants avoid excessive time and monetary costs by crossing borders unofficially, entering countries to work with nonwork visas, and overstaying work passes. Male Indonesians who migrate to Malaysia through irregular channels take less time to migrate and also face lower monetary costs than their counterparts who migrate through regular channels (figure O.10). Informal migration is a significant issue in ASEAN, where most migrants in Thailand and many in Malaysia are informal.

Labor mobility costs quantify the barriers that workers face when seeking to change jobs across firms, sectors, or countries. These barriers involve costs that are faced domes-tically and arise from job search, employment protection legislation, distance, and even mismatched skills. International migrants face the same costs as domestic migrants but confront additional ones as well, including direct monetary costs such as documenta-tion requirements and recruitment fees, indirect costs created by restrictive migration policies, and opportunity costs from wages not earned while complying with migration procedures. The overall costs faced by workers moving domestically and internationally can be approximated by comparing observed wage differences between jobs—a measure of their attractiveness—with data on actual job flows. For instance, if a country has high wages but few workers are moving to it for work, the labor mobility costs are likely high. In other words, labor mobility costs can be approximated by comparing how well work-ers are able to respond to signals—high wages—of economic opportunity.

FIGURE O.10
Average monetary migration costs for male Indonesian migrants in Malaysia

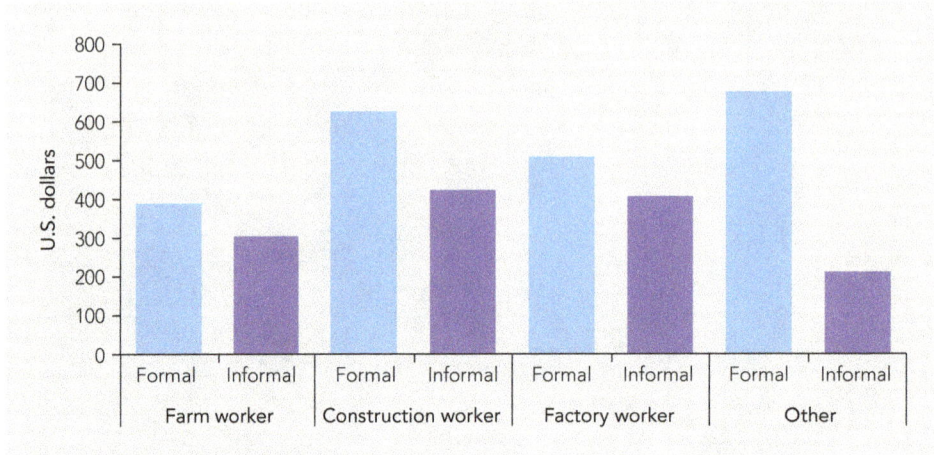

Source: World Bank 2016.
Note: 2014 exchange rate: US$1 = Rp 11,865.

ASEAN countries that are more open to globalization and have developed more advanced migration systems tend to have lower costs of international labor mobility. Malaysia and Singapore have the lowest international labor mobility costs in ASEAN (figure O.11).[2] In the 2000s, workers entering Malaysia faced labor mobility costs equal to 3 times the annual average wage, while those entering Singapore faced costs equal to

FIGURE O.11
International labor mobility costs in ASEAN countries, 2000s

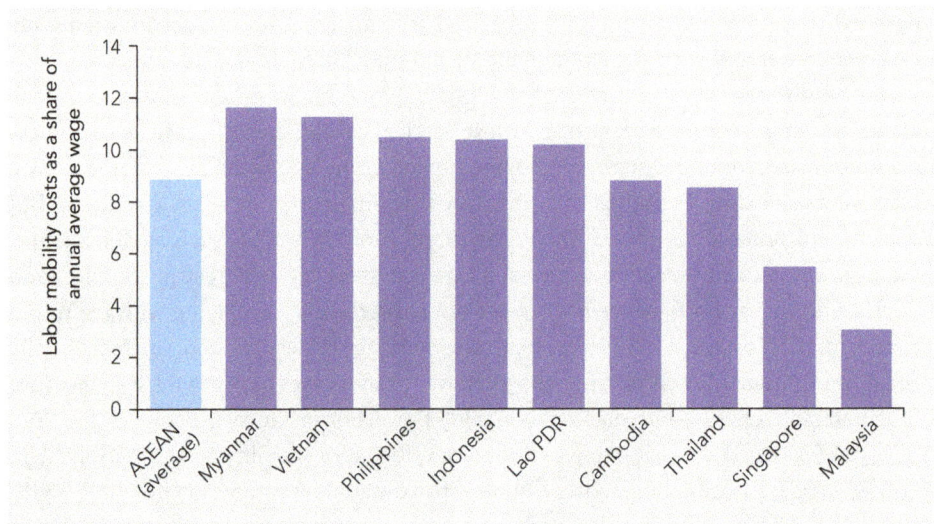

Source: Hollweg 2016.

5 times the annual average wage. Workers migrating to Myanmar and Vietnam, in contrast, confronted costs equal to more than 11 times the annual average wage. The lower costs of international mobility in Malaysia and Singapore reflect their openness to globalization, their efforts to develop migration systems that meet labor market needs, and their geographic centrality in the region. Thailand, another major migrant-receiving country in ASEAN, has a much less developed migration system, high levels of undocumented migration, and high costs of international labor mobility. ASEAN's major migrant-sending countries tend to impose restrictions on immigrants, including high-skilled workers, which is reflected in their high mobility costs. No matter where workers wish to migrate in ASEAN, they face mobility costs several times the annual average wage, suggesting that weaknesses in the migration process may make migrating for work difficult.

In summary, barriers to labor mobility, measured by labor mobility costs, are preventing ASEAN countries from reaping the full benefits of international migration. Lowering the barriers to mobility by decreasing the cost for workers to cross borders in search of economic opportunities would increase the welfare gains for workers as regional integration proceeds. What creates these barriers and how can they be lowered?

Weaknesses in migration systems increase migration costs

Migration systems reconcile the sometimes divergent needs of sending and receiving countries, employers, and migrants themselves. Receiving countries such as Malaysia, Singapore, and Thailand need both low- and high-skilled migrants to fill labor shortages. But policy makers are cautious of public attitudes, which can be skeptical of low-skilled migrants. Employers in receiving countries also use migrants to fill shortages, but their objective is to maximize profit. Sending countries such as Cambodia, Lao PDR, and Myanmar can gain from migration through skills transfers, lower unemployment, connections to international business networks, and remittances but also are concerned about the loss of human capital through brain drain and the treatment of their migrants while they are abroad (Ratha, Yi, and Yousefi 2016). Finally, migrants themselves benefit from employment opportunities and higher wages but often face significant up-front costs to migrate.

Migration systems are generally composed of the governance of the system and four additional components. These components work together to reconcile the needs of host and source countries, employers, and migrants:

- The **governance** of the migration system refers to the *legal* and *institutional framework* organizing the system, and to *bilateral agreements* between sending and receiving countries. The roles of actors in the migration system—migrants, employers, and sending and receiving countries—are structured by migration-related objectives included in national economic and migration plans and in national migration, labor, and other legislation and regulations. These roles are also coordinated by bilateral labor agreements, which govern migration between two countries.

• The **admissions component** determines who migrates and in what numbers through *entry paths*, *quantity restrictions*, and *recruitment*. Immigration systems in receiving countries frequently construct different paths for migrants of different skill levels. For low-skilled immigrants, in particular, entry paths can be restricted to certain source countries and/or to certain sectors or occupations of employment. Migration systems in sending countries can also influence entry paths through bilateral agreements. Quantity restrictions either set immigration targets or impose restrictions on the number of immigrant workers. These restrictions can be imposed in the form of numerical caps or in the form of levies that employers or foreign workers must pay. Recruitment is the process of matching migrant workers with employers. Though public recruitment occurs in some places, private recruitment by recruitment agencies and brokers, which charge a fee for facilitating labor migration, is dominant in ASEAN.

• The **employment component** involves the *terms* of employment and the *protection* provided to workers. Immigration policies governing the employment of migrant workers are closely related to admissions entry paths. Entry paths frequently determine the conditions of employment, with more generous employment terms—including contracts of longer duration and the ability to migrate with dependents—generally offered to more highly skilled migrants. Protections available to migrants while they are working in the host country include coverage by the minimum wage, the ability to change employers, eligibility for social protection benefits, and availability of complaint mechanisms in case of violations of these protections. Protections also include efforts by sending countries to prepare out-migrants for employment abroad prior to departure through predeparture training and vetting of employment contracts and after departure through labor attachés posted in the host country.

• The **exit component** involves the return of migrant workers to their source countries. The exit stage encompasses *sanctions and incentives* in the host country designed to punish temporary migrants who overstay their employment passes and to reward those who return; *diaspora engagement* undertaken by sending countries to form connections with diaspora; and *reintegration* policies used by sending countries to help returning migrant workers reenter labor markets.

• The **enforcement component** involves implementation of migration policy and oversight of the other components of the migration system. Enforcement involves oversight of the emigration and immigration processes to ensure that workers migrate legally; of recruitment agencies to ensure that recruitment is done legally; and of employers to ensure that migrants are treated according to the law. In particular, enforcement involves efforts to *coordinate* the implementation of migration policy across government agencies and levels of governments and the *targeting* of oversight to border and interior enforcement, and to employers and migrant workers.

Breakdowns and weaknesses in each component of the migration system increase the cost of international migration (figure O.12). Migration costs emerge from

Framework of the migration system and costs arising in each of its components

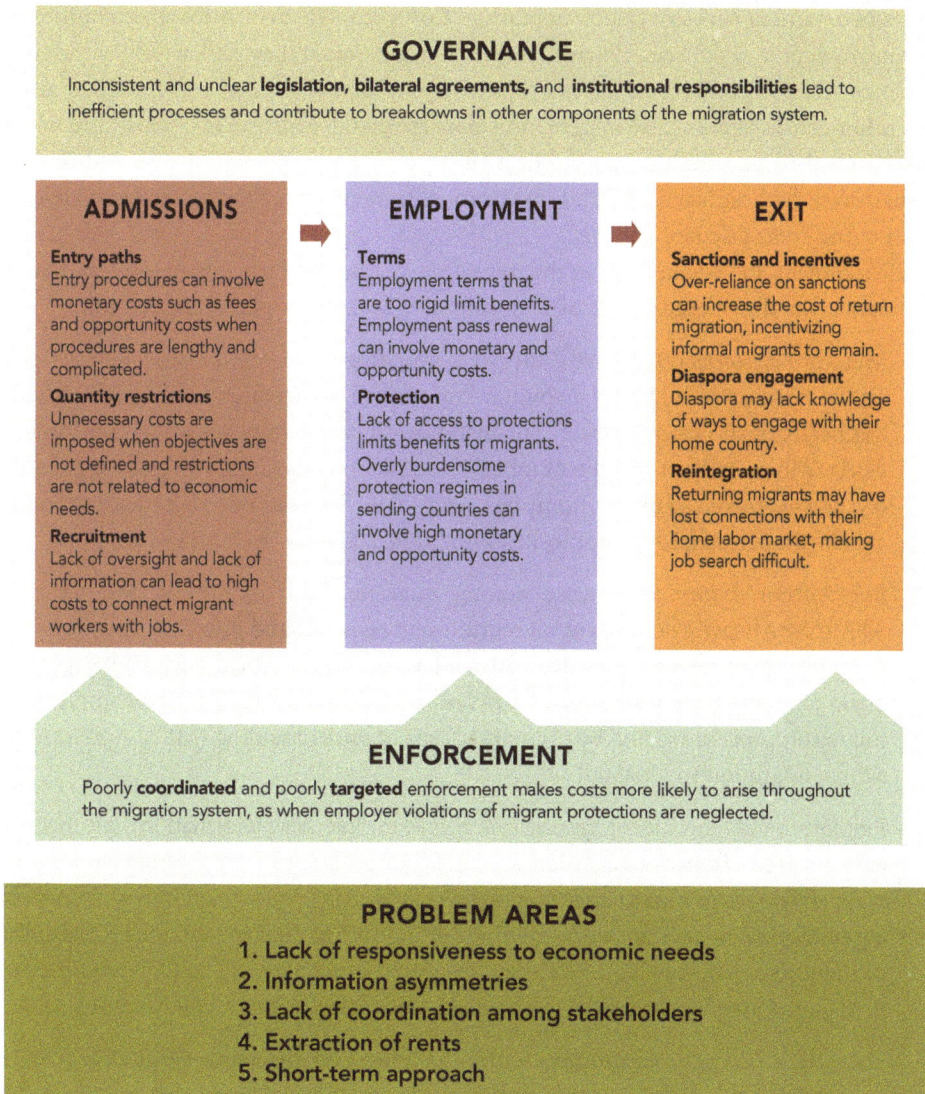

GOVERNANCE

Inconsistent and unclear **legislation, bilateral agreements,** and **institutional responsibilities** lead to inefficient processes and contribute to breakdowns in other components of the migration system.

ADMISSIONS

Entry paths
Entry procedures can involve monetary costs such as fees and opportunity costs when procedures are lengthy and complicated.

Quantity restrictions
Unnecessary costs are imposed when objectives are not defined and restrictions are not related to economic needs.

Recruitment
Lack of oversight and lack of information can lead to high costs to connect migrant workers with jobs.

EMPLOYMENT

Terms
Employment terms that are too rigid limit benefits. Employment pass renewal can involve monetary and opportunity costs.

Protection
Lack of access to protections limits benefits for migrants. Overly burdensome protection regimes in sending countries can involve high monetary and opportunity costs.

EXIT

Sanctions and incentives
Over-reliance on sanctions can increase the cost of return migration, incentivizing informal migrants to remain.

Diaspora engagement
Diaspora may lack knowledge of ways to engage with their home country.

Reintegration
Returning migrants may have lost connections with their home labor market, making job search difficult.

ENFORCEMENT

Poorly **coordinated** and poorly **targeted** enforcement makes costs more likely to arise throughout the migration system, as when employer violations of migrant protections are neglected.

PROBLEM AREAS

1. Lack of responsiveness to economic needs
2. Information asymmetries
3. Lack of coordination among stakeholders
4. Extraction of rents
5. Short-term approach

cumbersome entry procedures and quantity restrictions that do not reflect economic needs. Costs associated with recruitment can be significant, particularly fees for recruitment agents paid to match workers with employers. Employment terms that are too restrictive limit the benefits of migrating, as occurs when employment terms are overly short. Numerous costs are related to protection for migrants during employment abroad. Wages and benefits that are less than expected, particularly less than specified in a contract, or that violate a legal minimum wage create a cost for migrants, as do employment protections and benefits that are not enforced. Costs also arise prior to a migrant's departure as part of a sending country's protection regime. These include financial costs, such as contributions to migrant welfare funds, and the opportunity costs of obtaining necessary documentation. Costs are also incurred if opportunities to use newly acquired skills are not available to migrants when they return home. The governance and enforcement of the migration system impact the costs that arise in all of the other components of the system. This occurs when legislation is unclear and when institutional responsibilities are duplicative or misaligned. Weak enforcement undermines even the best legislative and institutional frameworks, allowing costs to arise in each of the areas discussed above.

Breakdowns and weaknesses in the migration system can be grouped into five major problem areas that increase the costs for migrants seeking employment abroad:

1. Migration systems often have difficulty *responding to economic needs*. Restrictions on the number of migrants a country can receive are frequently not aligned with the needs of the labor market. For instance, Malaysia imposes a levy on foreign workers in part to control the number of low-skilled migrants who enter the country; however, even as the economy has evolved, the levy has been left unadjusted for significant periods, for example, in 1999–2005, 2005–09, and 2011–16.

2. *Information asymmetries* arise among migrants and employers. Migrants in ASEAN are heavily dependent on recruitment agencies and informal labor brokers to reduce these asymmetries. Recruitment agencies are critical intermediaries that guide migrants from Cambodia, Lao PDR, and Myanmar through the complicated migration process created by memorandums of understanding (MOUs) governing formal migration to Thailand.

3. Employers and recruitment agencies are able to exploit these information asymmetries to *extract rents* from the migration system. Labor brokers capture a significant portion of the difference in wages between sending and receiving countries simply for connecting employers and migrant workers (Ahsan et al. 2014). In Thailand, labor brokerage fees are hundreds of dollars higher for migrants from Cambodia and Lao PDR who choose to migrate formally than for those who do so informally (Jalilian and Reyes 2012).

4. There is a *lack of coordination* within sending and receiving countries as well as among these countries, employers, trade unions, workers, and migrants. In Indonesia, a lack of clarity in the responsibilities of the main agencies responsible for migration has led to interagency disputes, uncertainty among migrants about which agency to seek out in case of need, and duplicative processes. Although some bilateral agreements have been formulated to coordinate migration between sending and receiving countries in ASEAN, the agreements often lack transparency and input from employers and migrants.

5. Both sending and receiving countries tend to focus on the *short-term benefits and costs* of migration. Thailand, for example, has struggled to formulate a long-term

migration policy. Periodic regularizations of undocumented migrants and a nationality verification process have been used as de facto migration policy. Sending countries have begun to consider the potential benefits of migration for labor markets and economic development more generally. However, programs to support returning migrants and to connect with their diaspora are in their infancy.

Better policies can lower the barriers to labor mobility

Interventions throughout the migration system can reduce labor mobility costs by addressing breakdowns and weaknesses in each component of the system. Appropriate policies vary across countries, depending on whether they primarily send or receive migrants, the maturity of their migration management system, and their level of development. This section discusses potential interventions in each component of the migration system that are broadly applicable across countries.

Reforms of domestic labor market policy can work alongside migration policies. While not the focus of this book, domestic labor market policies can reduce internal mobility costs by making it easier for local workers to switch sectors, occupations, or locations at home rather than abroad. Such reforms include reducing rigidities in labor markets such as the costs and requirements governing dismissal and restrictions on the use of temporary workers (World Bank 2014). These policies can help reduce any negative effect immigrants may have on locals.

Governance

National migration strategies. National migration strategies can guide policy making in both sending and receiving countries. A national migration plan should set both short- and long-term objectives for migration and be comprehensive in covering all aspects of migration and coordinating migration policy with other human capital strategies. In primarily receiving countries, a migration strategy could provide clarity to employers and other labor market stakeholders about how policy makers view immigrant workers and how they plan to adjust their numbers and skill levels to meet longer-term economic objectives. The plan could also acknowledge the potential negative impacts of immigration on some workers, particularly low-skilled ones, and highlight efforts to assist them. In East Asia, immigration systems were generally constructed assuming that immigration would be a temporary phenomenon. However, the increasing evidence that migration is a structural feature of the region's economy means that longer-term plans are needed to coordinate migration and other labor supply policies. A long-term vision for immigration can provide some clarity to employers and workers about the potential path of policy so that they are informed about the implications for production and employment. In primarily sending countries, a migration strategy could describe how policy makers view the role of out-migration and lay out strategies for protecting migrants while they are abroad. Such a document could also consider longer-term objectives such as using emigration as a strategy for economic development, which would involve setting out policies for diaspora engagement and reintegration of returning migrants.

The Republic of Korea's national migration plan and Cambodia's experience developing a national migration strategy provide models. Korea introduced a national migration strategy in 2008. Its First Basic Plan for Immigration Policy (2008–12) sought to improve cooperation among government agencies and lay out a longer-term, consistent immigration policy. The plan clearly states objectives, identifies priorities, lays out roles and responsibilities of different agencies, and identifies areas for collaboration. The Second Plan (2013–17) included an assessment of the First Basic Plan in relation to several targets. Cambodia has developed two national migration plans. The Policy on Labor Migration for Cambodia 2010–2015 establishes the main objectives for labor migration policy, while the 2015–18 policy introduces specific actions and the agencies responsible for implementing them. Unlike the first strategy document, the 2015–18 document was conceived with other national employment and development strategies in mind.

Institutional framework. Clearly defined institutional responsibilities are important to reduce time-consuming bureaucratic procedures and to better serve migrants. One receiving country (Singapore) and one sending country (the Philippines) are good examples of migration systems with clearly defined institutional responsibilities. In Singapore, the Ministry of Manpower develops and implements foreign labor policies. Divisions and departments within the ministry oversee issues related to the welfare of foreign labor, work permits, and enforcement of regulations regarding foreign manpower. In the Philippines, several migrant-focused agencies are housed mostly within the Department of Labor and Employment. Their roles and responsibilities are well defined, with the Philippine Overseas Employment Agency responsible mainly for managing migration and the Overseas Workers Welfare Administration responsible mainly for protecting migrants.

Bilateral agreements. Bilateral agreements can facilitate cooperation between sending and receiving countries. Sending and receiving countries have overlapping but different objectives for migration, which often result in inefficiencies in the migration process. Efforts to reduce these inefficiencies are constrained by the limited reach of domestic laws and regulations. Bilateral agreements and MOUs provide the basis for sending and receiving countries to reconcile their interests and align their legislative and institutional frameworks, although these agreements can suffer from the same inefficiencies. When they work best, these agreements formalize an ongoing process of negotiations related to the management and protection of migrant workers. The success of an agreement depends on its ability to adjust to emerging labor market needs, continued engagement between sending- and receiving-country representatives, and the complementarity of national migration and employment frameworks (KNOMAD 2014).

Model employment contracts, wage protection measures (such as mechanisms for the automatic deposit of wages into migrants' bank accounts), transparency about the content of MOUs, involvement of public employment services in sending and receiving countries, consideration of gender-specific issues, and concrete implementation and evaluation measures are all good practices in bilateral agreements and MOUs (Wickramasekara 2015).

Admissions

Entry paths. Admissions processes work best when they are transparent and when entry paths are clearly defined. Application processes that are confusing and opaque create inefficiencies, increase migration costs, and lead to doubts about the integrity of the admissions process. Increasing transparency and ensuring that both employers and migrants are aware of the eligibility requirements and the selection criteria for entry are critical. Systems that allow employers and migrant workers to track their progress toward entry can strengthen confidence in the system and help officials to make changes when bottlenecks are discovered. New Zealand has used an "expression of interest" system, which involves selecting qualified migrants from a pool of applicants who have registered their interest in migrating and meet an initial set of requirements. This system has helped to eliminate backlogs of applicants through the initial screening and periodic expiration of registrations (Bedford and Spoonley 2014). Clear criteria to differentiate entry paths can target different types of workers for different streams. Singapore has three well-defined entry streams for lower-, middle-, and higher-skilled workers, which use salary and education requirements to distinguish workers with different skill levels. These entry streams work in conjunction with employment terms, with the more stringent entry requirements linked to more beneficial employment terms.

Shortage lists are a useful mechanism to improve the responsiveness of the admissions system to labor market needs. Shortage lists address the question of which potential immigrants should be allowed entry. The lists are data-driven approaches to identifying labor market shortages, which draw on quantitative and qualitative evidence, including labor force surveys, administrative data, and stakeholder consultations. Using data to identify labor market shortages creates a feedback loop between the immigration system and the labor market, which helps to target migrant workers to the occupations in which they are most needed. Shortage lists can ensure that employers are able to fill gaps in both their high- and low-skilled workforces that cannot be filled by local workers. The lists also reassure the public that policy makers are closely monitoring the labor market and immigration. Finally, shortage lists can expedite the entry process by exempting employers from the requirement to advertise jobs locally. Shortage lists have been used in Australia, New Zealand, and the United Kingdom and in Malaysia. Malaysia's critical occupations list identifies sought-after, hard-to-fill, and strategic occupations by sector and is used to inform both immigration and human resource development policies.

Quantity restrictions. Quantity restrictions are immigration targets or, more frequently in ASEAN, caps or levies on the number of immigrant workers. Setting and revising quantity restrictions should rely on an evidence-based approach. Quantity restrictions should reflect economic needs and be adaptable to changing economic conditions. Setting the restrictions should rely on measurable indicators that come from survey data, administrative data (including programmatic and budgetary data), and innovative sources such as real-time labor market information. Analysis and input from stakeholders—including employers, unions, and other groups—are needed to determine a price for or a cap on immigrant labor. An independent research body can be charged with analyzing technical data and gathering input from stakeholders. A tripartite body can then review inputs from the independent research body and provide recommendations to policy makers.

Recruitment. Improved oversight of the recruitment industry, including additional licensing requirements, can both reduce labor mobility costs and improve protections for migrants. Additional licensing requirements and better monitoring of compliance can help to ensure that recruitment agencies provide good services to migrant workers, although the effectiveness of these measures depends on capacity and resources. In Singapore, recruitment agencies are required to undertake a training program prior to being licensed and must retake it if the agency commits a certain number of violations. In the Philippines, recruitment agencies must attend an orientation seminar prior to receiving a license and a continuing education seminar for license renewal. Finally, sending countries may consider making licensed agencies responsible for claims made by migrants against employers, as occurs in the Philippines. Still, any stricter licensing requirements must be balanced against the capacity for enforcement and deterrence of private sector involvement. Overly stringent rules may encourage informal brokers.

Expanding access to information can reduce information asymmetries, improving matches between employers and workers while also diminishing the need for recruitment agencies. Strategies to improve migrants' access to information include public employment services that provide potential migrants with job opportunities abroad and training courses that provide detailed information about migration procedures. Korea's Employment Permit System (EPS) has a user-friendly website that provides information for foreign workers in their native language. The Philippines provides a listing of job opportunities available abroad through the job advertising site JobStreet.com and offers an orientation program to workers who are contemplating migration. The Pre-Employment Orientation Seminar (PEOS) includes modules on working overseas, job search, illegal recruitment, allowable fees and the essential provisions of the employment contract, and country-specific information. The PEOS is mandatory for potential migrants, but can be completed online at no cost. As an example from outside the region, Morocco's National Agency for Promotion of Employment and Skill promotes the employment of skilled individuals and registers foreign employers and Moroccan youth for job matching.

Expanding access to information can also improve oversight of recruitment agencies and protections for migrants. Both sending- and receiving-country governments can use public information to improve oversight of recruitment agencies. Systems to license and regulate private recruitment agencies are the norm in ASEAN. However, public agencies charged with oversight frequently lack the staff and resources to conduct regular inspections of recruitment agencies. A low-cost complement to this approach is to make information about recruitment agencies publicly available. This information can include recruitment violations, the worker retention rate, and worker placement, as occurs in Singapore. Singapore has announced a system to allow employers of foreign household workers to rate employment agencies on their performance in explaining the application process, providing advice, and selecting workers. A more comprehensive system would also permit workers to rate the agency. Associations of recruitment agencies can be encouraged to adopt codes of conduct, rate the performance of individual agencies, and publish the results of these ratings. The International Labour Organization has worked with recruitment agencies in several ASEAN countries to do so. Good performers can be awarded publicly for their effectiveness, as in the Philippines, or even receive expedited processing of licenses or a waiver of license renewal obligations.

Employment

Employment terms. Well-designed employment terms are calibrated with entry paths to differentiate migrants by skills and productivity, have flexible terms, and are easily renewable. Receiving countries can offer more generous terms to more highly skilled migrants, including lengthier employment passes and the ability to bring dependents. Singapore follows this model, with employment terms dictated by different skill levels. More generous employment terms can also be used to reward improved productivity. Another improvement to employment terms would be the introduction of flexibility, allowing foreign workers to change employers rather than tying them to a single employer, as is currently the case for many foreign migrants. Such rigidity in the labor market for foreign workers likely limits productivity by preventing better matches between employers and workers, and it makes foreign workers vulnerable to mistreatment by employers, who can, in essence, revoke their employment passes. In Korea's EPS, foreign workers are able to change jobs up to three times, and both Malaysia and Singapore offer a type of employment pass for very highly skilled migrants that is not employer-specific.

Protections for migrant workers. Predeparture orientation and financial literacy programs may improve migrant workers' employment experience abroad. Most ASEAN countries provide orientation programs for migrants prior to their departure for employment abroad. These programs seek to improve protection for migrant workers by expanding their knowledge of their rights, of the destination country, and of available complaint mechanisms. The Philippines is generally lauded for its commitment to increasing the knowledge of migrant workers. Some good practices identified with orientation programs in the Philippines are involving local government partners and nongovernmental organizations to incorporate a rights perspective, creating a postarrival orientation seminar to ensure that learning does not stop at departure, developing orientation programs for recruiters, and providing migration information at the local level (Asis and Agunias 2012). Use of a standardized curriculum and oversight of implementation seem to be important elements of success. A pilot program providing financial literacy training to migrant domestic workers in the Greater Malang area and the Blitar District of East Java in Indonesia increased budgeting behavior, savings, financial knowledge, and awareness of mandatory migrant insurance among nonmigrating household members, although it did not increase the amount or frequency of remittances (Doi, McKenzie, and Zia 2014). Notably, effects were generally most pronounced when both the migrant and the family member received training, less pronounced when just the family member received training, and absent when only the migrant received training.

Sending countries could also consider providing loans to migrant workers to assist them with the cost of migration. Several sending countries have or are starting predeparture loan programs for migrants, including Bangladesh, Nepal, Sri Lanka, and Vietnam. There is some evidence that easing financial constraints may generate additional migration, suggesting that providing migration incentives may be effective in generating additional migration among households wishing to migrate (Angelucci 2015; Bryan, Chowdhury, and Mobarak 2014). However, experience with predeparture loans emphasizes the importance of implementation, as there have been reports of problems with repayment in Sri Lanka, and a loan program in the Philippines was terminated due to lack of repayment (Martin 2009). Information campaigns, in contrast, do not seem to increase out-migration (Beam, McKenzie, and Yang 2015).

Exit

Sanctions and incentives. Sanctions and exit incentives can work together in destination countries to encourage voluntary repatriation at the end of a migrant's employment term. In addition to negative incentives for employers to encourage on-time return, as in Malaysia and Singapore, wages might also be withheld or deposited in a compulsory savings scheme until workers return to their source country. In Korea, employers are required to enroll in departure guarantee insurance and workers to enroll in return cost insurance. The employer's monthly contribution is available to workers when they depart Korea or change employer, while return cost insurance is only available on completion of the employment term. Outside the region, Canada's Seasonal Agricultural Workers Program requires workers to contribute to a compulsory savings scheme that is only available on a worker's return to the source country. Careful design of such policies is critical, however, because withholding funds increases the risk for migrant workers who are employed by unscrupulous employers that allow the work permits of their employees to expire (OECD 2013). Positive incentives for return also exist and can be effective. This type of incentive includes tax rebates, guarantees of future employment, or assistance with transportation, medical examinations, and document preparation (OECD 2013). EPS workers in Korea can receive free vocational training and job counseling during employment, job-matching services with Korean employers in their home country, and access to returnee networks, which Korea has fostered to expand job opportunities.

Diaspora engagement. Sending countries can benefit from actively engaging their diaspora. Return migrants bring both financial and human capital resources with them. Members of the diaspora who remain abroad can be sources of learning for local experts and of financial connections to destination countries. Diaspora engagement policies help to construct diaspora networks, which circulate ideas, technology, and even capital (Dickerson and Özden, forthcoming). Programs such as Argentina's Research and Scientists Abroad program, Thailand's Reverse Brain Drain project, and Ethiopia's Diaspora Volunteer Program seek to create linkages with talented members of the diaspora to assist in the host country. Jamaica has a database of migrants currently working abroad, which employers can use to identify potential workers (McKenzie and Yang 2015). India's Overseas Indian Facilitation Center engages in investment facilitation and the creation of knowledge networks; the Financial Services Division in the Ministry of Overseas Indian Affairs provides advice on investing in India (Thimothy et al. 2016). Return migration policies seek to break down policy barriers to return and to incentivize return through tax benefits, citizenship or residency benefits for the returned migrant or their spouse or dependents, or recognition of professional qualifications (Dickerson and Özden, forthcoming). A recent impact analysis of Malaysia's Returning Expert Programme found positive results of such a policy. The program, which provides incentives for high-skilled Malaysians abroad to return, was found to increase the probability of return by 40 percent for applicants with an existing job offer, with only a modest fiscal impact (Del Carpio et al. 2016). Effective implementation of these programs is important to ensure cost-effectiveness. Clear objectives, a targeted diaspora group, a defined budget, and clear program terms are important elements of success (Dickerson and Özden, forthcoming).

Reintegration. More research into how sending countries can help to reintegrate returning workers into their labor markets is necessary. Source countries can offer reintegration benefits to returning migrants, including active labor market policies to help them to find jobs or start businesses on their return. This type of intervention may be necessary to reintegrate migrants into a labor force in which they have lost the networks to find jobs. However, little research has been conducted on the effectiveness of reintegration programs. Audits of programs offered in the Philippines have found significant challenges.

Enforcement

Coordination of enforcement. Enforcement of immigration laws should involve coordinated internal and border enforcement actions and coordinated use of data among agencies responsible for migration. Ensuring that immigrants do not enter and work without proper documentation requires more than border control, which, while effective in some cases, is also costly, particularly along lengthy borders like Thailand's borders with Lao PDR and Myanmar. Interior enforcement measures that target employers to ensure that they are using documented labor and are treating immigrant workers appropriately can be effective. Agencies charged with managing labor migration (which often hold data on migrant workers and their employers) and agencies charged with border enforcement (which hold data on the exit and entry of migrants) can leverage this knowledge to undertake joint enforcement efforts. Systems that are synchronized across agencies can assist with assessing risk and tracking noncompliance through the development of risk-based monitoring to guide enforcement. In low-capacity environments, coordination is even more important to ensure that limited staff and resources are leveraged to the greatest extent possible.

Targeting of enforcement. Targeting enforcement to employers in addition to migrant workers can improve compliance with immigration laws. Migrant workers are often at greater risk of sanction for immigration violations than their employers. Korea and Singapore have worked to strengthen enforcement of sanctions on employers. In Korea, the Ministry of Justice undertakes raids at job sites and fines employers found to be employing undocumented migrants. Those found violating labor laws or EPS-related rules are subject to fines and loss of eligibility to participate in EPS. Inspectors proactively seek to resolve conflicts between workers and employers. Singapore imposes significant fines on employers, with jail terms possible for repeat offenders. Efforts to increase compliance with migration regulations among employers should also involve policies to reward compliance. In some high-income countries, accreditation or sponsorship schemes are used for this purpose. These systems evaluate compliance with relevant employment and immigration laws, employers' history of approved applications, their recruitment of workers, their resources and training systems, and their recruitment and training of local workers (OECD 2013). Benefits of participating in the schemes vary. For example, New Zealand exempts accredited employers from the labor market test of whether a local can fill a job opening, while Australia offers priority processing.

Country-specific priorities: Destination countries

Destination countries should work to develop migration systems that are responsive to economic needs and consistent with domestic policies.

- With very low levels of informal migration and a sophisticated system of productivity-linked entry paths, **Singapore** will need to continue working to build public trust in the migration system and to improve protections for migrant workers.

- With high levels of informal migration but a less sophisticated admissions system than Singapore, **Malaysia** will need to work to make its immigration system more responsive to economic needs and to collaborate more closely with both employers and sending countries.

- With high levels of informal migration, **Thailand** will need to work to formalize its large population of undocumented migrants, rationalize entry procedures that are costly and time-consuming, and rethink immigration policies such as levies and a repatriation fund, which exist in law but not in practice, undermining the credibility of the migration system.

- As the country seeks to encourage private sector employment among locals, **Brunei Darussalam** will need to ensure that a relatively complex system of quotas and levies based on geography, sector, and employer supports this goal, while also meeting economic needs.

Country-specific priorities: Sending countries

Sending countries should work to balance protections for migrant workers with the needs of economic development.

- The **Philippines** has a highly developed support system for migrant workers that is a model for other sending countries. To build on this status, the country should continue to evaluate and improve its migration management system, including oversight of recruitment agencies, programs for returned migrants, and data sharing and interoperability.

- **Indonesia** should work to improve coordination among the agencies responsible for managing labor migration and to streamline exit procedures for migrants to encourage documented migration.

- **Vietnam** will need to evaluate its current policies for incentivizing out-migration to determine whether they are meeting the country's needs. While the intention of these policies is laudable, other reforms are also necessary, including review of recruitment agencies' frequent and at least tacitly sanctioned practice of requiring migrant workers to pay a security deposit to guarantee their return, which is frequently not repaid. A national migration strategy could help to guide reforms.

- Lower-capacity **Cambodia, Lao PDR,** and **Myanmar** should continue considering how migration can fit into their economic development strategies, shaping programs to make out-migration less costly and more formal, and creating connections with diaspora to facilitate the transfer of knowledge and capital. These countries can look to the experience of the Philippines in their efforts to develop institutions serving migrants and services such as predeparture orientation programs.

Regional priorities

The ASEAN Secretariat can support domestic efforts by serving as a clearinghouse for best practices and as a coordinating body. The secretariat could collect bilateral agreements and MOUs from ASEAN and the rest of the world to share best practices and provide technical assistance in the development of agreements and their key components. Drawing on the efforts of the ASEAN Forum on Migrant Labor and the Cebu Declaration, along with international conventions and regional best practices, it might consider developing a common, but flexible, framework for bilateral agreements;

guidelines for the protection of migrant workers; and even model contracts. Finally, ASEAN may consider creating a labor market information portal to provide potential migrants with information about job openings and employment regulations and practices in destination countries.

Notes

1. Enhanced trade integration within ASEAN is modeled as the removal of intraregional tariffs, the liberalization of nontariff barriers in goods and services, and the introduction of advanced trade facilitation measures. The model underpinning the simulations, unlike standard trade models, does not assume that workers can change jobs without friction. Mobility is possible, but costly.

2. The exact magnitude of the estimated labor mobility costs depends on several assumptions. Because of this sensitivity, comparison of the relative magnitude of labor mobility costs across countries is more informative than the absolute magnitude.

References

Adams, Richard H., and Alfredo Cuecuecha. 2014. "Remittances, Household Investment, and Poverty in Indonesia." In *Managing International Migration for Development in East Asia*, edited by Richard H. Adams and Ahmad Ahsan. Washington, DC: World Bank.

Adams, Richard H., and John Page. 2005. "Do International Migration and Remittances Reduce Poverty in Developing Countries?" *World Development* 33 (10): 1645–69.

Ahsan, Ahmad, Manolo Abella, Andrew Beath, Yukon Huang, Manjula Luthria, and Trang Van Nguyen. 2014. *International Migration and Development in East Asia and the Pacific*. Washington, DC: World Bank.

Angelucci, Manuela. 2015. "Migration and Financial Constraints: Evidence from Mexico." *Review of Economics and Statistics* 97 (1): 224–28.

Angrist, Joshua D., and Adriana D. Kugler. 2003. "Protective or Counter-Productive? Labour Market Institutions and the Effect of Immigration on EU Natives." *Economic Journal* 113 (488): F302–31.

ASEAN (Association of Southeast Asian Nations) Secretariat and World Bank. 2015. *ASEAN Services Integration Report*. Washington, DC: ASEAN Secretariat and World Bank.

Asia-Pacific RCM (Regional Coordination Mechanism) Thematic Working Group on International Migration Including Human Trafficking. 2015. *Asia-Pacific Migration Report 2015: Migrants' Contribution to Development*. Bangkok: International Organization for Migration, Regional Office for Southeast Asia.

Asis, Maruja M. B., and Dovelyn Rannveig Agunias. 2012. "Strengthening Pre-Departure Orientation Programmes in Indonesia, Nepal, and the Philippines." Migration Policy Institute, Washington, DC.

Batalova, Jeanne, Andriy Shymonyak, and Guntur Sugiyarto. 2017. *Firing up Regional Brain Networks: The Promise of Brain Circulation in the ASEAN Economic Community*. Manila: Asian Development Bank.

Beam, Emily A., David McKenzie, and Dean Yang. 2015. "Unilateral Facilitation Does Not Raise International Labor Migration from the Philippines." *Economic Development and Cultural Change* 64 (2): 323–68.

Bedford, Richard, and Paul Spoonley. 2014. "Competing for Talent: Diffusion of an Innovation in New Zealand's Immigration Policy." *International Migration Review* 48 (3): 891–911.

Beine, Michel, Frédéric Docquier, and Hillel Rapoport. 2008. "Brain Drain and Human Capital Formation in Developing Countries: Winners and Losers." *Economic Journal* 118 (528): 631–52.

Bryan, Gharad, Shyamal Chowdhury, and Ahmed Mushfiq Mobarak. 2014. "Underinvestment in a Profitable Technology: The Case of Seasonal Migration in Bangladesh." *Econometrica* 82 (5): 1671–748.

D'Amuri, Francesco, and Giovanni Peri. 2014. "Immigration, Jobs, and Employment Protection: Evidence from Europe before and during the Great Recession." *Journal of the European Economic Association* 12 (2): 432–64.

Del Carpio, Ximena, Çağlar Özden, Mauro Testaverde, and Mathis Wagner. 2015. "Local Labor Supply Responses to Immigration." *Scandinavian Journal of Economics* 117 (2): 493–521.

———. 2016. "Global Migration of Talent and Tax Incentives: Evidence from Malaysia's Returning Expert Program." Policy Research Working Paper 7875, World Bank, Washington D.C.

Dickerson, Sarah, and Çağlar Özden. Forthcoming. "Return Migration and Diaspora Engagement." In *Handbook of Migration and Globalisation*, edited by Anna Triandafyllidou. Cheltenham, U.K.: Edward Elgar Publishing.

Docquier, Frédéric, Çağlar Özden, and Giovanni Peri. 2014. "The Labour Market Effects of Immigration and Emigration in OECD Countries." *Economic Journal* 124 (579): 1106–45.

Docquier, Frédéric, and Hillel Rapoport. 2012. "Globalization, Brain Drain, and Development." *Journal of Economic Literature* 50 (3): 681–730.

Doi, Yoko, David McKenzie, and Bilal Zia. 2014. "Who You Train Matters: Identifying Combined Effects of Financial Education on Migrant Households." *Journal of Development Economics* 109 (C): 39–55.

Ducanes, Geoffrey. 2015. "The Welfare Impact of Overseas Migration on Philippine Households: Analysis Using Panel Data," *Asian and Pacific Migration Journal* 24 (1): 79–106.

Felbermayr, Gabriel J., and Wilhelm Kohler. 2009. "Can International Migration Ever Be Made a Pareto Improvement?" In *The Integration of European Labour Markets*, edited by Ewald Nowotny, Peter Mooslechner, and Doris Ritzberger-Grünwald, 32–50. Cheltenham, U.K.: Edward Elgar Publishing.

Hollweg, Claire. 2016. "Labor Mobility and Labor Market Integration in ASEAN." World Bank, Washington, DC.

Hollweg, Claire, Daniel Lederman, Diego Rojas, and Elizabeth Ruppert Bulmer. 2014. *Sticky Feet: How Labor Market Frictions Shape the Impact of International Trade on Jobs and Wages*. Washington, DC: World Bank.

ILO (International Labour Organization). 2014. *Global Wage Report 2014/15: Asia and the Pacific Supplement*. Bangkok: ILO.

ILO and ADB (Asian Development Bank). 2014. *ASEAN Community 2015: Managing Integration for Better Jobs and Shared Prosperity*. Bangkok: ILO and ADB.

IOM (International Organization for Migration). 2013. *Country Migration Report: The Philippines 2013*. Makati City: IOM.

Jalilian, Hossein, and Glenda Reyes. 2012. "Migrants of the Mekong." In *Costs and Benefits of Cross-Country Labour Migration in the GMS*, edited by Hossein Jalilian, 1–117. Singapore: ISEAS Publishing.

KNOMAD (Global Knowledge Partnership on Migration and Development). 2014. "Technical Workshop on Review of Bilateral Agreements Low-Skilled Labor Migration: Summary." KNOMAD, Kathmandu, December 1–2.

Lathapipat, Dilaka. 2014. "The Effects of Immigration on the Thai Wage Structure." In *Managing International Migration for Development in East Asia*, edited by Richard H. Adams and Ahmad Ahsan, 111–35. Washington, DC: World Bank.

Longhi, S., P. Nijkamp, and J. Poot. 2010. "Joint Impacts of Immigration on Wages and Employment: A Review and Meta-Analysis." *Journal of Geographical Systems* 12 (4): 355–87.

Martin, Philip. 2009. "Reducing the Cost Burden for Migrant Workers: A Market-Based Approach." University of California, Davis.

Martin, Philip, and Manolo Abella. 2014. "Reaping the Economic and Social Benefits of Labour Mobility: ASEAN 2015." Asia-Pacific Working Paper, International Labour Organization, Bangkok.

McKenzie, David, and Dean Yang. 2015. "Evidence on Policies to Increase the Development Impacts of International Migration." *World Bank Research Observer* 30 (2): 155–92.

Mishra, Prachi. 2007. "Emigration and Wages in Source Countries: Evidence from Mexico." *Journal of Development Economics* 82 (1): 180–99.

———. 2014. "Emigration and Wages in Source Countries: A Survey of the Empirical Literature." In *International Handbook on Migration and Economic Development*, edited by Robert E. B. Lucas, 241–66. Cheltenham, U.K.: Edward Elgar Publishing.

MMN (Mekong Migration Network) and AMC (Asian Migrant Centre). 2013. *Migration in the Greater Mekong Subregion Resource Book: In-Depth Study; Border Economic Zones and Migration*. Chiang Mai: MMN and AMC.

Nguyen, Cuong Viet. 2008. "Do Foreign Remittances Matter to Poverty and Inequality? Evidence from Vietnam." *Economics Bulletin* 15 (1): 1–11.

OECD (Organisation for Economic Co-operation and Development). 2013. *International Migration Outlook 2013*. Paris: OECD Publishing.

———. 2016. *Economic Outlook for Southeast Asia, China, and India: Enhancing Regional Ties*. Paris: OECD Publishing.

Özden, Çağlar, and David Phillips. 2015. "What Really Is Brain Drain? Location of Birth, Education, and Migration Dynamics of African Doctors." Working Paper 4, Global Knowledge Partnership on Migration and Development, Washington, DC.

Özden, Çağlar, and Mathis Wagner. 2016. "Immigrant versus Natives? Displacement and Job Creation." Unpublished manuscript, World Bank, Washington, DC.

Pholphirul, Piriya, Jongkon Kamlai, and Pungpond Rukumnuaykit. 2010. "Do Immigrants Improve Thailand's Competitiveness?" World Bank, Washington, DC.

Ratha, Dilip, Soonhwa Yi, and Seyed Reza Yousefi. 2016. "Migration and Development: The Asian Experience." In *The Routledge Handbook of Migration*, edited by Anna Triandafyllidou, 260–77. New York: Routledge.

Thimothy, Rakkee, S. K. Sasikumar, Padmini Ratnayake, and Alvin P. Ang. 2016. "Labour Migration Structures and Financing in Asia." International Labour Organization, Bangkok.

UN (United Nations). 2015a. *Trends in International Migrant Stock: The 2015 Revision*. United Nations database. New York: UN. POP/DB/MIG/Stock/Rev.2015.

———. 2015b. *World Population Prospects: The 2015 Revision*. DVD Edition. New York: United Nations, Department of Economic and Social Affairs, Population Division.

Wickramasekara, Piyasiri. 2015. "Bilateral Agreement and Memoranda of Understanding on Migration of Low-Skilled Workers: A Review." International Labour Organization, Geneva.

World Bank. 2014. *East Asia Pacific at Work: Employment, Enterprise, and Well-Being*. Washington: DC: World Bank.

———. 2016. "Indonesia's Global Workers: Juggling Opportunities and Risks." World Bank, Washington, DC.

PART I

Migration and Regional Integration in Southeast Asia

CHAPTER 1

Migration in Southeast Asia

Introduction

Migration in Southeast Asia is evolving. As in the rest of the world, workers from the region migrate to traditional receiving countries of the Organisation for Economic Co-operation and Development (OECD). But in recent years several Association of Southeast Asian Nations (ASEAN) countries have themselves become important destinations for migrants from the region. Malaysia, Singapore, and Thailand have developed into regional immigration hubs that receive migrants from Cambodia, the Lao People's Democratic Republic, Myanmar, and other countries in the region. Migration in Southeast Asia is diverse, with migrants in the region seeking out economic opportunity in a variety of ways. Cambodia is a well-known sender of migrants, but Vietnam also sends migrants across the long border with Cambodia to work in fishing and construction (MMN and AMC 2013). The Philippines is not only a significant sender of migrants to the Middle East and the United States but also the origin of about a quarter of the world's ship crews (IOM 2013). Malaysian workers commute each day across the narrow Straits of Johor to work in Singapore.

This chapter reviews the migration patterns and trends of the ten Southeast Asian countries[1] that make up ASEAN, a group that promotes regional cooperation. Data on migration patterns and trends are drawn from several sources, which are described in box 1.1. Several overarching trends are apparent:

- Migration in ASEAN is a growing factor in the movement of people globally and in East Asia and Pacific (EAP).

- Malaysia, Singapore, and Thailand are immigration hubs. Thailand receives most of its migrants from Cambodia, Lao PDR, and Myanmar; Malaysia from Indonesia; and Singapore from Malaysia. Indonesia, the Philippines, and Vietnam are migrant-sending countries, but migrants from these countries tend to migrate outside of the region.

- Most migration within ASEAN is low-skilled and occurs through informal channels.

BOX 1.1
Data sources, definitions, and concepts

The analysis in this chapter relies primarily on migration data from the United Nations' (UN) *Trends in International Migrant Stock: The 2015 Revision.*[a] The UN data are derived mostly from population censuses, but also incorporate population registers and nationally representative surveys. Data availability varies by region: 81 percent of countries in Africa have at least one data source on international migrant stock since the 2000 census round, 90 percent in Asia, 96 percent in Europe, 98 percent in Latin America and the Caribbean, 100 percent in Oceania, and 100 percent in North America. In Asian countries, however, the figures are lower for age and country of origin (70 and 74 percent, respectively).

Estimation techniques vary depending on the number of data sources. When countries lack any source of data, a model country is used. Age groups and countries of origin are standardized, requiring interpolation and other statistical and demographic estimation methods and the creation of aggregate groups (for example, "Other North" and "Other South").

Migrants are defined as *foreign-born persons*, whenever possible. However, the classification of *foreign citizenship* is used when necessary. This leads to three problems: (1) *overinclusion*, when a person is born in her country of residence but lacks citizenship; (2) *underinclusion*, when a person is born abroad but has naturalized; and (3) *overinclusion* or *underinclusion*, depending on a country's policy for granting citizenship to the children of international migrants.

Data exist for every ASEAN country. The foreign-born concept is used in half of the countries, and the foreign citizenship concept in the other half (table B1.1.1). The UN data incorporate estimates of refugee stocks from the Office of the UN High Commissioner for Refugees and the UN Relief and Works Agency for Palestine Refugees in the Near East. These estimates are added to the stock estimates of six ASEAN countries.

The analysis in this chapter relies primarily on UN data because they represent the most up-to-date portrait of migration in ASEAN and offer information about the age and gender of migrants. However, given the drawback of the definitions of migrants and the need for estimation techniques, the data do have inconsistencies with other sources. The World Bank has also produced bilateral estimates, though without gender or age information, with the most recent published in 2013. For intra-ASEAN migration, differences can be large in absolute terms but are generally quite small

box continues next page

BOX 1.1
Data sources, definitions, and concepts *(continued)*

TABLE B1.1.1
United Nations data for ASEAN countries: Basis for definition of migrant and inclusion of refugees

Country	Estimates based on...	Refugees added?
Brunei Darussalam	foreign-born persons	No
Cambodia	foreign-born persons	No
Indonesia	foreign-born persons	Yes
Lao PDR	foreign citizens	Yes
Malaysia	foreign citizens	Yes
Myanmar	foreign citizens	No
Philippines	foreign citizens	Yes
Singapore	foreign-born person	No
Thailand	foreign-born persons	Yes
Vietnam	foreign citizens	Yes

Source: UN 2015b.
Note: ASEAN = Association of Southeast Asian Nations.

relative to the size of the migrant population (table B1.1.2). Differences are larger in Brunei Darussalam and in Vietnam, where both UN and World Bank data show intra-ASEAN migration to be small.

There are large differences between the two datasets for Malaysia. In particular, there is a significant discrepancy for migration from the Philippines to Malaysia, which is estimated in the UN data to be 21,732 in 2015 and in the World Bank data to be 410,149 in 2013. Data from the Commission on Filipinos Overseas, a Philippine agency, suggest that the World Bank data may be more accurate, estimating the number of Filipinos in Malaysia to be 793,580 in 2013.

The prominence of undocumented migration to and from ASEAN countries is a significant issue for data reliability. Undocumented status likely makes individuals less likely to respond to population censuses and household surveys for fear of detection. The UN data, the World Bank data, and most other available data sources do not draw a distinction between documented and undocumented or informal migration.

Two other data sources are used to describe the characteristics of ASEAN migrants. The International Labour Organization's (ILO) International Labor Migration Statistics Database in ASEAN draws on population censuses, survey data, and administrative records to provide detailed information on ASEAN migration stocks and flows. However, the sources are not comparable across countries, and definitions used can vary significantly, making comparison useful only for illustrative purposes. This dataset is used to describe characteristics of *global* migrants to ASEAN destinations. The OECD's Database on Immigrants in OECD and Non-OECD Countries has detailed data on migration to many ASEAN countries for 2000, but updates are still ongoing for 2010. Access was provided to the 2010 update where available. This dataset is used to describe the characteristics of intra-ASEAN migrants in 2000 and in 2010 where available.

box continues next page

BOX 1.1
Data sources, definitions, and concepts *(continued)*

TABLE B1.1.2
Differences in intra-ASEAN migrant stocks between United Nations and World Bank data, by destination

Country	UN	World Bank	Difference (no.)	Difference (%)
Brunei Darussalam	83,832	32,199	51,633	62
Cambodia	68,106	69,579	−1,473	−2
Indonesia	49,930	44,858	5,072	10
Lao PDR	14,802	14,582	220	1
Malaysia	1,539,741	1,747,111	−207,370	−13
Myanmar	0	0	—	—
Philippines	6,499	6,252	247	4
Singapore	1,321,552	1,229,495	92,057	7
Thailand	3,762,393	3,618,373	144,020	4
Vietnam	40,537	25,614	14,923	37

Sources: UN 2015a; World Bank Bilateral Migration Matrix.
Note: — = not available; ASEAN = Association of Southeast Asian Nations.

Sources: UN 2015a; UN 2015b; World Bank Bilateral Migration Matrix.

a ILO and ADB (2014) includes an annex describing the wide discrepancies between the main sources of data on bilateral migration. Such migration is very difficult to estimate, but the importance of migration in ASEAN makes improved data collection critical.

Regional trends

During the past several decades, ASEAN countries have become a significant factor in the movement of people globally and throughout EAP. ASEAN countries are now the origin of 8 percent of the world's migrants, up from 6 percent in 1995; they are also the destination for 4 percent, up from 2 percent in 1995. As a result, the ratios of emigrants and immigrants to the total population of ASEAN countries are converging to global levels, though more quickly for emigration than immigration (figure 1.1). This growing significance is apparent at the regional level. Migrants from ASEAN origins represented 56 percent of all EAP emigration in 2015, an increase of 6 percentage points from 1995. ASEAN destinations represented 39 percent of EAP immigration in 2015, up from just 28 percent in 1990.

Migration within ASEAN is increasingly important. Many ASEAN countries have been part of EAP's impressive growth, but large within-region disparities in income, education, skills, and demographic patterns remain—making migration inside of ASEAN an attractive option. Indeed, ASEAN was one of the two global regions—the other one is EAP, of which ASEAN is part—in which the share of intraregional migration

FIGURE 1.1

Share of emigrants and immigrants per total population, 1995–2015

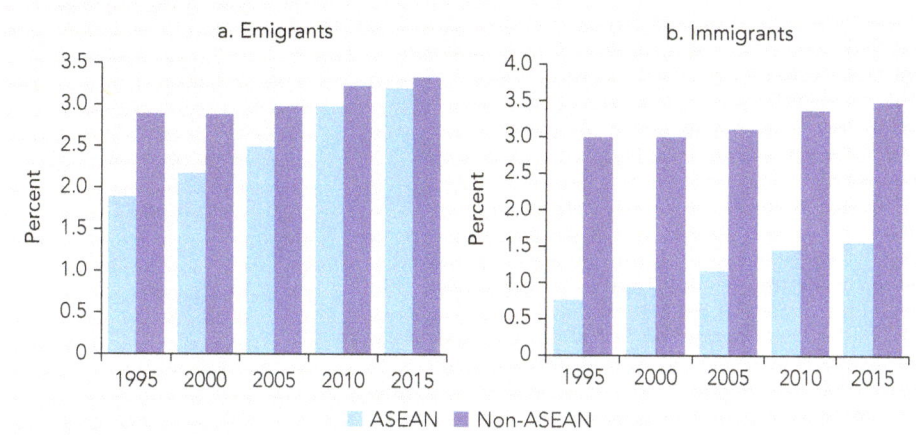

a. Emigrants

b. Immigrants

ASEAN   Non-ASEAN

Source: UN 2015a.
Note: ASEAN = Association of Southeast Asian Nations.

FIGURE 1.2

Change in the share of intraregional migration out of total migration in different regions, 1995–2015

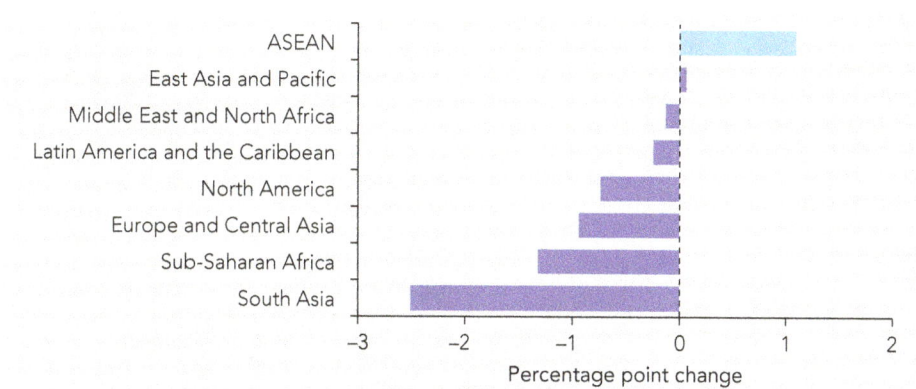

Source: UN 2015a.
Note: ASEAN = Association of Southeast Asian Nations.

increased between 1995 and 2015 (figure 1.2). The numerical increase in intra-ASEAN migrants between 1995 and 2015 was impressive: at 6.9 million, the figure was more than 3 times higher in 2015 than in 1995 versus 1.7 times for intra-EAP migrants outside of ASEAN (figure 1.3).

The migration profiles of ASEAN countries are diverse. ASEAN includes both regional hubs for immigrants and regional and global senders of emigrants, as shown in figure 1.4. Most migrants from Cambodia, Lao PDR, and Myanmar[2]

FIGURE 1.3

Intra-ASEAN and intra-EAP migrants, 1995–2015

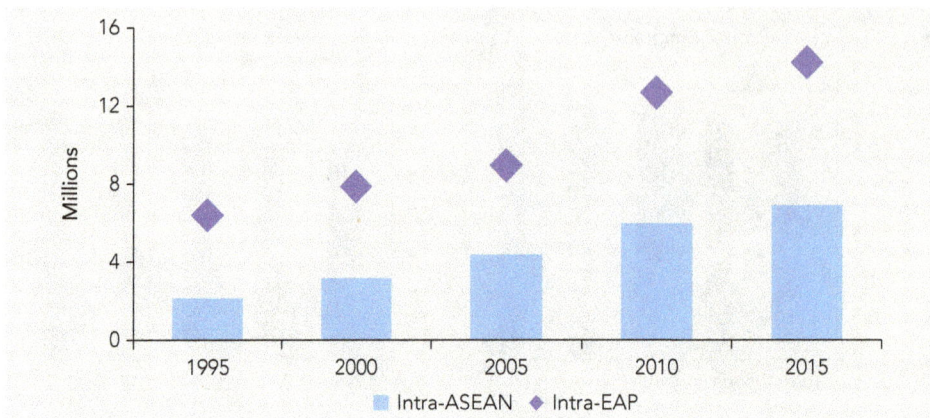

Source: UN 2015a.
Note: ASEAN = Association of Southeast Asian Nations; EAP = East Asia and Pacific.

FIGURE 1.4

Migration to and from ASEAN countries

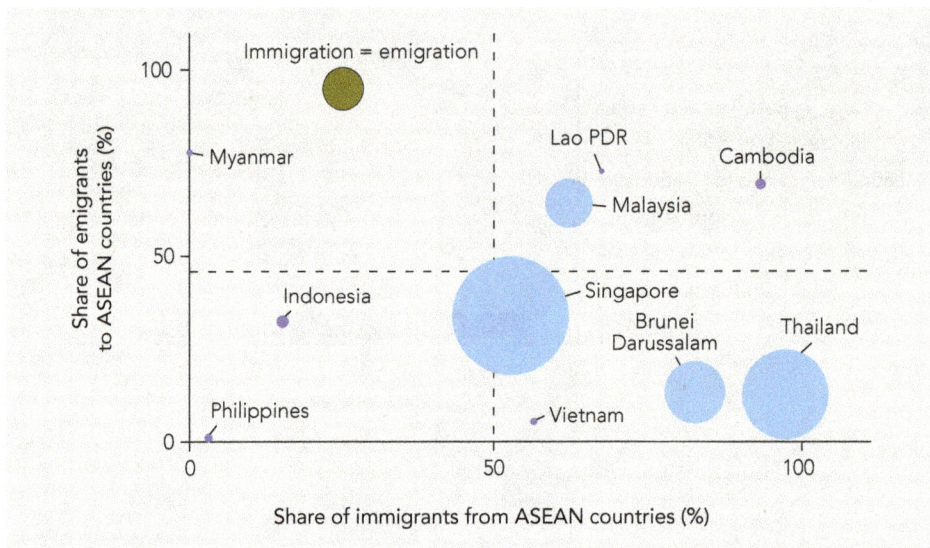

Source: UN 2015a.
Note: This figure shows the share of immigration to each ASEAN country from other ASEAN countries on the x axis, and the share of emigration from each ASEAN country to other ASEAN countries on the y axis. The size of each circle represents the ratio of migrants sent to that of migrants received, with the smallest purple circles indicating that more migrants are sent than received, and the larger blue circles indicating that more migrants are received than sent. The green circle shows the hypothetical case in which the number of immigrants equals the number of emigrants. ASEAN = Association of Southeast Asian Nations.

(all lower-middle-income economies that send many more migrants than they receive) migrate to other countries in ASEAN—namely, Malaysia, Singapore, and Thailand (all high- and upper-middle-income economies). Most of this migration is low-skilled and informal. Indonesia, the Philippines, and Vietnam (ASEAN's other lower-middle-income economies that also send more migrants than they receive) tend to send migrants outside of ASEAN, building on historical connections to the United States in the case of the Philippines and to the former Soviet Union in the case of Vietnam. Institutions in all three countries have supported out-migration.

ASEAN's regional immigration hubs are themselves also senders of migrants. Malaysia sends and receives a similar number of migrants, in both cases to and from ASEAN countries. Singapore receives many ASEAN migrants, but predominantly sends higher-skilled migrants outside of ASEAN for study and work. Thailand sends nearly all its migrants outside of ASEAN.

Immigration to and emigration from ASEAN countries

Thailand, Malaysia, and Singapore host most of ASEAN's immigrants. Thailand has the largest number of total migrants, with more than 3.9 million in 2015, about 50 percent more than Malaysia and Singapore's 2.5 million. These large migrant stocks distinguish these three countries from the other ASEAN countries, which have far fewer migrants. Thailand, for example, has 12 times the migrant stock of Indonesia and 175 times that of Lao PDR (figure 1.5). The size of the migrant stock relative to the destination country's total population generally follows the same pattern as the absolute levels of migrant stocks. Singapore (45 percent in 2015) and Brunei Darussalam (24 percent in 2015) host strikingly high proportions of migrants, while Malaysia (8 percent) and Thailand (6 percent) have substantial proportions as well (figure 1.6). In fact, in Singapore migrants make up the majority of the total population in each five-year age group between ages 25 and 49. In every other ASEAN country, the share of migrants relative to total population is 0.5 percent or lower.

Many ASEAN countries are significant senders of migrants globally. Seven ASEAN countries have more than 1 million out-migrants (figure 1.7). The Philippines and Indonesia lead the way, with 5.3 million and 3.9 million migrants, respectively. These significant stocks are reflected in and supported by the institutions that each country has created to govern out-migration. As a percentage of the population, however, the pattern changes somewhat (figure 1.8). With large populations overall, Indonesia and the Philippines are farther down the ASEAN ranking for emigration relative to the total population. Migrants from lower-middle-income Lao PDR and Cambodia make up 20 percent and 8 percent of the population, respectively, but out-migration is also significant for high-income Brunei Darussalam and Singapore and upper-middle-income Malaysia.

FIGURE 1.5
Total immigrants in ASEAN destinations, 1995 and 2015

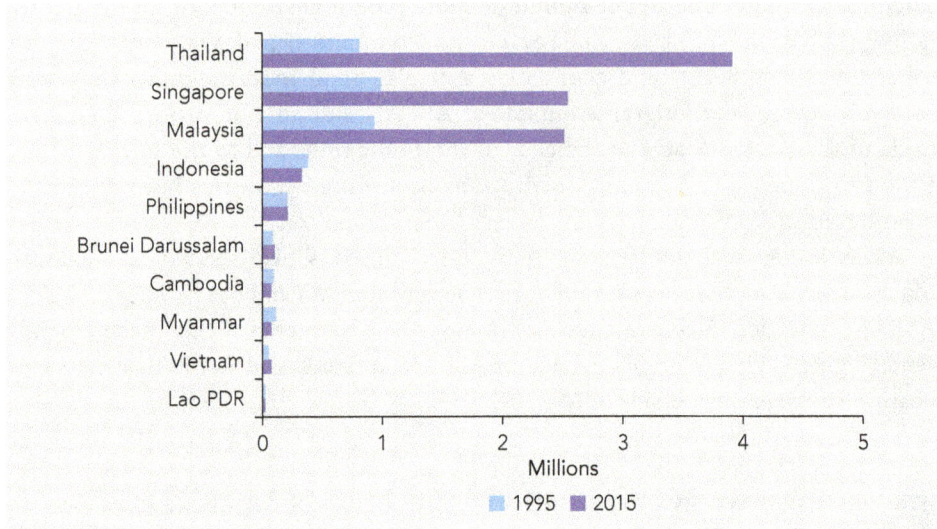

Source: UN 2015a.
Note: ASEAN = Association of Southeast Asian Nations.

FIGURE 1.6
Total immigrants relative to the total population in ASEAN destinations, 1995 and 2015

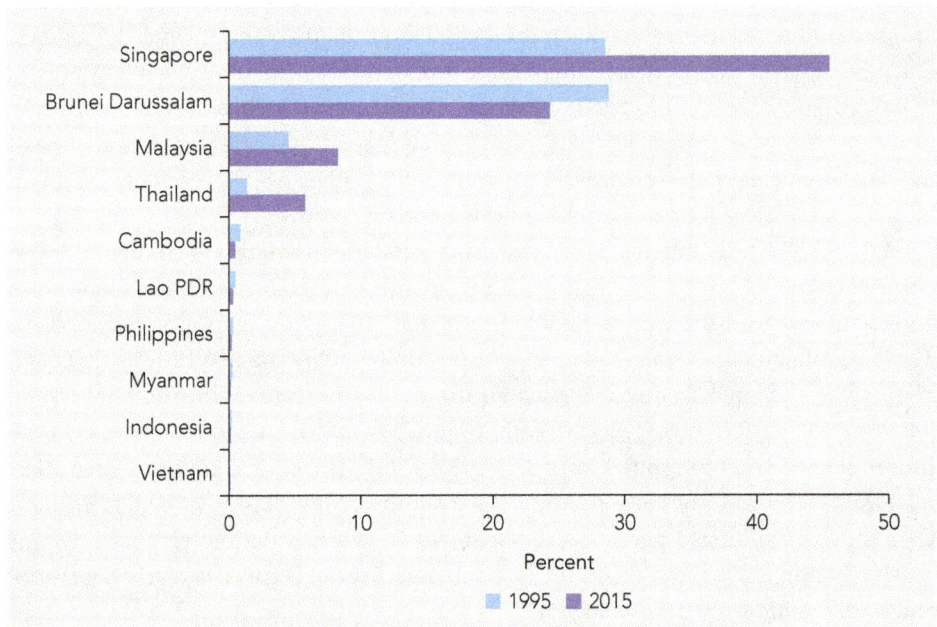

Source: UN 2015a.
Note: ASEAN = Association of Southeast Asian Nations.

FIGURE 1.7

Total emigrants from ASEAN origins, 1995 and 2015

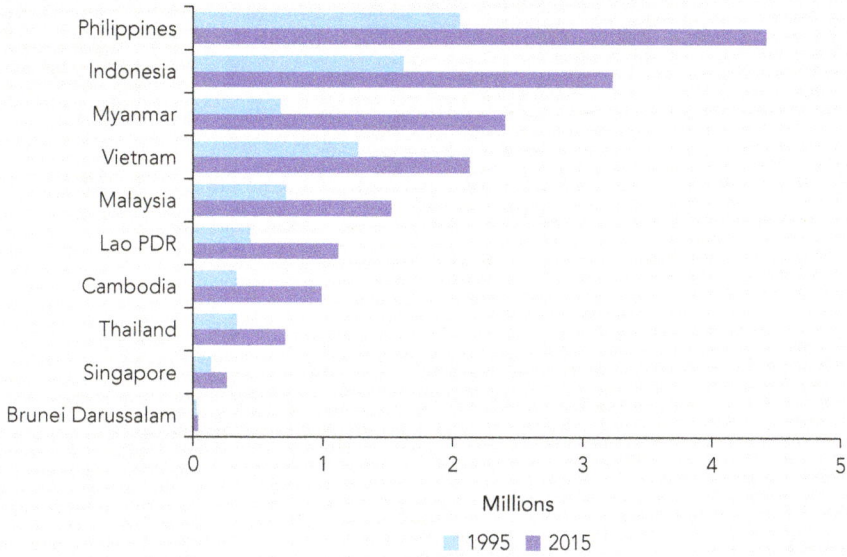

Source: UN 2015a.
Note: ASEAN = Association of Southeast Asian Nations.

FIGURE 1.8

Total emigrants relative to the total population in ASEAN origins, 1995 and 2015

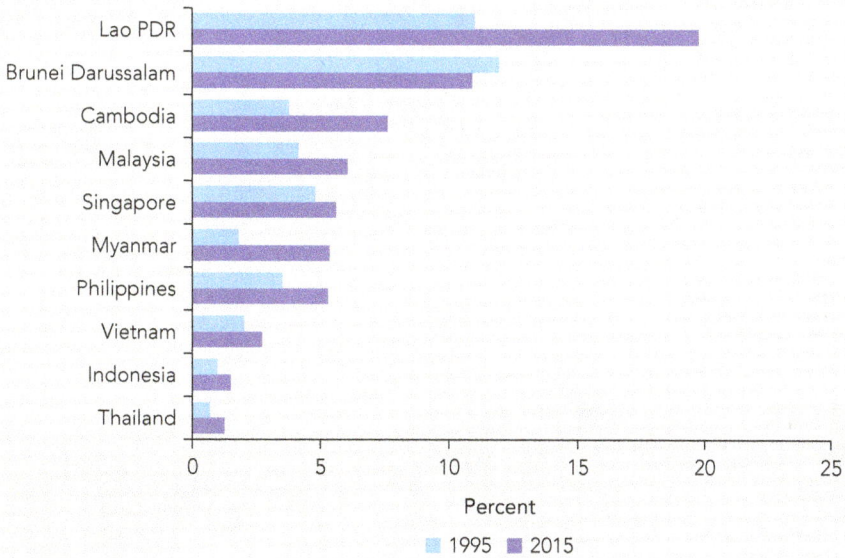

Source: UN 2015a.
Note: ASEAN = Association of Southeast Asian Nations.

Intra-ASEAN migration

ASEAN destinations

Malaysia, Singapore, and Thailand have the largest stocks of ASEAN migrants. The number of ASEAN migrants in ASEAN destinations was largest in Thailand in 2015, at more than 3.7 million (table 1.1). Malaysia and Singapore were next in line, with about 1.5 million and 1.3 million, respectively. The quantities in other ASEAN destinations were quite small in comparison, averaging about 36,000 (not including Myanmar for which no ASEAN migrants are recorded in the UN data). Between 1995 and 2015, the ASEAN migrant stock in Thailand increased by 3 million, or 394 percent, outpacing Singapore's 180 percent and Malaysia's 137 percent.

All ASEAN countries except Indonesia, Myanmar, and the Philippines receive most of their migrants from other ASEAN countries (figure 1.9). Notably, the share of migrants that Malaysia receives from other ASEAN countries has declined since 1995, as origin countries like Bangladesh and Nepal have become more important.

Except for Singapore, the ASEAN immigrant stock in the major ASEAN destination countries is primarily from poorer ASEAN origins (table 1.2). Of Thailand's ASEAN migrant stock, 53 percent originates from Myanmar, 26 percent from Lao PDR, and 21 percent from Cambodia. In Malaysia, 70 percent of the migrant stock originates from Indonesia and 16 percent from Myanmar. The story is different for Singapore, where 85 percent of ASEAN migrants are from neighboring Malaysia. Migrants from Indonesia, the Philippines, and Vietnam make up most of the ASEAN migrants in non-ASEAN destinations.

TABLE 1.1

Intra-ASEAN immigration by destination, 1995 and 2015

Destination	1995	2015	Change (no.)	Change (%)
Brunei Darussalam	69,078	83,832	14,754	21
Cambodia	82,910	68,106	−14,804	−18
Indonesia	9,713	49,930	40,217	414
Lao PDR	17,150	14,802	−2,348	−14
Malaysia	650,611	1,539,741	889,130	137
Myanmar	0	0	—	—
Philippines	18,584	6,499	−12,085	−65
Singapore	471,607	1,321,552	849,945	180
Thailand	761,559	3,762,393	3,000,834	394
Vietnam	44,755	40,537	−4,218	−9

Source: UN 2015a.

Note: — = not available; ASEAN = Association of Southeast Asian Nations.

FIGURE 1.9

Percentage of intra-ASEAN immigration relative to total immigration by destination

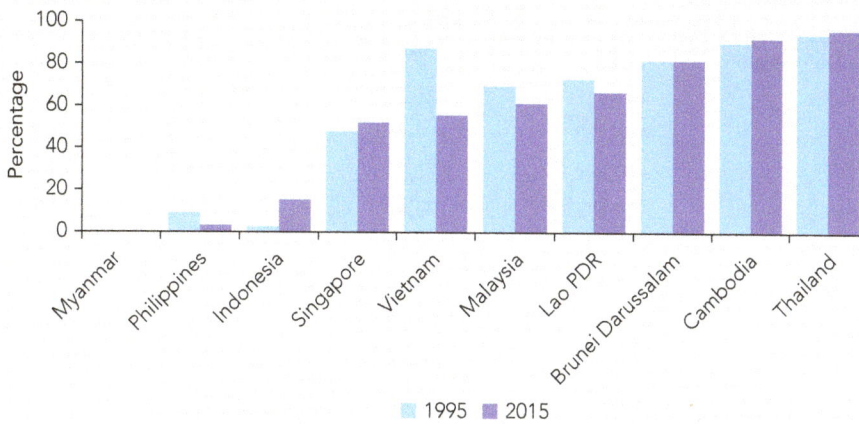

Source: UN 2015a.
Note: ASEAN = Association of Southeast Asian Nations.

TABLE 1.2

Primary origins of intra-ASEAN migrants by destination, 2015

Destination	Origin (>10% of migrants)
Brunei Darussalam	Malaysia (58%); Thailand (17%); Philippines (16%)
Cambodia	Vietnam (53%); Thailand (45%)
Indonesia	Singapore (44%); Thailand (44%)
Lao PDR	Vietnam (79%); Thailand (11%)
Malaysia	Indonesia (70%); Myanmar (16%)
Myanmar	n.a.
Philippines	Indonesia (51%); Singapore (13%); Malaysia (12%)
Singapore	Malaysia (85%); Indonesia (12%)
Thailand	Myanmar (53%); Lao PDR (26%); Cambodia (21%)
Vietnam	Thailand (28%); Myanmar (28%); Indonesia (19%); Lao PDR (17%)
Non-ASEAN	Philippines (39%); Indonesia (20%); Vietnam (18%)

Source: UN 2015a.
Note: n.a. = not applicable; ASEAN = Association of Southeast Asian Nations.

ASEAN origins

Indonesia, Myanmar, and Malaysia send the most migrants to other ASEAN countries. The largest number of ASEAN out-migrants was from Myanmar in 2015, at 2.2 million (table 1.3). Indonesia and Malaysia were next in line, at 1.3 million and 1.2 million, respectively. The numbers of migrants from Cambodia and Lao PDR to ASEAN destinations were both quite high, but less than 1 million.

TABLE 1.3

Intra-ASEAN emigration by origin, 1995 and 2015

Origin	1995	2015	Change (no.)	Change (%)
Brunei Darussalam	3,356	6,165	2,809	84
Cambodia	143,867	821,659	677,792	471
Indonesia	466,752	1,251,764	785,012	168
Lao PDR	210,294	976,770	766,476	364
Malaysia	479,872	1,176,428	696,556	145
Myanmar	450,230	2,242,549	1,792,319	398
Philippines	139,480	55,964	−83,516	−60
Singapore	39,326	106,284	66,958	170
Thailand	85,807	108,229	22,422	26
Vietnam	106,983	141,580	34,597	32

Source: UN 2015a.
Note: ASEAN = Association of Southeast Asian Nations.

FIGURE 1.10

Percentage of intra-ASEAN emigration relative to total emigration by origin, 1995 and 2015

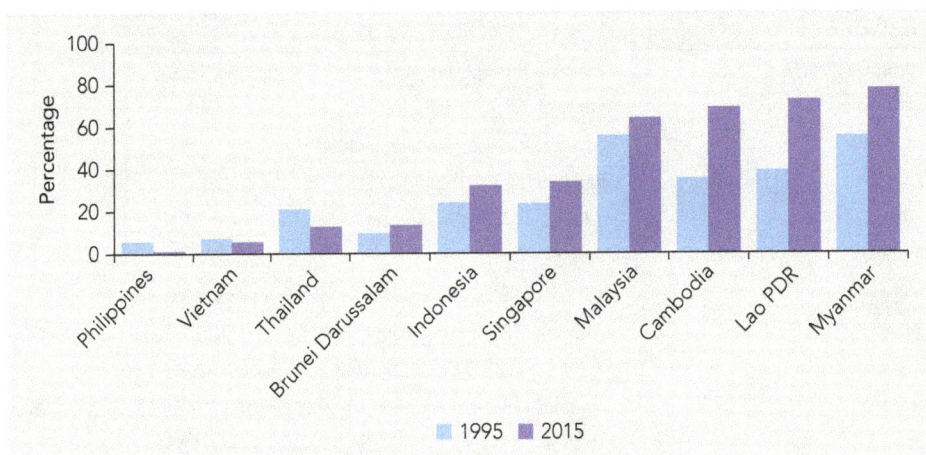

Source: UN 2015a.
Note: ASEAN = Association of Southeast Asian Nations.

Cambodia, Lao PDR, Malaysia, and Myanmar send most of their migrants to other ASEAN countries (table 1.3 and figure 1.10). For these four countries, the dominance of ASEAN destinations for their emigrants is a relatively new phenomenon with large increases in intra-ASEAN migration since 1995. Apart from Malaysia, which is positioned next to high-income Singapore, the destination for nearly all Malaysian intra-ASEAN migrants, the other three countries are the poorest in ASEAN. Nearly all intra-ASEAN migrants from Cambodia, Lao PDR, and Myanmar go to Thailand, which borders all three (table 1.4).

TABLE 1.4
Primary destinations of intra-ASEAN migrants by origin, 2015

Origin	Destination (>10% of migrants)
Brunei Darussalam	Malaysia (99%)
Cambodia	Thailand (98%)
Indonesia	Malaysia (86%); Singapore (13%)
Lao PDR	Thailand (99%)
Malaysia	Singapore (96%)
Myanmar	Thailand (88%); Malaysia (11%)
Philippines	Malaysia (39%); Singapore (28%); Brunei Darussalam (24%)
Singapore	Malaysia (75%); Indonesia (21%)
Thailand	Cambodia (28%); Indonesia (20%); Singapore (18%); Brunei Darussalam (13%)
Vietnam	Malaysia (62%); Cambodia (26%)
Non-ASEAN	Singapore (41%); Malaysia (33%)

Source: UN 2015a.
Note: ASEAN = Association of Southeast Asian Nations.

The Philippines and Vietnam are unique among sending countries because very few of their migrants go to ASEAN destinations. Nearly half of Philippine migrants go to North America, and a third go to the Middle East and North Africa, while about 1 percent go to other ASEAN countries. The intra-ASEAN share of Philippine emigration remains small (about 7 percent), even using the World Bank's larger estimate of the Philippine migrant stock in Malaysia. About 60 percent of migrants from Vietnam go to North America, whereas about 20 percent go to non-ASEAN East Asian countries and the remaining 20 percent go to Europe and Central Asia. Only the Philippines, Thailand, and Vietnam have fewer migrants in other ASEAN countries now than in 1995.

Most predominantly receiving countries send their ASEAN migrants to a single upper-middle or high-income ASEAN destination country. Brunei Darussalam sends them to Malaysia; Malaysia to Singapore; and Singapore to Malaysia. Thailand is unique, however. Of all ASEAN countries, Thailand has the most widespread distribution of ASEAN migrant destinations: 28 percent of migrants head to Cambodia; 20 percent to Indonesia; 18 percent to Singapore; and 13 percent to Brunei Darussalam.

ASEAN corridors

Migration within ASEAN is highly concentrated in several corridors. Three major groups of corridors run to ASEAN's three main destination countries.[3] These are the Thailand corridor for migration from Cambodia, Lao PDR, and Myanmar, making up 54 percent of ASEAN migration; the Singapore corridor for migration from Indonesia and Malaysia, making up 19 percent of ASEAN migration; and the slightly more diverse Malaysia corridor for migration from Indonesia, Myanmar, Singapore, and Vietnam, making up 22 percent of ASEAN migration. Together, these corridors account for 95 percent of all intra-ASEAN migration (table 1.5). These corridors were largely the same

TABLE 1.5
Intra-ASEAN migrant stocks in ASEAN's major migration corridors, 2015

Origin	Destination	Stock	Destination's migration (%)	ASEAN migration (%)
Myanmar	Thailand	1,978,348	53	29
Lao PDR		969,267	26	14
Cambodia		805,272	21	12
Total		*3,752,887*	*100*	*54*
Indonesia	Malaysia	1,070,433	70	16
Myanmar		252,292	16	4
Vietnam		87,272	6	1
Singapore		79,519	5	1
Total		*1,489,516*	*97*	*22*
Malaysia	Singapore	1,123,654	85	16
Indonesia		163,237	12	2
Total		*1,286,891*	*97*	*19*
Total of corridors		**6,529,294**		95

Source: UN 2015a.
Note: Some figures may not add up to 100 due to rounding. ASEAN = Association of Southeast Asian Nations.

in 2000. Migration in ASEAN is mostly, though not solely, from less developed to more developed countries. Notably, consistent with the strong historical ties and proximity of Malaysia and Singapore, ASEAN's main corridors include migration to and from two of ASEAN's wealthiest economies.

Characteristics of ASEAN migrants

Age

ASEAN's host countries tend to be aging countries, whereas its sending countries tend to be younger. Like East Asia more generally, ASEAN member states are diverse in their stage of population aging, and this is reflected in the region's migration flows. More than 10 percent of the local populations of Singapore and Thailand are at least 65 years old. Malaysia is slightly younger; 6 percent of its local population is 65 or older. All sending countries other than Vietnam have local populations in which 5 percent or less of the population is at least 65.

Migrant populations seem to fill gaps in the workforces of ASEAN's aging countries. Figure 1.11 plots the age distributions of local and migrant populations in ASEAN destination countries. All destination countries have migrant populations whose age distribution peaks between ages 25 and 39, the prime working years. This provides some evidence that migration is, in part, driven by a demand for workers in aging countries. Box 1.2 discusses the longer-term impact of migration on population aging in ASEAN countries. No recent comprehensive data are available on the age of intra-ASEAN migrants.

FIGURE 1.11

Age distribution of migrants and locals in ASEAN's main destination countries, 2015

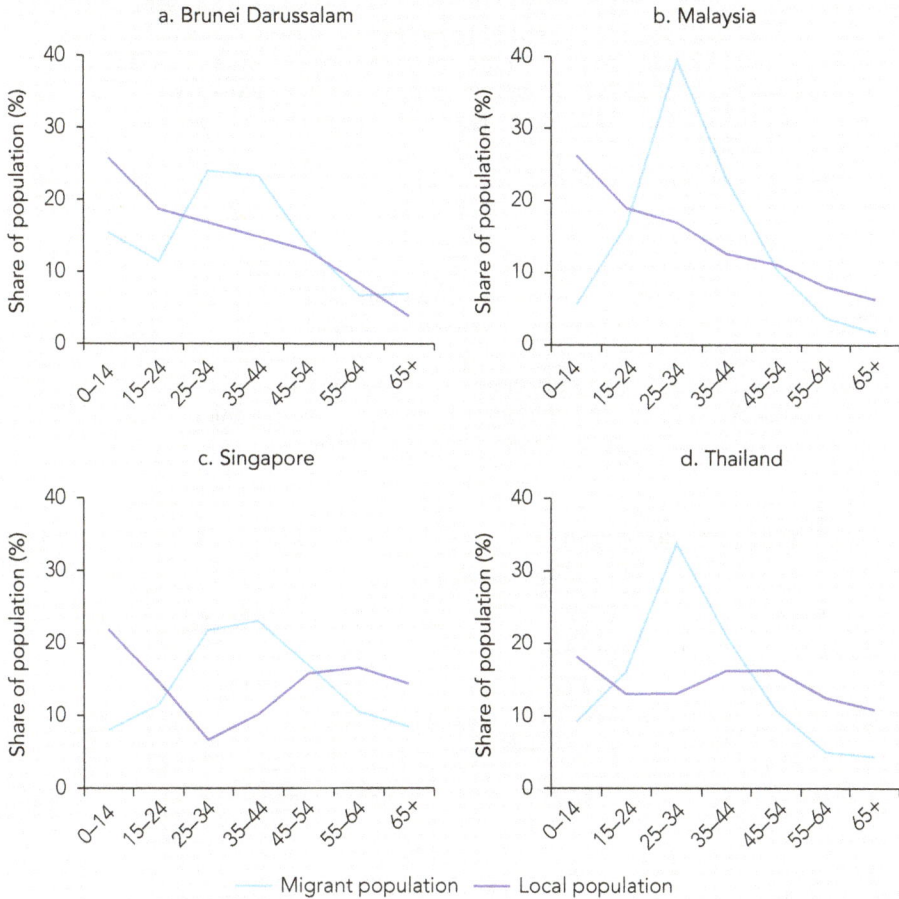

a. Brunei Darussalam

b. Malaysia

c. Singapore

d. Thailand

—— Migrant population —— Local population

Source: UN 2015a.
Note: ASEAN = Association of Southeast Asian Nations.

Gender

Just over half of EAP's total migrant stock (52 percent) is female, while just under half (48 percent) of ASEAN's total migrant stock is female. Although a trend toward a larger share of female migrants in EAP is well documented (Ahsan et al. 2014; Lee 2005), the female share of immigration to and emigration from ASEAN countries has remained about constant since 1995. Singapore is the only country in ASEAN whose migrant stock is mostly female (56 percent), while Thailand is at female–male parity (figure 1.12). The proportion of the stock that is female has increased 2 percentage points in both countries since 1995. In Malaysia, in contrast, the share of the stock that is female has

BOX 1.2
Migration and population aging in ASEAN

UN population projections provide an indication of the future impact that migration will have on population aging in ASEAN countries. The UN makes several important assumptions to estimate population growth, and publishes several variations of its projections. One of these variations estimates population growth without international migration, allowing for a comparison with the variation that does assume international migration.[a]

The impact of international migration on two of the three primary ASEAN destination countries is to increase the share of the working age population and decrease the share of the population that is 65 years old or older, thereby decreasing the median age in these countries (table B1.2.1). In Singapore, this effect is particularly significant, with the median age declining 2.2 years when migration is included. The effect is slightly smaller in Malaysia, where the median age declines about half a year. The other pronounced effect, however, is in the third destination country, Thailand, where the median age *increases* because of international migration and the working-age population *declines*. This is likely the effect of out-migration of working-age individuals from Thailand to countries outside of ASEAN.

TABLE B1.2.1
Impact of international migration on age distribution of ASEAN countries, 2050

Country	Age distribution			Change in median age
	0–14	15–64	65+	
Singapore	0.8%	2.1%	−3.0%	−2.2
Malaysia	0.2%	0.5%	−0.7%	−0.5
Brunei Darussalam	0.1%	0.4%	−0.5%	−0.4
Cambodia	0.3%	−0.6%	0.4%	−0.1
Lao PDR	0.1%	−0.5%	0.5%	0.0
Myanmar	0.0%	−0.1%	0.1%	0.0
Philippines	0.0%	−0.1%	0.1%	0.0
Indonesia	0.0%	−0.2%	0.2%	0.1
Vietnam	−0.1%	−0.2%	0.3%	0.3
Thailand	−0.2%	−0.4%	0.5%	1.3

Source: UN 2015c.
Note: This table shows the percentage point difference in age distribution and the difference in years between UN population projections in 2050 with and without international migration. ASEAN = Association of Southeast Asian Nations.

[a] UN projections without international migration do not permit comparison of the impact of intra-ASEAN migration alone on the age distribution and median age. Moreover, the projections include both immigration and emigration. See United Nations (2014) for a more detailed description of the methodology.

FIGURE 1.12
Female share of immigrant and emigrant stock of ASEAN countries, 1995 and 2015

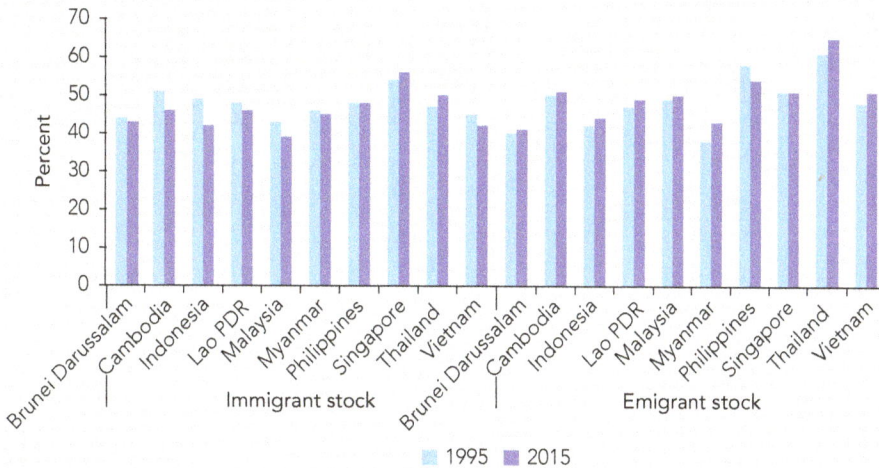

Note: ASEAN = Association of Southeast Asian Nations.

declined 4 percentage points. Notably, the share of ASEAN emigrants who are female has increased in every country except the Philippines; it is at or above parity in seven countries. The decline in female out-migration from the Philippines may have resulted in part from increased stringency imposed by the country's migration authorities on the terms of employment for domestic workers, who tend to be female.

The share of the intra-ASEAN migrant stock that is female rose from 46 percent in 1990 to 49 percent in 2015. This figure is lower than EAP's intraregional share of 53 percent. Most gains in female migration in ASEAN countries were made in the 1990s. In EAP, in contrast, the female share has increased steadily since 1990. Half of ASEAN countries sent a larger share of female migrants to other ASEAN countries than they did to non-ASEAN countries (table 1.6).

Skill level

Migrants help fill skills gaps. Relationships between origin and destination countries are often based on differences in the skill level of migrants and locals, with origin countries supplying migrants of a specific skill type in demand in destination countries. Within ASEAN, much of this migration involves the movement of less-educated individuals to work in lower-skilled occupations in the region's main destination countries.

Migrants in ASEAN's receiving countries tend to be less skilled than locals, whereas migrants in ASEAN's sending countries tend to be more skilled. Drawing on data from the ILO's newly created International Labour Migration Statistics Database in ASEAN (ILMS), figure 1.13 compares the education level of the migrant stock with the education level of locals in ASEAN countries where data are available. The educational level

TABLE 1.6
Female share of migration from ASEAN origins to ASEAN and non-ASEAN destinations, 2015
(Percent)

Origin	Destination	
	ASEAN	Non-ASEAN
ASEAN	49	50
Brunei Darussalam	39	42
Cambodia	52	50
Indonesia	42	44
Lao PDR	51	42
Malaysia	56	39
Myanmar	46	31
Philippines	58	53
Singapore	46	54
Thailand	50	67
Vietnam	42	51

Source: UN 2015a.
Note: ASEAN = Association of Southeast Asian Nations.

FIGURE 1.13
Education level of migrants and locals in ASEAN countries

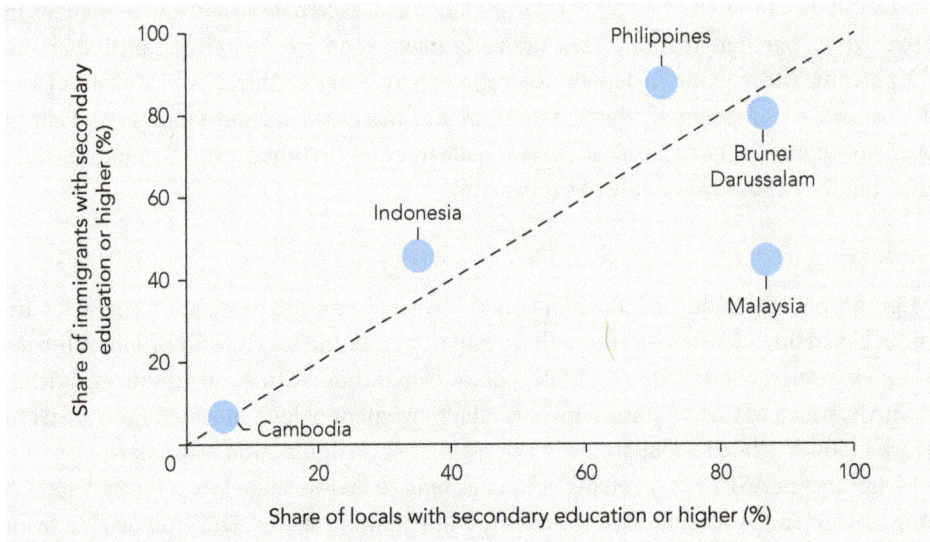

Source: International Labour Migration Statistics Database in ASEAN, ILO (ILMS).
Note: The share of working-age locals with at least secondary education is shown on the x axis and that of migrants with at least secondary education is on the y axis. The 45-degree line represents equal proportions of highly educated locals and migrants. The year is 2014 for Brunei Darussalam, 2013 for Cambodia, 2015 for Indonesia and Malaysia, and 2010 for the Philippines. ASEAN = Association of Southeast Asian Nations.

of the local population of Malaysia, one of ASEAN's main receiving countries, has grown significantly in recent decades, resulting in a highly educated population. In conjunction, most migration to Malaysia is low-skilled with 45 percent of migrants in 2015 having attained just basic education. Immigrants in Indonesia and the Philippines, both global senders of migrants, tend to be more highly skilled than their local counterparts. This highlights the fact that traditionally sending countries also need skilled workers to fill skills gaps in their labor markets.

The vast majority of intra-ASEAN migrants are less educated and so likely less skilled. Estimates of migration in 2000, the most recent year for which comprehensive intra-ASEAN data are available, suggest that 93 percent of intra-ASEAN migrants have less than a tertiary education and 83 percent have less than a secondary education. Emigrants from ASEAN's main sending countries tend to be less educated, with more than 90 percent of intra-ASEAN emigrants from Indonesia, Lao PDR, Myanmar, the Philippines, and Vietnam having less than a secondary education (figure 1.14a). Intra-ASEAN emigrants from the main destination countries, in contrast, tend to be more educated.

Intra-ASEAN immigrants in two of ASEAN's main destination countries tend to be less educated. In Thailand, 99 percent of immigrants have attained less than secondary education, while in Malaysia 95 percent have (figure 1.14b). Migrants are more educated

FIGURE 1.14

Educational composition of intra-ASEAN migrants by origin and destination, 2000

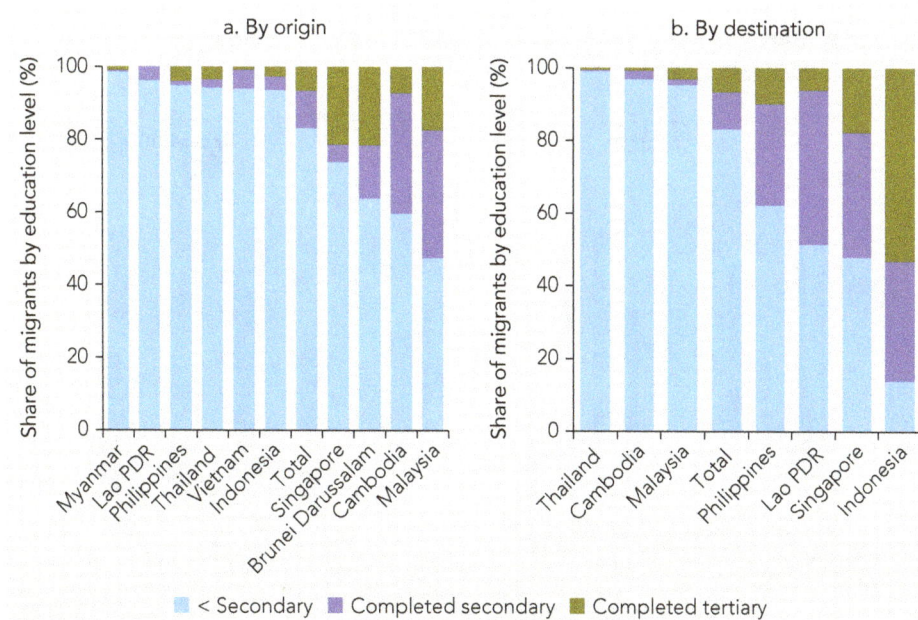

Source: Database on Immigrants in OECD and Non-OECD Countries, OECD (DIOC-E).
Note: Destination data are only available for Cambodia, Indonesia, Lao PDR, Malaysia, the Philippines, Singapore, and Thailand. ASEAN = Association of Southeast Asisan nations; OECD = Organisation for Economic Co-operation and Development.

in Singapore; 34 percent have completed their secondary education, likely reflecting the immigration of better-educated Malaysians. Newly available data for 2010 suggest that low-skilled migration continues to dominate in ASEAN.[4]

Migrants from every ASEAN country who have migrated to other ASEAN countries are less-educated than their counterparts who have migrated outside of the region (figure 1.15a). The difference between the skill levels of the two groups of migrants is large in all countries except Cambodia and particularly large in Indonesia and the Philippines, two significant senders of migrants outside of ASEAN. The same pattern is true for migrants to ASEAN countries: immigrants from other ASEAN countries tend to be less-skilled than their counterparts from outside the region in every country except Indonesia, where ASEAN migrants are more skilled (figure 1.15b).

Migrants also tend to work in lower-skilled occupations[5] in ASEAN's main destination countries. In Thailand, 90 percent of global migrants work in low-skilled elementary occupations compared to just 7 percent of locals (figure 1.16). In Malaysia, migrants are about evenly split between mid- and low-skilled jobs, though 47 percent are in low-skilled ones compared to 7 percent of the local population. The breakdown is similar in Brunei Darussalam, though there are slightly more high-skilled migrants. In Cambodia, the only sending country for which data are available,

FIGURE 1.15

Share of ASEAN and non-ASEAN migrants with at least a secondary education by origin and destination, 2000

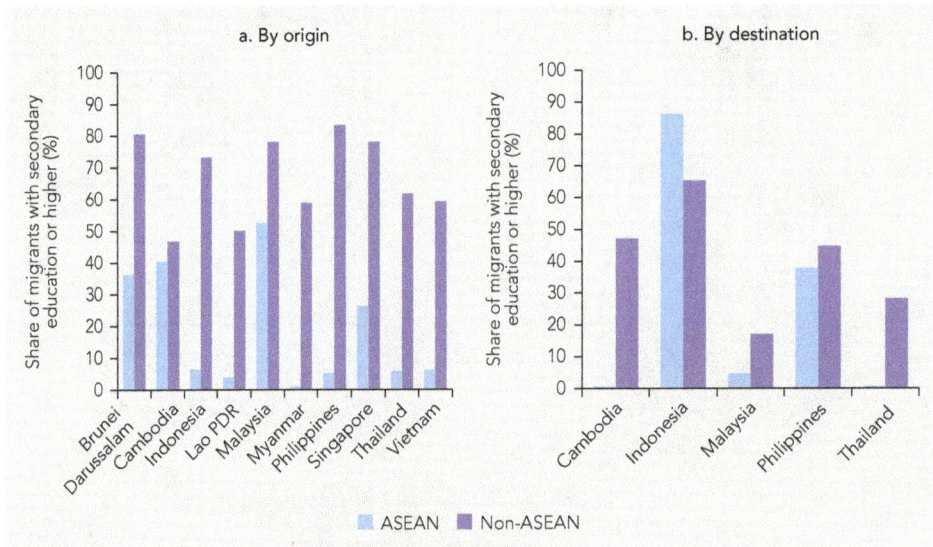

Source: Database on Immigrants in OECD and Non-OECD Countries, OECD (DIOC-E).
Note: Destination data are only available for Cambodia, Indonesia, Lao PDR, Malaysia, the Philippines, Singapore, and Thailand. ASEAN = Association of Southeast Asian Nations.

FIGURE 1.16

Skill level of migrants and locals in ASEAN destinations

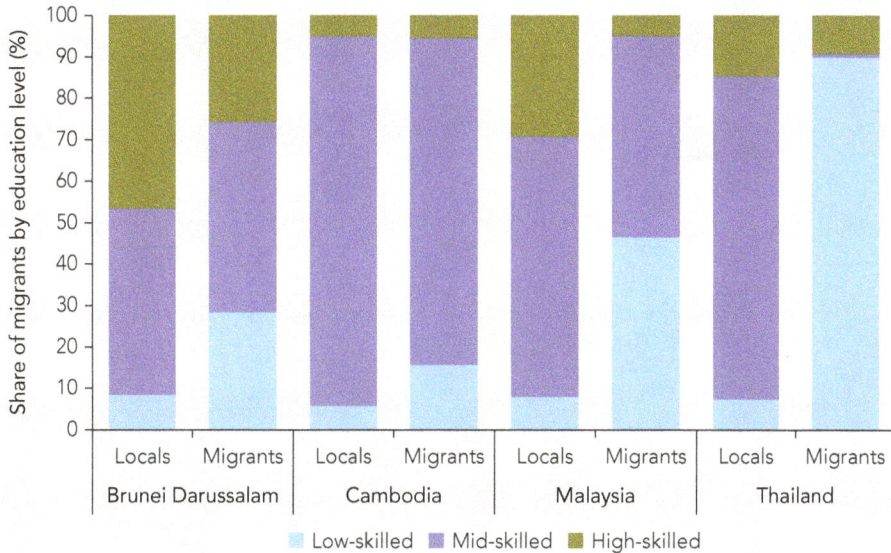

Source: International Labour Migration Statistics Database in ASEAN, ILO (ILMS).
Note: The year is 2014 for Brunei Darussalam, 2013 for Cambodia, 2015 for Malaysia, and 2015 for Thailand. Data are only available for these countries. ASEAN = Association of Southeast Asian Nations.

a much higher percentage of migrants work in mid-skilled jobs than in any of the other countries, and about equal percentages of locals and migrants work in high-skilled jobs.

Labor force characteristics

Employment and unemployment

In the main receiving countries in ASEAN, the employment rates[6] of migrants are high. In Brunei Darussalam, Malaysia, and Singapore, employment rates are at least 25 percentage points higher for migrants than for locals (table 1.7). This largely reflects migration policies that are designed primarily to attract temporary labor migrants.

Migrants who participate in the labor force in ASEAN seem to be fulfilling a demand for their skills. Unemployment rates were quite low among intra-ASEAN migrants in 2000, with rates in Indonesia, Lao PDR, Malaysia, and Thailand between 2 and 3 percent, comparable to the unemployment rates of the local population. Although data are limited for 2010, unemployment rates remained quite low and comparable to the unemployment rates of the local population. In Cambodia and Malaysia, the two ASEAN countries for which comparable rates are available, the unemployment rates were 3 percent and 2 percent, respectively.

TABLE 1.7
Employment rate of migrants and locals in ASEAN
(Percent)

Destination	Locals	Migrants	Difference
Brunei Darussalam	40	77	36
Cambodia	55	73	18
Indonesia	45	36	−9
Malaysia	43	72	29
Philippines	40	35	−5
Singapore	59	85	26

Source: International Labour Migration Statistics Database in ASEAN (ILMS), ILO.
Note: The year is 2014 for Brunei Darussalam, 2015 for Indonesia and Malaysia, and 2014 for the Philippines and Singapore. Data are only available for these countries.

TABLE 1.8
Sectoral distribution of migrants and locals in ASEAN
(% difference in distribution)

Destination	Agriculture	Industry	Services
Brunei Darussalam	0	16	−17
Cambodia	−26	6	21
Indonesia	5	−7	3
Lao PDR	−1	10	−9
Malaysia	21	10	−31
Singapore	−1	29	−29
Thailand	−19	29	−10

Source: International Labour Migration Statistics Database in ASEAN (ILMS), ILO.
Note: The year is 2006 for Lao PDR, 2014 for Brunei Darussalam, 2013 for Cambodia, and 2015 for Indonesia, Malaysia, Singapore, and Thailand. Data are only available for these countries. ASEAN = Association of Southeast Asian Nations.

Sector of employment

The sector in which global migrants to ASEAN countries work varies across countries and does not depend solely on whether the country is primarily a sender or receiver of migrants (table 1.8). Migrants in Malaysia, Singapore, and Thailand tend to work more in industry and less in services than locals. However, migrants are much more concentrated in the services sector in Singapore, which lacks a significant agricultural sector employing either locals or migrants. Thailand and Malaysia do have more robust agricultural sectors, but migrants play a different role in each. Malaysian palm oil plantations rely significantly on migrant labor, so migrants are much more prevalent in this sector than locals. In Thailand, in contrast, more locals work in agriculture, highlighting Thailand's more significant rural population. In 2015, for instance, about 50 percent of the population lived in rural areas in Thailand, compared to 25 percent in Malaysia.

Income

In ASEAN receiving countries, migrants seem to earn less than locals, although in its sending countries, migrants seem to earn more. Data on the employment-related income of migrants in ASEAN countries are limited to Brunei Darussalam, Cambodia, and Malaysia. Consistent with the evidence on the education and occupations of migrants in ASEAN receiving countries, migrants in Brunei Darussalam and Malaysia earn significantly less than their local counterparts. Migrants earn 50 percent of their local counterparts in Brunei Darussalam and 65 percent of their local counterparts in Malaysia (figure 1.17). In Cambodia, in contrast, migrants' median monthly wages are 133 percent of those of their local peers.

Undocumented migration

Undocumented migration is a significant feature of migration in ASEAN. Understanding this type of migration is limited by both a lack of data and the challenge of defining who is undocumented. Undocumented migrants are less likely to participate in population censuses and household surveys, and when they do identifying that they are undocumented is a challenge. Even when the undocumented can be identified, definitional issues arise. For instance, the Philippines regards out-migrants who do not use the country's formal migration channels as undocumented. However, if these migrants obtain a work permit in Singapore (which is possible without the use of formal channels in the Philippines), they are deemed to be documented and regular migrants by the Singaporean government. With these two challenges in mind, inferences about

FIGURE 1.17

Ratio of employment-related income of migrants relative to locals

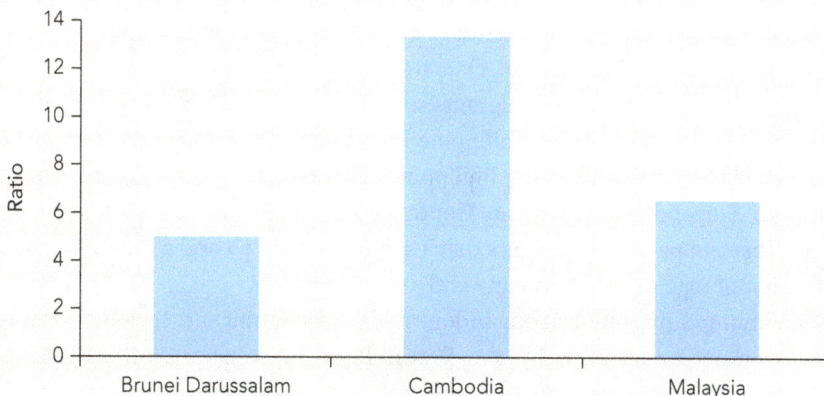

Source: International Labour Migration Statistics Database in ASEAN, ILO (ILMS).
Note: The year is 2014 for Brunei Darussalam, 2013 for Cambodia, and 2014 for Malaysia (data were only available for these countries).

the number of undocumented migrants in ASEAN can be made from regularization campaigns and other sources, though these are by nature not representative and provide only a lower bound to the total number of undocumented workers in a country.

Two of ASEAN's three migrant host countries receive significant numbers of undocumented migrants. Long borders between Thailand and Cambodia, Lao PDR, and Myanmar and between Indonesia and Malaysia make these corridors particularly vulnerable to informal migration. Migration from Cambodia, Lao PDR, and Myanmar, which accounts for most migration to Thailand, is mostly undocumented. Using data from Thai government sources, Huguet (2014) roughly estimates that there were 2.7 million migrants from these three countries in Thailand in 2013, of whom 1.6 million, or 58 percent, were irregular.[7] Reports from Malaysia's 6P amnesty and legalization program, which ran from 2011 to 2012, identified between 1.3 million and 2 million undocumented immigrants in Malaysia (World Bank 2015). This is about the same as the 1.6 million migrants with work permits for low-skilled employment in Malaysia in those years. About 49 percent of the undocumented migrants were from Indonesia, with 3 percent from the Philippines, 2 percent from Myanmar and Vietnam, and 1 percent or less from Cambodia and Thailand. In Malaysia, undocumented workers at times commute daily between Indonesian Kalimantan and the Malaysian state of Sarawak; borders are also porous between the Philippines and the Malaysian state of Sabah, which results in informal flows.

In contrast to Malaysia and Thailand, Singapore's advantageous geographical setting and strict enforcement result in limited undocumented migration to the city-state. The Immigration and Checkpoints Authority of Singapore identified just 310 undocumented immigrants and 1,591 overstayers in 2015 (ICA 2016). Though representing just those who were caught, this small number alongside Singapore's significant migration enforcement apparatus suggests that informal migration to Singapore is not a significant issue.

Although undocumented migration is normally thought of as an issue for host countries, sending countries also are interested in informal migration because they want to better protect their migrants abroad. Data from the Philippines suggest that 1.2 million, or 11 percent, of Philippine out-migrants were irregular in 2013, a significant decline from 22 percent in 2001. Most Philippine migrants to Malaysia were thought to be irregular (CFO 2016). Notably, the Philippines classifies 110,141, or 25 percent, of its migrants to Singapore as irregular. Contrasted with Singapore's data on irregular migrants, this comparison highlights that a sending country's and a receiving country's classification of regular migrants can conflict.

Undocumented migration from Indonesia is also significant. In a 2013 survey of migrant workers undertaken by the World Bank in collaboration with Statistics Indonesia, only 9 percent of current migrant workers were in full compliance with required documentation, and just 43 percent were in compliance with a more relaxed definition of these requirements (World Bank 2016a). This latter definition implies that 6.8 million migrants work abroad without the required documents (World Bank 2016b).

Undocumented migration is particularly significant for workers moving from Indonesia to Malaysia. Among the survey respondents, only 3.6 percent of current Indonesian migrant workers in Malaysia are fully compliant with required documentation (World Bank 2016a).

Though estimates are very rough, undocumented Vietnamese migrants are a significant presence abroad. For Vietnamese migrants, the issue of irregular migration seems most closely related to overstay after employment permits expire, but outmigration without the proper documents also occurs. Most estimates of the undocumented population relate to the share of Vietnamese workers who have overstayed their contracts. Research suggests that up to 57 percent of migrants overstay in the Republic of Korea, 30 percent in Japan, and 12 percent in Taiwan, China (Ahsan et al. 2014).

Notes

1. ASEAN consists of Brunei Darussalam, Cambodia, Indonesia, Lao PDR, Malaysia, Myanmar, the Philippines, Singapore, Thailand, and Vietnam

2. In 2015, the data show no recorded migrants in Myanmar from ASEAN countries.

3. If the World Bank's Global Migration Database were used, the corridor from the Philippines to Malaysia with 410,149 migrants in 2013 would rank as Malaysia's second-largest source and ASEAN's sixth-largest corridor.

4. Updated data on education are becoming available for 2010, though the data are still preliminary. Destination data are available in ASEAN only for Cambodia, Malaysia, and Thailand. These preliminary data suggest that intra-ASEAN migrants remain mostly less educated, with 97 percent of intra-ASEAN migrants to these countries having less than tertiary education and 86 percent having less than secondary education.

5. Low-skilled occupations are defined here as elementary occupations. Mid-skilled are defined as clerical support workers; service and sales workers; skilled agricultural, forestry, and fishery workers; craft and related trades workers; and plant and machine operators and assemblers. High-skilled occupations are defined as managers, professionals, and technicians and associated professionals.

6. The employment rate is used here because the size of the labor force was not available for all countries. The rate is calculated as the total of those employed age 15 and over divided by the population in the same age group.

7. Irregular is defined as either not having a work permit or not completing the nationality verification process, or both.

References

Ahsan, Ahmad, Manolo Abella, Andrew Beath, Yukon Huang, Manjula Luthria, and Trang Van Nguyen. 2014. *International Migration and Development in East Asia and the Pacific*. Washington, DC: World Bank.

CFO (Commission on Filipinos Overseas). 2016. *2014 CFO Compendium of Statistics on International Migration*. 4th ed. Manila: CFO.

Huguet, Jerrold W. 2014. "Thailand Migration Profile." In *Thailand Migration Report 2014*, edited by Jerrold W. Huguet, 27–43. Bangkok: United Nations Thematic Working Group on Migration in Thailand.

ICA (Immigration and Checkpoints Authority). 2016. *Annual Statistics Report 2015*. Singapore: ICA.

ILO (International Labour Organization) and ADB (Asia Development Bank). 2014. *ASEAN Community 2015: Managing Integration for Better Jobs and Shared Prosperity*. Bangkok: ILO and ADB.

IOM (International Organization for Migration). 2013. *Country Migration Report: The Philippines 2013*. Makati City: IOM.

Lee, June JH. 2005. "Human Trafficking in East Asia: Current Trends, Data Collection, and Knowledge Gaps." *International Migration* 43(1/2):165–201.

MMN (Mekong Migration Network) and AMC (Asian Migrant Centre. 2013. *Migration in the Greater Mekong Subregion Resource Book: In-depth Study: Border Economic Zones and Migration*. Chiang Mai, Thailand: MMN and AMC.

United Nations. 2014. "World Population Prospects: The 2012 Revision: Methodology of the United Nations Population Estimates and Projections." Working Paper No. 235. United Nations, New York.

———. 2015a. *Trends in International Migrant Stock: The 2015 Revision*. (United Nations database, POP/DB/MIG/Stock/Rev.2015). New York: United Nations.

———. 2015b. *Trends in International Migrant Stock: The 2015 Revision*. CD-ROM documentation. New York: United Nations.

———. 2015c. *World Population Prospects: The 2015 Revision*. DVD Edition. New York: United Nations, Department of Economic and Social Affairs, Population Division.

World Bank. 2015. *Malaysia Economic Monitor: Immigrant Labour*. Washington, DC: World Bank.

———. 2016a. "Features of Indonesian Overseas Migrant Workers." Background Paper 1. World Bank, Washington, DC.

———. 2016b. "Indonesia's Global Workers: Juggling Opportunities and Risks." World Bank, Washington, DC.

CHAPTER 2

The Determinants of Migration in ASEAN and the Importance of Labor Mobility Costs

Introduction

Migration decisions are made on the basis of the expected costs and benefits of migration. Migration scholars generally model the migration decision as motivated by an individual's desire to maximize income. The determinants of migration are, then, the benefits and costs that influence a migrant's decision to move. The benefits of migration are frequently conceptualized as economic gains in the form of increased wages, whereas costs are often captured using distance and other proxies.

In the Association of Southeast Asian Nations (ASEAN), higher-income countries with older populations tend to attract migrants by creating expectations for higher wages and employment opportunities. The presence of diaspora networks seems to attract more migrants to and from ASEAN countries, likely by lowering the cost of migration, whereas longer distances lower migration, likely by increasing the cost. Within ASEAN, these factors drive large one-way migration to a small number of countries, with migration to other countries being small in comparison.

While factors such as distance and presence of diaspora networks are important components of migration costs, these and other factors often used to describe migration costs do not capture the full range of costs faced by workers when they decide whether to migrate. These more comprehensive costs include skills mismatches, legal constraints to mobility, migrant workers' location preferences and job search costs, and many others. To overcome this limitation, the analysis in this chapter uses wage differentials and actual worker mobility to estimate migration costs. And, to capture the full range of alternatives available to migrants, domestic labor mobility costs—those faced by workers changing firms, sectors, and geographies within a country's borders—are also estimated. Estimation of both domestic and international labor mobility costs highlights the fact that frictions exist in labor markets in ASEAN that may lead workers to forgo wage gains, which has a negative impact on welfare (discussed in chapter 4).

In chapter 1, ASEAN countries were characterized as either senders or receivers of migrants, thus suggesting that there are underlying characteristics that make some countries more attractive to receiving migrants and others more likely to send them. In this chapter, these characteristics are explored. The first section reviews the literature on the determinants of migration. The second section provides descriptive evidence of the benefits of migrating in ASEAN.

The final section of the chapter is an innovative attempt to estimate the labor mobility costs for migrant workers in ASEAN. These costs are found to be lowest in Malaysia and Singapore and highest in the Lao People's Democratic Republic and Myanmar. Costs generally increased between the 1960s and the 1990s but then dropped in the 2000s, reflecting ASEAN's increased integration regionally and globally and improvements in the region's migration systems.

Existing evidence on the determinants of migration in ASEAN

An individual's decision to migrate is affected by several factors related to the expected benefits and costs of migration. These factors include economic, social, and demographic characteristics that affect the desirability of migration. Wage differentials and employment prospects are among the main "pull" factors. "Push" factors may include employment prospects in the sending country.

Income, distance, and demographic factors all affect migration decisions. Analyzing the determinants of international migration flows from 120 sending countries to 15 member countries of the Organisation for Economic Co-operation and Development (OECD), Ortega and Peri (2013) find that factors increasing bilateral flows include income differentials, common language and currency, looser entry laws, and a shared colonial past. Longer geographic distance and tighter entry laws decrease these flows. Larger existing stocks of immigrants also play a key role in determining migration flows by lowering migration costs through informational and financial support (Beine, Bertoli, and Fernández-Huertas Moraga 2015). Finally, a larger share of youth in the origin country's population increases migration both because young people are more likely to migrate[1] and because a larger youth share can affect employment prospects negatively by increasing labor market competition (Zaiceva and Zimmermann 2014). Beine and Parsons (2015) find that higher wage differentials, a larger diaspora, a lower dependency ratio at the origin (implying a younger population), shared linguistic roots, and shared borders all induce more migration. Although the authors do not find evidence of a direct effect of long-run climatic factors on migration, they note indirect evidence that environmental factors have an impact on migration through wages.

Immigration policies related to entry into the host country have important impacts on the quantity and characteristics of migrants admitted in that country, though these impacts are not always consistent with policy objectives. As mentioned previously, studies on the determinants of migration have examined the impact of policy on the decision to migrate. Visa waivers (Bertoli and Fernández-Huertas Moraga 2013; Beine and Parsons 2015; Bertoli and Fernández-Huertas Moraga 2015) and regional agreements (Beine, Bourgeon, and Bricongne 2013; Beine, Bertoli, and Fernández-Huertas Moraga 2015) seem to increase bilateral flows. However, Docquier, Peri, and Ruyssen (2014) find no effect, perhaps because of the similarities between countries with such agreements. Ortega and Peri (2013) find evidence that tighter entry rules decrease flows to OECD countries. Mayda (2010) finds similar results for OECD member countries, Hatton (2005) for the United Kingdom, and Clark, Hatton, and Williamson (2007) for the United States.

The impact of immigration policies on the skill mix of immigrants is of concern to ASEAN countries interested in attracting high-skilled foreign workers. Several studies have been skeptical about the impact that skill-based immigration policies can have, particularly where family reunification is significant (Beine, Docquier, and Özden 2011; Belot and Hatton 2012; Jasso and Rosenzweig 2008). However, gathering data on bilateral high-skilled immigration labor flows and policy instruments for 10 OECD countries, Czaika and Parsons (2016) find that points-based migration systems increase high-skilled migration in terms of both numbers and the skill share of immigrants. Points-based systems perform much better than alternatives (such as job offer requirements, labor market tests, and occupational shortage lists) in inducing and selecting high-skilled migrants. High-skilled migrants seem to compare the costs and benefits of skilled migration entry paths to other (general) entry paths. Facchini and Lodigiani (2014) and Coppel, Dumont, and Visco (2001) both note the tendency for skilled migrants to select general channels of entry when skill-specific ones seem too onerous. This suggests that—to be effective—skilled migration policies must provide additional value in comparison to other entry paths.

Other factors—including social networks, political conflict, and natural disasters—also play a role in migration decisions. Social networks have been shown to play a key role in lowering migration costs and facilitating flows by correcting for the asymmetry of information that potential migrants face (Beaman 2012; Munshi 2003). Social networks also help migrants integrate in the receiving country. Instability, civil conflict, and natural disasters in countries of origin may also lead individuals to migrate. Political conflict is part of the explanation for emigration from Myanmar in recent years; however, as the country undergoes political and economic transition, these flows may reverse (World Bank 2012).

The factors that may prevent migrants from moving include liquidity constraints and lack of demand. The poorest households in sending countries may not be able to send migrants because of the costliness of international migration. Indeed, evidence has been found of an inverse "U-shaped" relationship between migration and wealth—with the least wealthy households unable to afford migration and the wealthiest households having higher opportunity costs of migration (McKenzie and Rapoport 2007). Shrestha (2017) provides evidence of this relationship in Nepal, a country that sends migrants to India, Malaysia, and the Middle East. A rainfall shock that increases household income increases migration to India, a low-cost but also low-earnings destination, but not to other destinations such as Malaysia, a high-cost but high-earnings destination. This suggests that easing liquidity constraints could facilitate the migration of poorer households, though Shrestha (2017) notes that more significant resources may be needed to motivate migration to higher-earnings destination countries. At the same time, lack of demand can limit migration for households that would otherwise want to migrate. This is evidenced by the increase in migration to Malaysia and the Middle East following demand shocks in those countries.

Research from ASEAN largely supports these general findings on the determinants of migration. Income differences are found to be a key factor influencing migration in ASEAN. Jajri and Ismail (2014) suggest that the main determinants of migration to Malaysia from Indonesia, Thailand, and the Philippines are the real wage ratio between the countries, the unemployment rate in the source countries, and the real exchange rate ratio.[2] Sanglaoid, Santipolvut, and Thamma-Apiroam (2014) present evidence suggesting that the main determinants of migration to Thailand from ASEAN countries are the gross domestic product (GDP) ratio between Thailand and the origin countries, existing migrant stocks in Thailand, and Thailand's migration policy. There is some evidence suggesting that climatic factors play a role in migration in the region. Bylander (2016) finds that migration to Thailand from Cambodia, which experiences frequent floods and droughts, is related to droughts, poor rainfall, and past crop losses.

The benefits of migrating in ASEAN

Wages and GDP per capita

ASEAN countries vary significantly in their level of economic development. ASEAN's significant wage and GDP differentials suggest that individuals from lower-income countries could increase their income by migrating. Singapore's average monthly wage of US$3,694 is more than 30 times higher than Cambodia's average monthly wage of US$121 (ILO 2014). Average monthly wages in Malaysia are triple those in Indonesia, the Philippines, and Vietnam. Regional disparities in GDP per capita, which unlike the wage estimates are adjusted for purchasing power, are similarly large (figure 2.1). Indeed, there is a strong presence of migrants from lower-income ASEAN countries in higher-income ones. The receiving countries described above—Malaysia, Singapore, and Thailand—have the highest GDPs per capita in ASEAN. Their average GDP per capita is about $40,000 versus sending countries' $6,000.

FIGURE 2.1

GDP per capita of ASEAN countries, 2015

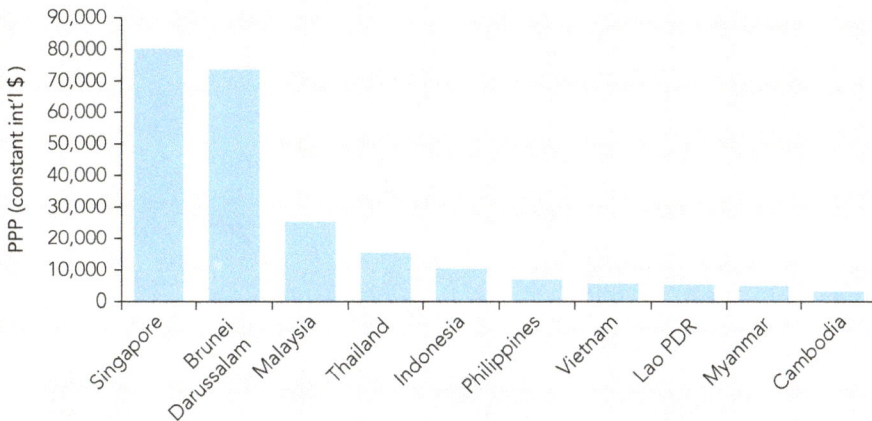

Source: World Development Indicators (database), World Bank.
Note: ASEAN = Association of Southeast Asian Nations; PPP = purchasing power parity.

GDP per capita is a strong determinant of migration to, from, and within ASEAN.[3] It is a proxy for the economic benefits migrants can expect in host countries. Figure 2.2a shows that, as GDP per capita increases, the share of an origin country's migrants in an ASEAN destination country increases. Figure 2.2b shows a similar relationship for migration from ASEAN countries. Notably, the relationship between GDP per capita and out-migration is stronger for ASEAN origin countries than for non-ASEAN ones, highlighting that ASEAN migrants are driven by the desire for better economic opportunities.

Migration to countries with higher GDPs per capita dominates ASEAN's three major migration corridors. The average ratio of destination-to-origin per capita GDP in these corridors is 3.8, with only migration from Singapore to neighboring Malaysia exhibiting a ratio of less than 1 (implying migration to a less wealthy country) (table 2.1).

Employment opportunities from population aging

Population aging also influences migration in ASEAN. Countries with aging populations and shrinking labor forces provide additional employment opportunities for migrants from countries with younger populations. The age distribution of total migrant stocks (presented in chapter 1) provides initial evidence that migration is, in part, driven by aging; it does so by showing that the migrant populations of destination countries tend to be younger than the local populations of those countries.

Evidence from the main migration corridors within ASEAN provides confirmation that population aging is a determinant. Singapore and Thailand have significantly older median ages than their main sending countries (at least 11 years older for Singapore and 10 for Thailand) (figure 2.3a). These differences are projected to become even more pronounced over time with the age gap between both

FIGURE 2.2

The relationship between GDP per capita and migration to and from ASEAN countries

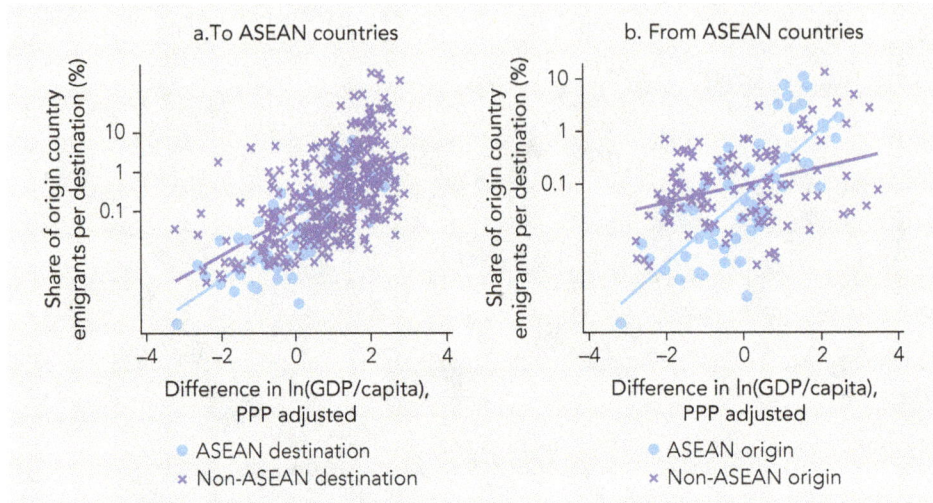

Source: UN 2015a and World Development Indicators, World Bank.
Note: The values are adjusted for log distance, contiguity, and origin country fixed effects. ASEAN = Association of Southeast Asian Nations; PPP = purchasing power parity.

TABLE 2.1

Migrant stocks and GDP per capita in ASEAN's major migration corridors, 2015

Origin	Destination	Stock	Ratio of D-to-O GDP per capita
Indonesia	Malaysia	1,070,433	2.4
Myanmar	Malaysia	252,292	5.1
Vietnam	Malaysia	87,272	4.5
Singapore	Malaysia	79,519	0.3
Malaysia	Singapore	1,123,654	3.2
Indonesia	Singapore	163,237	7.7
Myanmar	Thailand	1,978,348	3.1
Lao PDR	Thailand	969,267	2.9
Cambodia	Thailand	805,272	4.7

Sources: UN 2015a; World Development Indicators, World Bank.
Note: ASEAN = Association of Southeast Asian Nations; D-to-O GDP = destination-to-origin GDP.

Singapore and Thailand and their main sending countries increasing to at least 13 years (figure 2.3b). Interestingly, however, the tendency of sending countries to be older is not true for Malaysia, which receives many migrants from much *older* Singapore and many from Indonesia, Myanmar, and Vietnam, whose age distributions and median age are quite similar to those of Malaysia. Malaysia is expected to age only slightly more quickly than its main sending countries by 2050.

FIGURE 2.3
Median age in ASEAN's major migration corridors, 2015 and 2050

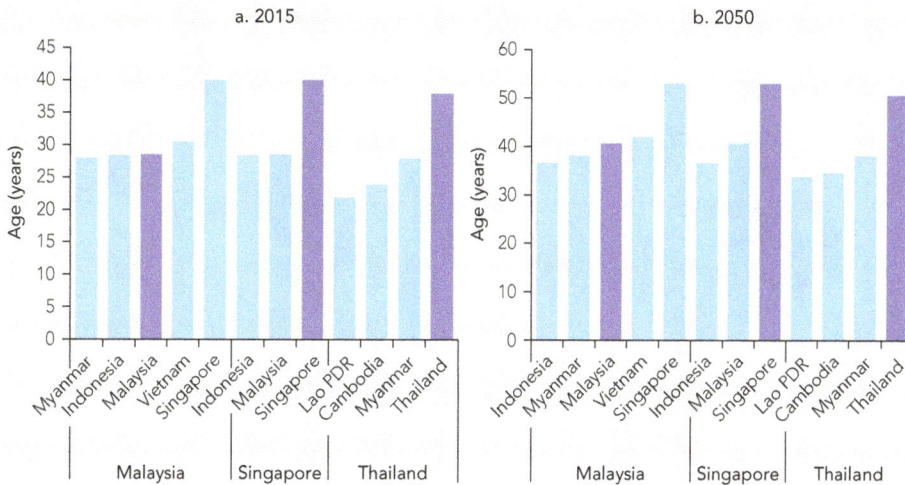

Source: UN 2015b.
Note: ASEAN = Association of Southeast Asian Nations.

The cost of migrating in ASEAN: Labor mobility costs

Labor mobility costs are costs incurred by workers when switching jobs. Workers incur these costs when they change firms and industries, whether domestically or abroad, upon perceiving alternative employment opportunities (Hollweg et al. 2014). Because taking advantage of these opportunities is costly, workers are often unable to do so. All workers face a range of costs when deciding to switch jobs. Domestically, workers must first consider job search costs, employment protection legislation, and distance costs. Skill mismatches, which arise when skills are not perfectly transferable across industries or firms, are also costly. The mismatches may mean that a worker's productivity is diminished in the new job, leading to lower wages.

International migrants consider the same costs as workers do domestically but face additional costs including restrictive migration policies, documentation costs, and recruitment fees. Table 2.2 lists the different financial costs faced by migrants from Vietnam to Malaysia, based on a survey of these migrants. Fees paid to recruiters on average make up the largest cost, though visa documentation costs are also significant. International migrants frequently face considerable time costs associated with waiting for documentation to be processed and approval for migration to be granted, which can be measured as wages lost while awaiting migration. In Thailand, a recent cost-benefit analysis of migration from Lao PDR and Cambodia to Thailand in the construction and domestic work sectors estimates that the time costs of migration increase overall migration costs about 40 percent (figure 2.4).

TABLE 2.2

Composition of migration costs for Vietnamese migrants to Malaysia
US$

Cost component	Average cost
Fees paid to recruiter	1,248
Visa	307
International travel	88
Local travel	69
Informal payments	30
Medical test	28
Passport	18
Health/life insurance	13
Security clearance	2
Average total cost	1,374

Source: ILO and KNOMAD 2015.

FIGURE 2.4

Estimated net benefit of migration to Thailand, by sector, with and without time costs

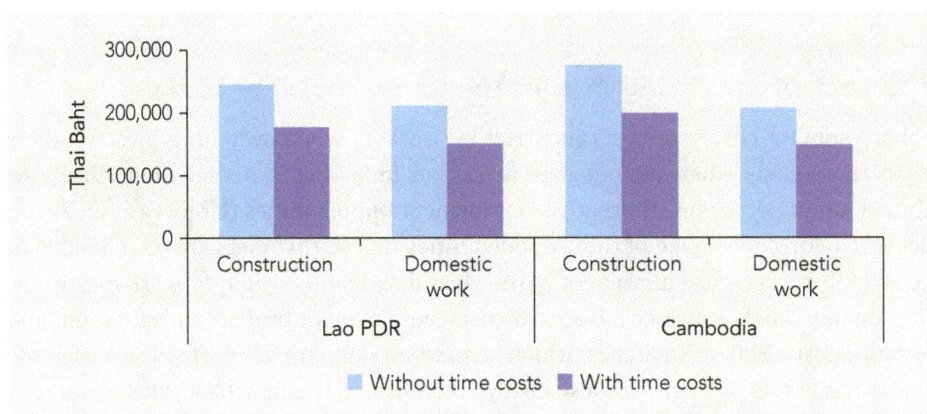

Source: Holumyong and Punpuing 2014.

In the absence of labor mobility costs, workers would be free to switch jobs in pursuit of the highest possible wage. Instead, workers frequently do not take advantage of large wage gains because the gains fail to outweigh the associated labor mobility costs (Hollweg et al. 2014). The previous section discussed the significant wage gains and employment opportunities available to migrants from ASEAN within the region. However, in 2015, just 3.2 percent of ASEAN's population were emigrants abroad, about the same as the global rate. Domestic migration rates are higher, but are still low in many Asian countries compared to other regions (UN 2013).

Workers make decisions to switch jobs on the basis of both domestic and international labor mobility costs. When deciding whether to migrate abroad, workers consider employment alternatives available both domestically and internationally. As such, although the focus of this book is on international migration, one must consider both domestic and international labor mobility costs to understand the full set of alternatives available to workers. The remainder of the chapter presents estimates of domestic and international labor mobility costs for ASEAN countries. Box 2.1 discusses how domestic and international labor mobility costs are estimated.

BOX 2.1

Estimating domestic and international labor mobility costs in ASEAN

Observed wage gaps between jobs are a measure of the attractiveness of different jobs. Comparison of this attractiveness with data on actual job flows provides an empirical indication of the labor mobility costs associated with accessing different jobs. For example, a certain type of job offering very high wages but attracting few workers implies very high labor mobility costs. At the sector level, if there are relatively large flows of labor into a low-paying sector (for example, agriculture), this suggests low mobility costs. This measure of labor mobility costs does not attempt to estimate each of the costs faced by individual workers, which may vary according to their characteristics and situation,[a] but rather estimates them indirectly.

As labor market frictions increase, workers become less responsive to differences in wages between industries. If labor mobility costs are high, workers are not expected to respond even to large wage differentials. In contrast, if these costs are low, workers are expected to respond even to small wage differentials; thus, in equilibrium, intersector wage differentials will be smaller. The estimated labor mobility cost is interpreted as the average cost a worker perceives to move between sectors for a given wage differential.

The framework to estimate labor mobility costs is based on a structural model of worker choice in sectoral employment when labor mobility is costly. Using this model, a worker employed in sector i can choose to (1) remain employed in sector i or (2) move to sector j but incur a cost (for simplicity, it is assumed here that the economy has only two sectors). This cost has a fixed component C (average mobility cost caused by labor market frictions) and a worker-specific component $\varepsilon^{i,j}$ (the idiosyncratic cost of moving from sector i to sector j) that captures personal circumstances, such as family constraints, or other preferences. The worker's expected welfare in sector i, EV^i, is the present discounted value of their real wage, a sector-specific fixed nonpecuniary benefit, and an option value reflecting the possibility of moving to a different sector with a higher wage. If the wage in sector j rises, a worker in sector i will experience an increase in welfare due to the higher option value, even if the worker never actually moves.

Wage, nonpecuniary benefit, and option value are sector-specific, whereas the idiosyncratic moving cost is specific to the worker. In each period, the worker decides whether to move, based on which sector offers a higher expected welfare benefit net

box continues next page

BOX 2.1
Estimating domestic and international labor mobility costs in ASEAN *(continued)*

of moving costs. The expected welfare benefit of moving from sector i to sector j, ($EV^j - EV^i$), depends on the wage differential between sectors. The worker will move from sector i to sector j if the expected welfare benefit of moving ($EV^j - EV^i$) exceeds the cost of doing so ($C + \varepsilon^{i,j}$), namely, if

$$EV^j - EV^i \geq C + \varepsilon^{i,j}$$

The model of sectoral employment choices generates flows of workers across sectors of the economy where the solution to the model is the employment allocation. The flows of workers across sectors depend on the model's parameters, inclusive of the mobility costs C. It is then possible to estimate these parameters by matching the predicted flows of workers simulated by the model with the flows of workers observed in the data for each country. Different estimation methodologies are used, depending on the data available.

Domestic labor mobility costs are estimated for workers transitioning across nine different sectors and joblessness (unemployment or out of the labor force). Transition data on movements across sectors and joblessness are combined with observed wage gaps between sectors to estimate the labor mobility cost of entering each sector as a ratio of the annual average sectoral wage. The estimations use panel data on employment sector, average sectoral wages, and individual worker characteristics. The mobility cost parameter is estimated by matching the worker flows predicted by the model with real data on observed average flows of workers and wages in each country.

Wages in the jobless sector are assumed to be zero. An underlying assumption is that labor mobility is solely motivated by economic considerations. Estimates of labor mobility costs are based on wage gaps at the average sectoral and skill level. That is, a single wage gap is estimated for each sector and skill, though there are many different types of workers in each sector. However, individual worker characteristics, including gender and skill level, are considered when measuring wage gaps, accounting for some of this heterogeneity.

Domestic labor mobility costs are estimated for Indonesia, Lao PDR, the Philippines, and Vietnam for all workers and by gender and skill level. Great care is taken to estimate domestic labor mobility costs at the same sectoral level across countries so that results are internationally comparable. To ensure comparability, skilled workers are defined as those who have completed vocational, university, or higher education.

International labor mobility costs are computed for workers transitioning across sectors and countries. International bilateral migration flows, calculated as decadal averages, are combined with decadal average country wages, expressed relative to the ASEAN average, to estimate the labor mobility costs of entering each country. As for domestic labor mobility costs, international labor mobility costs are expressed as a ratio of the annual average wage. The bilateral migration flows data, which do not distinguish between documented and undocumented flows, are obtained from the World Bank's Global Bilateral Migration Database. Decadal average country wages are obtained from the Conference Board's Total Economy Database, measured as labor productivity (GDP) per worker. Wage data were not available for Lao PDR and Brunei Darussalam, so employment per worker relative to the ASEAN average was used for these countries. The international labor mobility costs to enter a given

box continues next page

BOX 2.1

Estimating domestic and international labor mobility costs in ASEAN *(continued)*

ASEAN country are the same for migrants from all other ASEAN countries. International labor mobility costs were estimated for all ASEAN countries in each decade between 1960 and 2000. More details about the methodology are available in Hollweg (2016).

Sources: Hollweg et al. 2014; Hollweg 2016.

ª For example, in Mexico 86 percent of voluntary job exits were found to be motivated by marriage or family care, personal "costs" that make workers unresponsive to wage changes (Kaplan, Lederman, and Robertson 2013).

Domestic labor mobility costs

Understanding which sectors of an economy are the least costly to enter sheds light on which sectors may provide opportunities both to domestic workers and to workers who are mobile across ASEAN. The analysis takes into account the fact that costs associated with switching employment stem from various sources and vary across countries and sectors. Because of data limitations, only four countries—Indonesia, Lao PDR, the Philippines, and Vietnam—are considered along with nine sectors: (1) agriculture, forestry, and fishing; (2) mining and quarrying; (3) manufacturing; (4) utilities (electricity, gas, and water supply); (5) construction; (6) wholesale and retail trade, restaurants, and hotels; (7) transportation, storage, and communications; (8) finance, insurance, real estate, and business services; and (9) social services. Labor mobility costs are estimated by combining data on actual worker movements and wage gaps between sectors. Costs are estimated for workers entering each of these nine sectors, as well as for a state of joblessness that corresponds to either unemployment or inactivity (out of the labor force).

Labor mobility cost estimates are most useful for making comparisons across sectors and countries. The exact magnitude of the estimated labor mobility costs depends on several assumptions, including the level of sectoral disaggregation.[4] Because of this sensitivity, comparison of the relative magnitudes of labor mobility costs across sectors is more informative than their absolute magnitude. Labor mobility costs are expressed as a share of annual average wages.

Table 2.3 shows estimates of within-country labor mobility costs and their standard errors for Indonesia, Lao PDR, the Philippines, and Vietnam. The costs are expressed as a share of annual average wages. For instance, the value of 2.23 means that the average cost of entering the agriculture sector in Indonesia is equal to 2.23 times the annual average wage.

Domestic labor mobility costs in ASEAN can be several multiples of annual average wages. Workers faced with elevated labor mobility costs will likely weigh the decision to change jobs very carefully, even when the potential payoffs, such as higher wages, are strong. For example, workers entering Vietnam's utilities (electricity, gas, and water supply) sector face an average mobility cost of 22 times the annual average wage.

TABLE 2.3

Domestic labor mobility costs in ASEAN countries, by sector

Sector	Indonesia	Lao PDR	Philippines	Vietnam
Agriculture, forestry, and fishing	2.23	0.17	2.53	2.38
	(0.13)	(0.06)	(0.11)	(0.17)
Mining and quarrying	3.61	3.08	5.71	2.62
	(0.39)	(1.16)	(0.68)	(0.43)
Manufacturing	1.51	0.49	3.04	1.68
	(0.07)	(0.07)	(0.16)	(0.16)
Utilities (electricity, gas, and water supply)	4.92	3.86	5.76	22.28
	(0.49)	(1.30)	(0.62)	(0.52)
Construction	2.66	1.09	2.75	3.41
	(0.22)	(0.18)	(0.19)	(0.33)
Wholesale and retail trade, restaurants, and hotels	1.41	0.67	2.23	3.16
	(0.10)	(0.07)	(0.13)	(0.21)
Transportation, storage, and communications	2.90	0.98	3.45	3.58
	(0.33)	(0.26)	(0.12)	(0.35)
Finance/insurance, real estate, and business services	4.21	0.97	3.54	2.99
	(0.38)	(0.35)	(0.34)	(0.42)
Social services	1.59	0.73	2.84	4.19
	(0.12)	(0.14)	(0.10)	(0.22)
Unemployed/out of labor force	0.93	0.82	1.50	2.40
	(0.11)	(0.07)	(0.10)	(0.20)
Overall	2.78	1.28	3.54	3.60

Source: Hollweg 2016.
Note: Standard errors are shown in parentheses. The standard errors show that the labor mobility costs are estimated with low dispersion at the 95 percent confidence level. ASEAN = Association of Southeast Asian Nations.

Because this sector employs a small share of the workforce and has very little labor turnover, the costs of entering it are high. Thus, there are few chances for outsiders to enter.

Among the four ASEAN member countries for which adequate data are available, workers in Lao PDR face the lowest labor mobility costs, and workers in Vietnam and the Philippines the highest. Simple, unweighted averages across the nine sectors of the economy reveal that average labor mobility costs are 1.28 times the annual average wage in Lao PDR, compared to 2.78 times in Indonesia, 3.54 in the Philippines, and 3.60 in Vietnam. This finding is consistent with descriptive evidence of relatively more dynamism in Lao PDR's labor market, as well as this economy's comparatively low unemployment rates. Additionally, these findings largely agree with the rankings of the countries on the Employment Protection Legislation index, which measures the rigidity of labor markets, though Indonesia performs better in the case of labor mobility costs. Similarly, the ranking of the four countries is similar to that of the World Economic Forum's measure of labor market flexibility, though Lao PDR performs better in the case of labor mobility costs (table 2.4).

TABLE 2.4
Ranking of four ASEAN countries on different measures of labor mobility cost and flexibility

Labor mobility costs	EPL index	WEF labor market flexibility index
Lao PDR	Lao PDR	Indonesia
Indonesia	Philippines	Philippines
Philippines	Vietnam	Vietnam
Vietnam	Indonesia	Lao PDR

Sources: Hollweg (2016) for labor mobility costs, WEF Global Competitiveness Index 2015–6 for labor market flexibility index, and World Bank (2014) for the EPL index.
Note: EPL = employment protection legislation; WEF = World Economic Forum.

Leaving employment and either becoming unemployed or exiting the labor force generally involves the lowest labor mobility cost. The two exceptions are Lao PDR and Vietnam, where the agricultural sector absorbs new workers even more easily than joblessness. In fact, in all four countries the agriculture sector is one of the least costly sectors to enter. In Lao PDR, workers entering the sector incur a cost equivalent to 0.17 times the annual average wage. This is significantly lower than the labor mobility costs of entering other sectors in the same country and much lower than the cost of entering the agricultural sector in the other three countries. In Indonesia, these costs are 2.23 times the annual average wage, whereas in Vietnam and the Philippines, they are 2.27 times and 2.53 times annual average wages, respectively.

Costly sectors to enter include mining and quarrying; utilities; and the finance/insurance, real estate, and business services sectors. Social services, frequently provided by the public sector, are also costly. This finding is consistent with the very low turnover in public sector jobs prevalent across ASEAN. Outside of ASEAN, the labor mobility costs of entering manufacturing jobs are usually quite high. In contrast, manufacturing is among the least costly sectors to enter in Lao PDR and Vietnam. This difference likely reflects the type of manufacturing undertaken in Lao PDR and Vietnam. Workers entering manufacturing jobs in the two countries often need little or no sector-specific knowledge and experience. This results in low wages and relatively low labor mobility costs. In Indonesia and the Philippines, as for countries outside of ASEAN, entering manufacturing employment is relatively costly. This may reflect the geographical concentration of manufacturing in only a few metropolitan areas in the two archipelago countries.

International labor mobility costs

International migrants consider the same costs as domestic ones—job search costs, skills mismatches, and severance and hiring costs—and face additional costs, including restrictive migration policies and recruitment fees. International labor mobility costs can arise from economic and noneconomic factors that make it costly for workers to migrate internationally. Examples of such factors include not only distance, social networks in the destination, and language skills but also the monetary costs incurred to migrate abroad, which include transport and visa costs and recruitment agency fees. Many of these costs are the same as those affecting within-country labor mobility costs, and the difference between the two types of mobility costs is a matter of degree. However, there is a crucial factor that is typically present only for international labor mobility costs: laws limiting or restricting the free movement of workers.[5] Such laws are one reason why international labor mobility costs can be much higher than within-country mobility costs. At the same time, they also give governments a direct and powerful mechanism to influence international labor mobility costs.

Distance is a strong determinant of global migration to ASEAN countries. It is a key component of international labor mobility costs because migrants must normally pay more to travel farther; thus, in the presence of budget constraints, they will tend to migrate for employment less frequently to places that are farther away. Figure 2.5 shows that migration to ASEAN countries generally declines as distance increases. The relationship is stronger for ASEAN than for non-ASEAN destinations, reflecting the remoteness of and lack of migration to several ASEAN countries, such as Indonesia and the Philippines.

Distance is also a strong determinant of migration within ASEAN. The primary migration corridors in ASEAN tend to be relatively close. The average distance between countries in ASEAN is 1,610 kilometers; in contrast, among the countries in the primary corridors, the distance is about half that at 889 kilometers. Migration to Thailand,

FIGURE 2.5
Relationship between distance and migration to ASEAN

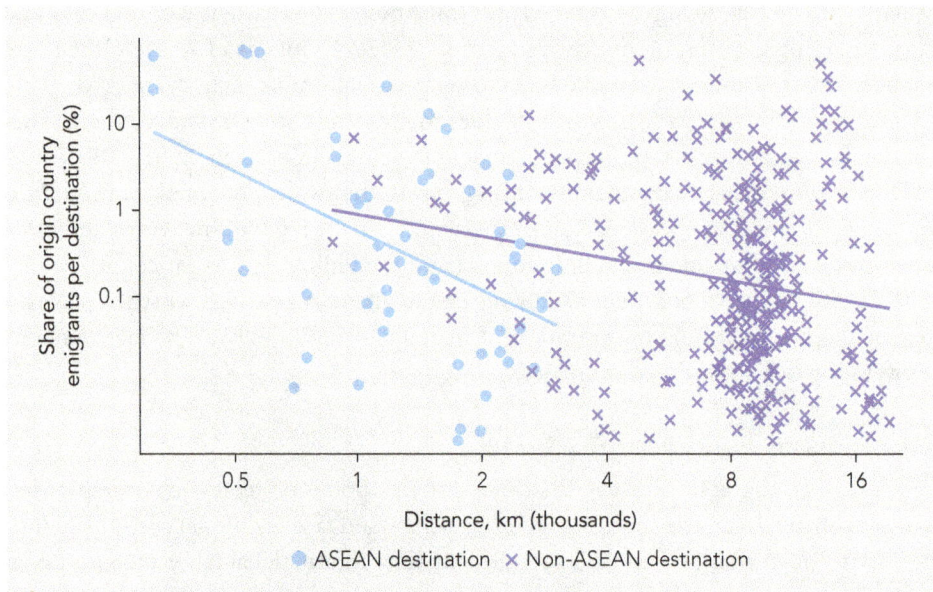

Sources: UN 2015a; GeoDist Database, CEPII.
Note: ASEAN = Association of Southeast Asian Nations; CEPII = Centre d'Études Prospectives et d'Informations Internationales; km = kilometers.

TABLE 2.5
Migrant stocks and distance in ASEAN's major migration corridors, 2015

Origin	Destination	Stock	Distance (km)
Indonesia	Malaysia	1,051,227	1,174
Myanmar	Malaysia	247,768	1,635
Vietnam	Malaysia	85,709	2,041
Singapore	Malaysia	78,092	316
Malaysia	Singapore	1,044,994	316
Indonesia	Singapore	152,681	886
Myanmar	Thailand	1,892,480	576
Lao PDR	Thailand	926,427	525
Cambodia	Thailand	750,109	536

Sources: UN 2015a; GeoDist Database, CEPII.
Note: ASEAN = Association of Southeast Asian Nations; CEPII = Centre d'Études Prospectives et d'Informations Internationales; km = kilometers.

in particular, is dominated by its neighbors. About 500 kilometers[6] separate the primary cities of Cambodia, Lao PDR, and Myanmar from that of Thailand. Fewer than 1,000 kilometers separate Singapore from the primary origins of its migrants (table 2.5). As with other determinants of migration, the story is different for Malaysia, which attracts migrants from a longer distance, including Vietnam, which is 2,041 kilometers from Malaysia, and Myanmar, which is 1,635 kilometers away.

Although distance is a key factor of international labor mobility costs, potential migrants are not always dissuaded by long distances. Figure 2.6 shows the share of emigration from each ASEAN country to every global destination by the distance to that destination, shown on the x axis. Cambodia, Lao PDR, and Myanmar (ASEAN's least-developed countries), and Malaysia all send most of their migrants to neighboring countries (Thailand in the case of the first three, and Singapore in the case of the Malaysia). However, the majority of migrants from all other ASEAN countries are in countries that are more than 5,000 kilometers or so away, about the distance from Manila (the Philippines) to Riyadh (Saudi Arabia). This suggests that distance is not the only important cost in migration decisions.

Networks play a key role in lowering international labor mobility costs by reducing migrants' lack of knowledge about the destination. Social networks not only ease mobility but also assist migrants in adjusting to and integrating into the destination country. Figure 2.7 shows the emigrant share from a given country in 1980 on the x axis, a proxy for established diaspora networks in a host country, and the emigrant share from a given country in 2015 on the y axis. The figure shows that migrant networks are strongly correlated with migration flows to ASEAN destinations.

Given the many factors influencing the costs of migrating, how costly is it for workers within ASEAN to move from one economy to another? The international labor mobility costs faced by workers crossing borders within ASEAN are estimated using data on international migration flows and wage gaps between countries.[7] As for

FIGURE 2.6

Cumulative distribution of migration from ASEAN countries over distance

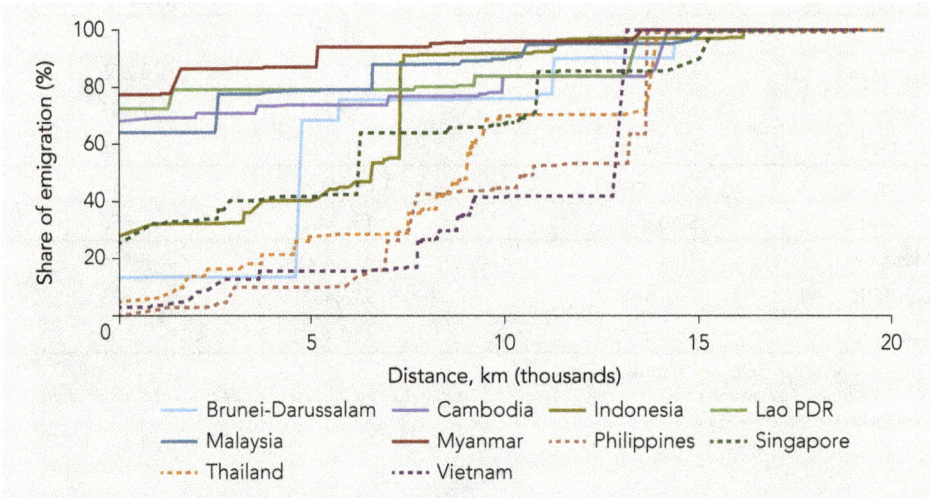

Sources: UN 2015a; GeoDist Database, CEPII.
Note: ASEAN = Association of Southeast Asian Nations; CEPII = Centre d'Études Prospectives et d'Informations Internationales.

FIGURE 2.7

Relationship between networks and migration to ASEAN, 1980 and 2015

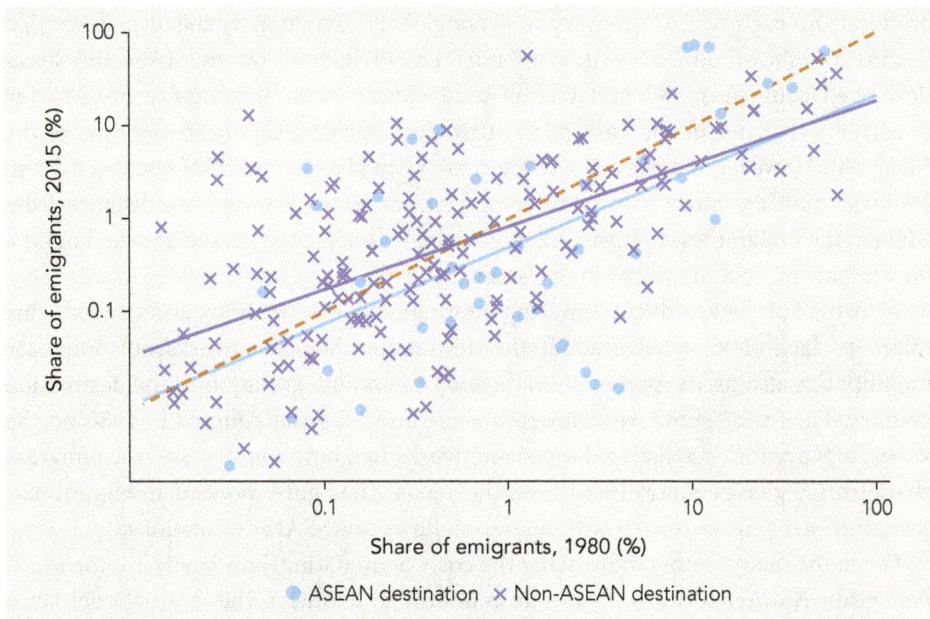

Sources: UN 2015a; Global Bilateral Migration Database, World Bank.
Note: ASEAN = Association of Southeast Asian Nations.

within-country labor mobility costs, international labor mobility costs can be expressed as a percentage of the average annual wage.[8] Costs were estimated for all ASEAN member countries for each decade between the 1960s and the 2000s (table 2.6). For example, in the 1960s the labor mobility cost of moving into Cambodia was 6.48 times its annual average wage.

ASEAN countries that are more open to globalization and that have developed more advanced migration systems tend to have lower international labor mobility costs. Malaysia and Singapore have the lowest international labor mobility costs in ASEAN. In the 2000s, workers entering Malaysia faced labor mobility costs equal to 3.02 times the Malaysian annual average wage, while those entering Singapore faced costs of 5.43 times the Singaporean annual average wage. Workers migrating to Myanmar and Vietnam, in contrast, confronted costs of more than 11 times the annual average wage. The lower international mobility costs in Malaysia and Singapore reflect their openness to globalization, their efforts to develop migration systems that meet labor market needs, and their geographic centrality in the ASEAN region.

TABLE 2.6

International labor mobility costs in ASEAN countries, 1960–2000

Country	1960	1970	1980	1990	2000
Cambodia	6.48	7.06	11.85	10.76	8.77
	(0.83)	(1.06)	(1.23)	(1.43)	(1.41)
Indonesia	10.65	10.81	10.59	10.35	10.33
	(0.81)	(0.69)	(0.68)	(0.76)	(0.77)
Lao PDR	8.96	9.04	9.28	10.33	10.15
	(0.94)	(1.10)	(1.32)	(1.52)	(1.45)
Malaysia	8.28	5.32	4.01	3.04	3.02
	(1.19)	(0.90)	(0.46)	(0.49)	(0.65)
Myanmar	9.85	11.30	10.94	11.90	11.58
	(1.04)	(0.92)	(1.04)	(1.28)	(1.20)
Philippines	11.57	11.27	9.65	11.12	10.44
	(0.91)	(0.67)	(0.65)	(0.76)	(0.63)
Singapore	7.15	4.64	4.87	5.75	5.43
	(1.09)	(1.00)	(0.40)	(0.36)	(0.47)
Thailand	7.52	8.34	10.17	9.77	8.50
	(0.95)	(0.91)	(0.82)	(0.99)	(1.17)
Vietnam	11.68	12.49	13.35	13.58	11.22
	(0.71)	(0.72)	(0.88)	(0.91)	(0.99)
ASEAN average	9.13	8.92	9.41	9.62	8.83

Source: Hollweg 2016.
Note: Standard errors are shown in parentheses. They show that the labor mobility costs are estimated with low dispersion at the 95% confidence level.

Thailand, another main migrant-receiving country in ASEAN, has a much less developed migration system, high levels of undocumented migration, and higher international labor mobility costs. ASEAN's major migrant-sending countries tend to impose restrictions on immigrants, including high-skilled workers, which is reflected in their high mobility costs. No matter where workers wish to migrate in ASEAN, they face mobility costs several times the annual average wage, suggesting potential weaknesses in the migration process that make migrating for work difficult.

The costs faced by workers to migrate from one country within the ASEAN region to another increased from the 1960s to the 1990s. The average international labor mobility cost across the sample of nine ASEAN member countries for which data were available was 9.13 times the annual average wage in the 1960s, compared to 9.62 times in the 1990s (table 2.6). As most ASEAN member countries grew rapidly between the 1960s and the 1990s, international migration flows did not increase proportionally to the countries' rapid internal development. In some countries—such as Cambodia, Myanmar, and Vietnam—fragility and conflict dampened in-migration. However, the trend of increasing international labor mobility costs between the 1960s and the 1990s did not hold for all ASEAN member countries. In Singapore, labor mobility costs declined between the 1960s and 1970s, before remaining relatively steady, whereas in Malaysia, labor mobility costs declined throughout this period. Both countries experienced significant economic growth during these periods, and both were more open to globalization than their ASEAN peers. As both came to rely on large inflows of low-skilled labor, both also developed sophisticated migration systems relative to other ASEAN countries, as chapter 6 shows.

Between the 1990s and the 2000s, the trend of generally rising international labor mobility costs that had previously dominated the ASEAN countries was reversed. During this period, average labor mobility costs fell from 9.62 to 8.83 times the annual average wage for ASEAN as a whole. Between the 1990s and the 2000s, labor mobility costs dropped for all countries in ASEAN. The reduction was most pronounced for Cambodia (18 percent), Thailand (13 percent), and Vietnam (17 percent). The reverse of the previous trend of rising labor mobility costs was due, at least in part, to the increased integration of ASEAN countries in the regional and world economy, which created increased opportunities for migration in several ASEAN countries. Moreover, all ASEAN countries, particularly the primary receiving ones, have worked in recent years to improve their immigration systems.

Low-skilled workers are likely the beneficiaries of reductions in international labor mobility costs that have made migration abroad less expensive. Generally, low-skilled migrants are more sensitive to migration costs. For example, low-skilled migrants, both from ASEAN countries to global destinations and within ASEAN, are more likely to migrate to a neighboring country and avoid more distant, more expensive destinations. About 30 percent of low-skilled migrants from ASEAN travel to neighboring countries (represented by the starting position on the vertical axis in figure 2.8), compared to a negligible share of high-skilled migrants. In fact, about 60 percent of ASEAN's high-skilled migrants travel more than 12,500 kilometers.

FIGURE 2.8

Cumulative distribution of migration from ASEAN countries over distance, by skill level

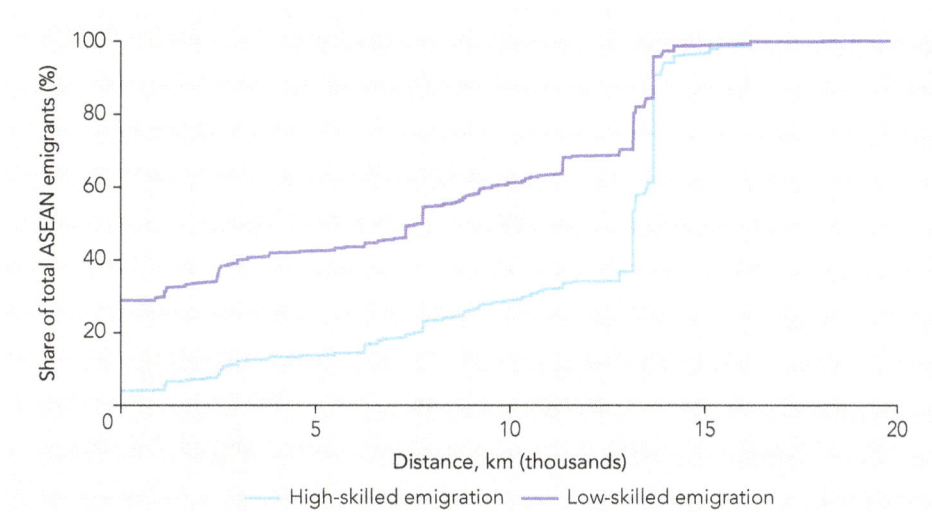

Sources: 2000 Skilled Migration Database (World Bank); GeoDist Database (CEPII).
Note: ASEAN = Association of Southeast Asian Nations; CEPII = Centre d'Études Prospectives et d'Informations Internationales; km = kilometers.

FIGURE 2.9

Cumulative distribution of intra-ASEAN migration over distance, by skill level

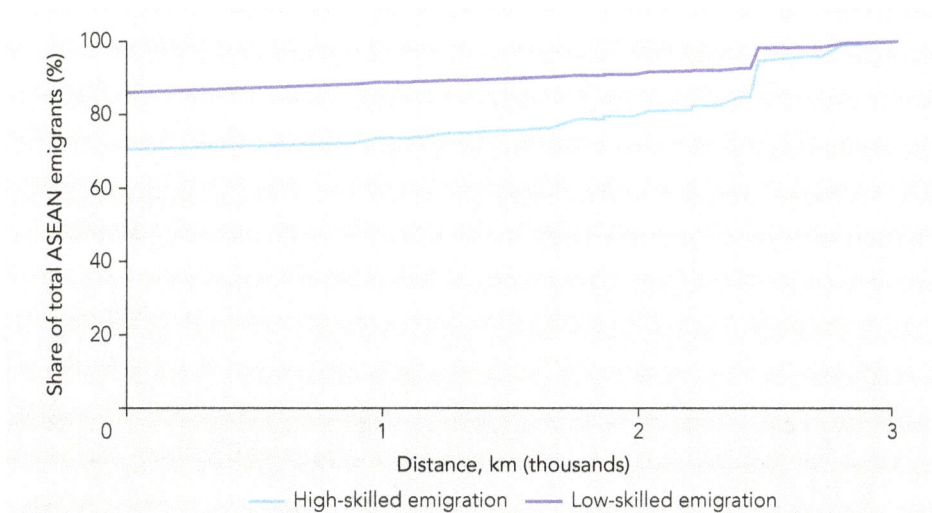

Sources: 2000 Skilled Migration Database (World Bank); GeoDist Database (CEPII).
Note: ASEAN = Association of Southeast Asian Nations; CEPII = Centre d'Études Prospectives et d'Informations Internationales; km = kilometers.

Even though distances are much shorter within ASEAN, the story remains the same within the region: high-skilled migrants tend to travel farther than low-skilled ones (figure 2.9). The increase in intra-ASEAN migration in recent years, mostly low-skilled, is consistent with lower migration costs resulting from increased integration and globalization benefiting mostly low-skilled migrants.

Notes

1. Young people are more likely to migrate in part because they have a longer working period over which to gain from migration compared to older people (Zaiceva and Zimmermann 2014).
2. A higher real exchange rate ratio decreases migration by increasing purchasing power in the origin relative to the destination.
3. All references to GDP and GDP per capita are PPP (constant 2011 international dollars) from the World Bank's World Development Indicators.
4. The higher the degree of sectoral disaggregation, the fewer the observed transitions and the higher the estimated mobility costs. An alternative disaggregation by sectors is presented in the online appendix, which is available on the World Bank's Open Knowledge Repository, at www.openknowledge.worldbank.org.
5. Examples of domestic restrictions on labor mobility include China's *hukou* system and Vietnam's *ho khau* system.
6. Distances refer to the distance in kilometers between the origin and the destination's largest city.
7. Chapter 1 describes the pros and cons of the different available data sources on bilateral migration flows. The data do not permit a distinction to be made between documented and undocumented migration flows.
8. As with domestic labor mobility costs, the relative magnitude of different international labor mobility costs is more informative than interpretation of their absolute magnitude.

References

Beaman, Lori A. 2012. "Social Networks and the Dynamics of Labour Market Outcomes: Evidence from Refugees Resettled in the U.S." *Review of Economic Studies* 79 (1): 128–61.

Beine, Michel, and Christopher Parsons. 2015. "Climatic Factors as a Determinants of International Migration." *Scandinavian Journal of Economics* 117 (2): 723–67.

Beine, Michel, Simone Bertoli, and Jesús Fernández-Huertas Moraga. 2015. "A Practitioners' Guide to Gravity Models of International Migration." *The World Economy* 39 (4): 496–512.

Beine, Michel, Pauline Bourgeon, and Jean-Charles Bricongne. 2013. "Aggregate Fluctuations and International Migration." Working Paper 4379, Center for Economic Studies and Ifo Institute, Munich.

Beine, Michel, Frédéric Docquier, and Çağlar Özden. 2011. "Diasporas." *Journal of Development Economics* 95 (1): 30–41.

Belot, Michèle V. K., and Timothy J. Hatton. 2012. "Immigrant Selection in the OECD." *Scandinavian Journal of Economics* 114 (4): 1105–28.

Bertoli, Simone, and Jesús Fernández-Huertas Moraga. 2013. "Multilateral Resistance to Migration." *Journal of Development Economics* 102: 79–100.

———. 2015. "The Size of the Cliff at the Border." *Regional Science and Urban Economics* 51: 1–6.

Bylander, Maryann. 2016. "Cambodian Migration to Thailand: The Role of Environmental Shocks and Stress." Working Paper 7, Global Knowledge Partnership on Migration and Development (KNOMAD), Washington, DC.

Clark, Ximena, Timothy J. Hatton, and Jeffrey G. Williamson. 2007. "Explaining U.S. Immigration 1971–1998." *Review of Economics and Statistics* 89 (2): 359–73.

Coppel, Jonathan, Jean-Christophe Dumont, and Ignazio Visco. 2001. "Trends in Immigration and Economic Consequences." Working Paper 284, Economics Department, Organisation for Economic Co-operation and Development, Paris.

Czaika, Mathias, and Christopher R. Parsons. 2016. "The Gravity of High-Skilled Migration Policies." KNOMAD Working Paper 13, Global Knowledge Partnership on Migration and Development (KNOMAD), Washington, DC.

Docquier, Frédéric, Giovanni Peri, and Ilse Ruyssen. 2014. "The Cross-Country Determinants of Potential and Actual Migration." *International Migration Review* 48 (S1): S37–S99.

Facchini, Giovanni, and Elisabetta Lodigiani. 2014. "Attracting Skilled Immigrants: An Overview of Recent Policy Developments in Advanced Countries." *National Institute Economic Review* 229 (1): R3–21.

Hatton, Timothy J. 2005. "Explaining Trends in UK Immigration." *Journal of Population Economics* 18(4): 719–40.

Hollweg, Claire. 2016. "Labor Mobility and Labor Market Integration in ASEAN." Background Paper, Washington, DC: World Bank.

Hollweg, Claire, Daniel Lederman, Diego Rojas, and Elizabeth Ruppert Bulmer. 2014. *Sticky Feet: How Labor Market Frictions Shape the Impact of International Trade on Jobs and Wages.* Washington, DC: World Bank.

Holumyong, Charampor, and Sureeporn Punpuing. 2014. "A Cost-Benefit Analysis of the Legal Status of Migrant Workers in Thailand." In *Managing International Migration for Development in East Asia*, edited by Richard H. Adams and Ahmad Ahsan, 263–282. Washington, DC: World Bank.

ILO (International Labor Organization). 2014. *Global Wage Report 2014/15: Asia and the Pacific Supplement.* Bangkok: ILO.

ILO and KNOMAD (Global Knowledge Partnership on Migration and Development). 2015. "Migration Cost Survey: Vietnamese Workers in Malaysia." Petaling Jaya, Malaysia.

Jajri, Idris, and Rahmah Ismail. 2014. "Determinants of Migration from ASEAN-3 into Malaysia." *Asian-Pacific Economic Literature* 28 (2): 56–62.

Jasso, Guillermina, and Mark R. Rosenzweig. 2008. "Selection Criteria and the Skill Composition of Immigrants: A Comparative Analysis of Australian and U.S. Employment Immigration." Discussion Paper 3564, Institute for the Study of Labor, Bonn.

Mayda, Ana Maria. 2010. "International Migration: A Panel Data Analysis of the Determinants of Bilateral Flows." *Journal of Population Economics* 23(4): 1249–74.

McKenzie, David, and Hillel Rapoport. 2007. "Network Effects and the Dynamics of Migration and Inequality: Theory and Evidence from Mexico." *Journal of Development Economics* 84 (1): 1–24.

Munshi, Kaivan. 2003. "Networks in the Modern Economy: Mexican Migrants in the US Labor Market." *Quarterly Journal of Economics* 118 (2): 549–99.

Ortega, Francesc, and Giovanni Peri. 2013. "The Effect of Income and Immigration Policies on International Migration." *Migration Studies* 1 (1): 47–74.

Sanglaoid, Utis, Sumalee Santipolvut, and Rewat Thamma-Apiroam. 2014. "The Impacts of ASEAN Labour Migration to Thailand upon the Thai Economy." *International Journal of Economics and Finance* 6 (8): 118–28.

Shrestha, Maheshwor. 2017. "Push and Pull: A Study of International Migration from Nepal." Policy Research Working Paper 7965, World Bank, Washington, DC.

UN (United Nations). 2013. *International Migration Policies: Government Views and Priorities*. New York: United Nations.

———. 2015a. *Trends in International Migrant Stock: The 2015 Revision*. United Nations database, POP/DB/MIG/Stock/Rev.2015.

———. 2015b. *World Population Prospects: The 2015 Revision*. Department of Economic and Social Affairs Population Division. DVD Edition.

World Bank. 2012. *Gaining from Migration: Migration Trends and Policy Lessons in the Greater Mekong Sub-region*. Policy Note. World Bank, Bangkok.

———. 2014. *East Asia Pacific at Work: Employment, Enterprise, and Well-being*. Washington, DC: World Bank.

Zaiceva, Anzelika, and Klaus F. Zimmermann. 2014. "Migration and the Demographic Shift." Discussion Paper 8743, Institute for the Study of Labor, Bonn.

CHAPTER 3

The Impacts of Migration in ASEAN Countries

Introduction

Countries in the Association of Southeast Asian Nations (ASEAN) have somewhat different concerns about the impacts of migration than do the Organisation for Economic Co-operation and Development (OECD) countries that dominate the migration literature. The migration systems of ASEAN host countries are designed to accept mostly temporary migrants, meaning that integration is less of a concern and the impact of undocumented migration is more of a concern. Malaysia and Thailand have become migration hubs before they have become high-income countries, provoking concerns that an overreliance on low-skilled migrants is impeding technological upgrading and escape from the middle-income trap. Concerns about remittances are largely unique to sending countries outside of the OECD.

This chapter reviews the impacts that migrants have on both origins and destinations to help illustrate the potential costs and benefits of migration in ASEAN countries. It draws on the international literature but focuses on ASEAN countries to address their unique concerns whenever possible. The chapter shows that migrants can fill labor shortages, facilitate skills upgrading, and generate economic growth in destination countries. In the case of labor market outcomes in destination countries, the impacts are generally quite small. In some cases, particularly where domestic labor market policies are rigid, negative impacts are observed. In origin countries, migrants and remittances can provide an important source of stabilizing income with significant effects on poverty.

Impacts on destination countries

Economic growth

Immigration can have important benefits for economic development. The impact of migration on economic growth is important because it determines whether those who gain from migration can compensate those who lose out (Felbermayr and Jung 2009; Felbermayr and Kohler 2009). Research from outside of ASEAN finds that the effect of immigration on gross domestic product (GDP) per capita and income per capita is generally small in the short run and other recent research finds negligible or slightly positive impacts of immigration on economic growth (Brunow, Nijkamp, and Poot 2015). There is evidence, however, that the impact varies by immigrant skill level; the human capital flowing into a country with immigrants can compensate for the dilution effect of immigrant labor on the capital-labor ratio, though the former does not always outweigh the latter. Orefice (2010), for instance, finds that skilled migration increases GDP per capita, but that low-skilled migration has a negative effect. Studying 22 OECD member countries between 1986 and 2006 and controlling for the skill composition of migrants, Boubtane, Dumont, and Rault (2016) find that permanent migration has a positive, though small, effect on economic growth. Ortega and Peri (2009) find that immigration increases GDP and employment at the same rate, resulting in a null effect of migration on GDP. Using a full set of bilateral migrant stocks for 2000, Felbermayr and Jung (2009) find that a 10 percent increase in migrant stocks leads to a gain of 2.2 percent in per capita income.

There is more evidence of positive impacts of migration on economic growth in the longer run. Brunow, Nijkamp, and Poot (2015) provide what they describe as "fairly weak" evidence that in the long run migration to high-income countries increases growth. A study of immigration to the United States between 1960 and 2006 found that a 1 percent increase in employment in a state resulting from immigration led to a 0.5 percent increase in income per worker in that state (Peri 2012). Ortega and Peri (2014) find that an increase in the share of immigrants in the population leads to an increase in long-run per capita income. The authors suggest that diversity of country of origin leads to more differentiated skills in the workforce of the host country, with positive impacts on productivity. Additionally, recent research suggests that unskilled migrants over time can increase economic growth as they become integrated into the host country and their educational levels increase (Dadush 2014). This is an important factor to consider in ASEAN countries, where most migration is temporary, restricting a potential channel for migration to have a positive impact on economic growth.

Evidence from ASEAN is generally consistent with the international findings. In Malaysia, computable general equilibrium (CGE) modeling finds that a 10 percent net increase in low-skilled immigrant workers increases real GDP by 1.1 percent (Ahsan et al. 2014). Low-skilled immigrants keep salaries low, which in turn lowers domestic prices and production costs and increases export growth (World Bank 2015). The result is that unskilled employment and profits increase, leading to increased investment and demand for (mostly Malaysian) skilled workers, who are complementary to the low-skilled migrants. Domestic demand is boosted through salary increases for skilled workers, which in turn boosts public revenue collection. Malaysia's tight labor market and the complementarity of the skills of local and migrant workers are key factors explaining these results. More generally, Malaysia's relatively open immigration policy has allowed investors to benefit from Malaysia's advanced infrastructure and reliable business environment while also having access to low-cost labor.

Research from other ASEAN receiving countries finds similar positive, though small, impacts of immigration on GDP (Ahsan et al. 2014). In Thailand, where labor markets are also tight, recent analysis estimates that without migrants in the labor force GDP would fall by 0.75 percent (Pholphirul, Kamlai, and Rukumnuaykit 2010). In another study, Sanglaoid, Santipolvut, and Phuwanich (2014) use a CGE model to analyze the impact of policies that would increase the number of foreign workers in Thailand. Each policy considered would result in an increase in GDP, though the increase is higher for policies impacting low-skilled migrants. Research on Singapore finds that immigrant labor has been responsible for a significant portion of the country's GDP growth, apart from the period after the 1997 Asian crisis (Ahsan et al. 2014). Recent modeling suggests that skilled immigrants promote growth in Singapore but that there are diminishing returns because the benefits of the complementarity between capital and skilled labor are exhausted (Thangavelu 2012; see also Thangavelu 2016). Though finding no impact of immigration on economic growth in the same decade, research finds that immigration into countries with high income or high net inward migration, or both—including Brunei Darussalam, Malaysia, and Singapore—has positive long-run impacts on growth in GDP per capita (Brunow, Nijkamp, and Poot 2015). The positive impacts seem to be related to increases in total factor productivity.

Competitiveness

International evidence suggests that, in the longer run, foreign workers may promote competitiveness. Studying immigration to U.S. states between 1960 and 2006, Peri (2012) finds that immigration is associated with growth in total factor productivity. Using migration to 20 OECD countries between 1960 and 2005, Mariya and Tritah (2009) find that migration increases labor productivity, likely by increasing total factor productivity in the long run. Also studying OECD countries, this time between 1986 and 2006, Boubtane, Dumont, and Rault (2016) find that a 50 percent increase in permanent net migration increases productivity growth by 0.3 percentage point.

There is some evidence that these positive productivity impacts result from the specialization of local and migrant workers. In certain contexts, low-skilled immigration seems to facilitate the efficient specialization of less educated local workers into occupations that require communication and of migrant workers into occupations that are manually intensive (D'Amuri and Peri 2011; Peri and Sparber 2012). The same seems to be true for highly educated immigrants and locals as well (Peri and Sparber 2011).

This implies that, instead of being substitutes, foreign and local workers at similar skill levels can be complements and enhance productivity. Cost savings and labor-intensive production techniques are other possible channels for immigration to impact productivity positively.

Some evidence suggests that positive productivity impacts are limited to high-skilled immigrants. Kangasniemi et al. (2012) find that migrant workers have a positive, long-term effect on productivity in the United Kingdom but a negative effect in Spain, suggesting that the former is superior at assimilating migrants or has better selectivity. Investigating Israeli manufacturing firms, Paserman (2008) finds that a firm's share of immigrants is negatively correlated with productivity in low-technology industries but positively correlated in high-technology industries. Finally, Huber et al. (2010) provide evidence that high-skilled migrants to the European Union positively impact productivity in skill-intensive industries.

Research from the United States and Europe shows that skilled migration is also associated with innovation and entrepreneurship. High-skilled migrants can lead to the formation of new businesses and to the introduction of new products and services (Nathan 2014). They can encourage trade and foreign direct investment (FDI) linkages, connect host and source countries through business networks, and facilitate the diffusion of technology (Docquier and Rapoport 2012).

The evidence on the productivity impacts of immigration is mixed in ASEAN. However, there is no strong evidence that low-skilled migrants have a negative impact on productivity. Several studies have been undertaken in Malaysia. Noor, Said, and Jalil (2011) find that immigration had a positive impact on productivity in the Malaysian manufacturing sector between 1972 and 2005. A 1 percent increase in immigrant labor led to a 0.17 percent increase in value added per worker. Bachtiar, Fahmy, and Ismail (2015) find impacts that vary by skill level, with unskilled immigrant workers having no impact on output growth in five manufacturing subsectors and higher-skilled workers generally having a positive impact. Ismail and Yuliyusman (2014) detect a negative impact of unskilled migrant workers on sectoral output growth in manufacturing, services, and construction between 1990 and 2010; but they find a positive impact for skilled and semi-skilled labor.

In Thailand, Pholphirul and Rukumnuaykit (2013) find that employing more unskilled workers does not affect participation in innovation activities but reduces the likelihood and amount of spending on research and development (R&D), though results lose statistical significance when broken down by firm size, into importers and exporters, and by domestic and foreign ownership. Employing more skilled workers has no effect on innovation or R&D spending. However, the study does not deal with the potential endogeneity of the share of migrants hired by a firm and spending on innovation and R&D. Anecdotally, there are reports that migrant fishery workers have been important in the development of fish production in Thailand by increasing the productivity of locals working as boat captains and boat builders. Overall, evidence from Thailand and similar evidence from the Republic of Korea is inconclusive or shows no impact of unskilled immigrants on productivity (Ahsan et al. 2014).

There is some evidence that immigration positively benefits competitiveness by increasing profitability even as labor productivity declines. Increased profitability allows firms to invest more, which could result in future productivity growth. In one study of manufacturing in Malaysia between 2000 and 2006, a 1 percent increase in the share of immigrant workers led productivity to decline by 0.6 percent on average. However, immigration also meant that unit labor costs declined, resulting in improvements to competitiveness and allowing future profits to be invested (Yean and Siang 2014). In Korea, unskilled migrants have been found to impact the profitability of Korean small and medium-size firms with no impact on productivity identified (Ahsan et al. 2014).

Countries that receive significant low-skilled immigration flows may be concerned that the presence of low-skilled migrants hinders the adoption of labor-saving technologies, perhaps even hindering the transition from middle- to high-income economies.[1] Though there is evidence that immigrants result in a decline in the capital-to-labor ratio in Malaysia and some other East Asian countries, low-skilled immigrants to Malaysia have also facilitated skills upgrading of locals by freeing them to pursue more education and more skilled occupations (Ahsan et al. 2014; World Bank 2015). While foreign workers in Malaysia remain mostly less educated, since 2001 the Malaysian population with at least some secondary education has increased by 20 percentage points (figure 3.1). At the same time, migrant workers in Malaysia first filled shortages in agriculture, as Malaysians shifted into high value-added manufacturing, and then in manufacturing, as Malaysians shifted to services. Additionally, although labor productivity has fallen in the manufacturing sector in Malaysia, low-wage foreign workers have allowed the country to sustain its trade competitiveness (Rasiah 2014). In Thailand,

FIGURE 3.1

The education level of Malaysian and migrant workers, 2001 and 2014

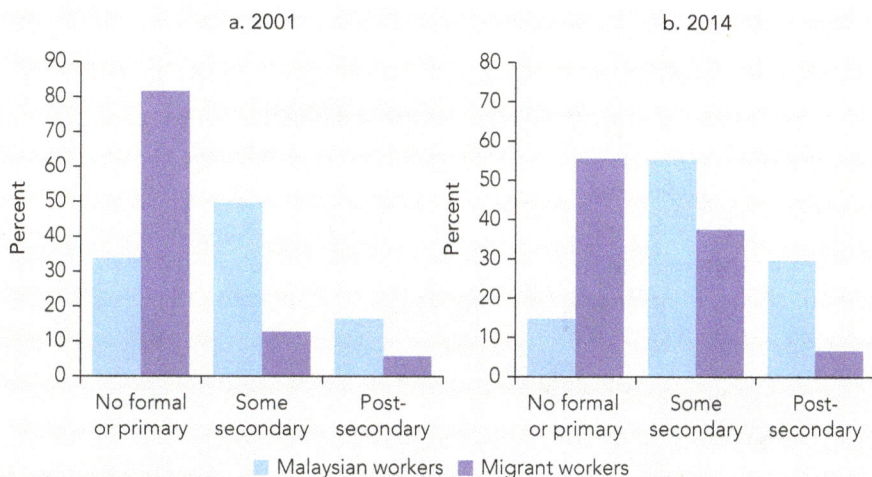

Source: World Bank 2015.

FIGURE 3.2

International students enrolled in tertiary education in ASEAN destinations

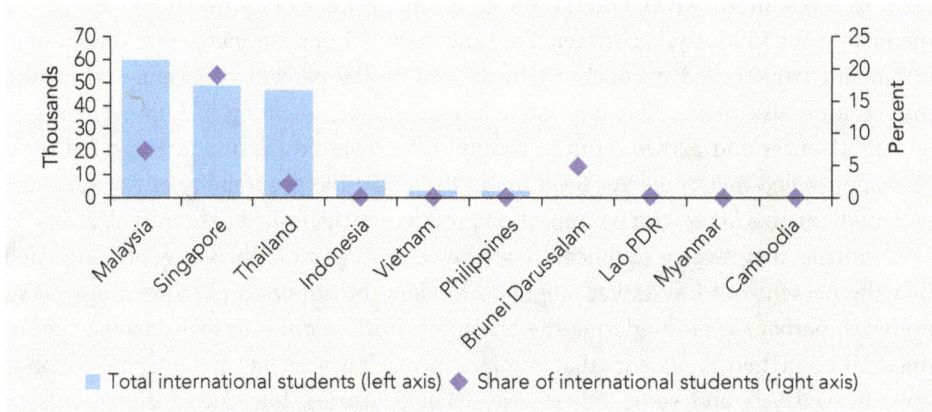

■ Total international students (left axis) ◆ Share of international students (right axis)

Source: UNESCO Institute for Statistics database.
Note: The year is 2015 for Brunei Darussalam, Lao PDR, Malaysia, Thailand, and Vietnam; 2013 for Singapore; 2012 for Indonesia and Myanmar; 2008 for the Philippines; and 2006 for Cambodia.

research suggests that additional workers who are less educated have not resulted in the expansion of labor-intensive sectors relative to skill-intensive ones (Ahsan et al. 2014).

ASEAN's growing student migrant population is a potential source of high-skilled labor that could increase competitiveness in the future. Several ASEAN destinations are becoming hubs for student migrants (figure 3.2). International students are increasingly seen as a source of high-skilled labor during and after education, in part because employers in host countries have more information about their qualifications. International students can also be an important market for the development of the domestic educational industry of host countries (ADBI, ILO, and OECD 2014). Malaysia hosts about 60,000 international students, and Singapore and Thailand about 50,000. This compares to the 55,000 international students hosted by Korea and the 150,000 hosted by Canada. Although in most ASEAN countries these numbers represent just a small share of students, in Singapore they represent as many as one-fifth. This compares with international students making up about 2 percent of tertiary enrollment in Korea. In some cases, these international students are from within ASEAN. The top three choices for students from Cambodia and the Lao People's Democratic Republic include Thailand and Vietnam, whereas students from Myanmar choose schools in Thailand. Malaysia is the third choice of migrants from Brunei Darussalam and Indonesia (Batalova, Shymonyak, and Sugiyarto 2017).

Employment and wages

Most evidence from high-income countries finds that migration has small impacts on the labor market outcomes of locals. Studying immigration to OECD member countries in the 1990s, Docquier, Özden, and Peri (2014) find that immigration had small, but positive, impacts on the wages and employment of both low-skilled and all local workers, even under pessimistic scenarios. A recent meta-analysis of seven studies, all of high-income countries, shows that increasing the share of immigrants by 1 percentage point in a local labor market results in declines in local employment of just 0.01 percent and in local wages of 0.03 percent (Longhi, Nijkamp, and Poot 2010).

Results are similarly small in East Asian countries, though positive impacts have been found in some cases. Ahsan et al. (2014) compile research from several East Asian countries and find that the impact of immigration on labor market outcomes is generally small; research in Korea shows that migrants do not adversely impact local employment and evidence from Singapore suggests that immigrants workers have a negligible impact on the wages of local workers. Recent research in Malaysia suggests that immigration has a positive impact on employment. Econometric techniques controlling for the possibility of reverse causality were used to isolate the causal impact of immigrants to Malaysia on the employment of locals (Del Carpio et al. 2015). Immigration to a given Malaysian state is found to increase the employment of local workers: an additional 10 immigrants in a state results in the inflow of 7.6 Malaysians to that state, more than 5 of whom are employed. Moreover, there is a a slight increase in the out-of-the-labor-force population. However, these individuals are almost entirely composed of women doing unpaid work at home or students. These results imply that immigration to a state induces demand for more local workers, who bring along their spouses and children.

Previous research on the impact of migrant workers on wages in Malaysia has found small, though negative, impacts (Athukorala and Devadason 2012; Narayanan and Yew-Wah 2014; Yean and Siang 2014). However, this literature did not distinguish between the effect on existing immigrant workers and Malaysians. Özden and Wagner (2016) analyze the impact of immigrants on the wages of Malaysian and immigrant workers separately. Consistent with the previous literature, the results show a small decrease in wages overall. However, when the impacts on Malaysians and immigrants are separated, the results are more nuanced: a 10 percentage point increase in immigration results in a small increase in the wages of Malaysian workers but a large decrease in the wages of immigrant workers (figure 3.3).

The results from Malaysia suggest a potential mechanism whereby immigrant arrivals generate employment. Concerns about the impact of immigration on employment and wages are often based on the assumption that immigrants and local workers are substitutes. An increase in the labor supply owing to increased immigration then implies more competition and wage declines. But lower production costs resulting from cheaper immigrant workers may result in an expansion of output. In Malaysia, immigration reduces the wages of foreign workers, lowering production costs and enabling output expansions. These expansions in output then demand the increases in employment described above (Özden and Wagner 2016).

Certain groups of local workers, particularly low-skilled ones, can be negatively affected by immigration, though these impacts are also generally small. The research in Korea presented in Ahsan et al. (2014) shows that a 1 percent increase in unskilled migrants is associated with a 0.09 percent reduction in the wages of unskilled locals but

FIGURE 3.3
Wage impacts of a 10 percent increase in immigrants in Malaysia

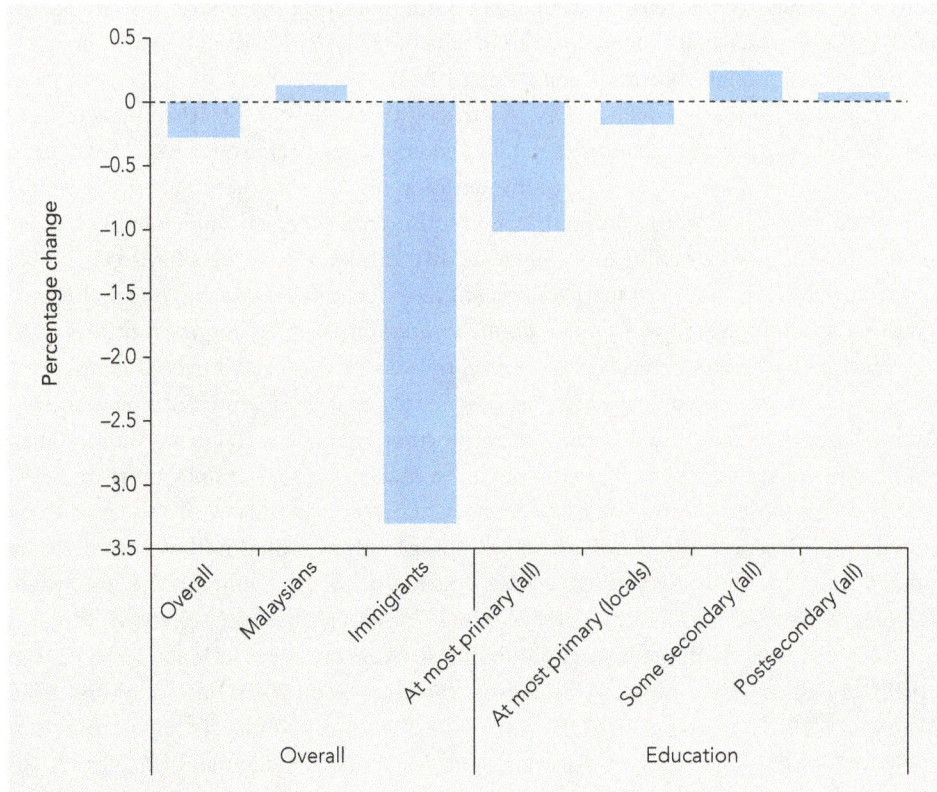

Source: Özden and Wagner 2016.

also a 0.3 percent increase in the wages of professionals. In Thailand, negative wage impacts from doubling the number of immigrant workers in five immigration-intensive provinces are isolated to less-skilled local workers. The wages of those with lower primary education fall by 0.03 percent and of those with upper primary education by 0.79 percent, whereas local workers with high school and college education benefit from wage increases of 0.56 and 0.57 percent, respectively (Lathapipat 2014) (figure 3.4). This suggests that low-skilled foreign workers increase the productivity of better-educated Thai workers. In Malaysia, the positive impacts of immigration on employment are smaller for the least educated locals who compete directly with immigrants (Del Carpio et al. 2015). Those with primary and lower secondary education gain the most in terms of employment from immigration, perhaps a signal that lower-middle-skilled locals have complementarities with immigrants, likely a result of language skills.[2] Similar to Thailand, the impact of immigration to Malaysia on wages is small and positive for more highly educated local workers but modestly negative for local workers with at most primary education (figure 3.3).

FIGURE 3.4

Change in the wages of Thai workers due to the doubling of the size of the immigrant workforce in five immigration-intensive provinces

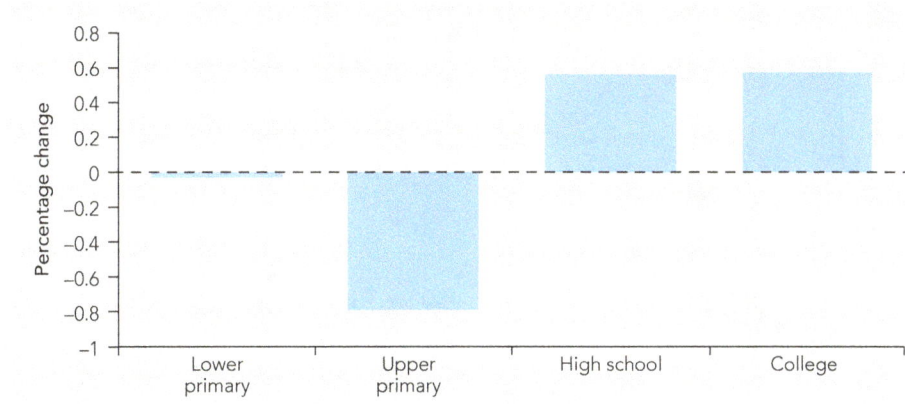

Source: Lathapipat 2014.

The impacts of migration on employment and wages depend on the rigidity of labor markets. Rigid labor markets characterized by strong employment protection legislation (EPL) (for instance, rules regarding firing, temporary employment, and collective dismissal) can make it more difficult for workers to switch jobs, firms, and geographic locations to adjust to, and benefit from, the presence of immigrant workers. In a meta-analysis of the impact of immigration on labor market outcomes, Longhi, Nijkamp, and Poot (2010) find that wage rigidity amplifies the negative impact of immigration on locals. In Europe, labor markets with high firing costs, rigid wages, and high business entry costs experience more job losses among locals owing to immigration (Angrist and Kugler 2003). There is evidence that these job losses arise because rigid labor markets disrupt the reallocation of less-skilled local workers to jobs requiring more complex skills as migrants increase the supply of less complex skills (D'Amuri and Peri 2014).[3]

Population aging

Migration is frequently suggested as a possible means to counteract the negative effects of population aging, which include smaller labor forces. As discussed in chapter 1, there is significant variation in the demographies of ASEAN countries. This suggests that younger countries, such as Indonesia, Lao PDR, and Myanmar, could boost the labor forces of older countries, such as Singapore, while providing relief to their slack labor markets. Simulations of the impact of permanent and temporary migration on the labor forces of migrant origins and destinations in East Asia and Pacific suggest that migration within East Asia could result in such an effect (Özden and Testaverde 2015). The simulations find that, compared with the baseline, migration will increase the labor forces of East Asian destinations in 2050 by 8 million people in the case of permanent migration and by 4.5 million people in the case of temporary migration (figure 3.5a). In contrast, the labor forces of East Asian

FIGURE 3.5

Impact of migration on the labor forces of East Asian destination and origin countries, 2010–50

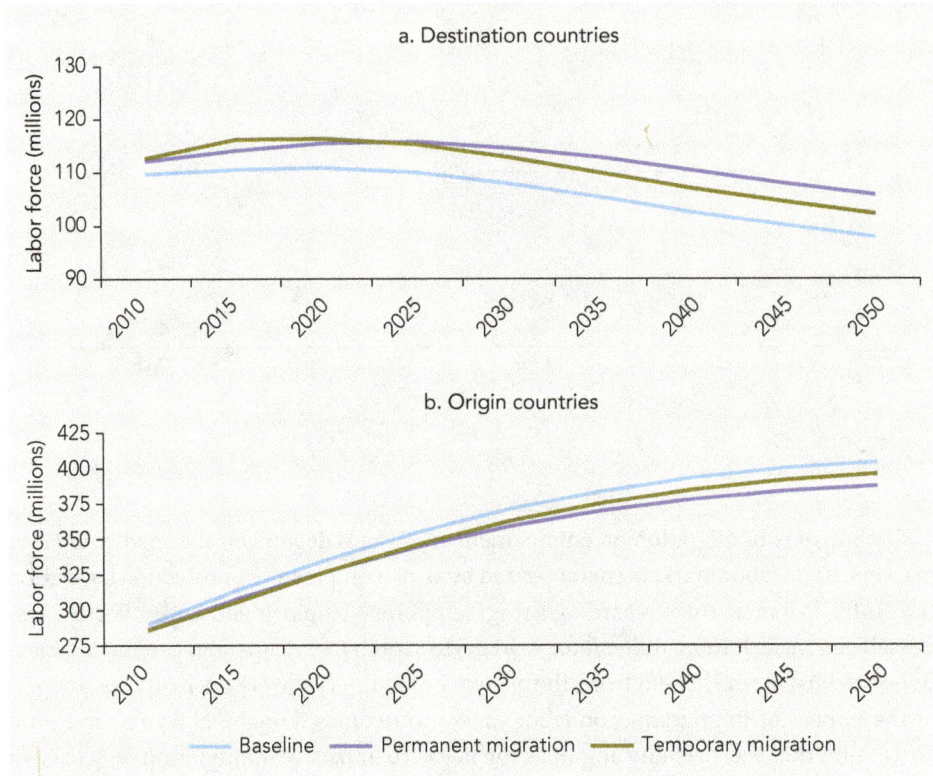

a. Destination countries

y-axis: Labor force (millions) — 90, 100, 110, 120, 130
x-axis: 2010, 2015, 2020, 2025, 2030, 2035, 2040, 2045, 2050

b. Origin countries

y-axis: Labor force (millions) — 275, 300, 325, 350, 375, 400, 425
x-axis: 2010, 2015, 2020, 2025, 2030, 2035, 2040, 2045, 2050

Baseline ——— Permanent migration ——— Temporary migration

Source: Özden and Testaverde 2015.
Note: The destination economies are Hong Kong SAR, China; Japan; Korea; Malaysia; and Singapore. The origin countries are Cambodia, Indonesia, Lao PDR, Mongolia, Myanmar, Papua New Guinea, the Philippines, Thailand, Timor-Leste, and Vietnam.

origins will be 17 million people smaller in the case of permanent migration and nearly 9 million people smaller in the case of temporary migration (figure 3.5b).

Migration may help counteract the shrinking of working age populations through indirect channels as well. It may help increase female labor force participation and, more speculatively, fertility rates. Low-skilled immigrants to the United States have eased the tradeoff between labor force participation, childbearing, and household work for high-skilled women (Cortes and Tessada 2011; Furtado and Hock 2010). The extension of work permits to foreign domestic workers was associated with an increased female labor force participation rate in Hong Kong SAR, China, for mothers with young children (Cortes and Pan 2013; see also Chan 2006; Suen 1994; Tan and Gibson 2013). Foreign domestic workers in the United States and Italy have been shown to allow highly skilled American and Italian women, respectively, to spend more time at work (Barone and Mocceti 2011; Cortes and Tessada 2011). The large presence of female

FIGURE 3.6

Age distribution in East Asian destination countries, 2050

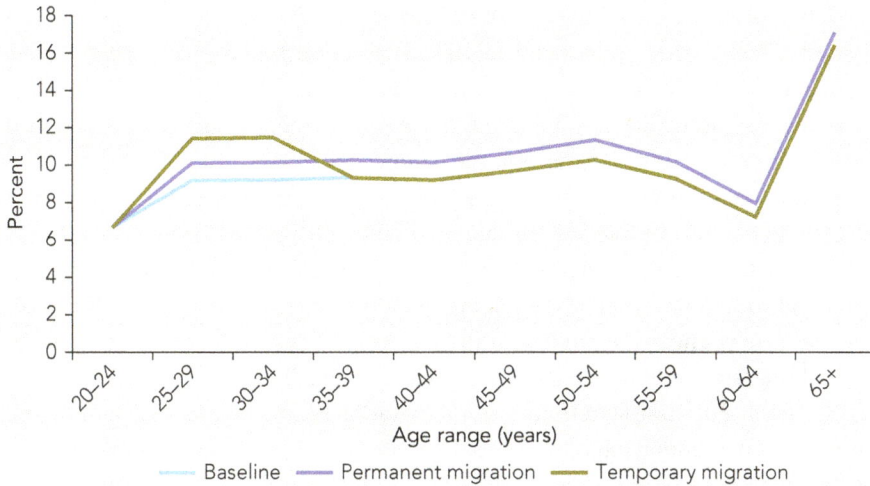

Source: Özden and Testaverde 2015.
Note: The destination economies are Hong Kong SAR, China; Japan; Korea; Malaysia; and Singapore. The temporary migration scenario and the baseline scenario converge at the 35–39 age group.

domestic workers in Malaysia, Singapore, and Thailand makes this channel particularly important in these economies. Singapore has even introduced a grant to help families employ foreign domestic workers to take care of the frail elderly (Østbye et al. 2013). Still, there is concern that the scale of migration may be insufficient to counteract the negative effects of population aging (Zaiceva and Zimmerman 2014).

The temporary nature of most migration in the ASEAN region means that some of the downsides of migration for population aging will not arise. Permanent migration can bring aging problems of its own because permanent migrants themselves age. Figure 3.6 shows the age distribution in East Asian destination countries in 2050 with temporary and permanent migration. Temporary migration does indeed boost the younger end of the population distribution. However, permanent migration shifts the distribution up along all age groups. This implies that permanent migration will likely boost the labor force of destination countries but also increase the older age population over time as migrants age and their behavior converges with that of locals. This issue is of less concern in ASEAN where most migration is temporary. Indeed, most evidence shows that higher fertility rates of immigrants converge quite quickly with those of locals (World Bank 2016).

Fiscal impacts

Migration imposes fiscal costs on destination country governments but also brings fiscal benefits. Most studies have found small impacts of between plus and minus 1 percent of GDP (UNDP 2009). Although immigrants do impose costs by increasing the demand for public services, they also have a positive fiscal impact through tax contributions. The fiscal impact of immigration depends on the generosity of the welfare state, particularly its generosity to immigrants, and on immigrants' tax and pension contributions (OECD 2013; Ratha, Mohapatra, and Scheja 2011). This is true of undocumented immigrants as well. In OECD countries, the tax and social security contributions of immigrants matter more than the benefits they receive in determining their fiscal impact (OECD 2013). Still, mismatches can occur because immigrants frequently receive services from providers at the local level but contribute taxes at the national level.

Although evidence of the fiscal impact of immigration in ASEAN is very limited, there is reason to believe that the effect should be small. Research from the OECD finds that impacts are more favorable when labor migration dominates, immigrants have higher employment rates, and immigrant populations are relatively young (OECD 2013). This is because younger migrants tend to be healthier and use fewer services, whereas employed migrants tend to use fewer services *and* contribute more in taxes and social security. All three of these factors are true of migration in ASEAN. As shown in chapter 1, employment rates among migrants are high in most cases. With the notable exception of Malaysia, migrants are significantly younger than the host country's population.

Prices

Immigration affects prices, particularly the cost of nontradable goods and services. In theory, the impact of immigration on prices is unclear—immigrants may increase prices by increasing demand or may lower prices if lower production costs are passed through to prices. However, most evidence shows that immigration lowers prices. Studies from the United Kingdom and the United States find that immigration leads to reductions of the prices of goods in sectors that are heavily reliant on immigrant labor and in the prices of immigrant-intensive services (Cortes 2008; Frattini 2014). In the case of the United States, the price reductions are particularly beneficial to the high-skilled locals who consume more of these services. Cross-country research finds that a 10 percent increase in the immigrant worker share can lead to declines in prices by as much as 3 percentage points. This evidence suggests that the findings of the studies from the United Kingdom and the United States are generalizable, though there is evidence that the result is explained by immigrant consumption habits rather than lower production costs (Zachariadis 2012).

Crime

Immigration can have an impact on crime for several reasons. Immigrants may differ from the local population in their likelihood to commit crimes, may improve or harm the opportunities of locals and so change crime rates among them, or may change the composition of an area, attracting or repelling locals who are likely to commit crimes. Both locals and immigrants who can find employment are less likely to commit crimes because the benefits of legal activity are more likely to outweigh the risk of loss from illegal activity, which in the case of immigrants, may involve deportation.

FIGURE 3.7
Impact of immigration on crime rates in Malaysia

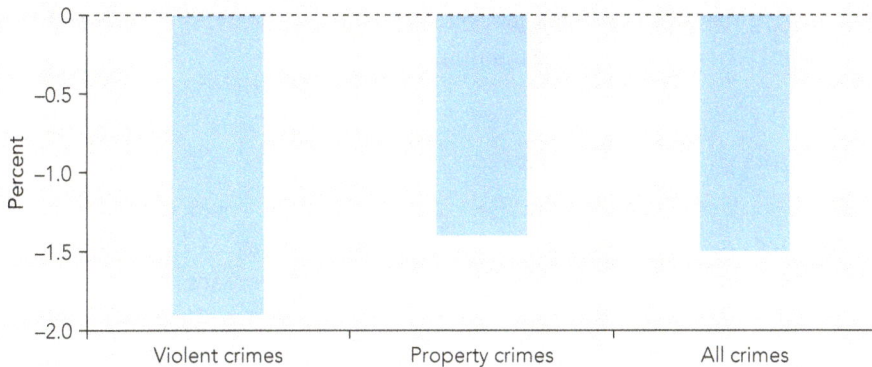

Source: Özden, Testaverde, and Wagner 2017.

International evidence tends to find that immigration has no effect on crime, particularly violent crime, and can even lead to a decrease in crime (Adelman et al. 2017; Bell 2014; Bell, Fasani, and Machin 2013; Bianchi, Buonanno, and Pinotti 2012; Spenkuch 2013). The labor market outcomes of migrants are particularly important, however. For instance, an increase in asylum seekers, who are generally prevented from seeking employment, was found to result in slight increases in property crime in the United Kingdom (Bell, Fasini, and Machin 2013).

Recent research from Malaysia is consistent with this international evidence. Studying crime rates based on data from the Royal Malaysian Police between 2003 and 2010 and controlling for potential endogeneity problems and potential undercounting of undocumented immigrants, Özden, Testaverde, and Wagner (2017) find that an increase of 100,000 immigrants to a Malaysian state reduces the total number of crimes committed by 1.5 percent (figure 3.7). Most of the reduction in crime is due to improved socioeconomic outcomes, particularly an increase in the local employment rate and a decrease in a state's share of less-educated men. This is especially true for property crimes. Immigration does not seem to affect violent crime through these socioeconomic channels, meaning that the reduction in violent crime is related to immigrants' lower propensity to commit crimes or to other factors, such as increased law enforcement activity in states with more immigrants.

Knowledge gaps

Although significant research exists on the wage and employment impacts of migration on host countries in the OECD area, the literature is much more limited in ASEAN countries, and research on the longer-term impacts of migration is limited everywhere. Except for some recent work in Malaysia, Singapore, and Thailand, rigorous analysis of the impacts of migration on receiving countries has been limited. Even in OECD member countries, only more recently has research tried to understand the impact of immigration on productivity and competitiveness, firm dynamics, prices, agglomeration, and other longer-term outcomes. As countries in ASEAN continue to develop, understanding the impact of immigration on firm productivity, skills upgrading, and technological advancement will be important.

Impacts on origin countries

Losing members of a country's workforce to out-migration would, on its own, lead to less economic growth as skilled individuals depart and the size of the economy shrinks (Bodvarsson and Van den Berg 2009a). However, such declines are not inevitable. Remittances, migrant networks, and changes in incentives to obtain more education mean that emigration can have important links to economic development in source countries.

Indeed, there is some evidence that, in the longer run, net emigration from developing countries has a positive impact on growth in those countries (Brunow, Nijkamp, and Poot 2015). Research on the impacts of migration on sending countries in ASEAN is limited. But recent work in East Asia, which includes findings from ASEAN countries, suggests that origins benefit from migration in the short run through remittances, although longer-run impacts and those related to brain drain, brain gain, and brain circulation are less clear (Ahsan et al. 2014).

Remittances

Remittances represent significant financial inflows in several ASEAN countries. About US$62 billion in remittances were sent to ASEAN countries in 2015, US$20 billion from them, and US$9 billion among them. In 2015 total remittances were 10 percent of GDP in the Philippines, 7 percent in Vietnam, 5 percent in Myanmar, and 3 percent in Cambodia (table 3.1). More than half of all remittances in these latter two countries originated in other ASEAN countries. Consistent with most of their migrants being outside of ASEAN, the other two large recipients of remittances—the Philippines and Vietnam—received more than 90 percent of remittances from outside of ASEAN. Households in Indonesia received the most remittances in U.S. dollar terms from other ASEAN countries. Several ASEAN countries are also significant sources of remittances, though households received about three times more remittances in ASEAN countries than they sent from them (table 3.2). Notably, 78 percent of remittances sent from Malaysia were sent within ASEAN, primarily to Indonesia and the Philippines. China is the primary recipient of remittances from Indonesia, Myanmar, the Philippines, Singapore, and Vietnam, which all send most of their remittances to outside ASEAN.

Macroeconomic impacts
Such sizable financial flows can be critical components of the economies of origin countries. Compared to other private and public financial flows, remittances are a relatively

TABLE 3.1
Remittances received in ASEAN countries, 2015
(Millions of 2015 US$)

Recipient	From ASEAN	From non-ASEAN	Total	% ASEAN	% of GDP
Brunei Darussalam	—	—	—	—	—
Cambodia	330	213	542	61	3
Indonesia	2,721	6,910	9,631	28	1
Lao PDR	63	30	93	68	1
Malaysia	1,068	575	1,643	65	1
Myanmar	1,832	1,405	3,236	57	5
Philippines	1,852	26,631	28,483	7	10
Singapore	—	—	—	—	—
Thailand	927	4,291	5,218	18	1
Vietnam	348	12,652	13,000	3	7

Source: Bilateral Remittance Matrix, World Bank.
Note: — = not available; ASEAN = Association of Southeast Asian Nations.

TABLE 3.2
Remittances sent from ASEAN countries, 2015
(Millions of 2015 US$)

Sender	To ASEAN	To non-ASEAN	Total	% ASEAN
Brunei Darussalam	148	512	660	22
Cambodia	264	15	279	95
Indonesia	103	731	834	12
Lao PDR	45	17	62	73
Malaysia	4,631	1,324	5,955	78
Myanmar	0	408	408	0
Philippines	10	510	520	2
Singapore	1,643	4,578	6,220	26
Thailand	2,268	2,210	4,478	51
Vietnam	26	82	107	24

Source: Bilateral Remittance Matrix, World Bank.
Note: ASEAN = Association of Southeast Asian Nations.

stable source of income that tends to be countercyclical: remittances tend to rise when the origin country has a negative economic outlook (Chami, Hakura, and Montiel 2012). The stable and compensatory nature of remittances means that they play a key role in stabilizing the aggregate economy of recipient countries. Because large flows of remittances increase a country's financial reserves, they boost confidence and expectations (Ahsan et al. 2014).

Remittances have other potential benefits. They can increase household consumption and, consequently, can increase the revenue that governments receive from taxes on consumption. Additionally, households receiving remittances are less compelled to take on debt, which can eventually boost the debt sustainability of the entire economy (Ahsan et al. 2014).

Remittances can also affect financial development. To explore the relationship between remittances and financial inclusion, Anzoategui, Demirgüç-Kunt, and Pería (2014) exploit household information from El Salvador and find that receiving remittances boosts the average likelihood of having a deposit account at a financial institution by 11 percentage points. One possible explanation is that recipients need bank accounts to safely store remittances that are "lumpy" in nature. This engagement with the banking system increases the chances of the recipient getting to know other financial products, which can lead to increased demand for them. At the same time, remittances may also increase an individual's probability of obtaining a loan. First, processing remittances flows provides financial institutions with better information on the recipient's income. Second, if remittances are used to purchase land or housing, these assets can be used as collateral to obtain loans.

However, remittances can have negative effects on the source country's economy when the flows are large and adequate policies are not in place. International remittances can transmit external business cycles (Chami, Hakura, and Montiel 2012). For example, in 2008 Vietnam had to cope with an interruption of remittance inflows due to the global economic downturn, which created macroeconomic imbalances in the economy (Ahsan et al. 2014). Rising inflows of remittances may also exert pressure to appreciate the real exchange rate in recipient countries, thereby increasing unit labor costs and reducing the competitiveness of exports. Consequently, resources might be reallocated from the tradable to the nontradable sector, leading to "Dutch disease" when a proactive, long-term approach to managing them is absent (Lartey, Mandelman, and Acosta 2012).

Income, consumption, and labor market impacts

Members of the household who do not migrate benefit from from the poverty-reducing effect of remittances. Using a novel database covering 71 developing countries, Adams and Page (2005) estimate that a 10 percent increase in remittances is associated with a 3.5 percent reduction in the proportion of poor households. In the Philippines, Rodriguez (1998) finds that households with a migrant abroad had roughly 6.5 percent more income than nonmigrant families. Using more recent data for the Philippines, Ducanes (2015) estimates that households that are able to send a member abroad have twofold or threefold greater odds of escaping poverty. Similarly, Yang and Martinez (2006) exploit the exchange rate shocks during the 1997 Asian financial crisis to measure how a drastic change in remittances inflows affected poverty. Results suggest that a rise in remittances of 10 percentage points is associated with a 2.9 percentage point decrease in the poverty headcount among migrant families. Similar results are found for Vietnam, where foreign remittances decreased the poverty headcount of recipients by approximately 2 percentage points (Viet 2008). A recent study by Adams and Cuecuecha

(2014) finds that in Indonesia families receiving remittances in 2007 but not in 2000 were less likely to be poor by almost 28 percent.

There are many reasons why remittances can reduce poverty. By injecting money into the household budget, remittances relax the credit constraints of stayers, allowing them to engage in entrepreneurship and income-generating activities and to invest in human capital accumulation and health care. Moreover, international remittances may act as insurance against income shocks and can smooth consumption during these periods. Studying emigration from the Philippines, Yang and Choi (2007) find that remittances fall when the income of the left-behind household rises, whereas they increase when that income falls, serving as a cushion against negative shocks. The size of this insurance effect appears to be very large: about 60 percent of negative income shocks are replaced by remittances.

The poorest households tend to use remittances as safety nets and spend them on consumption. Spending the additional income associated with remittances on consumption goods, such as food, is important to support poor families in the short term. However, spending the additional income on productive goods such as education and health may foster development in the medium and long term. In general, the use of remittances depends on household income. Remittances sent to families at the bottom of the income distribution are more likely to act as safety nets and be spent on consumption. For example, Adams and Cuecuecha (2014) find that recipients of remittances in Indonesia increase their marginal expenditures on food by almost 6 percent. Conversely, no effect is found on children's school enrollment and attendance (Nguyen and Purnamasari 2014).

Wealthier households are less likely to use remittances for consumption. Migrants from Vietnam and the Philippines, for example, typically do not belong to the poorest families. As a result, the money these migrants send home is more likely to be spent on productive and investment goods. Using data from the 2006 and 2008 Vietnam Household Living Standard Surveys, Cuong and Mont (2012) find that most of the international remittances received are spent on housing and land and on debt repayment and saving, with their impact on consumption-based poverty very limited. Similarly, Cabegin and Alba (2014) estimate a 40 percent decrease in food consumption for migrant households in the Philippines, while they find an increase of roughly 90 percent in expenditures on housing and 60 percent on education and health care. Additionally, when faced with exogenous rises in remittances, Filipinos mainly use the additional resources for investment rather than current consumption (Yang 2008).

Emigration and remittances may also alter work incentives by increasing household income. Using Labor Force Survey data for the Philippines, Rodriguez and Tiongson (2001) provide evidence that having a migrant in the family reduces the labor force participation of stayers by almost 28 percent. This finding appears to be particularly important for left-behind wives; in the absence of the migrant husband, women in the Philippines have been shown either to switch to part-time jobs or to completely withdraw from the labor force (Cabegin 2013). This decrease in labor supply, however, is mostly due to an increase in time spent in home production (for example, child care) rather than in time spent in consuming leisure. Yang (2008) also finds that recipients of remittances remove children from the labor force and keep them in school longer: one standard deviation increase in remittances is associated with a 1.6 percentage point increase in the probability of being in school. The study also finds that the remittances increase hours worked in self-employment and the likelihood that households undertake capital-intensive entrepreneurial activities.

Wages

Evidence from outside of ASEAN finds that emigration increases the wages of workers in source countries. The departure of a large number of migrant workers from a source country's labor force can result in a labor supply shift that increases the wages of those nonmigrant workers who remain in the source country. For instance, Hanson (2007) finds that, in Mexican states with significant levels of migration, wages rose 6 to 9 percent relative to those in states with low migration levels. Also in Mexico, Mishra (2007) estimates that a migration-induced 10 percent decrease in workers in a given skill group increased average wages by about 4 percent. Similar results have been found for Poland (Dustmann, Frattini, and Rosso 2015), Moldova (Bouton, Paul, and Tiongson 2011), Puerto Rico (Borjas 2008), and Honduras (Gagnon 2011). The increase in wages often varies across skill groups. In Mexico, the largest wage increases found by Mishra (2007) were among higher-wage earners. Though not found to explain the entire increase in wage inequality in Mexico, out-migration is likely a contributing factor (Mishra 2014).

Brain drain, brain gain, and brain circulation

The migration rates of high-skilled individuals are high in several ASEAN countries. The emigration rates of tertiary-educated individuals to OECD member countries in 2010 were quite high in several less-developed ASEAN countries, but also in more-developed ones like Singapore and Malaysia (figure 3.8). Fifteen percent of tertiary-educated individuals emigrated from Cambodia and Lao PDR in 2010, and 11 percent from Vietnam. The rates were also somewhat elevated in Malaysia, the Philippines, and Singapore compared to Indonesia and Thailand. Student migration is also a significant factor for several ASEAN countries (figure 3.9). Vietnam and Malaysia each had more than 40,000 students in the OECD in 2014 representing the 9th and 10th most important sources of student migrants globally. The high emigration rates and significant international student population of many ASEAN countries are consistent with a perception that several ASEAN countries have less capacity to retain talent, as measured by the World Economic Forum's Global Competitiveness Index (figure 3.10). While Singapore and Malaysia have comparable scores to the United States, the United Kingdom, and Canada, ASEAN's other countries have significantly lower scores.

FIGURE 3.8

Emigration rates of the tertiary educated from ASEAN to OECD countries, 2010

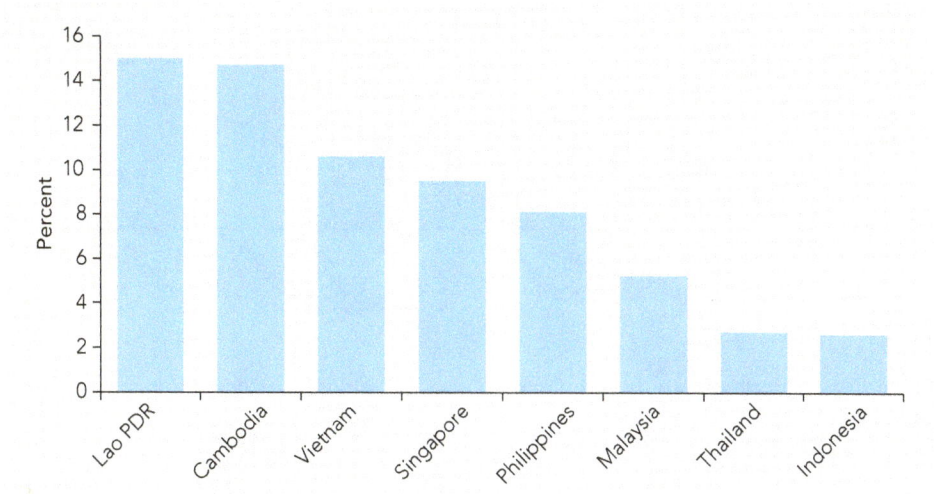

Source: ADBI, ILO, and OECD 2016.
Note: OECD = Organisation for Economic Co-operation and Development.

FIGURE 3.9

International students from ASEAN countries enrolled in tertiary education in OECD countries, 2014

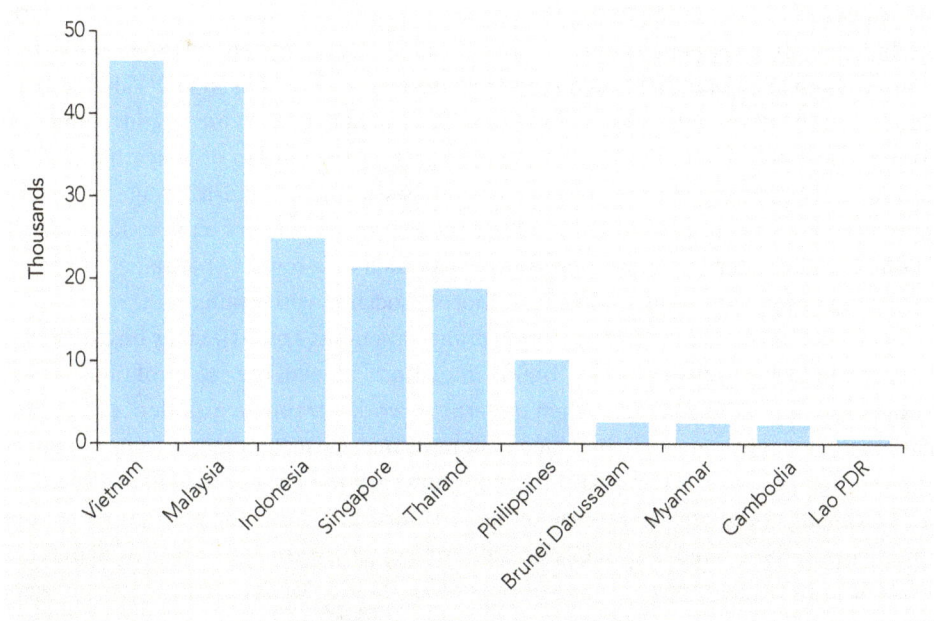

Source: OECD Education at a Glance, extracted from the OECD Education Database (http://www.oecd.org/education/database.htm).
Note: OECD = Organisation for Economic Co-operation and Development.

FIGURE 3.10

Capacity to retain talent in ASEAN and comparator countries, 2015–16

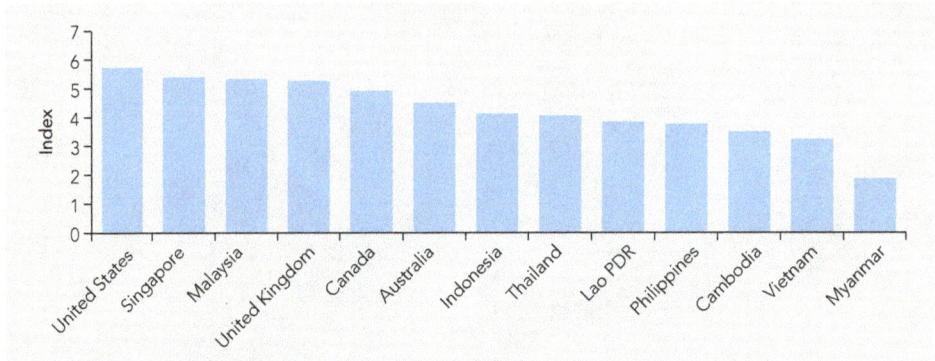

Source: Global Competitiveness Index, World Economic Forum 2015–2016 (http://reports.weforum.org/global
-competitiveness-index/).
Note: Highest capacity is designated by a score of "7." ASEAN = Association of Southeast Asian Nations.

The emigration of the highly skilled—or "brain drain"—is often perceived to be costly
for developing countries. The early literature on this type of emigration emphasized its
negative effects, including source countries paying for training that is then used abroad
and being depleted of the human capital necessary for technological upgrading, adapta-
tion, and, ultimately, economic growth (Bhagwati and Hamada 1974; Bhagwati and
Rodriguez 1975; Miyagiwa 1991; Wong and Yip 1999). This was viewed as particularly
problematic in developing countries, where scarce resources were invested in the creation of human capital that was not used domestically (Bodvarsson and Van den Berg
2009a). Student migration may also have detrimental effects for origin countries.
Though in this case host countries shoulder much of the burden of educating student
migrants, youth studying abroad have advantages in the foreign marriage and labor
markets compared to potential migrants educated in the origin country (Rosenzweig
2008). Obtaining tertiary education abroad may then be a route to permanent or long-
term emigration with similar impacts to those associated with brain drain.

However, the negative effects of "brain drain" in sending countries may be overstated
and may in fact be outweighed by "brain circulation." Indeed, the extent of high-skilled
emigration may be exaggerated when patterns of worker training, experience, and education are not considered. High-skilled emigrants may have complex patterns of education, work experience, and migration that obscure their impact on the welfare of sending
and receiving countries. In the case of doctors born or trained (or both) in Africa but
practicing in the United States, Özden and Phillips (2015) show that nearly 50 percent
of African-born doctors were trained outside of their birth country, 15 percent were
trained in Africa but born outside of the continent, and many gained experience working in their birth countries. Indeed, there does not seem to be strong evidence that
Africa suffers significant brain gain or brain loss (Docquier and Rapoport 2012).

Additionally, high-skilled emigration can have positive impacts on source countries by incentivizing human capital formation. In contrast to the earlier literature, which emphasized the downside to human capital of high-skilled emigration, newer research suggests that high-skilled emigration could actually increase human capital formation by increasing the perceived returns to education and encouraging current nonmigrants to invest more in education (Stark, Helmenstein, and Prskawetz 1998). Studying this possibility, Beine, Docquier, and Rapoport (2008) find that the prospect of high-skilled migration does in fact have a positive impact on human capital formation (see Beine, Docquier, and Oden-Defoort 2011). Overall, doubling the high-skilled emigration rate results in a 5 percent increase in the human capital formation of the local population in the sending country. However, the impact varies across countries. In Indonesia and Thailand, where high-skilled emigration rates are relatively low, high-skilled emigration is found to have increased the share of high-skilled workers (figure 3.11). Yet the very elevated high-skilled emigration rates in Cambodia, Lao PDR, and Vietnam are found to outweigh the incentive effect to acquire more human capital. In these countries, high-skilled emigration is found to have resulted in a smaller share of high-skilled workers.

Migration may also lead to "brain circulation" rather than "brain drain." In general, the likelihood of skilled professionals returning to source countries increases with source country characteristics such as growth prospects, though individual factors also seem to matter (Docquier and Rapoport 2012). Studying the "best and brightest academic performers" from Tonga, Papua New Guinea, and New Zealand, Gibson

FIGURE 3.11

Net effect of high-skilled emigration on the share of high-skilled workers in ASEAN source countries

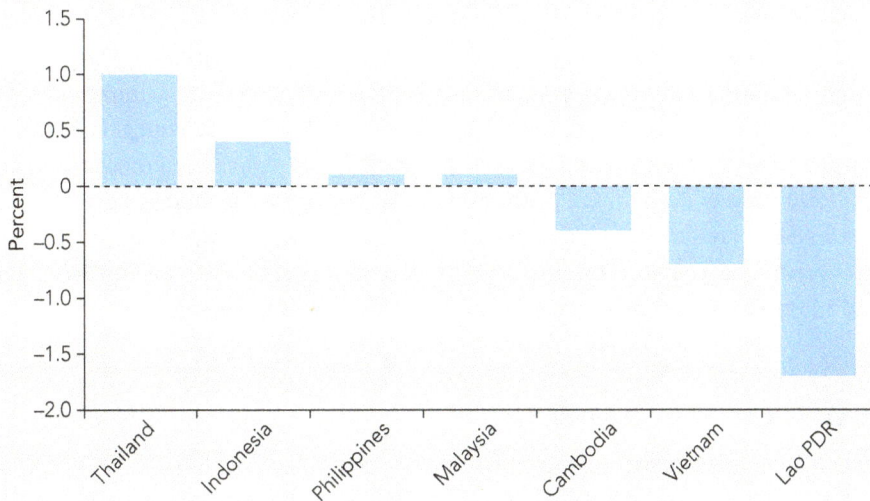

Source: Beine, Docquier, and Rapoport 2008.

and McKenzie (2011) show that return migration is motivated by family and lifestyle factors rather than income opportunities. Still, foreign-acquired skills can allow returnees to earn a wage premium compared with nonmigrants when they return to their origin countries (Wahba 2015a). International migration also raises the chances of upward occupational mobility of returnees compared to nonmigrants (Wahba 2015b). When migrants return to their country of origin, they often bring savings accumulated while abroad. Similar to remittances, the additional income can ease credit constraints and facilitate the creation of businesses or self-employment (McCormick and Wahba 2001; Wahba and Zenou 2012).

The presence of migrants in destination countries can reduce the cost of transferring knowledge, ideas, and capital (Docquier and Rapoport 2012). Migration is generally found to increase trade flows. For instance, Felbermayr and Jung (2009) find that a 1 percent increase in the bilateral stock of migrants increases bilateral trade by 0.11 percent, though there does not seem to be a difference in the pro-trade effects of low- and high-skilled migrants. Migrants, particularly high-skilled ones, can also result in higher FDI flows to their origin countries (Docquier and Rapoport 2012). For instance, Tong (2005) shows that ethnic Chinese networks help facilitate FDI flows in Southeast Asia. A similar effect occurs for technology diffusion across borders. Kerr (2008) uses patent citations to show that ethnic networks facilitate knowledge transfer, even increasing the labor productivity of manufacturing in home countries.

Skilled emigration may also have an impact on domestic institutions. Studying foreign-educated students, Spilimbergo (2009) finds that foreign students promote democracy in their source countries, but only if their education is obtained in democratic countries. Docquier et al. (2016) find that openness to emigration, as measured by the total emigration rate, improves institutional quality in source countries regardless of the skill level of emigrants. Similar to Spilimbergo (2009), the results only hold for emigration to wealthy democracies.

Knowledge gaps

Though substantial research has been done in ASEAN countries on the impact of remittances and emigration on origin countries, more work is necessary. Additional research is needed to understand the effect of remittances on longer-term outcomes and on the complex process of brain drain, gain, and circulation. Given the increasing importance of intra-ASEAN migration, further research on the interactions among education, emigration, and return could show how regional agreements could help maximize the benefits and minimize the costs associated with these three phenomena.

Attitudes toward migrants

Evidence on attitude formation

Understanding the drivers of public attitudes toward migrants is important to inform how policy makers can generate support for policies that take advantage of the benefits of migration. There has been increasing interest in understanding what drives attitudes toward migrants globally, with particular attention being paid to whether attitudes are driven by economic factors resulting from the impact of immigration on the well-being of locals or from noneconomic factors such as concerns about the social and cultural impacts of immigration. Where economic factors drive attitudes, policy makers can focus on ensuring that policies are in place to minimize negative effects from migration and to assist those who lose out. Where noneconomic factors drive these attitudes, there is some new evidence that information about migration can counteract concerns, creating room for policies that take advantage of the benefits of migration.

Concerns about labor market competition seem to play a role in the formation of attitudes toward migrants. Several prominent investigations of the drivers of attitudes toward immigration are based on theoretical models that posit that these attitudes depend on the relative supply of low- and high-skilled migrants. Increases in low-skilled immigrants are posited to reduce the wages of low-skilled local workers (and increase those of high-skilled workers) and lead to more negative (positive) attitudes toward immigrants among the low- (high-) skilled. Scheve and Slaughter (2001) find that lower skilled workers in the United States are more likely to prefer limiting immigration. Mayda (2006) finds cross-country evidence for this economic explanation, showing that skilled individuals are more likely to support immigration in countries in which locals are more skilled than immigrants. O'Rourke and Sinnott (2006) find further support for the conclusions of Mayda (2006).

The potential fiscal impacts of immigration also seem to play a role in attitude formation. Dustmann and Preston (2006) find support that immigration attitudes in Europe are based on concerns about the fiscal burden of immigration. Dustmann and Preston (2007) show that these concerns are held more strongly among the British by the more educated, who are most likely to be affected by immigrants with higher welfare dependency. Hanson, Scheve, and Slaughter (2007) corroborate this finding in the United States. Drawing on cross-country evidence, Facchini and Mayda (2009) find that preferences in countries where immigrants are less skilled than locals tend to become more favorable toward immigration as the skill level of locals increases but less favorable as their income increases. The implication is that the fiscal impact driver matters—higher-income individuals are assumed to bear a larger fiscal burden when immigration is low skilled—but so does the labor market competition driver: higher-skilled individuals are better off when there are more low-skilled immigrants. Facchini and Mayda (2012) then show evidence that this is true in Europe using a survey that directly measures attitudes toward skilled migration.

However, noneconomic factors such as concerns about the social and cultural impacts of immigrants are also important in attitude formation. As shown earlier in the chapter, the employment, wage, and fiscal impacts of immigration on locals are generally found to be quite small or even positive, leading to a question of why locals would be concerned about such effects. Further, the use of education as an indication of skill might be problematic as education is also correlated with support for cultural diversity and with less ethnocentrism (Hainmueller and Hopkins 2014). Indeed, much of the literature showing the importance of economic factors also finds that noneconomic variables such as concerns about immigrants' impact on crime and culture are correlated with attitudes toward migration (Dustmann and Preston 2007; Facchini and Mayda 2012 Mayda 2006; O'Rourke and Sinnott 2006). Like Facchini and Mayda (2012), Hainmueller and Hiscox (2010) use a direct survey of attitudes in the United States and show that both low- and high-skilled locals prefer high- over low-skilled immigrants, which runs contrary to the predictions of the labor competition model. Rich and poor locals are also found to be opposed to low-skilled immigration, which runs contrary to the prediction of the fiscal impact model. Hainmueller and Hiscox (2007) provide similar evidence for Europe. Finally, attitudes toward different types of migrants can be different. O'Rourke and Sinnott (2006) show that attitudes are generally more favorable toward refugees.

Information campaigns may help counteract noneconomic concerns related to migration. A recent large-scale randomized experiment presented Japanese citizens with information about positive economic and social impacts of immigration (Facchini, Margalit, and Nakata 2016). Those provided information about the potential effect of immigrants on Japan's pension crisis increased their support for allowing more immigrants by 21 percentage points. Those provided information about immigration's potential role in counteracting Japan's shrinking population increased support by 15 percentage points, while those provided information about immigration's potential role in alleviating Japan's caregiver shortage increased support by 19 percentage points. Similar increases were identified in support for increasing temporary work visas. There was also a positive impact on willingness to sign a petition of support for a more open immigration policy. The effects decreased, but remained positive, 10 to 12 days later. The authors suggest that the impact is driven by exposing participants to new information.

Attitudes toward migration in ASEAN

Attitudes toward migrants differ significantly across ASEAN countries, varying mostly according to whether a country is a host or sending country and generally, but not always, more positive in heavily migrant-dependent Singapore. In its periodic assessment of government views on migration, the United Nations found that most ASEAN countries view the level of immigration to their country to be satisfactory (table 3.3). However, Malaysia and Singapore, two of the region's receiving countries, viewed immigration to be too high. These two countries, in addition to Lao PDR, also view emigration to be too high. Cambodia and Indonesia, two of the region's sending countries, in addition to Vietnam and Thailand, which send migrants globally, view emigration as too low.

Individual attitudes toward migrants show a similar pattern. An ILO study of individual attitudes finds skepticism toward immigration in Malaysia, Singapore, and Thailand, though views are more moderate in Singapore (Tunon and Baruah 2012). Respondents in Singapore were more likely than respondents in Malaysia and Thailand

TABLE 3.3
Government attitudes toward migrants in ASEAN countries

Country	View on immigration	View on emigration
Brunei Darussalam	Satisfactory	Satisfactory
Cambodia	Satisfactory	Too low
Indonesia	Satisfactory	Too low
Lao PDR	Satisfactory	Too high
Malaysia	Too high	Too high
Myanmar	Satisfactory	Satisfactory
Philippines	Satisfactory	Satisfactory
Singapore	Too high	Too high
Thailand	Satisfactory	Too low
Vietnam	Satisfactory	Too low

Source: UN 2013.
Note: ASEAN = Association of Southeast Asian Nations.

to think that migrants make a positive economic contribution and less likely to think they have a negative social impact. In Malaysia and Thailand, about 80 percent of respondents believed that migrants commit a large number of crimes, versus 52 percent in Singapore. Beliefs about cultural impacts were different: respondents in Malaysia and Singapore were more likely to believe that immigrants threatened culture and heritage, and about 80 percent of survey respondents in each country expressed an interest in making government immigration policies more restrictive. There was significantly less support for reducing high-skilled immigration.

Further evidence on attitudes toward immigrants comes from the World Values Survey, which is a compilation of similar nationally representative surveys about human beliefs and values. Data are available for six ASEAN countries for the two most recent survey waves (2005–09 and 2010–14). About 60 percent of respondents in Malaysia and Thailand mentioned immigrants or foreign workers when asked whom they would *not* like to have as neighbors (figure 3.12a). Substantially less than half of respondents mentioned immigrants or foreign workers in the four other ASEAN countries for which data are available. Attitudes are more positive in Indonesia, the Philippines, and Vietnam, which send many migrants, but also in Singapore, a receiving country.

Across ASEAN countries, most respondents agree that employers should prioritize hiring "people of this country over immigrants" when jobs are scarce. Agreement is highest in Malaysia and Thailand, at about 90 percent, somewhat lower at 74 percent in Singapore, and lowest in the Philippines and Vietnam, which are sending countries (figure 3.12b). In Malaysia and Thailand, the most popular immigration policy is "strict limits," whereas respondents in Vietnam are the only ones who prefer a lax immigration policy of "let[ting] anyone come" (figure 3.12c).

FIGURE 3.12

Attitudes toward migrants and migration policy in ASEAN countries

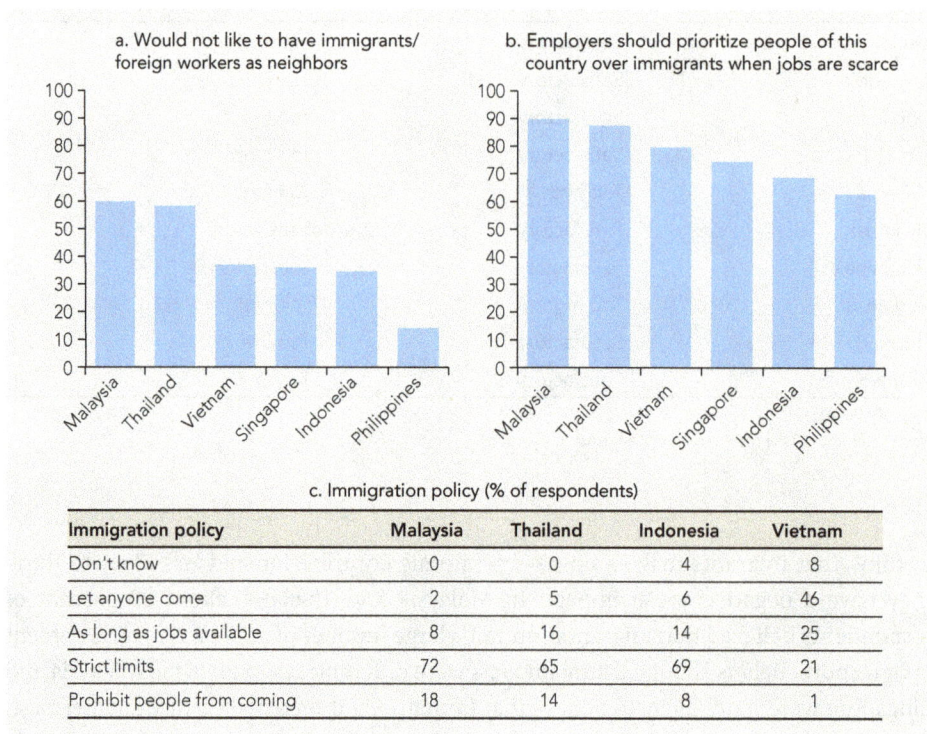

a. Would not like to have immigrants/foreign workers as neighbors

b. Employers should prioritize people of this country over immigrants when jobs are scarce

c. Immigration policy (% of respondents)

Immigration policy	Malaysia	Thailand	Indonesia	Vietnam
Don't know	0	0	4	8
Let anyone come	2	5	6	46
As long as jobs available	8	16	14	25
Strict limits	72	65	69	21
Prohibit people from coming	18	14	8	1

Source: World Values Survey 2015.
Note: The darker cells indicate the most frequent response. The wave is 2010–14 for Malaysia, the Philippines, Singapore, and Thailand, and 2005–09 for Indonesia and Vietnam for panels a and b. The wave is 2005–09 for panel c. For access to the survey, visit http://www.worldvaluessurvey.org/wvs.jsp.

Finally, an electronic survey[4] of ASEAN countries undertaken for this book, which included mostly highly educated individuals who visited World Bank Group websites, showed individuals to have fairly skeptical views of migration (figure 3.13). Respondents were about evenly split in their views on whether labor immigration is good or bad. Fifty-one percent of people believed that immigration would be somewhat or very good for their country, whereas 47 percent believed that more people coming would be somewhat or very bad (figure 3.13a). Opinions were about evenly split between whether immigration or emigration was a cause for concern, though worries about low-skilled immigration and high-skilled emigration dominated. Of the respondents surveyed, 29 percent worried most about unskilled immigrants and 17 percent about skilled immigrants, whereas 36 percent worried most about skilled emigrants and 5 percent about unskilled emigrants (figure 3.13b).

FIGURE 3.13

Attitudes toward migration and emigration in ASEAN countries
(% of respondents)

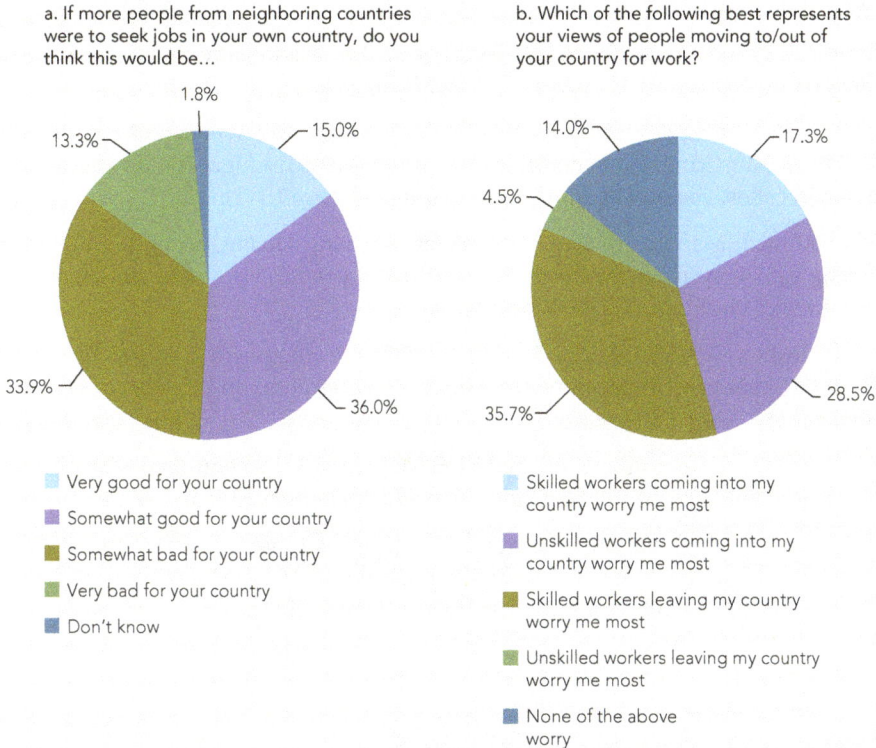

a. If more people from neighboring countries were to seek jobs in your own country, do you think this would be…

1.8%
13.3%
15.0%
33.9%
36.0%

b. Which of the following best represents your views of people moving to/out of your country for work?

14.0%
17.3%
4.5%
35.7%
28.5%

- Very good for your country
- Somewhat good for your country
- Somewhat bad for your country
- Very bad for your country
- Don't know

- Skilled workers coming into my country worry me most
- Unskilled workers coming into my country worry me most
- Skilled workers leaving my country worry me most
- Unskilled workers leaving my country worry me most
- None of the above worry

Source: Based on World Bank survey data.
Note: ASEAN = Association of Southeast Asian Nations.

Notes

1. See, for instance, Bank Negara Malaysia (2010).

2. Investigating the Malaysian manufacturing sector, Jajri and Ismail (2006) find that whether Malaysian and migrant workers are substitutes or complements depends on the manufacturing subsector's skill mix and product type.

3. Rigid labor markets can also have an impact on the ability of existing migrants to react to further immigration. D'Amuri, Ottaviano, and Peri (2010) find that immigration to Germany in the 1990s had a small or no effect on the employment and wages of locals but negative impacts on the employment and small negative impacts on the wages of existing immigrants. The relatively larger impacts on existing immigrants were found to be the result of wage rigidities such as generous unemployment benefits.

4. The electronic survey was posted in February 2016 on the World Bank Group country sites of Cambodia, Indonesia, Lao PDR, Malaysia, Myanmar, the Philippines, Singapore, Thailand, and Vietnam. There were 1,139 respondents from all countries.

References

Adams, R. H., and A. Cuecuecha. 2014. "Remittances, Household Investment and Poverty in Indonesia." In *Managing International Migration for Development in East Asia*, edited by R. Adams and A. Ahsan. Washington, DC: World Bank.

Adams, R. H., and J. Page. 2005. "Do International Migration and Remittances Reduce Poverty in Developing Countries?" *World Development* 33 (10): 1645–69.

Adelman, Robert, Lesley Williams Reid, Gail Markle, Saski Weiss, and Charles Jaret. 2017. "Urban Crime Rates and the Changing Face of Immigration: Evidence across Four Decades." *Journal of Ethnicity in Criminal Justice* 15 (1): 52–77.

Ahsan, Ahmad, Manolo Abella, Andrew Beath, Yukon Huang, Manjula Luthria, and Trang Van Nguyen. 2014. *International Migration and Development in East Asia and the Pacific*. Washington, DC: World Bank.

Angrist, Joshua D., and Adriana D. Kugler. 2003. "Protective or Counter-Productive? Labour Market Institutions and the Effect of Immigration on EU Natives." *Economic Journal* 113 (488): F302–F331.

Anzoategui, D., A. Demirgüç-Kunt, and M. S. M. Pería. 2014. "Remittances and Financial Inclusion: Evidence from El Salvador." *World Development* 54: 338–49.

ADBI (Asia Development Bank Institute), ILO (International Labor Organization), and OECD (Organisation for Economic Co-operation and Development). 2014. *Labor Migration, Skills & Student Mobility in Asia*. Tokyo: ADBI.

———. 2016. *Labor Migration in Asia: Building Effective Institutions*. Tokyo: ADBI; Bangkok: ILO; and Paris: OECD.

Athukorala, Prema-Chandra, and Evelyn S. Devadason. 2012. "The Impact of Foreign Labor on Host Country Wages: The Experience of a Southern Host, Malaysia." *World Development* 40 (8): 1497–510.

Bachtiar, Nasri, Rahmi Fahmy, and Rahmah Ismail. 2015. "The Demand for Foreign Workers in the Manufacturing Sector in Malaysia." *Jurnal Ekonomi Malaysia* 49 (2): 135–47.

Bank Negara Malaysia. 2010. *Annual Report 2009*. Kuala Lumpur: Bank Negara Malaysia.

Barone, Guglielmo, and Sauro Mocetti. 2011. "With a Little Help from Abroad: The Effect of Low-Skilled Immigration on the Female Labour Supply." *Labour Economics* 18 (5): 664–75.

Batalova, Jeanne, Andriy Shymonyak, and Guntur Sugiyarto. 2017. *Firing Up Regional Brain Networks: The Promise of Brain Circulation in the ASEAN Economic Community*. Manila: Asian Development Bank.

Beine, Michel, Frédéric Docquier, and Cecily Oden-Defoort. 2011. "A Panel Data Analysis of the Brain Gain." *World Development* 39 (4): 523–32.

Beine, Michel, Frédéric Docquier, and Hillel Rapoport. 2008. "Brain Drain and Human Capital Formation in Developing Countries: Winners and Losers." *Economic Journal* 118 (528): 631–52.

Bell, Brian. 2014. "Crime and Immigration: Do Poor Labor Market Opportunities Lead to Migrant Crime?" *IZA World of Labor* 33: 1–10.

Bell, Brian, Francesco Fasani, and Stephen Machin. 2013. "Crime and Immigration: Evidence from Large Immigrant Waves." *Review of Economics and Statistics* 95 (4): 1278–90.

Bhagwati, Jagdish, and Koichi Hamada. 1974. "The Brain Drain, International Integration of Markets for Professionals and Unemployment: A Theoretical Analysis." *Journal of Development Economics* 1 (1): 19–42.

Bhagwati, Jagdish, and Carlos Rodriguez. 1975. "Welfare-Theoretical Analyses of the Brain Drain." *Journal of Development Economics* 2 (3): 195–221.

Bianchi, Milo, Paolo Buonanno, and Paolo Pinotti. 2012. "Do Immigrants Cause Crime?" *Journal of the European Economic Association* 10 (6): 1318–47.

Bodvarsson, Örn B., and Hendrik Van den Berg. 2009a. "Immigration in the Source Country," in *The Economics of Immigration*, edited by Örn B. Bodvarsson and Hendrik Van den Berg, 183–219. New York: Springer.

Borjas, George. 2008. "Labor Outflows and Labor Inflows in Puerto Rico." *Journal of Human Capital* 2 (1): 32–68.

Boubtane, Ekrame, Jean-Christophe Dumont, and Christophe Rault. 2016. "Immigration and Economic Growth in the OECD Countries, 1986–2006." *Oxford Economic Papers* 68 (2): 340–60.

Bouton, Lawrence, Saumik Paul, and Erwin R. Tiongson. 2011. "The Impact of Emigration on Source Country Wages: Evidence from the Republic of Moldova." Policy Research Working Paper 5764, World Bank, Washington, DC.

Brunow, Stephan, Peter Nijkamp, and Jacques Poot. 2015. "The Impact of International Migration on Economic Growth in the Global Economy." In *Handbook of the Economics of International Migration*, vol. 1B, edited by Barry R. Chiswick and Paul W. Miller, 1027–75. Elsevier (North Holland).

Cabegin, E. C. A. 2013. "Gendered Labor Supply Response to Filipino Spouses' Overseas Migration and Remittances." *Asian and Pacific Migration Journal* 22 (2): 147–75.

Cabegin, E., and M. Alba. 2014. "More or Less Consumption? The Effect of Remittances on Filipino Household Spending Behavior." In *Managing International Migration for Development in East Asia*, edited by R. Adams and A. Ahsan. Washington, DC: World Bank.

Chami, R., D. S. Hakura, and P. J. Montiel. 2012. "Do Worker Remittances Reduce Output Volatility in Developing Countries?" *Journal of Globalization and Development* 3 (1): 1–23.

Chan, Annie Hau-nung. 2006. "The Effects of Full-Time Domestic Workers on Married Women's Economic Activity Status in Hong Kong, 1981–2001." *International Sociology* 21 (1): 133–59.

Cortes, Patricia. 2008. "The Effect of Low-Skilled Immigration on US Prices: Evidence from CPI Data." *Journal of Political Economy* 116 (3): 381–422.

Cortes, Patricia, and Jessica Pan. 2013. "Outsourcing Household Production: Foreign Domestic Helpers and Native Labor Supply in Hong Kong." *Journal of Labor Economics* 31 (2): 327–71.

Cortes, Patricia, and Jose Tessada. 2011. "Low-Skilled Immigration and the Labor Supply of Highly Skilled Women." *American Economic Journal: Applied Economics* 3 (3): 88–123.

Cuong, N. V., and D. Mont. 2012. "Economic Impacts of International Migration and Remittances on Household Welfare in Vietnam." *International Journal of Development Issues* 11 (2): 144–63.

D'Amuri, Francesco, and Giovanni Peri. 2011. "Immigration, Jobs and Employment Protection: Evidence from Europe." *Journal of the European Economic Association* 12 (2): 432–64.

———. 2014. "Immigration, Jobs and Employment Protection: Evidence from Europe Before and During the Great Recession." *Journal of the European Economic Association* 12 (2): 432–64.

D'Amuri, Francesco, Gianmarco I. P. Ottaviano, and Giovanni Peri. 2010. "The Labor Market Impact of Immigration in Western Germany in the 1990s." *European Economic Review* 54 (4): 550–70.

Dadush, Uri. 2014. "The Effect of Low-Skilled Labor Migration on the Host Economy." Working Paper 1, Global Knowledge Partnership on Migration and Development (KNOMAD), Washington, DC.

Del Carpio, Ximena, Çağlar Özden, Mauro Testaverde, and Mathis Wagner. 2015. "Local Labor Supply Responses to Immigration." *Scandinavian Journal of Economics* 117 (2): 493–521.

Docquier, Frédéric, and Hillel Rapoport. 2012. "Globalization, Brain Drain, and Development." *Journal of Economic Literature* 50 (3): 681–730.

Docquier, Frédéric, Çağlar Özden, and Giovanni Peri. 2014. "The Labour Market Effects of Immigration and Emigration in OECD Countries." *Economic Journal* 124 (579): 1106–145.

Docquier, Frédéric, Elisabetta Lodigiani, Hillel Rapoport, and Maurice Schiff. 2016. "Emigration and Democracy." *Journal of Development Economics* 120: 209–223.

Ducanes, G. 2015. "The Welfare Impact of Overseas Migration on Philippine Households: Analysis Using Panel Data." *Asian and Pacific Migration Journal* 24 (1): 79–106.

Dustmann, Christian, and Ian Preston. 2006. "Is Immigration Good or Bad for the Economy? Analysis of Attitudinal Responses." Discussion Paper CDO 06/04, Centre for Research and Analysis of Migration, London.

———. 2007. "Racial and Economic Factors in Attitudes to Immigration." *B.E. Journal of Economic Analysis & Policy* 7 (1): 1–39.

Dustmann, Christian, Tommaso Frattini, and Anna Rosso. 2015. "The Effect of Emigration from Poland on Polish Wages." *Scandinavian Journal of Economics* 117 (2): 522–64.

Facchini, Giovanni, Yotam Margalit, and Hiroyuki Nakata. 2016. "Countering Public Opposition to Immigration: The Impact of Information Campaigns." Discussion Paper 10420, Institute of Labor Economics, Bonn.

Facchini, Giovanni, and Anna Maria Mayda. 2009. "Does the Welfare State Affect Individual Attitudes Toward Immigrants? Evidence across Countries." *Review of Economics and Statistics* 91 (2): 295–314.

———. 2012. "Individual Attitudes Towards Skilled Migration: An Empirical Analysis Across Countries." *The World Economy* 35 (2): 183–96.

Felbermayr, Gabriel J., and Benjamin Jung. 2009. "The Pro-Trade Effect of the Brain Drain: Sorting Out Confounding Factors." *Economics Letters* 104 (2): 72–75.

Felbermayr, Gabriel J., and Wilhelm Kohler. 2009. "Can International Migration Ever Be Made a Pareto Improvement?" In *The Integration of European Labour Markets*, edited by Ewald Nowotny, Peter Mooslechner, and Doris Ritzberger-Grünwald, 32–50.

Frattini, Tommaso. 2014. "Impact of Migration on UK Consumer Prices." Report for the Migration Advisory Committee, Home Office of the United Kingdom, London.

Furtado, Delia, and Heinrich Hock. 2010. "Low Skilled Immigration and Work-Fertility Tradeoffs Among High Skilled US Natives." *American Economic Review: Papers & Proceedings* 100 (May): 224–28.

Gagnon, Jason. 2011. "Stay with US? The Impact of Emigration on Wages in Honduras." Development Centre Working Paper 300, Organisation for Economic Co-operation and Development, Paris.

Gibson, John, and David McKenzie. 2011. "Eight Questions about Brain Drain." Policy Research Working Paper 5668, World Bank, Washington, DC.

———. 2012. "The Economic Consequences of 'Brain Drain' of the Best and Brightest: Microeconomic Evidence from Five Countries." *Economic Journal* 122 (560): 339–75.

Hainmueller, Jens, and Michael J. Hiscox. 2007. "Educated Preferences: Explaining Attitudes Towards Immigration in Europe." *International Organization* 61 (2): 399–442.

———. 2010. "Attitudes toward Highly Skilled and Low-Skilled Immigration: Evidence from a Survey Experiment." *American Political Science Review* 104 (1): 61–84.

Hainmueller, Jens, and Daniel J. Hopkins. 2014. "Public Attitudes Toward Immigration." *Annual Review of Political Science* 17: 225–49.

Hanson, Gordon. 2007. "Emigration, Labor Supply and Earnings in Mexico." In *Mexican Immigration to the United States*, edited by George Borjas, 289–328. Chicago: University of Chicago Press.

Hanson, Gordon H., Kenneth Scheve, and Matthew J. Slaughter. 2007. "Public Finance and Individual Preferences over Globalization Strategies." *Economics & Politics* 19 (1): 1–33.

Huber, Peter, Michael Landesmann, Catherine Robinson, and Robert Stehrer. 2010. "Migrants' Skills and Productivity: A European Perspective." *National Institute Economic Review* 213 (1): R20–R34.

Ismail, Rahmah, and Ferayuliani Yuliyusman. 2014. "Foreign Labour on Malaysian Growth." *Journal of Economic Integration* 29 (4): 657–75.

Jajri, Idris, and Rahmah Ismail. 2006. "Elasticity of Substitutions between Foreign and Local Workers in the Malaysian Manufacturing Sector." *Pertanika Journal of Social Sciences & Humanities* 14(1): 63–76.

Kangasniemi, Mari, Matilde Mas, Catherine Robinson, and Lorenzo Serrano. 2012. "The Economic Impact of Migration: Productivity Analysis for Spain and the UK." *Journal of Productivity Analysis* 38 (3): 333–43.

Kerr, William R. 2008. "Ethnic Scientific Communities and International Technology Diffusion." *Review of Economics and Statistics* 90 (3): 518–37.

Lartey, E. K., F. S. Mandelman, and P. A. Acosta. 2012. "Remittances, Exchange Rate Regimes and the Dutch Disease: A Panel Data Analysis." *Review of International Economics* 20 (2): 377–95.

Lathapipat, Dilaka. 2014. "The Effects of Immigration on the Thai Wage Structure." In *Managing International Migration for Development in East Asia*, edited by Richard H. Adams and Ahmad Ahsan, 111–35. Washington, DC: World Bank.

Longhi, S., P. Nijkamp, and J. Poot. 2010. "Joint Impacts of Immigration on Wages and Employment: A Review and Meta-Analysis." *Journal of Geographical Systems* 12 (4): 355–87.

Mariya, Aleksynska, and Ahmed Tritah. 2009. "Immigration, Income and Productivity of Host Countries: A Channel Accounting Approach." Working Paper 2009–23, Centre d'Etudes Prospectives et d'Informations Internationales (CEPII), Paris.

Mayda, Ana Maria. 2006. "Who Is Against Immigration? A Cross-Country Investigation of Individual Attitudes Towards Immigrants." *Review of Economics and Statistics* 88 (3): 510–30.

McCormick, B., and J. Wahba. 2001. "Overseas Work Experience, Savings and Entrepreneurship amongst Return Migrants to LDCs." *Scottish Journal of Political Economy* 48 (2): 164–78.

Mishra, Prachi. 2007. "Emigration and Wages in Source Countries: Evidence from Mexico." *Journal of Development Economics* 82 (1): 180–99.

———. 2014. "Emigration and Wages in Source Countries: A Survey of Empirical Literature." In *International Handbook on Migration and Economic Development*, edited by Robert E. B. Lucas, 241–66. Cheltenham UK: Edward Elgar.

Miyagiwa, Kaz. 1991. "Scale Economies in Education and the Brain Drain Problem." *International Economic Review* 32 (3): 743–59.

Narayanan, Suresh, and Lai Yew-Wah. 2014. "Migration and Development in Malaysia: The Impact of Immigrant Labour on the Manufacturing Sector, 1986–2010."

Paper presented at the National Population Conference on the Inter-Relationship between Population Dynamics and Development at Universiti Sains Malaysia, Penang, Malaysia, June 26.

Nathan, Max. 2014. "The Wider Economic Impacts of High Skilled Migrants: A Survey of the Literature for Receiving Countries." *IZA Journal of Migration* 3.

Noor, Zaleha Mohd, Noraina Isa, Rusmawati Said, and Suhaila Abd Jalil. 2011. "The Impact of Foreign Workers on Labour Productivity in Malaysian Manufacturing Sector." *International Journal of Economic and Management* 5 (1):169–178.

Nguyen, T., and R. Purnamasari. 2014. "Impacts of International Migration and Remittances on Child Outcomes and Labor Supply in Indonesia: How Does Gender Matter?" In *Managing International Migration for Development in East Asia*, edited by R. Adams and A. Ahsan. Washington, DC: World Bank.

Orefice, Gianluca. 2010. "Skilled Migration and Economic Performance from OECD Countries." *Swiss Society of Economics and Statistics* 146 (4): 781–820.

OECD (Organisation of Economic Co-operation and Development). 2013. *International Migration Outlook* 2013. Paris: OECD.

O'Rourke, Kevin H., and Richard Sinnot. 2006. "The Determinants of Individual Attitudes towards Immigration." *European Journal of Political Economy* 22 (4): 838–61.

Ortega, Francesc, and Giovanni Peri. 2009. "The Causes and Effects of International Migrations: Evidence from OECD Countries 1980–2005." Working Paper 14833, National Bureau of Economic Research, Cambridge, MA.

———. 2014. "Openness and Income: The Roles of Trade and Migration." *Journal of International Economics* 92 (2): 231–51.

Østbye, Truls, Rahul Malhotra, Chetna Malhotra, Chandima Arambepola, and Angelique Chan. 2013. "Does Support from Foreign Domestic Workers Decrease the Negative Impact of Informal Caregiving? Results from Singapore Survey on Informal Caregiving." *Journals of Gerontology, Series B: Psychological Sciences and Social Sciences* 68 (4): 609–21.

Özden, Çağlar, and David Phillips. 2015. "What Really Is Brain Drain? Location of Birth, Education, and Migration Dynamics of African Doctors." Working Paper 4, KNOMAD, Washington, DC.

Özden, Çağlar, and Mauro Testaverde. 2015. "International Migration in Aging Societies: Impacts and Benefits in East Asia and Pacific Countries." Background paper for *Live Long and Prosper: Aging in East Asia and Pacific*, World Bank, Washington, DC.

Özden, Çağlar, and Mathis Wagner. 2016. "Immigrant versus Natives? Displacement and Job Creation." World Bank, Washington, DC.

Özden, Çağlar, Mauro Testaverde, and Mathis Wagner. 2017. "How and Why Does Immigration Affect Crime? Evidence from Malaysia," *World Bank Economic Review*. lhx010, https://doi.org/10.1093/wber/lhx010.

Paserman, M. Daniele. 2008. "Do High-Skill Immigrants Raise Productivity? Evidence from Israeli Manufacturing Firms, 1990–1999." IZA Discussion Paper 3572, Institute for the Study of Labor, Bonn.

Peri, Giovanni. 2012. "The Effect of Immigration on Productivity: Evidence from U.S. States." *Review of Economics and Statistics* 94 (1): 348–58.

Peri, Giovanni, and Chad Sparber. 2011. "Highly Educated Immigrants and Native Occupation Choice." *Industrial Relations: A Journal of Economic and Society* 50 (3): 385–411.

———. 2012. "Task Specialization, Immigration, and Wages." *American Economic Journal: Applied Economics* 1 (3): 135–69.

Pholphirul, Piriya, Jongkon Kamlai, and Pungpond Rukumnuaykit. 2010. "Do Immigrants Improve Thailand's Competitiveness?" World Bank, Washington, DC.

Pholphirul, Piriya, and Pungpong Rukumnuaykit. 2013. "Does Immigration Promote Innovation in Developing Countries? Evidence from Thai Manufacturers." Working Paper 14–009, Asian Institute of Management, Manila.

Rasiah, Rajah. 2014. "Economic Implications of ASEAN Integration for Malaysia's Labour Market." Asia-Pacific Working Paper Series, International Labor Organization, Bangkok.

Ratha, Dilip, Sanket Mohapatra, and Elina Scheja. 2011. "Impact of Migration on Economic and Social Development: A Review of Evidence and Emerging Issues." Policy Research Working Paper 5558, World Bank, Washington, DC.

Rodriguez, E. R. 1998. "International Migration and Income Distribution in the Philippines." *Economic Development and Cultural Change* 46 (2): 329–50.

Rodriguez, E. R., and E. R. Tiongson, 2001. "Temporary Migration Overseas and Household Labor Supply: Evidence from Urban Philippines." *International Migration Review* 35 (3): 709–25.

Rosenzweig, M. R. 2008. "Higher Education and International Migration in Asia: Brain Circulation." In *Annual World Bank Conference on Development Economics: Regional 2008*, edited by Justin Yifu Lin and Boris Pleskovic, 58–85. Washington, DC: World Bank.

Sanglaoid, Utis, Sumalee Santipolvut, and Laemthai Phuwanich. 2014. "The Impacts of ASEAN Labour Migration to Thailand upon the Thai Economy." *International Journal of Economics and Finance* 6 (8): 118–28.

Scheve, Kenneth F., and Matthew J. Slaughter. 2001. "Labor Market Competition and Individual Preferences over Immigration Policy." *Review of Economics and Statistics* 83 (1): 133–45.

Spenkuch, Jörg L. 2013. "Understanding the Impact of Immigration on Crime." *American Law and Economic Review* 16 (1): 177–219.

Spilimbergo, Antonio. 2009. "Democracy and Foreign Education." *American Economic Review* 99 (1): 528–43.

Stark, Oded, Christian Helmenstein, and Alexia Prskawetz. 1998. "Human Capital Depletion, Human Capital Formation, and Migration: A Blessing or a 'Curse'?" *Economics Letters* 60 (3): 363–67.

Suen, Wing. 1994. "Market-Procured Housework: The Demand for Domestic Servants and Female Labor Supply." *Labour Economics* 1 (3–4): 289–302.

Tan, Peck-Leong, and John Gibson. 2013. "Impact of Foreign Maids on Female Labor Force Participation in Malaysia." *Journal of the East Asian Economic Association* 27 (2): 163–83.

Thangavelu, Shandre Mugan. 2012. "Economic Growth and Foreign Workers in ASEAN and Singapore." *Asian Economic Papers* 11 (3): 114–36.

———. 2016. "Productive Contribution of Local and Foreign Workers in Singapore Manufacturing Industries." *Journal of Economic Studies* 43 (3): 380–99.

Tong, Sarah Y. 2005. "Ethnic Networks in FDI and the Impact of Institutional Development." *Review of Development Economics* 9 (4): 563–80.

Tunon, Max, and Nilim Baruah. 2012. "Public Attitudes towards Migrant Workers in Asia." *Migration and Development* 1 (1): 149–62.

UN (United Nations). 2013. *International Migration Policies: Government Views and Priorities*. New York: United Nations.

UNDP (UN Development Programme). 2009. *Human Development Report 2009: Overcoming barriers: Human mobility and development*. New York: UNDP.

Viet, Cuong Nguyen 2008. "Do Foreign Remittances Matter to Poverty and Inequality? Evidence from Vietnam." *Economics Bulletin* 15 (1): 1–11.

Wahba, Jackline and Yves Zenou. 2012. "Out of Sight, Out of Mind: Migration, Entrepreneurship and Social Capital." *Regional Science and Urban Economics* 42 (5): 890–903.

———. 2015a. "Selection, Selection, Selection: The Impact of Return Migration." *Journal of Population Economics* 28 (3): 535–63.

———. 2015b. "Who Benefits from Return Migration to Developing Countries?" *IZA World of Labor* 123: 1–10.

Wong, Kar-yiu, and Chong Kee Yip. 1999. "Education, Economic Growth, and Brain Drain." *Journal of Economic Dynamics and Control* 23 (5–6): 699–726.

World Bank. 2015. *Malaysia Economic Monitor: Immigrant Labour*. Washington, DC: World Bank.

———. 2016. *Live Long and Prosper: Aging in East Asia and Pacific*. Washington D.C.: World Bank.

Yang, D. 2008. "International Migration, Remittances and Household Investment: Evidence from Philippine Migrants' Exchange Rate Shocks." *Economic Journal* 118 (528): 591–630.

Yang, D., and H. Choi. 2007. "Are Remittances Insurance? Evidence from Rainfall Shocks in the Philippines." *World Bank Economic Review* 21(2): 219–48.

Yang, D., and A. Martínez. 2006. "Remittances and Poverty in Migrants' Home Areas: Evidence from the Philippines." In *International Migration, Remittances, and the Brain Drain*, edited by Ç. Özden and M. Schiff. Washington, DC: World Bank.

Yean, Tham Siew, and Liew Chei Siang. 2014. "The Impact of Foreign Labor on Productivity and Wages in Malaysian Manufacturing, 2000–2006." In *Managing International Migration for Development in East Asia*, edited by Richard H. Adams Jr. and Ahmad Ahsan. Washington, DC: World Bank.

Zachariadis, Marios. 2012. "Immigration and International Prices." *Journal of International Economics* 87(2): 298–311.

Zaiceva, Anzelika, and Klaus F. Zimmermann. 2014. "Migration and the Demographic Shift." Discussion Paper 8743, Institute for the Study of Labor, Bonn.

CHAPTER 4

Trade Integration and Labor Mobility in the ASEAN Economic Community

Introduction

The trade integration measures adopted as part of the ASEAN Economic Community (AEC) will not substitute for the flows of workers among ASEAN countries. ASEAN member states created the AEC to deepen economic integration and trade within ASEAN through the creation of a single market. The AEC, formally established in late 2015, is working to establish a single market by removing tariffs and liberalizing nontariff barriers to trade.[1] A natural assumption might be that these measures to enhance trade integration would lead to less migration among ASEAN countries because freer cross-border trade reduces the need for people to migrate across borders. Indeed, economic theory has traditionally taken this view. As the first part of this chapter shows, however, the experience of two other regional trade blocs—the European Union (EU) and the North American Free Trade Agreement (NAFTA), which both include free mobility provisions—contradict these expectations. Both regions experienced temporary increases in international migration following integration. Consistent with other structural factors driving migration, increased integration under the AEC is then not likely to lead to a decline in migration, though it will likely not lead to persistently larger flows either.

Online appendixes are available in the World Bank's Open Knowledge Repository at www.openknowledge.worldbank.org

NAFTA and the EU also represent different models of how to address regional mobility in the context of trade integration. The AEC envisions skilled workers moving freely among ASEAN countries. However, its efforts to facilitate this movement have thus far been limited, and its focus on high-skilled workers alone ignores the vast majority of intra-ASEAN migrants. Like the AEC, NAFTA has special mobility provisions only for high-skilled workers, though its approach is more expansive. The EU, in contrast, has implemented policies with the explicit objective of overcoming obstacles to migration between member countries. For ASEAN countries, the EU is a more ambitious model of how to foster the free flow of labor, while NAFTA is a model of a more cautious, limited approach that, nonetheless, goes beyond what is currently envisioned for the AEC.

The second part of this chapter investigates how welfare is affected by trade integration under different assumptions about how the AEC's policies on labor mobility evolve. Building on economic theory, experience from other regional free trade blocs, and formal economic modeling, simulations are used to investigate how ASEAN will best be able to maximize the gains from the interplay between enhanced trade liberalization and freer migration. The simulations make it possible to investigate how the labor market effects of enhanced trade integration across the ASEAN region differ under two distinct scenarios: (1) the AEC's measures to reduce labor mobility costs for skilled services workers are fully implemented and reduce labor mobility costs for these workers; and (2) the AEC expands its mobility facilitation measures so that labor mobility costs are reduced for all workers regardless of skill and sector of employment.

The simulations are innovative because, unlike previous models of trade integration, they consider how the costs for workers to move within and across countries affect the gains from this integration. For the ASEAN region as a whole, the effects of enhanced trade integration on wages differ across simulations and are negative in some cases. In contrast, the simulation results point to unambiguously more positive effects on employment and worker welfare when trade liberalization includes a reduction in labor mobility costs. For welfare in particular, the simulations show a positive impact of efforts to lower international labor mobility costs for skilled workers. Welfare gains will be even larger and more broad-based, however, if measures are taken to reduce labor mobility costs for all workers, not just skilled services workers. These results imply that the AEC can maximize the gains from trade by combining trade liberalization with comprehensive reductions in labor mobility costs for all workers.

Migration and regional integration

Economic theory

The theoretical literature analyzing the relationship between international trade and labor migration has typically treated trade and migration as substitutes. In other words, models assumed that freer trade would reduce economic incentives to migrate and that freer mobility would reduce economic incentives to trade. The most influential early academic paper is by Mundell (1957) and is based on the canonical Heckscher-Ohlin model (Heckscher 1919; Ohlin 1933). The central assumption of Mundell's theory is that the relative abundance of factors of production differs across countries, as in the Heckscher-Ohlin model. This assumption explains why international trade might be worthwhile: countries with a relative abundance of labor can gain from exporting goods that require a relatively high proportion of labor input in exchange for importing relatively capital-intensive goods. Importantly, under this and five other assumptions made by Mundell,[2] free trade leads to an equalization of wages between countries, even if labor cannot move freely between them. Thus, under the premise that international migration is solely motivated by economic considerations and, in particular, by the exploitation of wage gaps between countries, liberalizing international trade exhausts any incentive for labor migration. Conversely, Mundell's theoretical model implies that, if international mobility of capital and labor between countries is possible, then the resulting capital and migration flows will lead to an equalization of the relative abundances of production factors across countries. This, in turn, implies that trade is no longer worthwhile.

However, more recent theoretical literature has shown that trade and migration can in fact be complements. In the 1980s, Markusen (1983) and other economists began to challenge the prevailing view that trade and migration were necessarily substitutes. In his paper, Markusen presents five simple models that, in contrast to the Heckscher-Ohlin model, all assume an identical relative abundance of factors of production across countries. At the same time, Markusen successively relaxes each of the other five basic assumptions underlying Mundell's theory. Markusen shows that two important results hold in each of his five models. First, gains from trade and migration arise even with an identical relative abundance of factors of production across countries. Second, trade and migration are not substitutes but, in fact, complements. In other words, Markusen's models imply that the gains from trade can be maximized if the liberalization of trade and migration go hand in hand.[3]

Much of the policy debate about migration and trade, at least implicitly, rests on Mundell's substitution result: trade liberalization is frequently expected to reduce migration flows (Schiff 2006). Indeed, this was the expectation before the establishment of two important regional free trade blocs, the EU and NAFTA, which many policy makers and pundits believed would lead to a reduction in migration flows. Evidence that such a reduction did not occur is presented next. Moreover, the new strand of theory allows for data-driven investigations of the relationship between trade and migration and of how gains from trade depend on the mobility of labor. The simulations in the second section of this chapter undertake such an investigation.

Mobility in the AEC

As chapter 8 will discuss in detail, ASEAN member states have taken steps to reduce the barriers to labor mobility as part of their efforts to promote deeper regional integration (figure 4.1). The 1995 ASEAN Framework Agreement on Services provided for the

FIGURE 4.1

ASEAN actions to facilitate labor mobility, 1995–2015

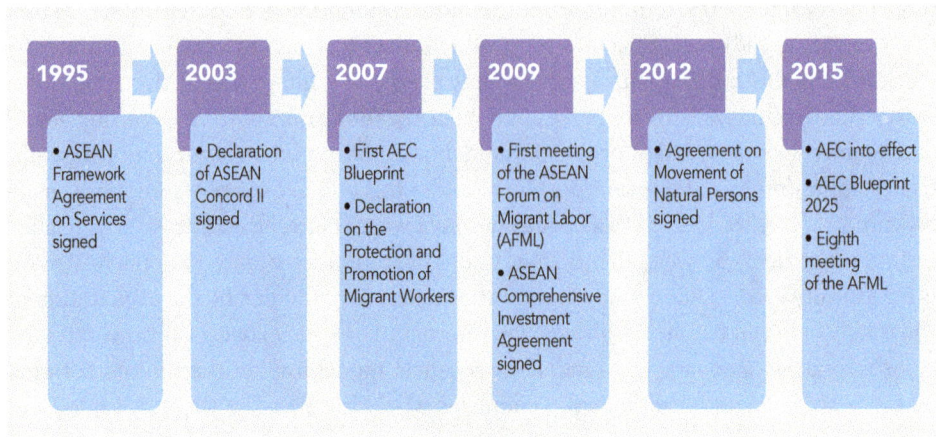

1995	2003	2007	2009	2012	2015
• ASEAN Framework Agreement on Services signed	• Declaration of ASEAN Concord II signed	• First AEC Blueprint • Declaration on the Protection and Promotion of Migrant Workers	• First meeting of the ASEAN Forum on Migrant Labor (AFML) • ASEAN Comprehensive Investment Agreement signed	• Agreement on Movement of Natural Persons signed	• AEC into effect • AEC Blueprint 2025 • Eighth meeting of the AFML

Note: ASEAN = Association of Southeast Asian Nations; AEC = ASEAN Economic Community.

temporary movement of skilled professionals across borders. Mobility-related commitments were later collected in the ASEAN Agreement on Movement of Natural Persons. One of the five pillars of the AEC, which envisions a single regional market, is the free movement of skilled workers alongside the free movement of goods, services, and investment and the freer flow of capital. In laying out the vision for the AEC in the Declaration of ASEAN Concord II in 2003, ASEAN member states pledged to "facilitate movement of business persons, skilled labor, and talents" in order to promote economic integration. The 2007 AEC Blueprint laid out specific actions to accomplish this, including facilitating the issuance of visas and employment passes and working to harmonize and standardize qualifications. The AEC Blueprint 2025 envisions reducing and standardizing documentation requirements and improving the mutual recognition of professional qualifications.

However, progress on implementing regional commitments related to labor mobility has been limited. Mutual recognition arrangements, in which multiple countries agree to recognize professional qualifications and facilitate the mobility of professionals in those fields, are the major steps the AEC has taken in this direction; but these arrangements are limited in scope. They currently cover only doctors, dentists, nurses, engineers, architects, accountants, and tourism professionals, who account for about 5 percent of employment in ASEAN countries (Batalova, Shymonyak, and Sugiyarto 2017). Relatively onerous qualification and verification processes remain in place even for the covered professions. Finally, and perhaps most important, each state's migration procedures remain paramount, meaning that the decision regarding how many and what type of work visas to grant and whether to accept or reject an application for a visa continues to rest with individual ASEAN member countries. For instance, Thailand bans migrants from working in 39 occupations, including engineering, accounting, and architecture, which are covered by mutual recognition arrangements.

Moreover, the AEC's focus on high-skilled migration ignores the majority of ASEAN migrants, who are low-skilled and often undocumented. The AEC does not have plans to facilitate the migration of low- or mid-skilled migrants, although some regional dialogue has taken place. In the 2007 Declaration on the Protection and Promotion of the Rights of Migrant Workers (Cebu Declaration on Migrant Workers), ASEAN member states agreed to promote the dignity of migrant workers, including those who are not documented, and to set forth the obligations of receiving and sending countries and of ASEAN itself. The ASEAN Forum on Migrant Labor was created to promote implementation and has representatives from member states, employers, workers, and civil society (Asia-Pacific RCM Thematic Working Group 2015). However, the Cebu Declaration is nonbinding, and the instrument to protect migrant workers envisioned in it has not been adopted (Asia-Pacific RCM Thematic Working Group 2015; Martin and Abella 2014).

Mobility in NAFTA and the EU

NAFTA and the EU, the world's most important regional free trade blocs, are particularly useful models of regional integration to study in the context of the AEC because of their size and their contrasting approaches to labor mobility.[4] NAFTA and the EU were created under very different circumstances and with very different economic and policy objectives. However, both have faced the challenge of managing the movement of people to harness the growth opportunities created by regional integration. And each adapted policies for the management of international migration to its unique framework for regional governance and economic cooperation.

NAFTA and the EU have implemented policies that are similar in some regards, such as the recognition of migrants' professional qualifications and the facilitation of free trade. However, the two regional free trade blocs exemplify very different models of how to manage labor mobility and its interplay with trade liberalization, with each approach corresponding to the bloc's own economic and policy objectives. Although NAFTA has focused on trade integration and includes relatively narrow provisions for the free movement of skilled labor, the EU has implemented more ambitious free mobility policies with the explicit objective of overcoming obstacles to migration among its member countries. The different experiences of NAFTA and the EU are summarized on the next page in Table 4.1.

TABLE 4.1
Mobility in NAFTA and the EU

Policy	Impacts on migration	
	NAFTA	EU
Facilitating free movement for citizens of member states	*Minimal effects on migration:* Though the Treaty NAFTA (TN) visa was created in the United States, liberalizing entry requirements for Canadian and Mexican nationals, uptake has been limited, though it has grown in recent years	*Minimal effects on migration:* The addition of new EU member states has only been associated with a small and temporary increase in migration
Facilitating free movement for nationals from outside the trade bloc	n.a.	*Variable effects on migration:* The introduction of the Blue Card program has had mixed results. Although uptake has been high in some countries, overall the program has not been very popular
Recognizing professional qualifications	*Variable effects on migration:* The TN visa category has facilitated the mutual recognition of professional qualifications across NAFTA, but uptake has varied among professions. Many migrants may have been able to enter NAFTA countries even without a TN visa	*Minimal effects on migration:* Despite significant efforts to strengthen specific and general directives on qualifications recognition across EU member states, their use has generally been low

Note: n.a. = not applicable; EU = European Union; NAFTA = North American Free Trade Agreement; TN = Treaty NAFTA.

North American Free Trade Agreement

NAFTA established a regional free trade bloc across North America. Its three signatories are Canada, Mexico, and the United States. The agreement became effective in 1994, with the primary objective of reducing barriers to trade and investment among the three signatory countries. Facilitating the free movement of labor was much less of an explicit objective. No provision on the movement of low-skilled labor was included in the agreement.

NAFTA did establish a new migration category in the United States, the Treaty NAFTA (TN). This new category is available exclusively to workers from Mexico and Canada pursuing jobs in 70 highly skilled occupations, including accountants, architects, computer systems analysts, economists, engineers, and hotel managers. Applicants from Canada and Mexico with college degrees and job offers in the United States are eligible to apply. In contrast to the U.S. H1-B visa program, the TN program has no quota on the number of migrants who can be admitted (Martin 2015).[5] Employment is for three years, and the visa is renewable indefinitely. Migrants can bring their dependents through the NAFTA dependent, or TD, classification. The application process for Canadians is particularly easy, allowing migrants to apply on entry to the United States with only proof of a job offer and proof of education; the process does not impose any labor market test on employers to certify that U.S. workers are unavailable to fill positions. The application process is somewhat more involved for Mexicans because they must apply for a visa in Mexico (Martin and Abella 2014). Their employer must go through some of the same requirements required of applicants to the H1-B program, such as a labor market test. Overall though, the TN visa combines temporary entry, residency, and work permits in a single document, and offers much faster and less costly application and approval procedures than regular work visas for non-NAFTA nationals.

The number of TN visas issued has increased significantly and steadily since NAFTA's implementation. Between 2004 and 2009, several thousand TN visas were issued each year, with more than 13,000 issued in 2015 (figure 4.2). The lack of a quota and an easier application process has made the TN visa more attractive than the H1-B, which caps professionals in specialized occupations from all countries at 65,000.

Before 1994, many policy makers expected NAFTA to foster economic growth in all three signatory countries and to be an instrument for easing migration pressures, particularly between Mexico and the United States. NAFTA's impact was widely expected to be particularly strong in Mexico, the signatory with the lowest level of economic development and the United States' largest source of immigrants. Before NAFTA, Mexican migrant workers represented about 30 percent of immigrant workers in the

FIGURE 4.2

Total Treaty NAFTA and H1-B visas issued to Canadians and Mexicans by the United States, 1994–2015

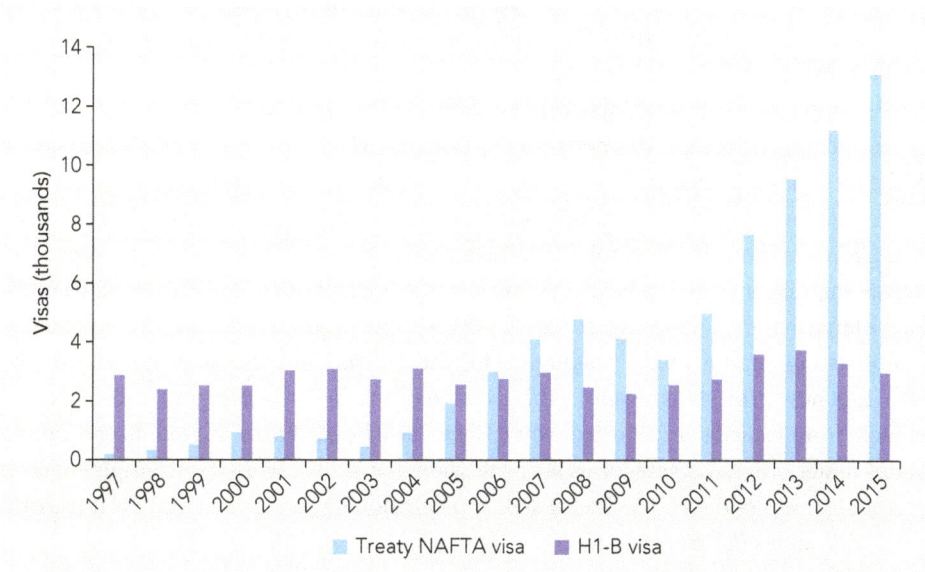

Source: Nonimmigrant Visa Statistics, United States Department of State (https://travel.state.gov/content/visas/en /law-and-policy/statistics/non-immigrant-visas.html).
Note: NAFTA = North American Free Trade Agreement.

United States, and the majority of them were unauthorized or irregular workers (Martin 1993). On the basis of the widespread view of trade and migration as substitutes, many policy makers hoped that NAFTA would lead to increased trade, which in turn would allow Mexico to achieve significant levels of economic growth and convergence with Canada and the United States. The job creation and wage increases resulting from the agreement were expected to reduce international worker flows, particularly those of low-skilled, irregular migrants. For instance, in 1993 the U.S. attorney general, Janet Reno, stated that "NAFTA is our best hope for reducing illegal immigration, in the long haul" (DOJ 1993).

Some economists and migration experts did not share the widespread view of trade and migration as substitutes.[6] Instead, on the basis of theoretical and empirical evidence, they considered trade and migration to be complementary and predicted that freer trade in North America would increase both low- and high-skilled migration in the region.

The available evidence suggests that migration flows increased after the implementation of NAFTA before easing in later years. No comprehensive review of NAFTA's impact on migration has been carried out. However, the available evidence suggests that those who predicted an increase in migration flows after NAFTA's inception were correct. Both the absolute number of migrants moving within NAFTA and the share of highly skilled migrants increased (Globerman 2000; Wasem 2005). But as predicted by Martin (1993), the surge in migration flows among NAFTA's three signatory states, particularly between Mexico and the United States, eventually subsided. Annual migration from Mexico to the United States generally increased between 1991 and 2000, before declining steadily, particularly after 2005 (figure 4.3). In fact, net migration between Mexico and the United States was minimal in the second half the 2000s and the first half of the 2010s (Gonzalez-Barrera 2015). Of course, secular trends and business cycles in Canada, Mexico, the United States, and even non-NAFTA countries are also important determinants of NAFTA's migration patterns. Nevertheless, NAFTA's experience suggests that Mundell's theory does not always provide a good description of the interplay between trade and migration: complementarities can exist.

Despite lowering the costs of migrating to the United States for high-skilled workers, NAFTA's provisions for the mobility of high-skilled labor likely had a muted impact on overall migration flows. At NAFTA's inception, workers with relatively low skills made up the large majority of the migrant stock of Mexicans in the United States. Consequently, most existing migrants were not eligible for the TN visa and thus were not affected by NAFTA's new provisions. Even in the absence of the TN visa category, most TN visa holders from Canada and Mexico would likely have been able to migrate to the United States under other visa categories for professional or skilled workers. Examples of such visa categories are the H-1B visa for skilled professionals and the L-1 visa for intracompany transferees (Globerman 2000).

NAFTA does not include specific provisions to facilitate the movement of low-skilled labor. Independently of NAFTA, Canada and the United States offer limited avenues for the legal temporary employment of foreign low-skilled workers. Canada has

FIGURE 4.3

Annual migration from Mexico to the United States, 1991–2010

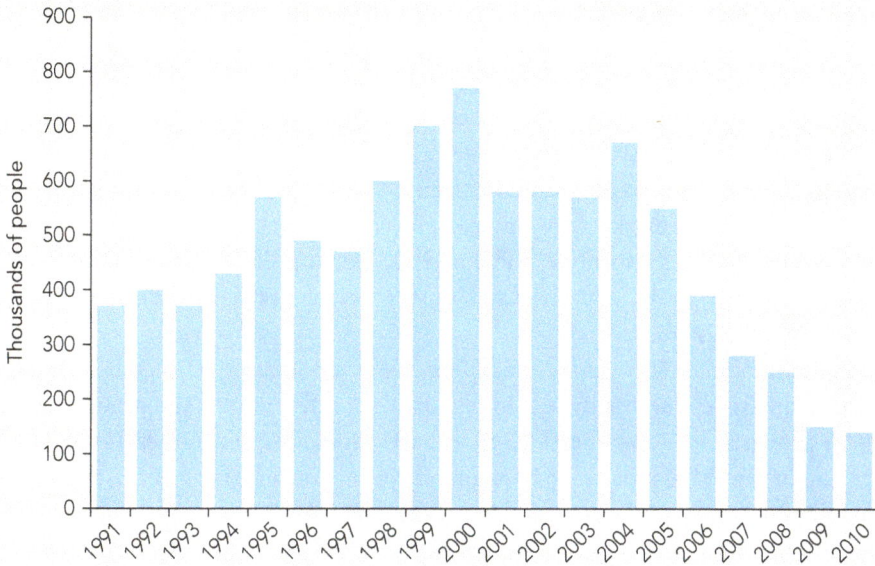

Source: Passel, Cohn, and Gonzalez-Barrera 2012.

a bilateral agreement with Mexico for the employment of seasonal agricultural workers. In the United States, foreign workers from a list of eligible countries, which is updated yearly but has up to now always included Mexico and Canada, can apply for temporary employment through H-2A visas for agricultural work and H-2B visas for nonagricultural jobs. Both types of visas allow employers to hire seasonal or temporary workers for up to three years. The quantity of H-2B visas that can be issued each year is limited, but there is no fixed quota for the annual number of H-2A visas. Until 2006, the H-2A visa category always had fewer applicants than the H-2B visa category. This occurred even though significant numbers of Mexican migrants worked in the United States irregularly in the agriculture sector. Having increased since 2006, applications for H-2A visas are now greater than those for H-2B visas. The United States' increased border controls along the Mexican border since 2006 are one possible reason for this trend (Lee et al. 2013).

European Union

The EU is a political and economic confederation of 28 member countries. The EU guarantees four fundamental freedoms: the free movement of goods, capital, workers, and services. The right to free movement of workers is codified in the 1997 Treaty Establishing the European Community, which was a predecessor to the EU, and is fully elaborated in the European Parliament's Directive 2004/38/EC. Citizens of any country in the EU and their relatives have the right to live in any other EU member country for up to three months; afterward, they must be working, enrolled in full-time education, or able to demonstrate financial independence. After five years of residence, these intra-EU migrants earn the right to permanent residence in their host country. Citizens of any EU member country are also generally permitted to work freely in the job and country of their choosing. At the same time, there are limits on the free movement of workers across the EU: (1) EU member countries may restrict access to civil service jobs to national citizens; (2) EU member countries may restrict access to their labor markets "in an emergency" with approval from the European Commission, the EU's executive body; and (3) existing EU member countries may impose temporary mobility restrictions on the citizens of newly admitted member countries (Brady 2008).

Despite the policies in place to facilitate migration among EU member countries and stark differences across the EU in employment rates, wages, and other economic variables, migration flows across Europe have generally been rather subdued. The accession to the EU of a relatively large number of countries from Central and Eastern Europe in 2004 and 2007 changed this pattern somewhat, but only temporarily. The stock of migrants in the "old" EU (originating from the eight countries admitted to the trade bloc in 2004) rose from 900,000 before enlargement to about 1.9 million in 2007. During the same period, the stock of migrants from Bulgaria and Romania, which joined in 2007, rose from about 700,000 to about 1.9 million (EIC 2009; Martin and Abella 2014). However, the initially large increases in migration flows slowed over time. Galgóczi, Leschke, and Watt (2009) show that overall intra-EU migration increased by just 0.2 percent after the accession of the eight other new countries in 2004 and Bulgaria and Romania in 2007. This pattern is broadly similar to what was observed in North America following the implementation of NAFTA and provides additional evidence that trade and migration are complements but that freer trade induces only modest increases in migration.

The EU takes a very different approach than NAFTA to managing the movement of people. In addition to guaranteeing the free movement of workers, the EU has implemented various policies to overcome obstacles to migration among member countries and to facilitate the movement of workers of any skill level. Bureaucratic and institutional procedures match the policies they are meant to operationalize. This includes the mutual recognition of common forms of documentation and the relative streamlining of entry processes. Additionally, there is portability across EU member countries of various social rights and entitlements, including access to health care, social welfare, and pensions, as well as any other locally available social protection programs such as childcare allowances. Moreover, intra-EU migrant workers are subject to the same taxation regimes as host country nationals. A common currency among many EU member countries and a shared job-search infrastructure also significantly reduce migration costs (Recchi 2008). Altogether, both the monetary and nonmonetary costs of migrating from one EU member country to another are comparatively low.

The EU's focus on the free mobility of workers of any skill level is a departure from the emphasis that most regional integration agreements put on the movement of highly skilled workers. However, the underlying premise of the EU as a political and economic confederation also goes beyond that of any other regional free trade blocs, including NAFTA and ASEAN. Nevertheless, the provisions for the free mobility of labor within the EU have at times been contested by member countries. There have been substantive debates on whether these policies have a positive or negative impact on national economies and labor markets, particularly in countries that have seen a net inflow of intra-EU migrants. Debates have been especially intense when new member countries with below-average income have joined the EU, first those in Southern Europe and later those in Central and Eastern Europe and the Balkans.

While the EU has concentrated on limiting the costs of moving across borders, migrants still face costs related to adjusting to local labor markets. Migrants from one EU member country to another tend to be concentrated initially in low-skilled, low-wage employment. Over time, however, migrants move on to jobs that demand higher skills and offer better pay. One implication of this finding is that many intra-EU migrants go through an adjustment process that allows them to gain the country-specific human capital, such as language skills or knowledge about local norms and customs, which is a prerequisite for accessing improved employment opportunities. Another implication is that there is a need to facilitate the adjustment process and to better match workers to suitable jobs. Otherwise, many skilled migrants are at least temporarily forced to take on jobs that do not make good use of their capabilities, resulting in "brain waste" (de la Rica, Glitz and Ortega 2013; Galgóczi, Leschke and Watt 2009; Recchi, 2008).

The EU has made some progress in facilitating migration with countries outside the regional bloc. As a customs union as well as a regional free trade bloc, the EU can enter into agreements with third countries. The EU has taken over most responsibilities regarding trade policies from its member countries, but is much less active in managing migration relations with non-EU countries. Most agreements with third countries continue to be reached, administered, and implemented by individual EU member states. However, progress has been made in streamlining this process. The European Commission has established a number of "mobility partnerships" with third countries such as Armenia, Azerbaijan, Georgia, and Moldova. Mobility partnerships are the EU's most complete framework for bilateral cooperation with its partners. The partnerships are based on mutual offers of commitment that cover mobility, migration, and asylum issues. In general, they are meant to better manage migration flows into the EU. In practice, the EU's partners agree to cooperate in managing flows of irregular migrants or in devising policies to promote the return of temporary labor migrants. In exchange, their citizens are granted preferential conditions for migration into the EU.

EU and NAFTA: Two models for ASEAN

The EU and NAFTA offer two models that are useful for ASEAN to consider when contemplating how to manage the relationship between trade integration and migration. The EU has established a comprehensive system to reduce the costs of, and barriers to, migration and is proactively managing migration relations with other countries. This makes this regional bloc well placed to benefit from complementarities between trade and international migration. The EU is a model worth studying for ASEAN if the association decides to go beyond the measures currently envisaged to foster the free flow of skilled labor across its member states. NAFTA focuses on facilitating high-skilled migration through an entry process that is more relaxed for Mexicans and very streamlined for Canadians, but does not include provisions to facilitate low- or mid-skilled workers. NAFTA provides a model of a more cautious, limited effort that nevertheless goes beyond what is currently implemented or planned in ASEAN.

Simulating trade integration with labor mobility costs

The previous section showed that the EU and NAFTA experienced moderate, temporary increases of international migration following deeper trade integration. This implies that deeper regional integration in ASEAN under the AEC is unlikely to result in a decline in migration, though a large increase in migration is similarly unlikely. The question then becomes how migration flows can be best managed to maximize the benefits from trade integration. This section uses simulations to investigate the impact on welfare gains from trade integration if commitments to facilitate the free movement of skilled services workers across ASEAN are implemented and effective, as currently envisioned under the AEC, and if they are expanded to include all workers.

Following Plummer, Petri and Zhai (2014), enhanced trade integration within ASEAN is modeled as the removal of remaining intraregional tariffs, the liberalization of nontariff barriers in goods and services, and the introduction of advanced trade facilitation measures. However, the model underpinning the simulations presented in this analysis is innovative in that, unlike standard trade models, it relaxes the assumption that workers change jobs without friction in response to changing incentives. The simulations of the effects of enhanced trade integration within ASEAN are performed under different assumptions about how the labor mobility costs presented in chapter 2 affect the free movement of workers. That is, mobility between countries, sectors, and skill levels is possible but costly. Box 4.1 describes how the labor mobility costs presented in chapter 2 are used in the simulations.[7]

The simulations begin with a baseline scenario that models trade integration in ASEAN assuming that the AEC's measures to reduce labor mobility costs for skilled services workers are not implemented or are not effective. Labor market outcomes before and after trade integration are compared. Scenario I models trade integration assuming that the AEC's measures are implemented and effectively reduce labor mobility costs for high-skilled services workers. Labor market outcomes are compared to the baseline scenario. Scenario II models trade integration assuming that the AEC expands

BOX 4.1
Labor mobility cost estimates in the simulations

The costs for workers to switch jobs across sectors and countries are needed to simulate the labor market impacts of trade integration under different scenarios of labor mobility in the AEC. However, data on migration into and out of different sectors and countries are not available. Thus, it is not possible to estimate the transition cost of entering sector i in country a from sector i or sector j in country b. Instead, the domestic and international labor mobility costs estimated in chapter 2 are combined to approximate the labor mobility costs of migrants entering different sectors across different ASEAN countries. International labor mobility costs are first estimated for all countries. Then, for the four countries for which domestic labor mobility costs are available, the relative differences in domestic labor mobility costs by sector are applied to the estimates of international labor mobility costs. For the remaining countries without estimates of domestic labor mobility costs, domestic labor mobility costs are assumed to be the same across sectors. The labor mobility costs for a migrant worker to enter a given ASEAN country are the same for migrants from all other ASEAN countries. However, *bilateral* wage differentials as well as *within-country* wage differentials across sectors shift after the simulated trade shock.

In the simulations, a model is calibrated to a pre-trade shock steady state that matches existing data parameters. A shock is then imposed on trade, and economies adjust to a post-trade shock steady state in which workers face costly mobility. The change in relative prices and real wages following the shock induces some workers to reallocate their labor across sectors. The magnitude of this reallocation depends on the size of the labor mobility costs. The resulting market-clearing employment and wage path solutions reflect workers' optimization of their utility, which in turn depends on expected wages and costs to change sectors. See Hollweg (2016) for additional methodological details.

Source: Hollweg 2016.

the scope of its labor mobility facilitation measures such that labor mobility costs are reduced for all workers. Labor market outcomes are compared to Scenario I.

The baseline scenario provides a point of reference for investigating how labor market outcomes are affected by less restrictive labor mobility policies in Scenario I and Scenario II. Results are purely driven by the price changes induced by enhanced trade integration and ensuing labor reallocations. Productivity and population growth or a pattern of structural change are not considered. The model assumes no adjustment costs to capital.[8] Adjustment paths to the new equilibrium following a trade-related shock are simulated. They include both the immediate changes in relative prices and real wages following immediately after the trade-related shock, as well as second-round effects. Second-round effects happen because the changes in relative prices and real wages brought about by the trade-related shock induce some workers to move across countries, sectors, and skill levels.

Enhanced trade integration is simulated for the ASEAN region as a whole and for individual countries within ASEAN. Simulation results are presented separately for skilled and unskilled jobs as well as for five different sectors.[9] These sectors are agriculture and mining; manufacturing; finance and business services (including insurance and real estate services); social services; and other services (utility supply, construction, trade and accommodation, and transportation and communication services). A residual "jobless" sector is also included that encompasses both being unemployed and being out of the labor force. To ensure comparability, skilled workers are defined as those who have completed vocational, university, or higher education. A distinction cannot be made between formal and informal flows of migrant labor.

The simulations shed light on the specific labor market channels through which gains from trade can be achieved under less restrictive labor market policies. The simulations investigate three labor market outcomes. First, employment rates within countries and the distribution of employment among countries are investigated. After the trade integration shock, some workers enter employment from the jobless sector (employment growth), while others switch sectors (change in the distribution of employment). Although the simulations do not allow explicit predictions of bilateral migration flows, comparison of the differences in the employment share of individual countries among overall employment in ASEAN provides an indication of net migration flows. Second, real wage levels are measured relative to the average ASEAN wage level. Finally, impacts on worker welfare are simulated.

Worker welfare is defined as a combination of three variables: wages, nonwage benefits associated with a sector, and the potential gains from moving to a different sector offering a higher wage.[10] Thus, welfare could be different in the baseline simulation and in Scenarios I and II for various reasons. For instance, wage levels might be different across jobs. This would have a direct effect on worker welfare even where workers did not change their job, because they have the potential to move to a job with a higher wage. Another possibility is that differences in labor mobility costs between the scenarios make it more or less costly for a worker to react to changes in relative wages between sectors by switching to a new job with high wages. This possibility of moving from one job to another with higher wages is a key factor contributing to worker welfare. The welfare measure provides a means of assessing the overall impact of trade integration under different scenarios of labor mobility costs. The model is simulated for a representative worker, though in reality, workers are heterogenous so some may benefit while others will may lose out.

Overall the simulations show that trade integration that is accompanied by measures to reduce mobility costs for workers increases gains from trade. Table 4.2 describes the simulations and summarizes the results. The direction of the results—whether employment, wages, and welfare increase or decrease—is more important than their exact magnitude because the shock to labor mobility costs is imposed exogenously. Of all of the scenarios, welfare gains are largest when measures to reduce labor mobility costs are extended to all workers. In this scenario (Scenario II), employment gains are also largest, though declines

TABLE 4.2
Summary of simulation results

	Baseline	Scenario I	Scenario II
Comparison	Compare labor market outcomes before and after trade integration	Compare labor market outcomes with baseline	Compare labor market outcomes with Scenario I
Policy scenario	Policies to reduce labor mobility costs for high-skilled services workers are not implemented/not effective	Policies to reduce labor mobility costs for high-skilled services workers are implemented and effective	Policies to reduce labor mobility costs are expanded to include all workers
Labor mobility costs	Labor mobility costs exist at levels comparable to the recent past	Labor mobility costs are 20% lower than the base year for skilled services workers	Labor mobility costs are 20% lower than the base year for all workers
Objective	To serve as the baseline for comparisons	To show how the labor market effects of enhanced trade integration would differ if integration occurred with a reduction of labor mobility costs for skilled services workers	To show how the labor market effects of enhanced trade integration would differ if integration occurred with a reduction of labor mobility costs for all workers
Interpretation	Show the impact of enhanced trade integration assuming that labor facilitation measures for skilled services workers are neither implemented nor effective, meaning that labor mobility costs are at levels comparable to the recent past	Show how outcomes of enhanced trade integration would be different if policies (such as mutual recognition arrangements) reduced mobility costs for skilled services workers	Show how outcomes of enhanced trade integration would be different if policies to reduce labor mobility costs were extended to all workers
Impact on employment in ASEAN	Employment is higher after the trade-related shock	Scenario I is associated with a higher employment rate than the baseline	Scenario II is associated with an even higher employment rate than Scenario I
Impact on wages in ASEAN	Real wages are higher after the trade-related shock	Scenario I is associated with lower real wages than the baseline	Scenario II is associated with lower real wages than Scenario I
Impact on welfare in ASEAN	Welfare in ASEAN is higher after the trade-related shock	Scenario I is associated with a more positive effect on welfare than the baseline	Scenario II is associated with a more positive effect on welfare than Scenario I

in wages are also seen. Compared to the baseline simulation with no reductions in labor mobility costs, welfare is improved when measures to reduce labor mobility costs for skilled services workers are fully implemented and effective. This scenario (Scenario I) also sees employment gains, though wage declines are also observed. The online appendix summarizes the main channels of transmission behind the results presented in the chapter.

Baseline scenario

The wage, employment, and welfare effects of the trade-related shock of enhanced trade integration within ASEAN are simulated under the assumption that the AEC's measures to facilitate the mobility of skilled workers are neither implemented nor effective. This simulation serves as a benchmark to look at how changes to labor mobility affect trade integration efforts, and it should not be used to predict the impact of enhanced trade integration on ASEAN member countries. As noted earlier, enhanced trade integration in the baseline is modeled as the removal of remaining intraregional tariffs, the liberalization of nontariff barriers in goods and services, and the introduction of advanced trade facilitation measures.[11] Trade integration, as a whole, brings many benefits. It is noteworthy that there are both winners and losers from integration and that an adjustment process that is at times protracted is often necessary for these benefits to materialize. Policy action is important to compensate those who lose out. Whereas more detailed results will be presented for Scenario I and Scenario II, results for the baseline scenario are only summarized for reference. Complete results are available in the online appendix.

When trade integration occurs without reductions in mobility costs for any workers:

- Real wages rise in the ASEAN region as a whole, especially for workers employed in sectors that are already relatively open to trade.

- The impact on the ASEAN employment rate is very small, but there are nonnegligible impacts on the distribution of employment across countries that is driven in part by reallocation toward countries with higher wages and lower mobility costs. ASEAN, as a whole, would experience an employment reallocation from sectors with low wages, high initial levels of protectionism, and/or high labor mobility costs (agriculture and mining, social services, and other services) to sectors with high wages, low initial levels of protectionism, and/or low labor mobility costs (manufacturing, finance, and business services).

- In ASEAN as a whole, the share of skilled workers would increase. However, some countries would experience a decline in the share of skilled workers because of large wage declines following the reduction in high trade barriers such as nontariff barriers.

- Welfare would improve, on average, in all ASEAN countries and for all categories of workers.

Scenario I: Policy measures reduce labor mobility costs for skilled services workers

Scenario I compares the impact of enhanced trade integration that occurs alongside efforts to facilitate labor mobility for skilled services workers to the impact of enhanced trade integration without such efforts. Policies to facilitate labor mobility for skilled services workers are assumed to reduce labor mobility costs for these workers by 20 percent.[12]

This reduction is a rough approximation because the objective of the simulations is to determine whether labor mobility costs matter for how economies respond to trade integration rather than to predict exact magnitudes of impacts.[13] Labor mobility costs in the model are exogenously reduced for all skilled services workers, including those transitioning domestically across sectors and internationally between countries. Practical steps to decrease international mobility costs and, hence, increase between-country labor mobility for skilled services workers include the closing of loopholes in the mutual recognition arrangements (MRAs) agreed by ASEAN countries and the ratification and implementation of these MRAs by all ASEAN member countries. Domestic labor mobility costs can also be eased through labor market, social protection, education, and other domestic policies. Policies to reduce labor mobility costs will be discussed in chapter 9.

Compared to no reduction in labor mobility costs, enhanced trade integration occurring with reductions for skilled services workers results in the following:

- Employment rates would be higher across ASEAN.

- In all ASEAN countries, the services sector would account for a larger share of employment, while agriculture and mining and manufacturing would account for a smaller share.

- In line with the sectoral shift toward services, skilled workers would account for a higher share of employment in all ASEAN countries.

- More skilled workers would move to countries offering wage premiums in their services sectors to take advantage of the opportunities resulting from lower labor mobility costs for skilled services workers.

- Because of a higher overall employment rate, real wages would increase by a smaller magnitude in ASEAN as whole. At the country level, real wage increases would be smaller in countries that would now account for higher shares of ASEAN total employment after enhanced migration of skilled services workers.

- Welfare would be higher on average in all ASEAN countries and for all categories of workers.

Employment

Enhanced trade integration would result in a higher employment rate in ASEAN if it occurred with reduced labor mobility costs for skilled services workers, though employment would be lower among the unskilled. Despite the reduction in unskilled employment, overall employment in the ASEAN region is 1.2 percent higher in Scenario I than in the baseline (figure 4.4). In fact, the employment rate in all ASEAN member countries is higher in Scenario I than in the baseline (figure 4.5). Differences are sizable in Singapore, where a reduction of labor mobility costs is associated with an employment rate that is 2.1 percent higher under Scenario I than the baseline.

FIGURE 4.4

Differences in the employment rate in ASEAN and across skill levels between Scenario I and the baseline

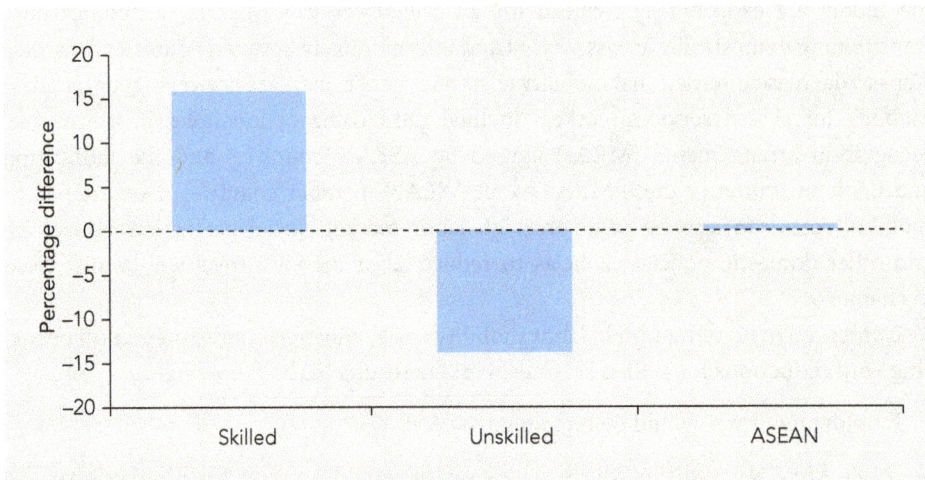

Source: World Bank simulations based on Hollweg 2016.
Note: Positive numbers indicate higher employment rates under Scenario I than the baseline. ASEAN = Association of Southeast Asian Nations.

FIGURE 4.5

Differences in the employment rate within countries between Scenario I and the baseline

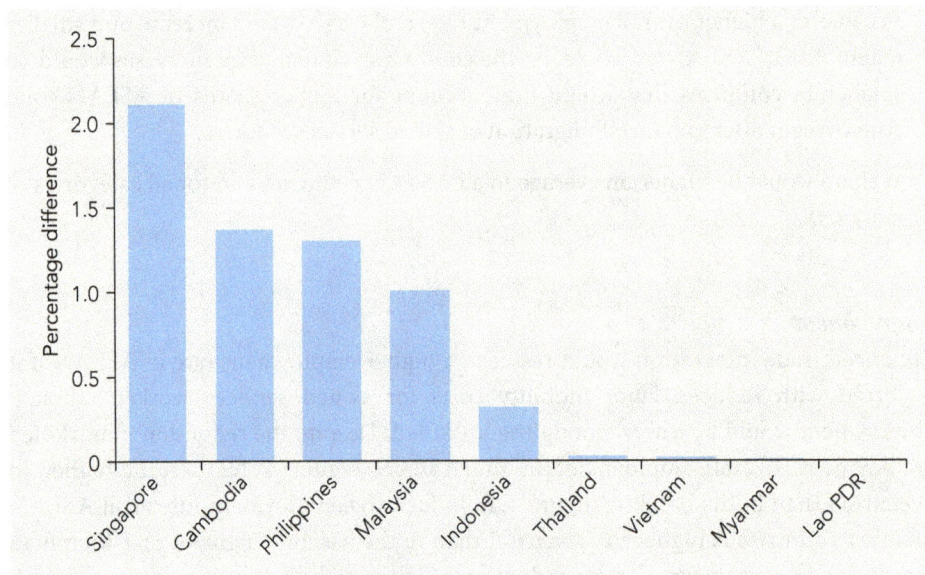

Source: World Bank simulations based on Hollweg 2016.
Note: Positive numbers indicate higher employment rates under Scenario I than the baseline.

When labor mobility costs are lower, individuals have stronger incentives to leave joblessness in response to the higher real wages following enhanced trade integration. Intuitively, given that labor mobility costs are reduced only for skilled workers, the share of skilled jobs among all jobs is 16 percent higher under Scenario I than the baseline (figure 4.4). Conversely, the share of unskilled jobs is 13.8 percent lower. The reason for the shift toward skilled work is that Scenario I makes it relatively less costly to enter skilled employment in services, either from joblessness or from unskilled employment. This is true across countries.

Countries that receive more migrants with trade integration would attract even more if integration occurred with reduced mobility costs for skilled services workers. The distribution of employment across countries and sectors changes between the baseline and Scenario I (figures 4.6 and 4.7). Countries in which enhanced trade integration alone would lead to a net inflow of employed migrants would receive an even larger proportion of net immigrants. The reason is that lower labor mobility costs lead to both stronger incentives to migrate to attractive migration destinations and lower costs of doing so. As a result, in Scenario I Singapore and Malaysia capture a greater share of overall ASEAN employment, but the share for both Vietnam and the Lao People's Democratic Republic is lower. However, a counterbalancing effect is also at work. Lower labor mobility costs for skilled services workers to enter their sectors domestically could also keep these workers from leaving their country in search of better employment opportunities. This is the case in Cambodia. The smaller number of Cambodian out-migrants results in less net immigration to Thailand.[14]

Employment in ASEAN member countries shifts toward the services sectors when labor mobility costs are reduced for skilled services workers. The employment share of all three services sectors across ASEAN is higher under Scenario I than the baseline (figure 4. 7). This is because Scenario I assumes relatively lower labor mobility costs of entering the skilled services sector, making it relatively less costly for workers exiting joblessness, the mining and agriculture sector, and the manufacturing sector to access services sector jobs. In contrast, under Scenario I, the shares of workers in the mining and agriculture sector and the manufacturing sector are lower than in the baseline. This again reflects the fact that, under Scenario I, workers find it relatively easier to head for services jobs.

Within-country differences in sectoral employment shares largely mirror those documented for ASEAN as a whole. The shares of employment in the agriculture and mining sector and in the manufacturing sector are lower. The share is higher in the three services sectors combined when enhanced trade integration happens under Scenario I (figure 4.8). Because of heterogeneity in sectoral wage premiums across countries, the services sectors that expand most differ across countries. In Cambodia, Lao PDR, Myanmar, and Vietnam, for instance, finance and business services see the largest difference between Scenario I and the baseline, whereas in Malaysia and Singapore, this is the case for social and other services, perhaps reflecting the restrictions on high-skilled migrants working in those sectors that are currently in place.

FIGURE 4.6
Differences in the employment share across countries between Scenario I and the baseline

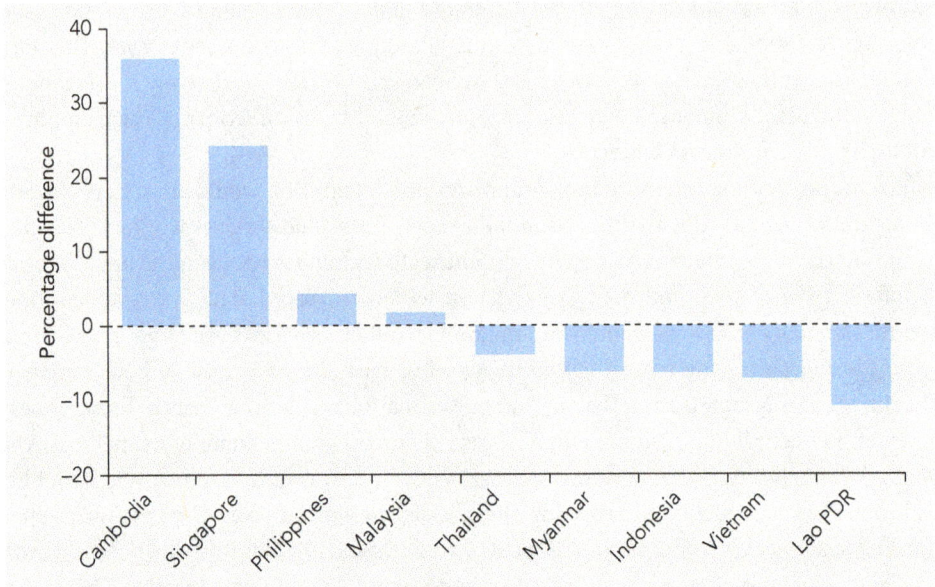

Source: World Bank simulations based on Hollweg 2016.
Note: Positive numbers indicate higher employment shares under Scenario I than the baseline.

FIGURE 4.7
Differences in the employment share across sectors in ASEAN between Scenario I and the baseline

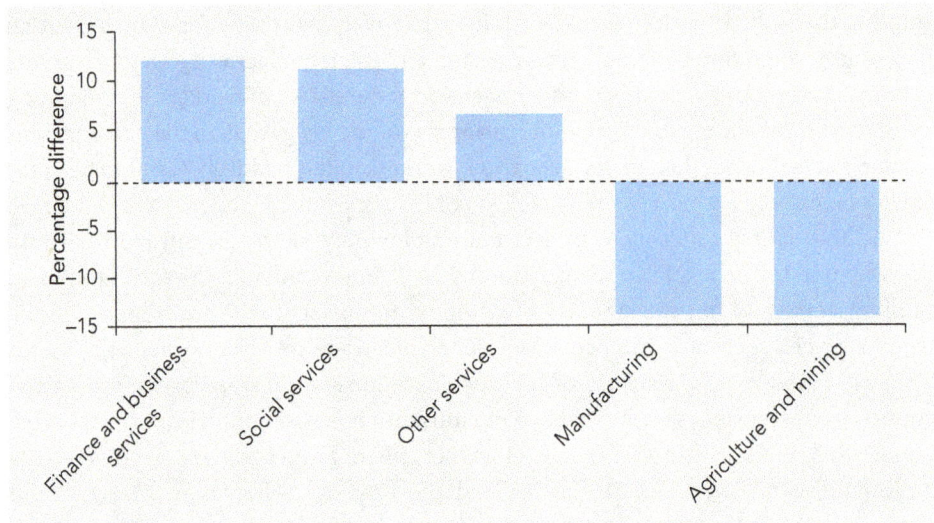

Source: World Bank simulations based on Hollweg 2016.
Note: Positive numbers indicate higher employment share under Scenario I than the baseline. ASEAN = Association of Southeast Asian Nations.

FIGURE 4.8

Differences in the sectoral employment share within countries between Scenario I and the baseline

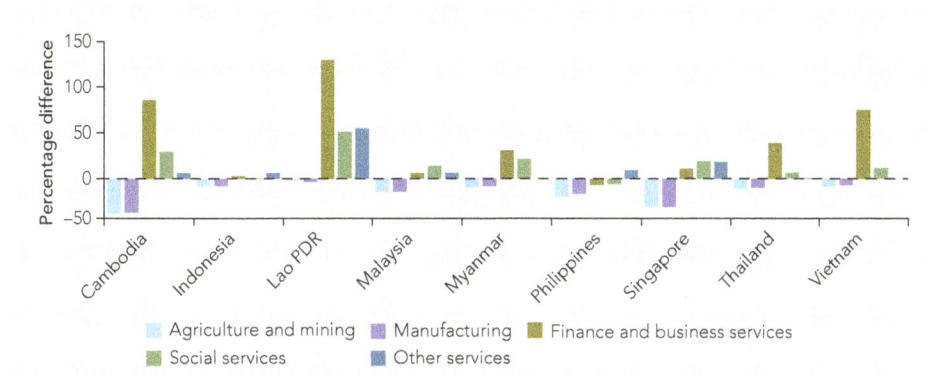

Source: World Bank simulations based on Hollweg 2016.
Note: Positive numbers indicate higher employment shares under Scenario I than the baseline.

Wages

Real relative wages in ASEAN would increase less if enhanced trade integration occurred with reduced labor mobility costs for skilled services workers, though unskilled workers would see wage gains. The real relative wage level in Scenario I is 1.2 percent lower for the ASEAN region as a whole (figure 4.9). However, wage impacts vary by skill levels and contrast with the employment results: real wages are 11 percent higher for unskilled workers, but 11 percent lower for skilled workers. There are also varying impacts on the wage rate by country and sector. For example, wages are higher in Indonesia, Lao PDR, Myanmar, Thailand, and Vietnam (figure 4.10). They are also higher for jobs in agriculture and mining, as well as in manufacturing (figure 4.11).

Higher employment rates have trade-offs with wage levels, though wage levels are higher in both the baseline and Scenario I than without trade integration. As discussed in the previous section, wage and employment effects are closely linked. Enhanced trade integration leads to an increase in real wages, which incentivizes individuals to leave joblessness and enter employment. This process is present in both the baseline and Scenario I. The difference between the two is that the lower mobility costs in Scenario I mean that workers face lower costs when they leave joblessness and, thus, more workers are willing to enter employment. Consequently, in ASEAN, labor markets are more dynamic and employment rates are higher. This provides a strong rationale for making sure that MRAs and similar policies envisaged in the initial AEC blueprint are implemented effectively to reduce mobility costs for skilled services workers. The higher employment rates in Scenario I also influence nominal wage levels. Under the assumption that there are decreasing marginal returns to labor and that wages equal the marginal returns to labor, higher employment rates in Scenario I imply lower marginal returns to labor and thus lower nominal wages. Although in both

FIGURE 4.9
Real wage differences in ASEAN and across skill levels between Scenario I and the baseline

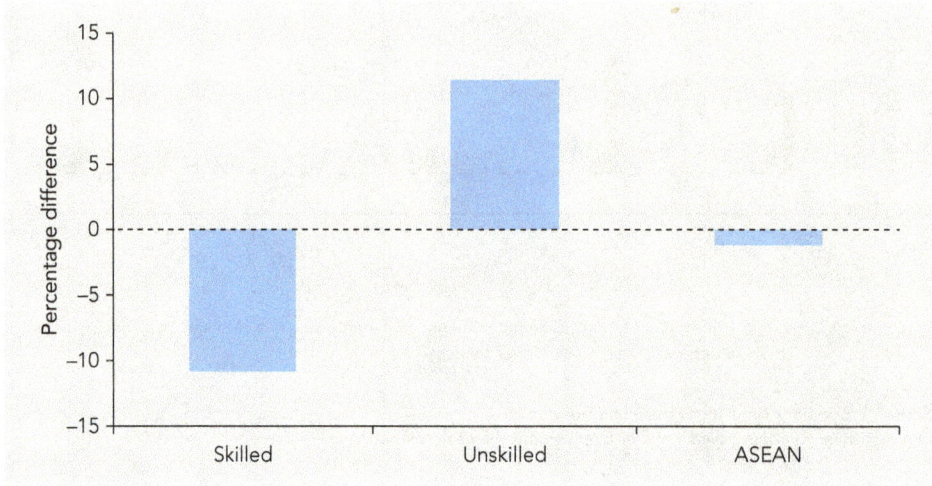

Source: World Bank simulations based on Hollweg 2016.
Note: Positive numbers indicate higher real wages under Scenario I than the baseline. ASEAN = Association of Southeast Asian Nations.

FIGURE 4.10
Real wage differences across countries between Scenario I and the baseline

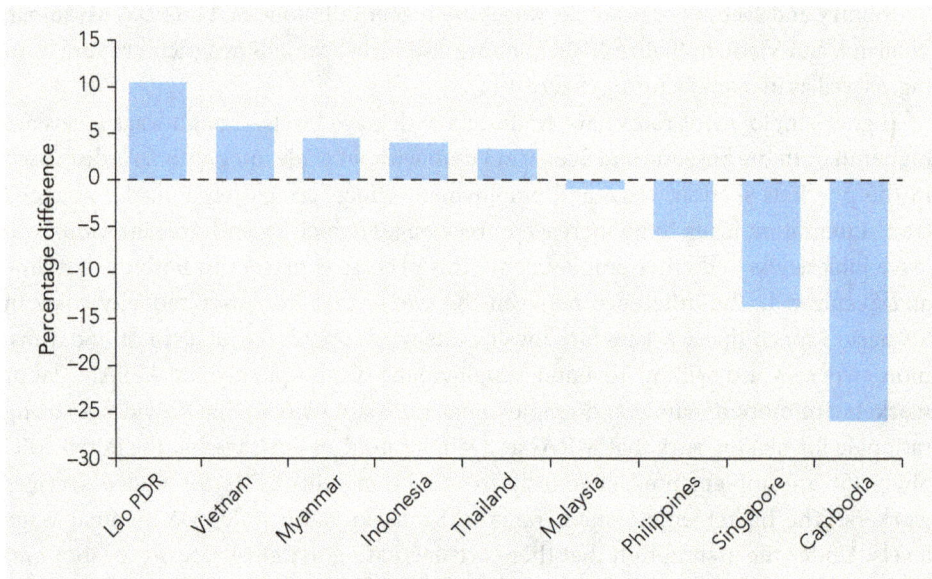

Source: World Bank simulations based on Hollweg 2016.
Note: Positive numbers indicate higher real wages under Scenario I than the baseline.

FIGURE 4.11
Real wage differences across sectors between Scenario I and the baseline

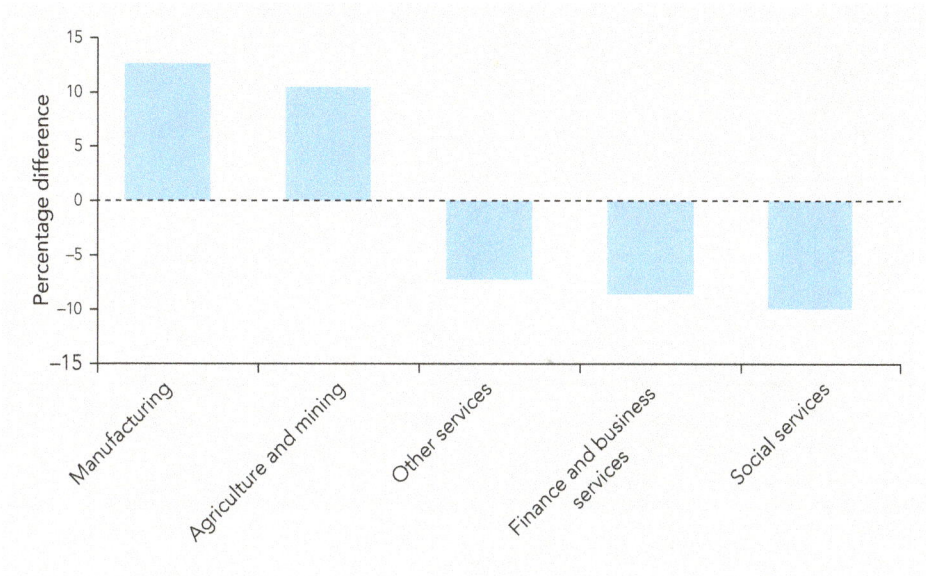

Source: World Bank simulations based on Hollweg 2016.
Note: Positive numbers indicate higher real wages under Scenario I than the baseline.

scenarios real wages are higher post-trade integration than before because of the decrease in prices that accompanies integration, this countervailing decrease is identical under both scenarios. Therefore, for ASEAN as a whole, wage levels are lower under Scenario I than the baseline. Similar mechanisms explain real wage differences by worker type and sector.

Welfare

Trade integration would increase welfare across ASEAN and in each ASEAN country more if labor mobility costs were reduced for skilled services workers. The effect of enhanced trade integration on welfare across the ASEAN region is 14.1 percent higher under Scenario I than the baseline (figure 4.12). Under Scenario I, unskilled labor undergoes particularly pronounced welfare gains, explained by their higher real wages. This is true for ASEAN, for skilled and unskilled workers, and across all ASEAN countries. Welfare differences between Scenario I and the baseline range from 11 percent in Myanmar to 16 percent in Lao PDR (figure 4.13). These results suggest that welfare gains will be left on the table if trade integration is not undertaken alongside efforts to reduce mobility costs for skilled services workers. This gives all countries in ASEAN a strong incentive to implement the policies envisaged by the AEC to promote the free mobility of skilled labor.

FIGURE 4.12

Welfare differences in ASEAN and across skill levels between Scenario I and the baseline

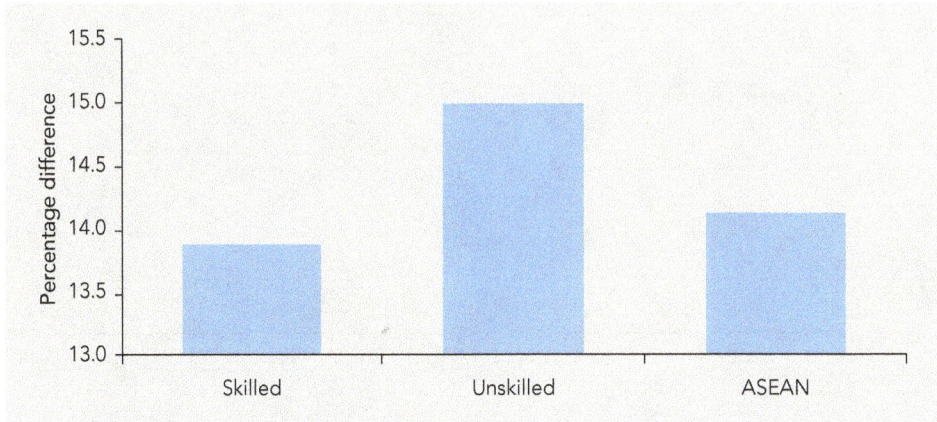

Source: World Bank simulations based on Hollweg 2016.
Note: Positive numbers indicate higher welfare under Scenario I than the baseline. ASEAN = Association of Southeast Asian Nations.

FIGURE 4.13

Welfare differences across countries between Scenario I and the baseline

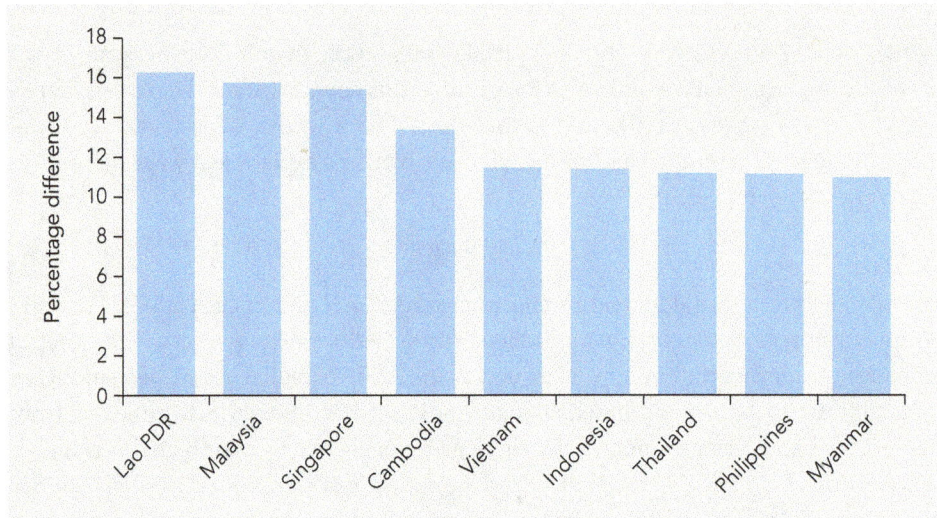

Source: World Bank simulations based on Hollweg 2016.
Note: Positive numbers indicate higher welfare under Scenario I than the baseline.

Scenario II: Policy measures reduce labor mobility costs for all workers

Scenario II simulates the impact of enhanced trade integration that occurs alongside policies to reduce labor mobility costs for all workers. To understand whether the gains from enhanced trade integration would be higher or lower if efforts to reduce mobility costs were extended to all workers, the results of Scenario II are compared to those of Scenario I in which mobility costs are lower only for skilled services workers. In Scenario II, policies to facilitate labor mobility are assumed to reduce labor mobility costs for all workers by 20 percent.[15] Examples of practical steps to decrease international labor mobility costs for all workers include better oversight of employment agencies to reduce recruitment fees and increased use of bilateral agreements to facilitate the entry of low-skilled workers into destination countries. Approaches to reducing both domestic and international labor mobility costs are discussed in chapter 9.

Compared to reductions in labor mobility costs for skilled services workers alone, enhanced trade integration combined with reductions for all workers would result in the following:

- Employment rates would be higher across ASEAN.

- In all ASEAN countries, agriculture and mining and manufacturing would account for most of the new jobs created.

- The benefits from trade would be shared more broadly with lower-skilled workers who would account for higher shares of employment.

- A larger number of workers would take advantage of the opportunities in the manufacturing sector by moving to countries that have lower migration costs and a relatively high wage for low-skilled workers.

- Because of a higher employment rate, real wages would be lower in ASEAN as a whole. Real wages would be lower in countries that would account for a higher share of total employment in ASEAN after full labor market integration.

- Welfare would be higher on average in all ASEAN countries and for all categories of workers.

Employment

Enhanced trade integration would have an even more positive effect on ASEAN-wide employment if it happened alongside a reduction of labor mobility costs for all workers. The simulations in Scenario I showed that enhanced trade integration would have a more positive effect on the overall employment rate in ASEAN if the integration happened under a partial reduction of labor mobility costs rather than with no reductions. Figure 4.14 shows that this positive result would be even larger if labor mobility costs were reduced for all workers. In Scenario II, lower labor mobility costs across all sectors and job types (as opposed to just skilled service jobs) incentivize even more labor market entries from joblessness in response to the higher real wages

FIGURE 4.14

Differences in the employment rate in ASEAN and across skill levels between Scenario I and Scenario II

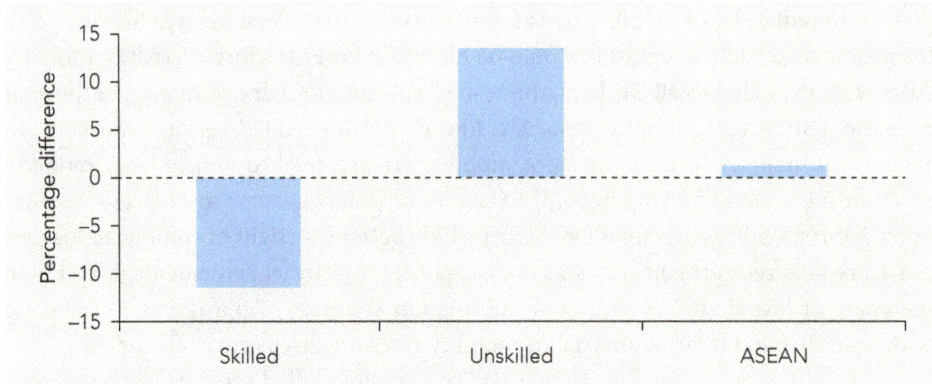

Source: World Bank simulations based on Hollweg 2016.
Note: Positive numbers indicate higher employment rates under Scenario II than Scenario I. ASEAN = Association of Southeast Asian Nations.

generated by enhanced trade integration. As a result, for the ASEAN region as a whole the employment rate is 1.2 percent higher under Scenario II than under Scenario I. The additional gains in employment under Scenario II accrue primarily to unskilled workers, whose share increases 13 percent. This is generally true across ASEAN countries, with the most pronounced increase in the unskilled share in Singapore.

The employment rate is higher in all ASEAN countries in Scenario II than in Scenario I. The greatest difference in employment rates between the two scenarios is found in Singapore, though Cambodia, Malaysia, and the Philippines also see sizable differences in employment rates (figure 4.15). In Lao PDR, Myanmar, Thailand, and Vietnam the differences are much smaller. With all workers facing lower labor mobility costs, individuals are better able to leave joblessness and enter the workforce in response to the new opportunities created by enhanced trade integration. This is an important result for ASEAN countries like Indonesia and the Philippines, where unemployment rates are high for the region and labor force participation rates are low, and Malaysia, where labor force participation rates are low. This finding provides a strong rationale for pursuing enhanced trade integration in conjunction with a policy agenda designed to reduce international and domestic labor mobility costs for workers of all skill levels.

The effects of enhanced trade integration on net migration within ASEAN and the resulting employment distributions across countries would be different if efforts to lower labor mobility costs were expanded to cover all workers (figure 4.16). The simulations suggest that Singapore would see even more immigration and, as a result, gain an even greater share of ASEAN employment. The main reason is that Singapore offers higher wages relative to other ASEAN member countries. The incentive for

FIGURE 4.15

Differences in the employment rate within countries between Scenario I and Scenario II

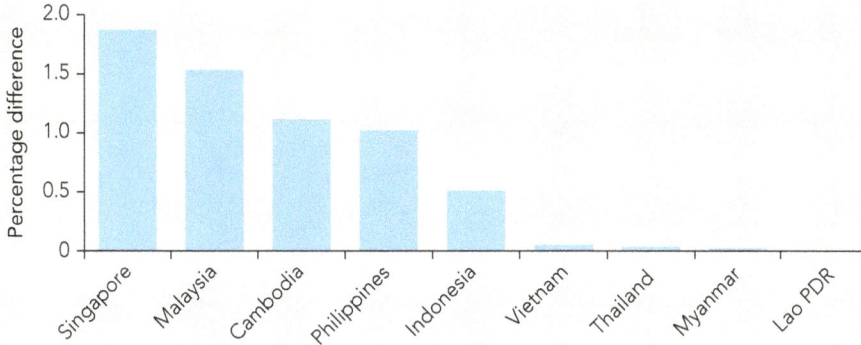

Source: World Bank simulations based on Hollweg 2016.
Note: Positive numbers indicate higher employment rates under Scenario II than Scenario I. ASEAN = Association of Southeast Asian Nations.

FIGURE 4.16

Differences in employment share across countries between Scenario I and Scenario II

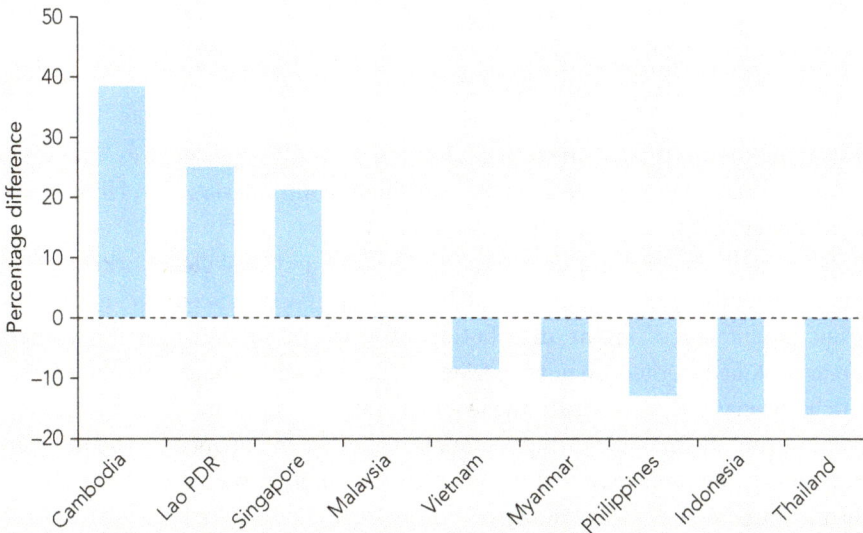

Source: World Bank simulations based on Hollweg 2016.
Note: Positive numbers indicate higher employment shares under Scenario II than Scenario I.

workers of all types to take advantage of these high wages by migrating to Singapore is stronger when the costs of doing so are lower for skilled and unskilled workers alike. Cambodia and Lao PDR would also have substantially greater shares of overall employment in ASEAN if labor mobility costs were reduced for all workers. This is driven by fewer workers leaving these countries, though they remain net sending

FIGURE 4.17

Differences in employment share across sectors in ASEAN between Scenario I and Scenario II

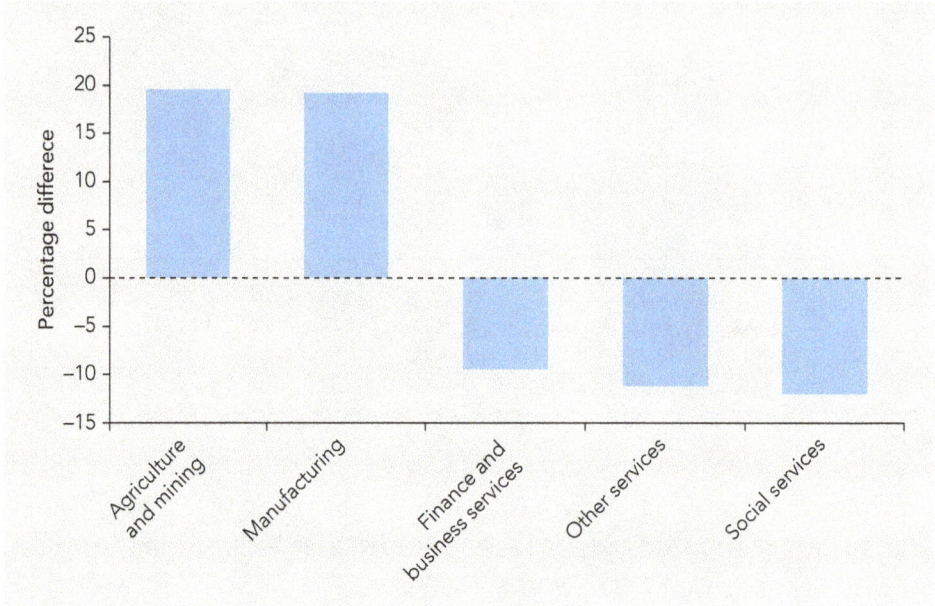

Source: World Bank simulations based on Hollweg 2016.
Note: Positive numbers indicate higher employment shares under Scenario II than Scenario I.

countries in the simulations. In contrast, Indonesia would experience even more pronounced net out-migration. This can be explained by Indonesia's high labor mobility costs relative to other countries in the region.

Differences in the sectoral distribution of skilled and unskilled workers who are affected differently by the reductions in labor mobility costs in Scenario I and Scenario II result in differences in the distribution of employment between the scenarios. Whereas unskilled workers do not experience reductions in mobility costs in Scenario I, they do in Scenario II. As a result, the share of ASEAN employment in the agriculture and mining and the manufacturing sectors is higher when enhanced trade integration occurs under a comprehensive reduction of labor mobility costs (figure 4.17). The same pattern is found across most countries (figure 4.18). The results by sector, as well as those for unskilled labor, underline that gains from trade would be more broad-based if enhanced trade integration occurred alongside a reduction of labor mobility costs for all workers.

Wages

Real relative wages in ASEAN would increase by less overall if enhanced trade integration occurred with reduced labor mobility costs for all workers, though skilled workers would see wage gains. Figure 4.19 depicts the real wage differences in ASEAN across

FIGURE 4.18

Differences in the sectoral employment share within countries between Scenario I and Scenario II

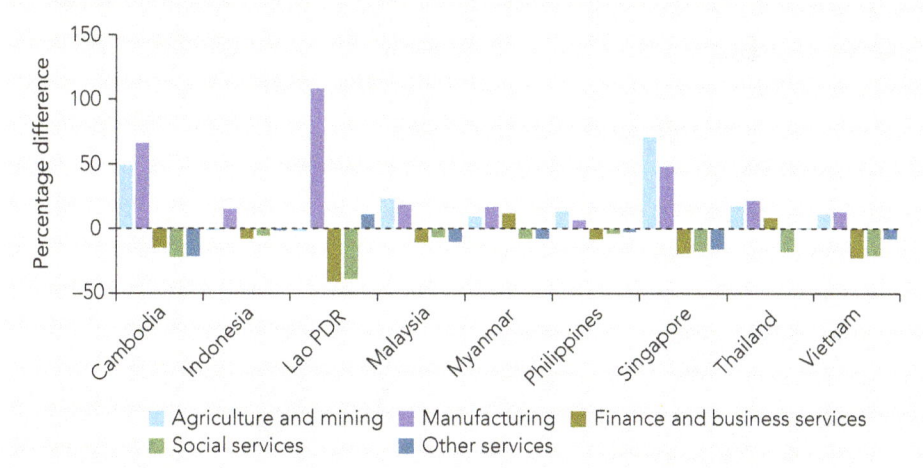

Source: World Bank simulations based on Hollweg 2016.
Note: Positive numbers indicate higher employment shares under Scenario II than Scenario I.

FIGURE 4.19

Real wage differences in ASEAN and across skill levels between Scenario I and Scenario II

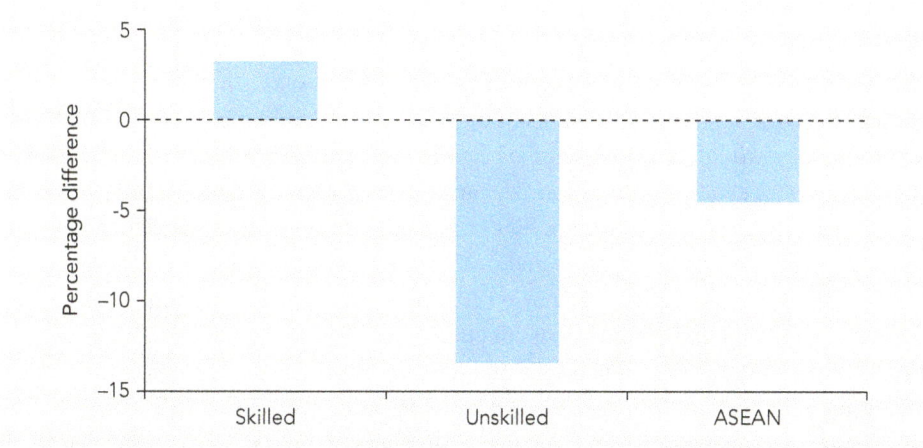

Source: World Bank simulations based on Hollweg 2016.
Note: Positive numbers indicate higher real wages under Scenario II than Scenario I. ASEAN = Association of Southeast Asian Nations.

FIGURE 4.20

Real wage differences across countries between Scenario I and Scenario II

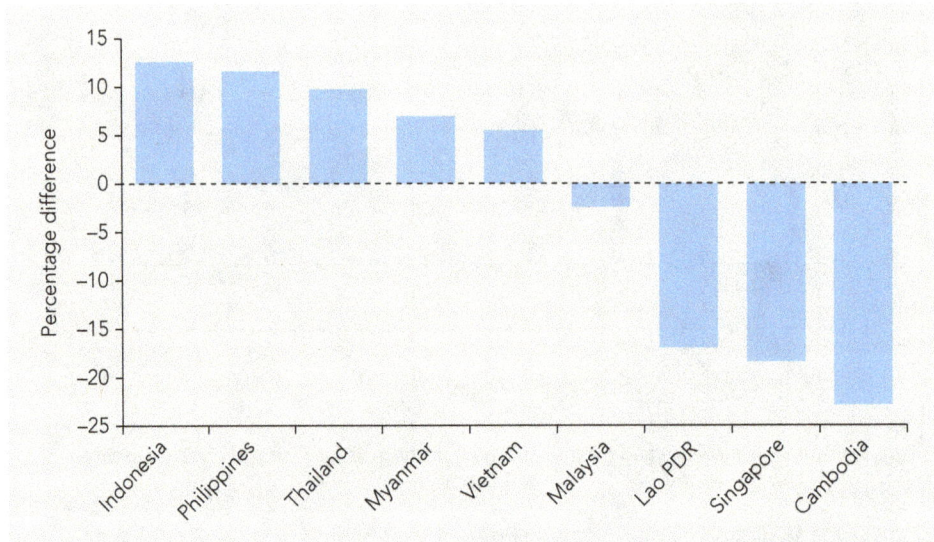

Source: World Bank simulations based on Hollweg 2016.
Note: Positive numbers indicate higher real wages under Scenario II than Scenario I.

skill levels between Scenario I and Scenario II. Real wages are higher in ASEAN after enhanced trade integration in both Scenarios I and II. However, real wages for ASEAN as a whole increase less when trade integration occurs with a reduction of labor mobility costs for all workers than they do when the reduction is for skilled services workers only. The same result is observed for unskilled workers, though the wages of skilled workers would be higher. The impacts on the wage rate vary by country (figure 4.20). Although Indonesia, Myanmar, the Philippines, Thailand, and Vietnam would see higher real wages under Scenario II, wages in Cambodia, Lao PDR, Malaysia, and Singapore would be lower. There is also substantial heterogenity in the real wage differences between Scenario II and Scenario I across sectors (figure 4.21). For example, wages in the services sector are higher under Scenario II than Scenario I.

Higher employment rates have trade-offs with wage levels, though wage levels are higher in both Scenario II and Scenario I than without trade integration. As discussed for Scenario I, wage and employment effects are closely linked. Enhanced trade integration leads to an increase in real wages that incentivizes individuals to leave joblessness and enter employment. This process is present in both Scenario I and Scenario II. The difference between the two is that the lower mobility costs for all workers in Scenario II mean that all workers face lower costs when they leave joblessness; thus, more workers than in Scenario I are willing to enter employment. Consequently, labor markets are more dynamic, and employment rates in ASEAN are higher. This provides a strong rationale for ensuring that ASEAN's measures for reducing labor mobility costs are expanded to cover all workers. The higher employment rates in Scenario II also have an

FIGURE 4.21

Real wage differences across sectors between Scenario I and Scenario II

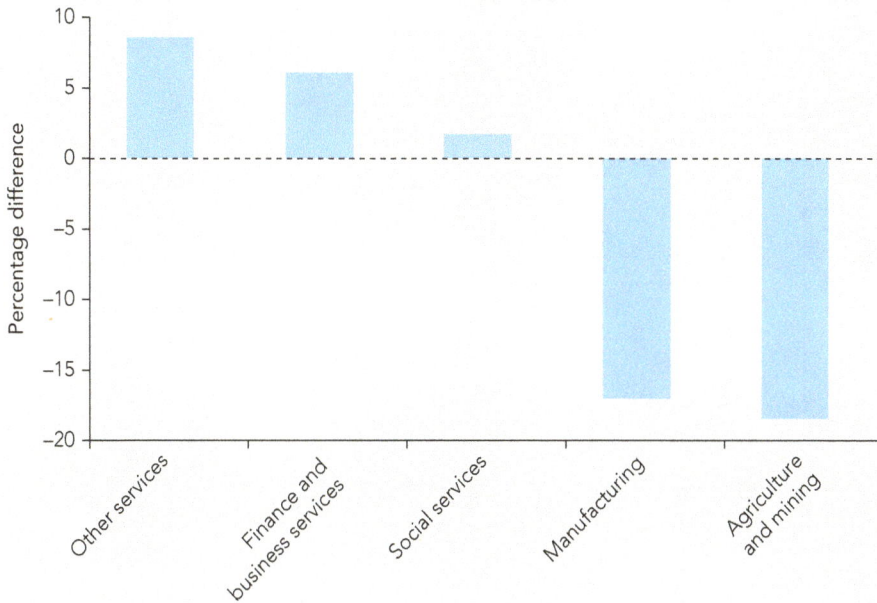

Source: World Bank simulations based on Hollweg 2016.
Note: Positive numbers indicate higher real wages under Scenario II than Scenario I.

effect on nominal wage levels. Under the assumption that there are decreasing marginal returns to labor and that wages equal the marginal returns to labor, higher employment rates in Scenario II imply lower marginal returns to labor and thus lower nominal wages. Though in both Scenario I and Scenario II real wages are higher post-trade integration than before because of the decrease in prices that accompanies integration, this countervailing decrease is identical under both scenarios. Thus, for ASEAN as a whole, wage levels are lower under Scenario II than Scenario I. Similar mechanisms explain real wage differences by worker type and sector.

Welfare

Trade integration increases welfare more across ASEAN and in each ASEAN country when labor mobility costs are reduced for all workers rather than for skilled workers alone. Aggregate welfare levels within ASEAN are 29 percent higher in Scenario II than in Scenario I (figure 4.22). Skilled workers would experience even greater welfare gains than unskilled workers, driven by greater wage differences for these workers. The still significant welfare gains of unskilled workers are a result of this group's greater employment opportunities under Scenario II as compared to Scenario I. Welfare gains are consistently large across countries (figure 4.23). Lao PDR, Malaysia, and Singapore have the largest positive welfare gains. The other countries are not far behind.

FIGURE 4.22

Welfare differences in ASEAN and across skill levels between Scenario I and Scenario II

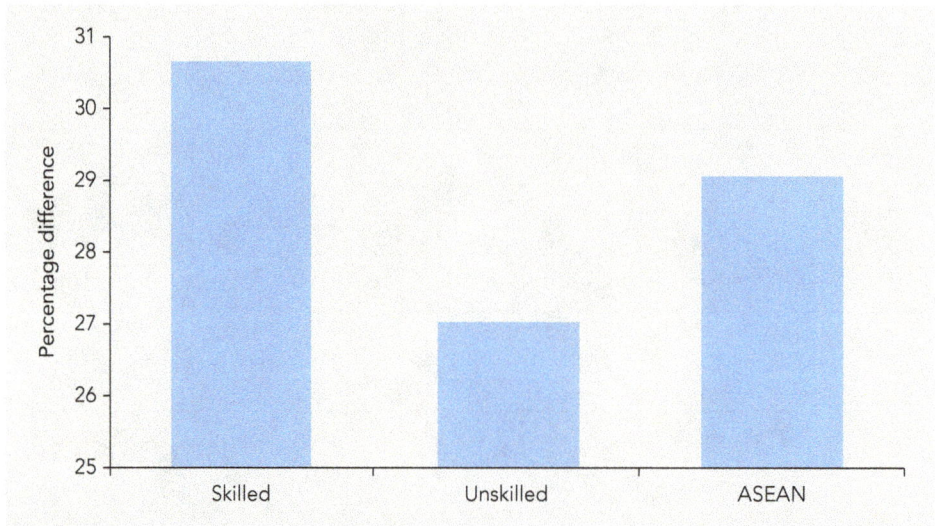

Source: World Bank simulations based on Hollweg 2016.
Note: Positive numbers indicate higher welfare under Scenario II than Scenario I. ASEAN = Association of Southeast Asian Nations.

FIGURE 4.23

Welfare differences across countries between Scenario I and Scenario II

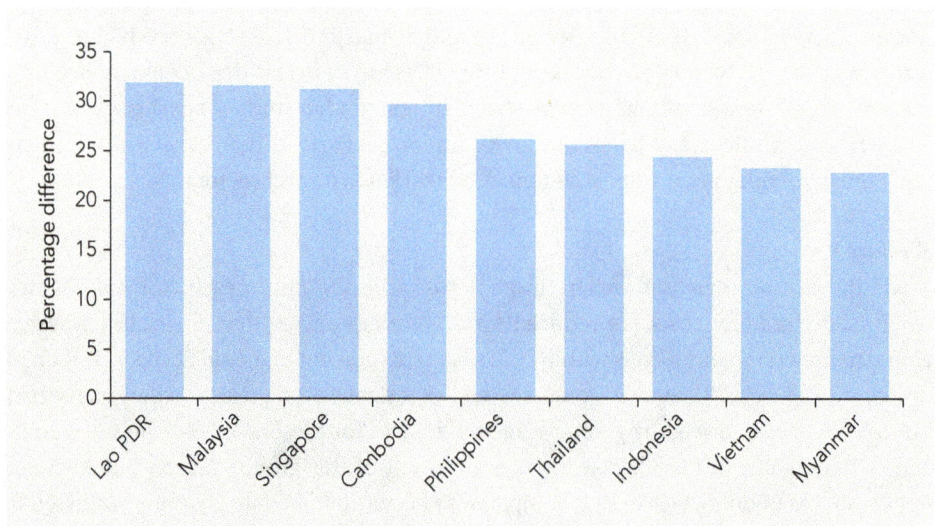

Source: World Bank simulations based on Hollweg 2016.
Note: Positive numbers indicate higher welfare under Scenario II than Scenario I.

Key takeaways from the simulations

The simulations discussed above show that, both across the ASEAN group of countries as a whole and within all countries in the region, enhanced trade integration and freer migration are likely to have complementary welfare effects. Enhanced trade integration would have a more positive effect on welfare if it occurred alongside a reduction of mobility costs for skilled workers in the services sector. Even larger welfare gains would be possible if labor mobility costs were lowered for all workers and not only skilled services workers as currently envisaged under the AEC. Importantly, welfare gains would be more broad-based if labor mobility costs were lowered for all workers.

For the ASEAN region as a whole, the effects of enhanced trade integration on wages differ across simulations and are negative in some cases. In contrast, the simulation results point to more positive effects on employment. All countries experience a lower share of the working age population that is jobless under the scenario that assumes a reduction in labor mobility costs for skilled services workers. All countries realize an even lower share of the working age population that is jobless when labor mobility costs are reduced for all workers. Given that unemployment is increasingly an issue in Southeast Asia, this provides evidence in favor of lowering barriers to international and internal labor mobility.

Reducing labor mobility costs for all workers would spread the gains from trade more widely. If enhanced trade integration occurred under a scenario in which reduced labor mobility costs were limited to skilled services workers, most welfare gains from trade would be reaped by these workers. In contrast, if labor mobility costs were reduced for all workers, the welfare gains from trade would be enjoyed more widely. The generally positive impacts of immigration on employment, wages, and economic growth that were presented in chapter 3 provide evidence of how welfare gains manifest themselves and suggest that these gains are economically significant. These results imply that comprehensive measures to free up the movement of labor are necessary to ensure that enhanced trade integration benefits not just a select few but the population as a whole.

The simulations also demonstrate the likely effect of enhanced trade integration on intra-ASEAN migration. A comparison of employment shares across countries before and after enhanced trade integration reveals that enhanced trade integration would create opportunities for workers to find more productive employment both within their home countries and abroad. Reducing labor mobility costs would amplify this effect. During this process, enhanced trade integration could, to a certain extent, amplify existing migration patterns. Under a more comprehensive reduction of labor mobility costs, the amplification of some (but not all) existing net migration patterns would be somewhat more pronounced. If properly managed, larger net migration flows are likely to benefit migrants and both labor-receiving and labor-sending countries.

Overall, this chapter's findings suggest that lowering barriers to labor mobility would benefit ASEAN countries. The chapters in part II discuss how these barriers arise and how they can be lowered to maximize the gains from migration and enhanced trade integration.

Notes

1. Trade-related barriers restricting economic integration within ASEAN remain, and the realization of enhanced trade integration remains an ongoing effort. Still, ASEAN member countries have made substantial progress in liberalizing trade. Particularly noteworthy are the tariff reductions that happened through the 2009 ASEAN Trade in Goods Agreement. However, services sector trade liberalization has so far been modest, and the identification and removal of nontariff barriers in goods has also been limited (ILO and ADB 2014).

2. The other five basic assumptions underlying Mundell's stylized theory are (1) technologies are identical across countries; (2) returns to scale are constant (if the inputs of all factors of production are increased by a factor of two, output doubles); (3) competition is perfect (there is a large number of buyers and sellers and producers have no market power to set prices); (4) there are no domestic distortions; and (5) consumer preferences are identical across countries and are homothetic (the relative demand for different goods depends on their prices but not on consumers' income or wealth).

3. More recently, theoretical models have been developed in which trade and migration are no longer necessarily either substitutes or complements, but more complex interactions between international flows of goods and production factors can emerge. See, for example, Iranzo and Peri (2009).

4. For a detailed discussion of regional agreements with labor components, see ILO and ADB (2014), Martin and Abella (2014), and Jurje and Lavenex (2015).

5. There was a quota on the entry of Mexican TNs between 1994 and 2004 (Martin and Abella 2014).

6. A prominent voice in this debate was Martin (1993) who predicted that NAFTA would lead, at the very least, to a migration hump.

7. The simulation results presented in this chapter are based on the application in Hollweg (2016) of the Trade Shocks and Labor Adjustments Toolkit recently developed by the World Bank (Hollweg et al. 2014). The toolkit encompasses a general equilibrium model for simulating the effects of trade-related shocks on wages, employment, and welfare. For a summary of the data used by Hollweg (2016), see the online appendix.

8. The firm's production function is assumed to be Cobb-Douglas, so that the substitution between capital and labor is unity.

9. These sectors reflect the level of aggregation necessary for comparability across data sources.

10. More formally, the worker's expected welfare in sector i, EV^i, is the present discounted value of the worker's real wage, a sector-specific fixed nonpecuniary benefit, and an option value reflecting the possibility of moving to a different sector with a higher wage based on the structural model of the worker's choice of employment sector.

11. The mechanics of the model are more simplified than other computerized general equilibrium (CGE) models such as the Plummer, Petri, and Zhai (2014) model used in ILO and ADB (2014). Additionally, the model underlying the simulations presented here differs substantially from the one used by Plummer, Petri, and Zhai (2014), which (1) uses a CGE model that allows for a richer modeling of the interactions among actors within and across countries and (2) models structural transformations and compares outcomes between no enhanced and enhanced trade integration. In contrast, the model underlying this chapter is used to

simulate how effects of enhanced trade integration depend on whether trade integration happens under partially or comprehensively reduced labor mobility costs. Nevertheless, the aggregate results of the baseline do not differ significantly from those in ILO and ADB (2014).

12. This chapter does not explicitly discuss the effects of enhanced trade integration within ASEAN under Scenario I. At least qualitatively, the effects of enhanced trade integration under the baseline scenario and Scenario I are very similar. For instance, under Scenario I, enhanced trade integration again leads to higher wages, employment, and welfare across ASEAN; to a reallocation from unskilled to skilled employment; and to positive real wage increases in all countries expect Lao PDR (and practically no wage changes in Indonesia and Vietnam). The purpose of the simulations is to show that the effects of trade integration could be different under different assumptions of labor mobility, rather than to anticipate the effects of enhanced trade integration.

13. Robustness tests, which use reductions of 10 percent and 30 percent, were also undertaken and show results that are generally consistent with those presented in the chapter. The results of these robustness tests are available from the authors upon request. Labor mobility costs exist for a variety of reasons that are unrelated to the efforts of the AEC to facilitate labor mobility, for example, skills mismatches or geographic relocation. As such, efforts to enhance labor mobility within the AEC would only be expected to partially affect labor mobility costs. Without existing evidence of how efforts to enhance labor mobility within the AEC could affect labor mobility costs, and given significant variability in changes in international labor mobility costs after integration in other regions, a 20 percent reduction in labor mobility costs was chosen for the simulations, along with the robustness tests of 10 and 30 percent. The magnitude of the decline in labor mobility costs is imposed exogenously and does not reflect any attempt to predict the impact of existing or future labor mobility initiatives on labor mobility costs.

14. The differences in net migration flows between the baseline and Scenario I result largely from differences in the effects of enhanced trade integration on the movement of skilled labor under the two scenarios.

15. This chapter does not explicitly discuss the effects of enhanced trade integration within ASEAN under Scenario II. At least qualitatively, the effects of enhanced trade integration under the baseline and Scenario II are very similar.

References

Asia-Pacific RCM (Regional Coordination Mechanism) Thematic Working Group on International Migration Including Human Trafficking. 2015. *Asia-Pacific Migration Report 2015: Migrants' Contribution to Development.* Bangkok: International Organization for Migration, Regional Office for Southeast Asia.

Batalova, Jeanne, Andriy Shymonyak, and Guntur Sugiyarto. 2017. *Firing Up Regional Brain Networks: The Promise of Brain Circulation in the ASEAN Economic Community."* Manila: Asian Development Bank.

Brady, Hugo. 2008. *EU Migration Policy: An A–Z.* London: Centre for European Reform.

de la Rica, Sara, Albrecht Glitz, and Francesc Ortega. 2013. "Immigration in Europe: Trends, Policies and Empirical Evidence." Discussion Paper 7778, Institute for the Study of Labor, Bonn.

DOJ (U.S. Department of Justice). 1993. "United States Attorney General Janet Reno: Discussion: North American Free Trade Agreement and U.S. Immigration Issues." Washington, DC: DOJ.

EIC (European Integration Consortium). 2009. *Labour Mobility within the EU in the Context of Enlargement and the Functioning of the Transitional Arrangements.* Brussels: European Commission.

Galgóczi, Bela, Janine Leschke, and Andre Watt, eds. 2009. *EU Labour Migration since Enlargement: Trends, Impacts and Policies.* Aldershot, England: Ashgate.

Globerman, Steven. 2000. "Trade Liberalization and the Migration of Skilled Professionals and Managers: The North American Experience." *World Economy* 23(7): 901–22.

Gonzalez-Barrera, Ana. 2015. *More Mexicans Leaving Than Coming to the U.S.* Washington, DC: Pew Research Center.

Heckscher, Eli. 1919. "The Effect of Foreign Trade on the Distribution of Income." *Ekonomisk Tidskrift* 21: 497–512.

Hollweg, Claire. 2016. "Labor Mobility and Labor Market Integration in ASEAN." Background paper, World Bank, Washington, DC.

Hollweg, Claire, Daniel Lederman, Diego Rojas, and Elizabeth Ruppert Bulmer. 2014. *Sticky Feet: How Labor Market Frictions Shape the Impact of International Trade on Jobs and Wages.* Washington, DC: World Bank.

ILO (International Labour Organization) and ADB (Asia Development Bank). 2014. *ASEAN Community 2015: Managing Integration for Better Jobs and Shared Prosperity.* Bangkok: ILO and ADB.

Iranzo, Susana, and Giovanni Peri. 2009. "Migration and Trade: Theory with an Application to the Eastern-Western European Integration." *Journal of International Economics* 79 (1): 1–19.

Jurje, Flavia, and Sandra Lavenex. 2015. "ASEAN Economic Community: What Model for Labour Mobility?" Working Paper 105/02, Swiss National Centre of Competence in Research, Swiss National Science Foundation, Bern.

Lee, Erik, Christopher E. Wilson, Francisco Lara-Valencia, Carlos A. de la Parra, Rick Van Schoik, Kristofer Patron-Soberano, Eric L. Olson, and Andrew Selee. 2013. *The State of the Border Report: A Comprehensive Analysis of the US-Mexico Border.* Edited by Christopher E. Wilson and Erik Lee. Washington, DC: Woodrow Wilson International Center for Scholars.

Markusen, James. 1983. "Factor Movements and Commodity Trade as Complements." *Journal of International Economics* 14 (3–4): 341–56.

Martin, Philip. 1993. *Trade and Migration: NAFTA and Agriculture.* Washington, DC: Institute for International Economics.

———. 2015. "Low-Skilled Labour Migration and Free Trade Agreements." In *The Palgrave Handbook of International Labour Migration: Law and Policy Perspectives,* edited by M. Panizzon, G. Zurcher, E. Fornale, and G. Zurcher, 205–30. New York: Palgrave Macmillan.

Martin, Philip, and Manolo Abella. 2014. "Reaping the Economic and Social Benefits of Labour Mobility: ASEAN 2015." Asia-Pacific Working Paper Series, International Labour Organization, Bangkok.

Mundell. Robert. 1957. "International Trade and Factor Mobility." *American Economic Review* 47 (3): 321–35.

Ohlin, Bertil. 1933. *Interregional and International Trade.* Cambridge, MA: Harvard University Press.

Passel, Jeffrey S., and Cohn D'Vera. 2016. "Overall Number of U.S. Unauthorized Immigrants Holds Steady Since 2009." Pew Research Center, Washington, DC.

Passel, Jeffrey S., D/Vera Cohn, and Ana Gonzalez-Barrera. 2012. "Net Migration from Mexico Falls to Zero—and Perhaps Less." Pew Research Center, Washington, DC.

Plummer, Michael, Peter Petri, and Fan Zhai. 2014. "Assessing the Impact of ASEAN Economic Integration on Labour Markets." Asia-Pacific Working Paper Series, September 2014, International Labour Organization, Bangkok.

Recchi, Ettore. 2008. "Cross-State Mobility in the EU." *European Societies* 10 (2): 197–224.

Schiff, Maurice. 2006. "Substitution in Markusen's Classic Trade and Factor Movement Complementarity Models." Policy Research Working Paper 3974, World Bank, Washington, DC.

Wasem, Ruth. 2005. "Immigration Issues in Trade Agreements." Washington, DC: Congressional Research Service, U.S. Congress.

PART II

Migration Policy in Southeast Asia

CHAPTER 5

A Framework for Migration Systems and Migration Costs

Introduction

This second part of the book turns to the management of migration. The first part showed the significant role that migration plays in the Association of Southeast Asian Nations (ASEAN) region and discussed the generally positive impact of migration for sending countries, receiving countries, and migrants themselves. Simulations showed how different policy regimes related to the mobility of workers within and across borders are likely to affect ASEAN countries as they continue to integrate. However, the specific ways in which labor mobility costs arise, and specific policy interventions to reduce these costs, were not addressed. The second part of the book investigates the channels through which policy affects the ability of workers to change jobs, focusing on migrants crossing borders in search of employment opportunities.

This chapter presents a framework that breaks down migrations systems into their components and discusses how mobility costs can emerge from each component when management policies are absent, weak, or ineffective. Chapter 6 focuses on migration policies in ASEAN's main receiving countries, chapter 7 on migration policies in its main sending countries, and chapter 8 on regional migration policies. Analyzing the immigration and out-migration systems of each ASEAN country would be ideal, but data and information limitations make this impractical in most cases. Thus, the migration systems of ASEAN's main receiving and main sending countries are reviewed with information about other countries included where possible. The concluding chapter of the book provides policy recommendations to help policy makers reduce international labor mobility costs to maximize the benefits of migration.

The migration system

Managing international migration requires reconciling the needs of sending and receiving countries, employers, and migrants themselves (figure 5.1). The needs of these actors are not always aligned. Receiving countries such as Malaysia, Singapore, and Thailand need both low- and high-skilled migrants to fill labor shortages, but governments are cautious of public attitudes that can be skeptical of low-skilled migrants. Employers in receiving countries also use migrants to fill shortages. Their objective, however, is profit maximization rather than economic growth. Sending countries, such as Cambodia, the Lao People's Democratic Republic, and Myanmar, can gain from migration through skill transfers, reduced unemployment, international business networks, and remittances; nonetheless, these countries are also concerned about the loss of human capital through brain drain and the treatment of their migrants abroad (Ratha, Yi, and Yousefi 2016). Finally, migrants themselves benefit from employment opportunities and higher wages, but face often significant upfront costs to migrate.

FIGURE 5.1
Actors in migration management

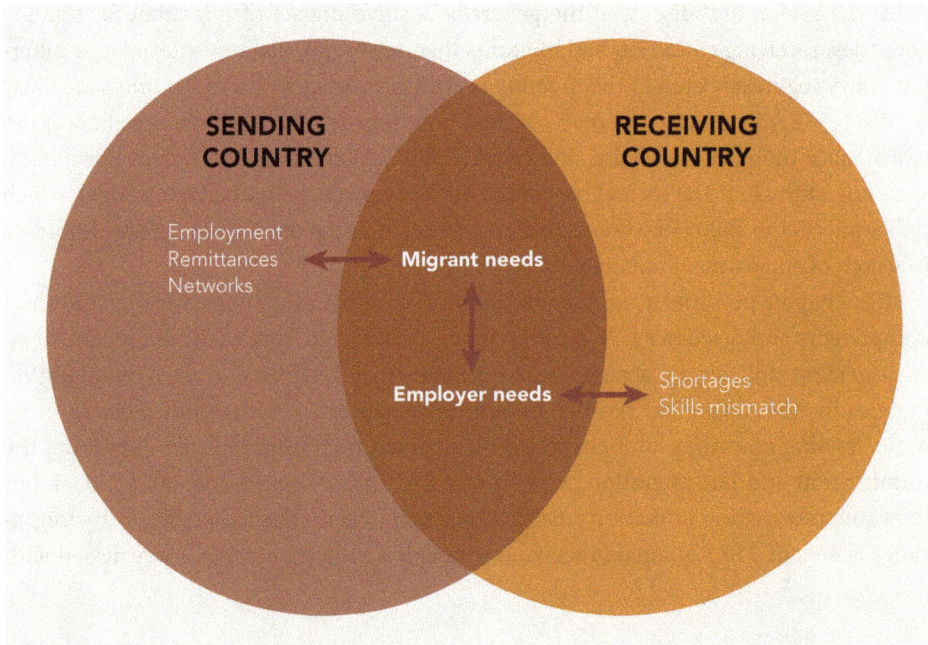

Migration systems are generally composed of the governance of the system and four additional components (figure 5.2). These components work together to reconcile the needs of host and source countries, employers, and migrants.

- The **governance** of the migration system refers to the *legal* and *institutional* framework organizing the system, and to *bilateral agreements* between sending and receiving countries. The roles of actors in the migration system—migrants, employers, and

FIGURE 5.2
Framework of the migration system and costs arising in each of its components

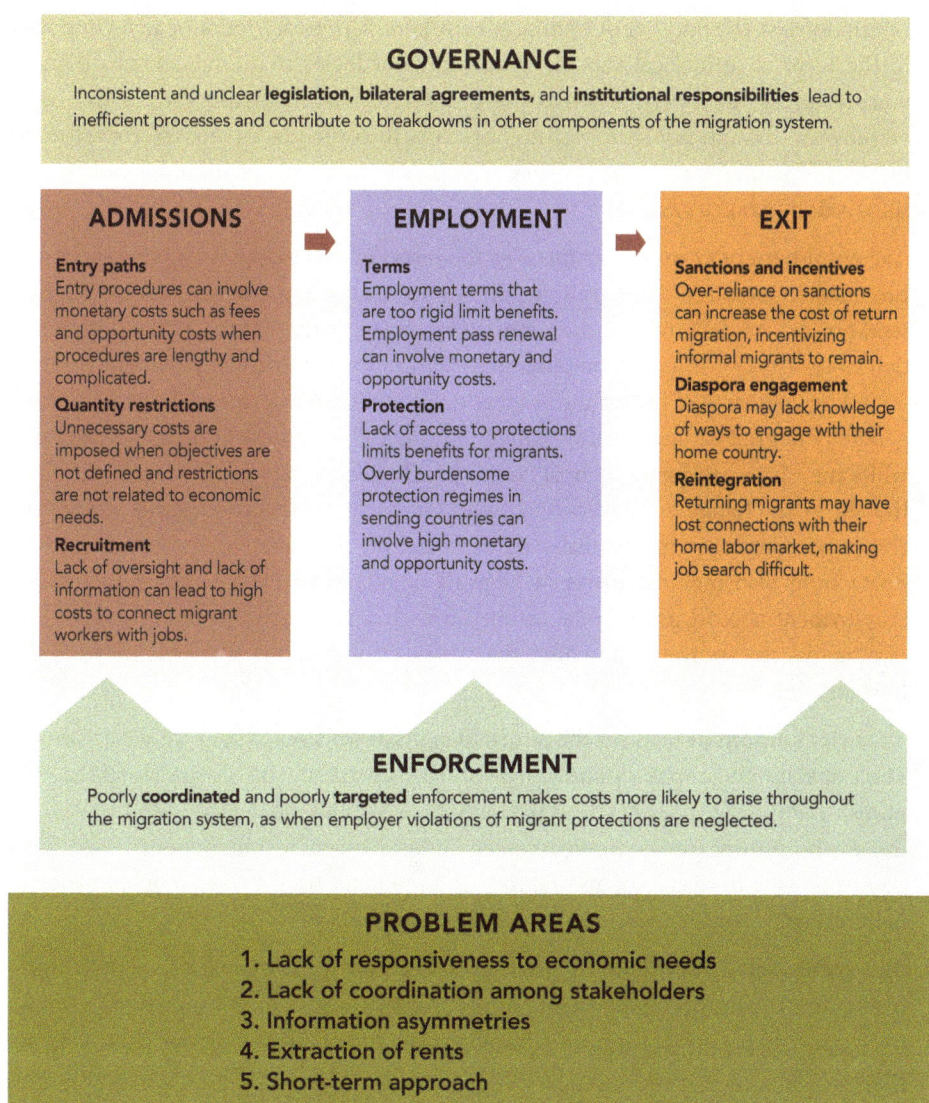

GOVERNANCE

Inconsistent and unclear **legislation, bilateral agreements,** and **institutional responsibilities** lead to inefficient processes and contribute to breakdowns in other components of the migration system.

ADMISSIONS

Entry paths
Entry procedures can involve monetary costs such as fees and opportunity costs when procedures are lengthy and complicated.

Quantity restrictions
Unnecessary costs are imposed when objectives are not defined and restrictions are not related to economic needs.

Recruitment
Lack of oversight and lack of information can lead to high costs to connect migrant workers with jobs.

EMPLOYMENT

Terms
Employment terms that are too rigid limit benefits. Employment pass renewal can involve monetary and opportunity costs.

Protection
Lack of access to protections limits benefits for migrants. Overly burdensome protection regimes in sending countries can involve high monetary and opportunity costs.

EXIT

Sanctions and incentives
Over-reliance on sanctions can increase the cost of return migration, incentivizing informal migrants to remain.

Diaspora engagement
Diaspora may lack knowledge of ways to engage with their home country.

Reintegration
Returning migrants may have lost connections with their home labor market, making job search difficult.

ENFORCEMENT

Poorly **coordinated** and poorly **targeted** enforcement makes costs more likely to arise throughout the migration system, as when employer violations of migrant protections are neglected.

PROBLEM AREAS

1. Lack of responsiveness to economic needs
2. Lack of coordination among stakeholders
3. Information asymmetries
4. Extraction of rents
5. Short-term approach

sending and receiving countries—are structured by migration-related objectives included in national economic and migration plans and in national migration, labor, and other legislation and regulations. These roles are also coordinated by bilateral labor agreements that govern migration between two countries.

- The **admissions component** determines who migrates and in what numbers through *entry paths, quantity restrictions,* and *recruitment.* Immigration systems in receiving countries frequently construct different paths for migrants of different skill levels. For low-skilled immigrants, in particular, entry paths can be restricted to certain source countries and/or to certain sectors or occupations of employment. Migration systems in sending countries can also influence entry paths through bilateral agreements. Quantity restrictions either set immigration targets or impose restrictions on the number of immigrant workers. These restrictions can be imposed in the form of numerical caps or in the form of levies that employers or foreign workers must pay. Recruitment is the process of matching migrant workers with employers. Though public recruitment occurs in some places, private recruitment by recruitment agencies and brokers, who charge a fee for facilitating labor migration, is dominant in ASEAN.

- The **employment component** involves the *terms* of employment and the *protection* provided to workers. Immigration policies governing the employment of migrant workers are closely related to admissions entry paths. Entry paths frequently determine the conditions of employment, with more generous employment terms—including contracts of longer duration and the ability to migrate with dependents—generally offered to more highly skilled migrants. Protections available to migrants while they are working in the host country include coverage by the minimum wage, the ability to change employers, eligibility for social protection benefits, and availability of complaint mechanisms in the case of violations of these protections. Protections also include efforts by sending countries to prepare out-migrants for employment abroad prior to departure through predeparture training and vetting of employment contracts, and after departure through labor attachés posted in the host country.

- The **exit component** involves the return of migrant workers to their source countries. The exit stage encompasses *sanctions and incentives* in the host country designed to punish temporary migrants who overstay their employment passes and to reward those who return; *diaspora engagement* undertaken by sending countries to form connections with diaspora; and *reintegration* policies used by sending countries to help returning migrant workers reenter labor markets.

- The **enforcement component** involves implementation of migration policy and oversight of the other components of the migration system. Enforcement involves oversight of the emigration and immigration processes to ensure that workers migrate using formal channels, of recruitment agencies to ensure that recruitment is done legally, and of employers to ensure that migrants are treated according to the law. In particular, enforcement involves efforts to *coordinate* the implementation of migration policy across government agencies and levels of governments and the *targeting* of oversight to border and interior enforcement, and to employers and migrant workers.

Migration costs and the migration system

Breakdowns and weaknesses in each component of the migration system increase the cost of international migration (figure 5.2). Migration costs include the direct monetary costs of fees charged by recruitment agencies for placing migrants in jobs and by migration authorities for exit and entry visas. They also include opportunity costs that arise when migration procedures are complex and time-consuming. But these costs also arise less directly when regulations and institutions do not function appropriately, the immigration system is not well aligned with economic needs, and protections for migrant workers are inaccessible.

In the admissions component, migration costs emerge from cumbersome entry procedures and quantity restrictions that do not reflect economic needs. Entry procedures frequently involve monetary costs to obtain necessary documents and time costs to comply with necessary procedures. When procedures are complex or require the involvement of many different agencies, these time costs can be high and represent significant lost wages. High-skilled migrants, in particular, are likely to be dissuaded by lengthy or cumbersome entry procedures because of their higher opportunity costs. When quantity restrictions are not calibrated to economic needs, they may be overly restrictive and impose unnecessarily high costs for their objectives. Lack of input from stakeholders is one reason the restrictions may not reflect economic needs. Additionally, entry paths and quantity restriction that lack transparency and predictability can create uncertainty for migrants and decrease their expected benefits.

Migration costs associated with the recruitment subcomponent of admissions can be significant. Fees for recruitment agents paid for job placements are some of the most significant costs. Important drivers of this cost are information asymmetries between workers who are familiar with their own skills but not with available jobs and employers who are familiar with available jobs but not with worker skills (Ahsan et al. 2014). Intermediaries are then able to intervene to link the two parties, charging a fee to bridge the information gap. Recruiters also provide services beyond intermediation, including helping migrants navigate complex migration processes, obtain necessary documentation, and travel domestically and internationally. The fee charged by recruiters often bundles these services together, thus obscuring the actual cost to migrants (Abella, Martin, and Yi 2015). Migrants also incur opportunity costs during the process of searching for employment abroad.

Migration costs also arise in the employment component of the migration system. Migration systems often set employment terms that restrict occupations, sectors, and employers. Restrictions that are too rigid limit the benefits that migrants can obtain from migrating, as occurs when migrants are not able to switch employers even if a higher wage is available. Employment terms that are overly short limit the benefits migrants can receive from work abroad. Renewing terms of employment can involve similar costs to those associated with entry procedures. The cost of sending remittances is an important financial cost incurred by migrants during employment.

Numerous costs can arise in the protection subcomponent. Wages and benefits that are less than expected, particularly less than those specified in a contract or that violate a legal minimum wage, create a cost for migrants, along with employment protections and benefits that are not enforced. Additionally, benefits that are not portable are lost to migrants who return to their host country. Migrants face additional costs when their qualifications are not recognized and when they work in jobs that do not deploy their skills. Costs also arise before departure as part of a sending country's protection regime. These include financial costs (for instance, contributions to migrant welfare funds, predeparture training fees, and health examination fees) and the opportunity costs of obtaining the necessary documentation and attending mandatory predeparture training.

Costs are incurred to migrants during exit if they are prevented from remigrating to a destination country where they have developed country-specific skills such as language competencies. "Cooling off" periods that prevent remigration for a certain time period impose similar costs. The absence of mechanisms to facilitate return and to create opportunities for migrants upon return can make return financially costly and waste skills gained abroad.

Governance and enforcement impact the costs that arise in all of the other components of the migration system. When legislation is unclear and institutional responsibilities are duplicative or misaligned, costs arise in various components of the migration system. Excessive bureaucracy may affect the efficiency of entry procedures while loopholes may arise in the oversight of private recruitment agencies. Costs can also arise when bi- and multilateral agreements are inconsistent with existing regulations. Patchwork legislation and ill-defined, ill-equipped institutions often translate into migrant protections that go unenforced or only partially enforced. Enforcement that is poorly coordinated and poorly targeted undermines even the best legislative and institutional frameworks, allowing costs to arise in each of the areas discussed above.

Breakdowns and weaknesses in the migration system can be grouped into five major problem areas that increase the costs for migrants seeking employment abroad (figure 5.2).

1. Migration systems often have difficulty *responding to economic needs.* Restrictions on the number of migrants a country can receive are frequently not aligned with the needs of the labor market. For instance, Malaysia imposes a levy on foreign workers in part to control the number of low-skilled migrants that enter the country; however, even as the economy has evolved, the levy has been left unadjusted for significant periods, for example, in 1999–2005, 2005–09, and 2011–16.

2. There is a *lack of coordination* within sending and receiving countries as well as among these countries, employers, trade unions, workers, and migrants. In Indonesia, lack of clarity in the responsibilities of the main agencies responsible for migration has led to interagency disputes, uncertainty among migrants about which agency to seek out in case of need, and duplicative processes. Although some bilateral agreements have been formulated to coordinate migration between sending and receiving countries in ASEAN, the agreements often lack transparency and input from employers and migrants.

3. *Information asymmetries* arise among migrants and employers. Migrants in ASEAN are heavily dependent on recruitment agencies and informal labor brokers to reduce these asymmetries. Recruitment agencies are critical intermediaries that guide migrants from Cambodia, Lao PDR, and Myanmar through the complicated migration process created by memorandums of understanding (MOUs) governing formal migration to Thailand.

4. Employers and recruitment agencies are able to exploit these information asymmetries to *extract rents* from the migration system. Labor brokers capture a significant portion of the difference in wages between sending and receiving countries simply for connecting employers and migrant workers (Ahsan et al. 2014). In Thailand, labor brokerage fees are hundreds of dollars higher for migrants from Cambodia and Lao PDR who choose to migrate formally (Jalilian and Reyes 2012).

5. Both sending and receiving countries tend to focus on the *short-term benefits and costs* of migration. Thailand, for example, has struggled to formulate a long-term migration policy. Periodic regularizations of undocumented migrants and a nationality verification process have been used as de facto migration policy. Sending countries have begun to consider the potential benefits of migration for labor markets and economic development more generally. However, programs to support returning migrants and to connect with their diaspora are in their infancy.

Migration costs in practice

Chapter 2 indirectly estimated the costs for workers to migrate across borders for work. This approach permitted cross-country comparisons of the costliness of labor mobility, but could not reveal the individual costs that migrants face when moving internationally for work or how these costs vary across different types of migrants. Comprehensive data on these costs are generally not available. However, recent surveys undertaken in many migration corridors and other research on migration costs suggest several features about the composition and drivers of migration costs (Abella and Martin 2016; Abella, Martin, and Yi 2015; Ahsan et al. 2014).

- Costs vary significantly across origins and destinations, gender, and even individuals. In the sample of countries investigated in Abella, Martin, and Yi (2015), the existence of bilateral agreements was associated with lower migration costs and the presence of labor supply companies with higher costs. Experience working abroad and unemployment were migrant characteristics associated with lower migration costs.

• The monetary costs of migration can be quite high relative to the income earned in the destination country.

• Migration costs tend to be higher as a proportion of wages for low- than for high-skilled migrants.

• Recruitment fees are often higher than legal limits.

• Because of the large supply of and lack of differentiation among low-skilled migrants, these migrants, and not their employers, often pay much of the recruitment fee component of migration costs.

Several recent analyses provide estimates of overall migration costs for migrants in ASEAN. Recent surveys of Vietnamese foreign workers in Malaysia and of Indonesian migrants to Malaysia who had repatriated, and several rough estimates from nongovernmental organizations and other sources provide an indication of the range of total migration costs from several countries to Malaysia (figure 5.3). Of the Vietnamese migrants to Malaysia, nearly all (95 percent) migrated via recruitment agents or brokers, with mean migration costs at $1,374 (in 2014 US$), equivalent to 3.5 months of earnings in Malaysia (ILO and KNOMAD 2015).[1] Migration costs for Vietnamese

FIGURE 5.3

Migration costs to Malaysia by source country

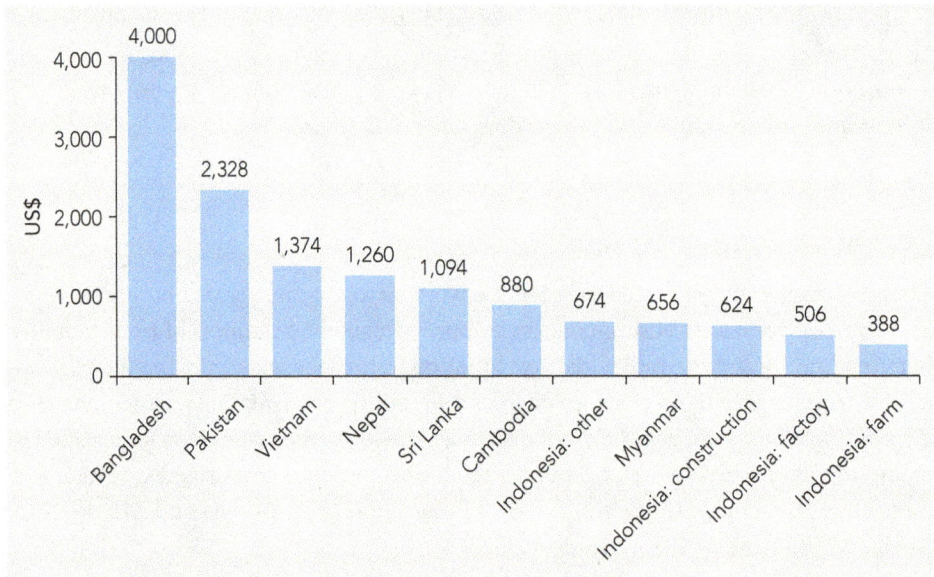

Source: Wickramasekara 2016 for Bangladesh; Siddiqui 2011 for Pakistan, Nepal, and Sri Lanka; ILO and KNOMAD 2015 for Vietnam; Bormann, Krishnan, and Neuner 2010 for Cambodia; World Bank 2016a for Indonesia; and Verité 2014 for Myanmar.

workers are significantly higher than those faced by Indonesian workers, likely reflecting in part the proximity of Indonesia and Malaysia.[2] Migration costs from Cambodia and Myanmar, which reflect only the recruitment fee paid by the migrant, lie between these two. Costs from Bangladesh and Pakistan are much higher than those from ASEAN countries, though a recent government-to-government agreement between Bangladesh and Malaysia seems to have reduced these costs significantly (Wickramasekara 2016).

The survey of Vietnamese migrants in Malaysia shows the importance of the recruitment fee in the total cost of migration. The survey is able to provide only a rough decomposition of migration costs because migrants, who frequently pay a lump sum to recruiters, are often unaware of the cost of each component (for instance, only 3 percent were aware of the cost of a visa). The survey suggests that recruitment fees, visa costs, and international and local travel are the primary drivers of migration costs (table 5.1). In the survey, eighty percent of the Vietnamese migrants reported borrowing money to pay the cost of migrating. Seventy percent reported that their employers paid their migration costs, and of these 96 percent had to repay their employer through deductions, including for recruitment fees. Most work between 25 and 36 months to repay their employers.

High migration costs are closely linked to undocumented migration. When migration costs are high, whether because of high financial costs or a lengthy admissions process, migrants are incentivized to seek out informal channels. A 2013 survey of Indonesian migrants conducted by the World Bank in collaboration with Statistics Indonesia shows that migration costs are particularly high for regular relative to irregular migrants (figure 5.4). High (documented) migration costs give migrants an incentive to break the law and migrate informally to avoid fees associated with documentation

TABLE 5.1

Composition of migration costs for Vietnamese migrants to Malaysia
(US$)

Cost component	Mean	Median	SD
Fees paid to recruiter	1248	1260	224
Visa	307	377	273
International travel	88	88	88
Local travel	69	40	87
Informal payments	30	16	38
Medical test	28	25	17
Passport	18	10	23
Health/life insurance	13	13	10
Security clearance	2	1	4
Total cost	1374	1370	280

Source: ILO and KNOMAD 2015.
Note: SD = standard deviation.

FIGURE 5.4

Average monetary migration costs for male Indonesian migrants in Malaysia

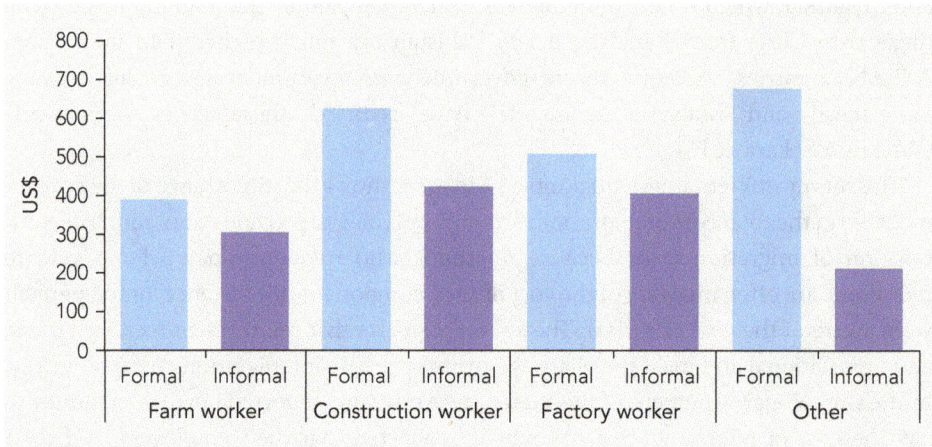

Source: World Bank 2016a.
Note: 2014 exchange rate 1US$ = 11,865 rupiah.

and to avoid losing wages while waiting for migration paperwork to be processed. Migration costs were higher for regular male migrant workers in every occupation covered in the survey, including by as much as 50 percent for construction workers.

Similarly, migration costs for migrants to Thailand from Cambodia and Lao PDR are much lower for irregular workers. A study of migrants to Thailand from Cambodia and Lao PDR estimates that migration costs are US$626 for regular migrants from Lao PDR and US$747 for those from Cambodia, several times higher than the costs for irregular migrants with and without documentation (table 5.2). For the regular immigrants, labor brokerage and passport fees are particularly significant. Brokerage costs, which may include other fees for documents or transportation if migrants paid in a lump sum, make up at least three-quarters of the cost in both cases. Transportation and passports make up the second- and third-largest costs for migrants from Lao PDR, and passport and physical checkups for those from Cambodia. Irregular migrants pay hundreds of dollars less in brokerage fees and, particularly in the case of migrants from Cambodia, much less for passports.

However, simply finding that the costs of regular migration to Thailand are high does not itself explain the prevalence of irregular migration to Thailand. After all, regular migrants likely earn more, are eligible for additional benefits, and may feel less vulnerable, meaning that the net benefit of migrating regularly may still be positive. A recent cost benefit analysis of migrants from Lao PDR and Cambodia to Thailand in the construction and domestic work sectors provides evidence that irregular migration remains a rational choice for migrants even after taking these potential benefits into account (Holumyong and Punpuing 2014). The net benefits of migration are never highest for migrants using the formal migration pathway

TABLE 5.2

Composition of migration costs for migrants to Thailand from Lao PDR and Cambodia
(US$)

Cost component	Lao PDR			Cambodia		
		Irregular			Irregular	
	Regular	With documentation	Without documentation	Regular	With documentation	Without documentation
Brokerage fee	484	15	96	625	33	136
Passport	42	14	0	110	4	0
Border pass	0	1	0	0	26	0
Physical checkup	37	4	0	10	0	0
Transportation	47	9	10	2	77	81
Other	16	13	0	0	10	0
Total	626	56	106	747	150	217

Source: Jalilian and Reyes 2012.

established in MOUs between Thailand and each country (figure 5.5). Irregular migration is preferable for domestic workers from both Lao PDR and Cambodia, while registration—irregular migration with subsequent legal registration in Thailand—is preferable for construction workers from both countries. The cost-benefit analysis also highlights the importance of addressing migration costs related to lengthy processing times. When the time costs associated with completing the MOU process are not considered—in other words, if the time costs were minimal—formal MOU pathways offer the largest net benefits in every case except that of domestic workers from Cambodia (figure 5.6).

Though these analyses of overall migration costs do not include the cost of sending remittances, remittance costs are a particularly important component of overall migration costs because they affect how earnings abroad are translated into benefits for non-migrating household members. In general, remittance costs are lower in corridors with larger migrant flows and more competition and are higher in corridors that are wealthier and have more banks in remittance markets (Beck and Martínez Pería 2009). In ASEAN, remittance costs to the three main destination countries averaged 8.4 percent of the total cost of sending US$200 in remittances in the third quarter of 2016, higher than both the global average of 7.4 percent and the East Asia and Pacific average of 8.2 percent (World Bank 2016b). The average remittance cost was lowest from Singapore at 4.6 percent followed by from Malaysia at 6.2 percent (table 5.3). Specifically, average remittance costs were lowest in the Singapore-to-Philippines corridor at 3.0 percent and in the Malaysia-to-Myanmar corridor at 3.5 percent. Thailand's average remittance cost was significantly higher at 14.4 percent, with high costs to send money to this country's three most important source countries, Cambodia, Lao PDR, and Myanmar.

FIGURE 5.5

Net benefits of migrating to Thailand with time costs

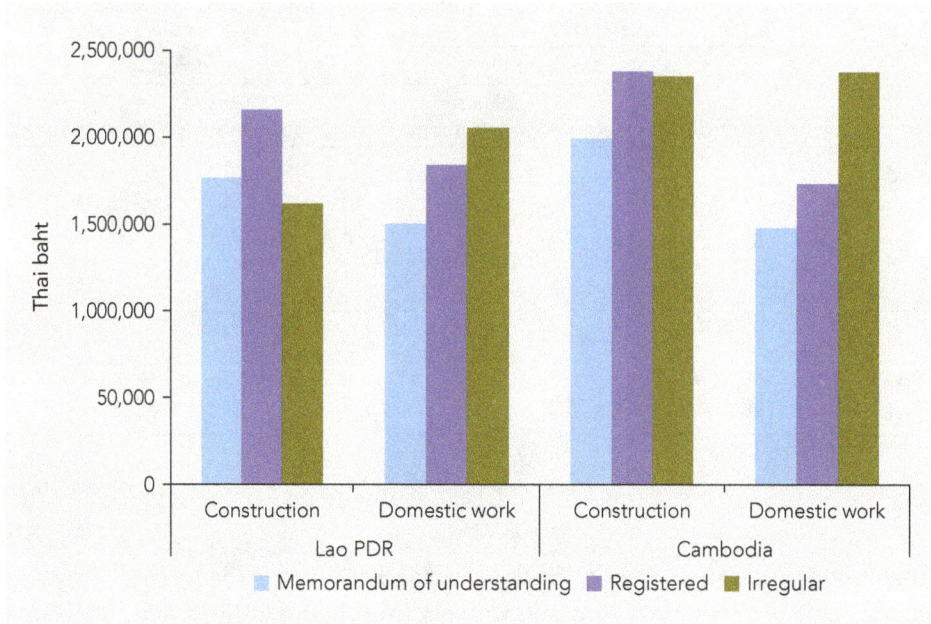

Source: Holumyong and Punpuing 2014.

FIGURE 5.6

Net benefits of migrating to Thailand without time costs

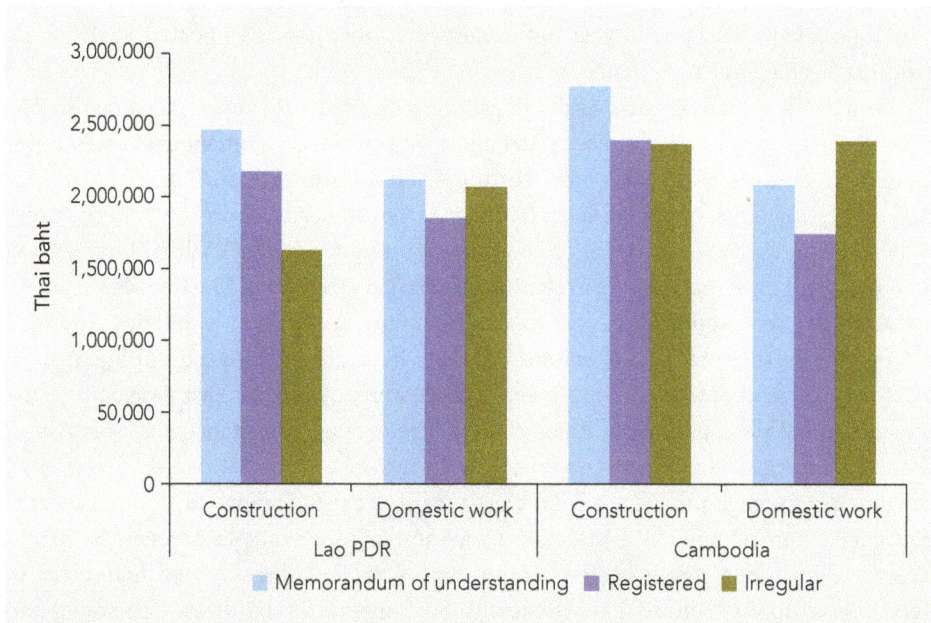

Source: Holumyong and Punpuing 2014.

TABLE 5.3
Remittance costs in ASEAN and comparator countries
(Cost to send US$200, expressed as a percentage of the total amount sent)

		To								
		IDN	KHM	LAO	MMR	MYS	PHL	THA	VNM	Ave
From	MYS	5.6			3.5		4.4	10.5	6.8	6.2
	SGP	4.8				5.1	3.0	5.5		4.6
	THA	15.2	14.1	14.4	12.3				16	14.4
	AUS	8.3				13.1	5.4	11.3	9.1	9.4
	CAN						6.2		8.0	7.1
	KOR								4.7	4.7
	USA	8.1					5.3	11.7	4.6	7.5

Source: Remittance Prices Worldwide, World Bank, http://remittanceprices.worldbank.org.
Note: AUS = Australia; CAN = Canada; IDN = Indonesia; KHM = Cambodia; KOR = Korea; LAO = Lao PDR; MMR = Myanmar; MYS = Malaysia; PHL = Philippines; SGP = Singapore; THA = Thailand; USA = United States; VNM = Vietnam.

Notes

1. These costs include fees for brokerage, passports, visas, health insurance, medical exams, police clearance, contract approval, training, skills tests, food, housing, and local and international transportation costs.

2. Indonesian migrants were asked, "How much was the total cost for working abroad?"

References

Abella, Manolo, and Philip Martin. 2016. *Guide on Measuring Policy Impact in ASEAN.* Geneva: International Labour Organization.

Abella, Manolo, Philip Martin, and Soonhwa Yi. 2015. "Why are Migration Costs High for Low-Skilled Workers? Evidence from Migrant Surveys."

Ahsan, Ahmad, Manolo Abella, Andrew Beath, Yukon Huang, Manjula Luthria, and Trang Van Nguyen. 2014. *International Migration and Development in East Asia and the Pacific.* Washington, DC: World Bank.

Beck, Thorsten, and María Soledad Martínez Pería. 2009. "What Explains the Cost of Remittances? An Examination across 119 Country Corridors." Policy Research Working Paper 5072, World Bank, Washington, DC.

Bormann, Sarah, Pathma Krishnan, and Monika E. Neuner. 2010. *Migration in a Digital Age: Migrant Workers in the Malaysian Electronics Industry: Case Studies on Jabil Circuit and Flextronics.* Berlin: World Economy, Ecology and Development.

Holumyong, Charampor, and Sureeporn Punpuing. 2014. "A Cost-Benefit Analysis of the Legal Status of Migrant Workers in Thailand." In *Managing International Migration for Development in East Asia*, edited by Richard H. Adams and Ahmad Ahsan, 263–82. Washington, DC: World Bank.

ILO (International Labour Organization) and KNOMAD (Global Knowledge Partnership on Migration and Development). 2015. "Migration Cost Survey: Vietnamese Workers in Malaysia."

Jalilian, Hossein, and Glenda Reyes. 2012. "Migrants of the Mekong." In *Costs and Benefits of Cross-Country Labour Migration in the GMS*, edited by Hossein Jalilian, 1–117. Singapore: ISEAS Publishing.

Ratha, Dilip, Soonhwa Yi, and Seyed Reza Yousefi. 2016. "Migration and Development: The Asian Experience." In *The Routledge Handbook of Migration*, edited by Anna Triandafyllidou, 260–277. New York: Routledge.

Siddiqui, Tasneem. 2011. "Cost in Bangladesh: Challenges of Governing Migration in the Countries of Origin," Working Paper Series No. 25, Refugee and Migratory Movements Research Unit (RMMRU), Dhaka.

Verité. 2014. *Forced Labor in the Production of Electronic Goods in Malaysia: A Comprehensive Study of Scope and Characteristics* Amherst, MA.

Wickramasekara, Piyasiri. 2016. "Review of the Government-to-Government Mechanism for the Employment of Bangladeshi Workers in the Malaysian Plantation Sector," International Labour Organization, Geneva.

World Bank. 2016a. "Indonesia's Global Workers: Juggling Opportunities and Risks." World Bank, Washington, DC.

World Bank. 2016b. "Remittance Prices Worldwide," Issue No. 19, World Bank, Washington, DC.

CHAPTER 6

Migration Policy in Receiving Countries

Introduction

Migrant-receiving countries in the Association of Southeast Asian Nations (ASEAN) are faced with the challenge of managing the inflow of migrant workers to fill labor shortages and skills gaps while also considering political constraints. The need for low-skilled workers to fill labor market demand, concerns about displacement of local workers by less-skilled immigrants, and a desire to benefit from the knowledge and skills of high-skilled immigrants often influence admissions policy. Receiving countries are also concerned about protecting immigrants from exploitative recruitment and employment practices that may make them less attractive destinations and put local populations into unfair competition with migrants. Because most migration in ASEAN is temporary, consideration must also be given to how to design migrant worker schemes to manage contract renewal or exit once employment contracts expire.

The framework of the migration system presented in the previous chapter can be applied to receiving countries to benchmark their migration systems (figure 6.1). Receiving countries set entry paths and quantity restrictions for incoming migrants and regulate recruitment agencies operating within their borders. They also set the terms of employment contracts, at times in conjunction with sending countries through bilateral agreements, and determine the availability of protections such as social protection and treatment under labor law. Finally, receiving countries establish exit policies in an attempt to ensure that temporary migrant workers return home when their employment terms expire.

FIGURE 6.1

Framework of the migration system in receiving countries

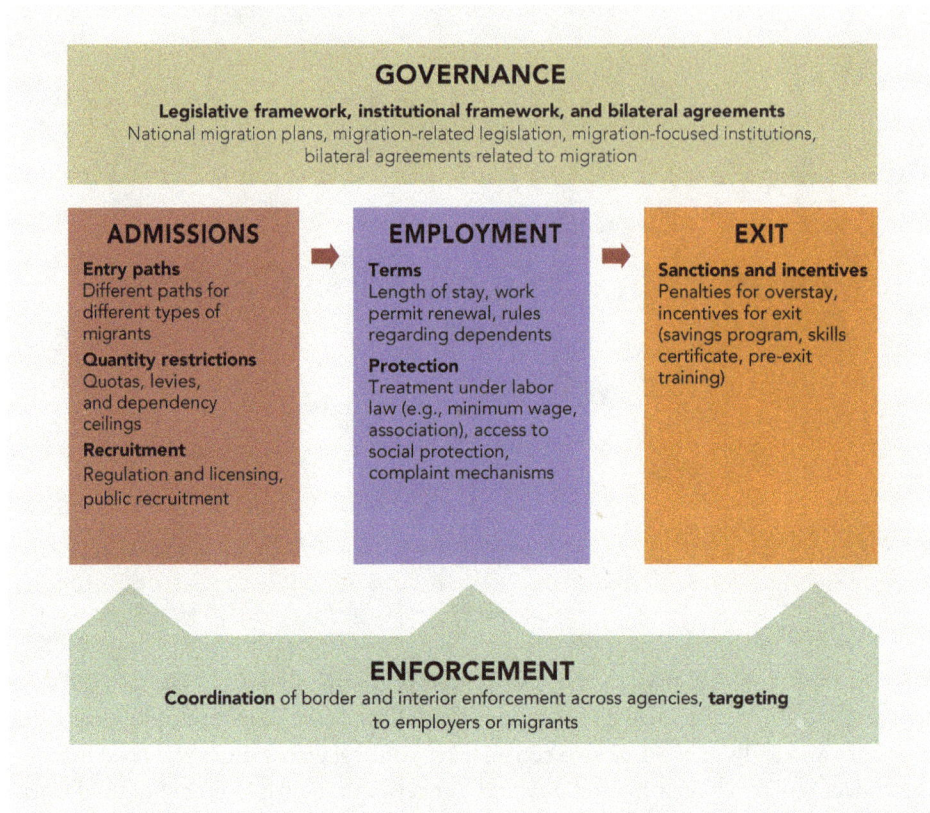

The rest of this chapter benchmarks the immigration systems of ASEAN's main receiving countries using this framework.[1] Singapore is a model in many respects, having achieved a migration system with high formality and strong links between the migration system and economic needs. The city-state's concerns focus mainly on managing an economy that is highly reliant on low- and mid-skilled workers to fill labor shortages resulting from strong economic growth and a shrinking working-age population, while addressing concerns about sluggish productivity growth and a perceived overreliance on foreign workers. Thailand, in contrast, has not been able to achieve a highly formal migration system. The system lacks mechanisms to respond to economic needs, permits high rents to recruitment agencies that navigate a complex migration bureaucracy, and is stuck in a cycle of short-term registrations and regularizations of informal migrants. The large presence of undocumented migrants and the continued preference of migrants from Cambodia, the Lao People's Democratic Republic, and Myanmar for irregular channels has made addressing undocumented migration a top priority. Still, the country has made some progress in engaging with its main sending countries. Malaysia lies somewhere between Singapore and Thailand.

Malaysia's migration system has elements designed to respond to economic needs. However, short-termism in migration decisions and a lack of coordination among stakeholders have resulted in ad hoc decision making that has undermined trust in and the effectiveness of the migration system. In Brunei Darussalam, the government's migration policy is shaped by a push to prioritize local employment in the private sector as concerns grow about overreliance on public sector employment, a result of significant oil revenues. Skilled migrants are often subject to the same restrictions as their lower-skilled counterparts, as the focus of migration policy is less on attracting the highly skilled and more on facilitating a transition to domestic employment across a range of sectors and skill-levels.

Table 6.1 summarizes areas for improvement and indicates the countries in which they are a particular concern.

TABLE 6.1
Priority areas for improvement in the migration systems of ASEAN's main receiving countries

	SGP	MYS	THA	BRN
GOVERNANCE				
Legislation				
No national migration plan	X	X	X	—
Patchwork legislation and regulation	O	X	X	—
Institutions				
Lack of coordination/clear institutional roles	O	X	X	—
Weak tripartite relationship	O	X	X	—
Bilateral agreements				
MOUs not responsive to economic needs	n.a.	X	X	—
ADMISSIONS				
Entry paths				
Unclear application process	O	X	X	—
Complicated and cumbersome procedures	O	X	X	—
Not well-differentiated by skill level	O	O	X	X
Quantity restrictions				
Not implemented or not binding	O	X	X	—
Unclear objectives	O	X	n.a.	—
Not responsive to economic needs	O	X	n.a.	—
Lack transparency and predictability	O	X	n.a.	—
Recruitment				
Lack of oversight of private agencies	O	O	X	—
Ineffective licensing	O	X	—	—
High recruitment costs	X	X	X	—

table continues next page

TABLE 6.1
Priority areas for improvement in the migration systems of ASEAN's main receiving countries (continued)

	SGP	MYS	THA	BRN
EMPLOYMENT				
Terms				
Overly rigid	X	X	X	—
Not well-differentiated by skill level	O	O	X	—
Lengthy and time-consuming renewal	O	X	X	—
Protection				
Protections/access different for migrants and locals	X	X	X	—
Weak protections for domestic workers	X	X	X	X
EXIT				
Sanctions and incentives				
Employer-driven process	X	X	O	X
Lack of coordination with sending countries	X	X	O	—
Moral hazard related to regularization	O	X	X	—
ENFORCEMENT				
Coordination				
Lack of coordination with sending countries	X	X	O	—
Lack of proactive enforcement	X	X	X	—
Targeting				
Focus on migrant worker more than employer	O	X	X	—
Focus on security more than protections	O	X	O	—

Note: — = not available; X = problem area is a priority for a given country; O = problem area is not a priority; n.a. = not applicable. BRN = Brunei Darussalam; MOU = memorandum of understanding; MYS = Malaysia; SGP = Singapore; THA = Thailand.

Governance

Legislative framework

ASEAN's main receiving countries have not published national strategy documents outlining priorities for migration policy. Malaysia has gone the farthest toward articulating an official migration policy. The 11th Malaysia Plan includes improving the management of foreign workers as a strategy to enhance labor market efficiency and accelerate economic growth. The Plan calls for placing a cap on foreign workers at 15 percent of the population, clarifying responsibilities for managing migrant workers, and improving the recruitment system. In Singapore, the prime minister announced a slowdown in immigrant worker flows in 2009, and the government has a soft target to keep migrant workers at 30 percent of the workforce; however, no public plan for managing migration has been produced (Singapore, ESC 2010). Thailand has not produced a migration strategy.

Despite its lack of a national strategy, Singapore manages migration through a comprehensive legislative framework, whereas Malaysia does so through a patchwork of legislation and policy pronouncements. Separate legislation governs entry and exit into Singapore (Immigration Act, last amended in 2008); the management of foreign workers, including issuance of work permits, the obligations of employers, and punishment for illegal employment (Employment and Foreign Manpower Act, last amended in 2012); and the regulation of recruitment agencies (Employment Agencies Act, last amended in 2011) (Yue 2011). These laws, in conjunction with several others governing employment conditions, provide a comprehensive system of rules for a migrant's entry into, employment in, and exit from Singapore.

Although Malaysia has developed a full set of employment permits to allow low-, mid-, and high-skilled migrants to work in the country, no comprehensive law or system of laws has guided the creation of these permits. Current legislation deals primarily with overseeing entry into the country and punishing undocumented migrants and their employers (Immigration Act 1959/63 with amendments in 1998 and 2002); ensuring that local employees are not disadvantaged by the employment of foreign workers (Employment Act 1955, with an amendment in 1998); and regulating recruitment (Private Employment Agencies Act 1981).[2] In part as a result of the lack of a comprehensive legislative framework, migration policy making has frequently occurred through pronouncements of new policies by the Malaysian Ministry of Home Affairs or the Ministry of Human Resources as problems have emerged. On several occasions, these policies have been quickly reversed, revised, or delayed because of public reaction. This occurred twice in 2016 with the announcement of a large increase to the foreign worker levy, which was then reduced, and with the announcement that the foreign worker levy would no longer be deductible from migrant workers' salaries, which was delayed for a year.

Components of Thailand's main migration-related legislation have never been implemented, and important policy decisions have been made through cabinet resolutions. The 1979 Immigration Act regulates entry into Thailand, while the 2008 Alien Employment Act is the main legislation regulating the employment of migrants. The latter act regulates the occupations in which migrants are permitted to work and establishes tools for hiring workers from Cambodia, Lao PDR, and Myanmar (Paitoonpong 2011). However, implementation of the 2008 Act has been limited with important elements not applied, such as a foreign worker levy and committees to review the employment of migrants. Registrations and regularizations of undocumented migrants from Cambodia, Lao PDR, and Myanmar have been undertaken on an as-needed basis by cabinet resolutions that have been issued regularly but sporadically. This has created uncertainty for existing undocumented migrants but has also incentivized further undocumented migration by suggesting that regularizations will continue to happen.

Institutional framework

Thailand and Malaysia both have inter-ministerial committees charged with policy making. Until 2014, Thailand's inter-ministerial Illegal Alien Workers Management

Committee was charged with policy making for irregular migrants and low-skilled immigration more generally. However, the conflicting priorities of different ministries—facilitating migration or regularization in the case of the Ministry of Labor and the Ministry of Health versus security concerns in the case of the Ministry of the Interior and the National Security Council—undermined the effectiveness of the Committee (World Bank 2006; Hall 2011). The military-led government National Council for Peace and Order replaced the Illegal Alien Workers Management Committee with the Committee and Subcommittee on Solving Problems of Migrant Workers. The impact of this change is still uncertain. In Malaysia, the Cabinet Committee on Foreign Workers and Illegal Immigrants, an inter-ministerial committee of 13 ministers, is chaired by the deputy prime minster with the Ministry of Home Affairs as secretariat. The Cabinet Committee is responsible for setting migration policy including recruitment criteria, sectors and source countries that are eligible for migrant workers, and other requirements. In Singapore, responsibility for migration policy making generally lies with the Ministry of Manpower, though the policy making process is less clear (Koh et al. 2017).

For managing foreign workers, Singapore and Thailand have single agencies in charge of the various functions involved. In Singapore, the Ministry of Manpower is responsible for the overall management and regulation of foreign workers. Different divisions are charged with issuing work passes (Work Pass Division); overseeing working conditions and the well-being of foreign workers, enforcing policy, and regulating recruitment (Foreign Manpower Management Division); attracting global talent (International Manpower Division); and overseeing policy (Manpower Planning and Policy Division) (Teng 2014). In Thailand's Ministry of Labor, the Office of Foreign Workers Administration in the Department of Employment regulates recruitment, oversees migrant worker registration, issues work permit applications, and coordinates with various agencies.

Two ministries share responsibility for different aspects of foreign worker management in Malaysia, an arrangement that can lead to duplicative roles and misaligned objectives. First, the Ministry of Home Affairs houses the Department of Immigration, which manages admissions; the Foreign Worker Management Division, which manages applications for foreign workers from employers; and the police department that has responsibility for law enforcement matters, such as criminal cases against migrant workers, border patrol, and undocumented workers. Second, the Department of Labor of the Ministry of Human Resources regulates recruitment agencies and is responsible for employment-related issues concerning migrants.[3] While the 11th Malaysia Plan seeks to clarify these roles, the ministries are currently responsible for similar tasks: both must approve an employer's application to hire a foreign worker, and both are involved in licensing agencies that participate in the recruitment of foreign workers. The overlapping responsibilities complicate applications for foreign workers and undermine the agencies' ability to determine which and how many migrant workers should be admitted. Instances of joint enforcement operations are rare.

Tripartite relationships vary in ASEAN's receiving countries. In Singapore, the government is known for a close relationship with employers and labor[4] that allows for negotiation on matters related to foreign workers (Teng 2014). In Malaysia, the relationship between employers and the government is less institutionalized. Negotiations about policy changes seem to play out in public, as when levy changes have been announced and have prompted strong reactions from the Malaysian Employers Federation. Still, dialogue does occur between industry associations and the government as the associations provide input on decisions about dependency ceilings (Abella and Martin 2016). Similarly, labor unions do not have an institutionalized role in Malaysia. The extent of collaboration between private sector employers and migration officials in Thailand is less clear. The 2008 Alien Employment Act envisioned committees of employers and trade unions to review the employment of migrant workers, though these do not seem to have been created. However, the government's regularization campaigns have been in part a reaction to employers' continued demand for lower-skilled workers.

Singapore and Malaysia both have special public agencies devoted to attracting and keeping global talent. In Malaysia, the Expatriate Services Division within the Immigration Department of the Ministry of Home Affairs is responsible for managing the immigration of mid- and high-skilled workers[5]. The Expatriate Services Division collaborates with TalentCorp, a specialized agency with a mandate to attract highly skilled foreign talent to Malaysia and to run the Malaysia Expatriate Talent Service Centre (MYXpats Centre) that issues employment passes to mid- and high-skilled workers. TalentCorp seeks to engage with talented Malaysians abroad and encourage their return and to retain particularly talented expatriates who have short-term employment passes for longer periods. Singapore's International Manpower Division within the Ministry of Manpower has offices throughout the world to attract talented expatriates to Singapore. The National Population and Talent Division in the Prime Minister's Office develops strategies for engaging Singaporeans overseas.

Bilateral agreements and memorandums of understanding

Thailand employs memorandums of understanding (MOUs) to manage low-skilled immigration flows from its main sending countries. MOUs were signed with its main sending countries: Lao PDR in 2002 and Cambodia and Myanmar in 2003.[6] The MOUs govern all aspects of the migration process from admissions to employment and exit, and pay particular attention to efforts to prevent irregular migration. They established a formal migration process from Cambodia, Lao PDR, and Myanmar to Thailand for the first time; they also set the stage for regularization programs for informal migrants in Thailand. The MOUs have also provided a venue for regular meetings between the governments of Cambodia, Lao PDR, and Myanmar and that of Thailand on migration-related issues.

Malaysia supplements its regulatory framework for migration with MOUs, while Singapore has not used the bilateral approach. Malaysia has signed MOUs with Bangladesh, Cambodia, China, India, Indonesia, Pakistan, the Philippines, Sri Lanka, Thailand, and Vietnam (Blomberg and Sothear 2015). These agreements supplement Malaysia's legislated immigration system, and they include elements such as recommended recruitment fees (in the case of Indonesia and Bangladesh); standard contracts for foreign workers (Bangladesh, Indonesia, and Vietnam); a minimum wage (Bangladesh);

migrant protections such as preventing employers from keeping a worker's passport (Indonesia and Bangladesh); and responsibilities of different parties (India and Indonesia) (Wickramasekara 2015). Malaysia also signed a government-to-government recruitment agreement with Bangladesh that seemed to reduce migration costs significantly. The MOU governed immigration into the palm oil sector and replaced private recruitment agencies with a public recruitment model. Migration costs declined as much as 8 to 10 times; however, the scope of the agreement was limited by a cap imposed by the Malaysian government, and fewer than 10,000 workers were ultimately recruited despite the interest expressed by 1.4 million Bangladeshis (Wickramasekara 2015, 2016). A more recent MOU has reportedly allowed private recruitment agencies to participate in the process. Singapore, in contrast, does not currently have any bilateral agreements or MOUs governing immigration.

Despite some successes, Malaysia and Thailand's MOUs are overly procedural and do not do enough to reflect economic needs. In both countries, the MOU negotiation process has not been transparent, and it has incorporated limited input from stakeholders. In both cases, this reflects an over-emphasis on the procedural aspects of migration and a lack of emphasis on using the agreements to reflect economic needs. In Thailand, the MOU migration channel involves a months-long application process and payment of fees to recruiters to help migrants navigate the process. This had led most migrants to shun formal for informal migration pathways with many not seeing any benefit from migrating through the MOU channel (MMN and AMC 2013). Malaysia has experienced a similar situation. Its 2011 MOU with Indonesia governing domestic workers established fixed recruitment fees that appear to have led migrant domestic workers to seek out informal channels (Harkins 2016). Data collection and sharing and monitoring and evaluation have been inadequate in the agreements of both countries. In Malaysia, MOUs are generally not made public. Additionally, it is not clear how Malaysian labor standards and migrant quotas included in MOUs fit with existing legislation and regulations.

One of ASEAN's primarily sending countries, Lao PDR has used bilateral agreements to fill skills gaps for high-skilled labor and for migration-related technical assistance. For instance, Lao PDR has an agreement for the Philippines to provide technical assistance on migration and other labor-related areas (MMN and AMC 2013).

Admissions

Entry paths

Singapore has well-defined entry paths for different types of workers. Workers receive passes according to their skill level, and each pass includes well-defined tracks that further differentiate foreign workers by skill and other characteristics. The stringency of entry requirements and the generosity of terms and rights both increase with skill level. Lower-skilled workers are eligible for work permits that are issued in the construction, manufacturing, marine shipyard, process, services, and domestic work sectors, all of which are considered to have difficulty attracting local workers (Teng 2014). There is no minimum salary to obtain a permit, but migrants from only certain countries of origin are allowed to work in certain sectors. Mid- or semi-skilled workers who earn at least S$2,200 each month and have a degree or diploma and relevant work experience can obtain S Passes. There is no restriction on country of origin. Higher-skilled workers are eligible for the Employment Pass, which has the most stringent entry requirements but also the most generous terms of stay in Singapore. Employment Passes are for foreign professionals, managers, and executives who have a job offer in Singapore; earn at least S$3,600 each month (with an expectation that more experienced workers will have higher salaries); and have certain minimum qualifications.[7]

Malaysia also has well-defined entry paths for different types of workers. Low-skilled migrants, who generally earn less than RM2,400 a month, enter Malaysia by obtaining a Visitors Pass (Temporary Employment), or VP(TE). VP(TE)s are only issued in manufacturing, construction, plantations, agriculture, services, and domestic work. Passes are restricted by country for certain sectors. For mid- and high-skilled migrants, Malaysia has three main entry paths, differentiated by salary. Employment Pass (Category I) is for migrant workers earning a basic monthly salary of at least RM5,000 per month with an employment contract of at least two years. Employment Pass (Category II) is for migrant workers with the same minimum monthly salary but with employment contracts of less than two years. Finally, Employment Pass (Category III) is for migrant workers earning between RM2,500 and RM5,000 with employment contracts that do not exceed one year.

Entry paths are less differentiated in Thailand and Brunei Darussalam. Only low-skilled migrants from Cambodia, Lao PDR, and Myanmar can enter Thailand legally via the admissions process established in Thailand's MOUs with each country. There is, however, no definition of a low-skilled migrant, and there is no entry path for mid-skilled migrants. High-skilled migrants, including intracompany transferees, can obtain a work permit if they have a prospective employer. They must have a job offer, at least a bachelor's degree, and be paid an occupation-specific minimum wage. These migrants are not permitted to work in 39 occupations, including accounting, engineering, and architecture, that are covered by ASEAN's mutual recognition agreements. Brunei Darussalam has a single entry path for all foreign workers (Ruhs 2016). The country has recently embarked on a rationalization of the application process that consolidates two separate entry procedures into one, in an attempt to facilitate entry.

Entry into Thailand through the MOU channel involves numerous and complicated procedures that result in lengthy application times. This path requires 25 steps and the involvement of numerous agencies in Thailand as well as in Cambodia, Lao PDR, and Myanmar. Private recruitment agencies have become necessary to fill information gaps and help employers and migrants navigate the recruitment process even though it is nominally government-sponsored. The process takes an estimated 89 days for migrants from Myanmar, a minimum of 62 working days for those from Cambodia, and a minimum of 55 for those from Lao PDR (ILO 2015). These processing times are significantly longer than those in many Organisation for Economic Co-operation and Development (OECD) countries and much longer than the few days that are required to migrate informally (figure 6.2). These lengthy procedures are responsible in part for the low uptake of the MOU channel: migrants can find cheaper alternatives, such as irregular migration with the possibility of registration. As of February 2016, about 300,000 migrants had used the MOU channel compared to about 1 million informal migrants who had been regularized through Thailand's national verification program (IOM 2016).

FIGURE 6.2

Processing times for employment passes in Malaysia, Thailand, and OECD countries

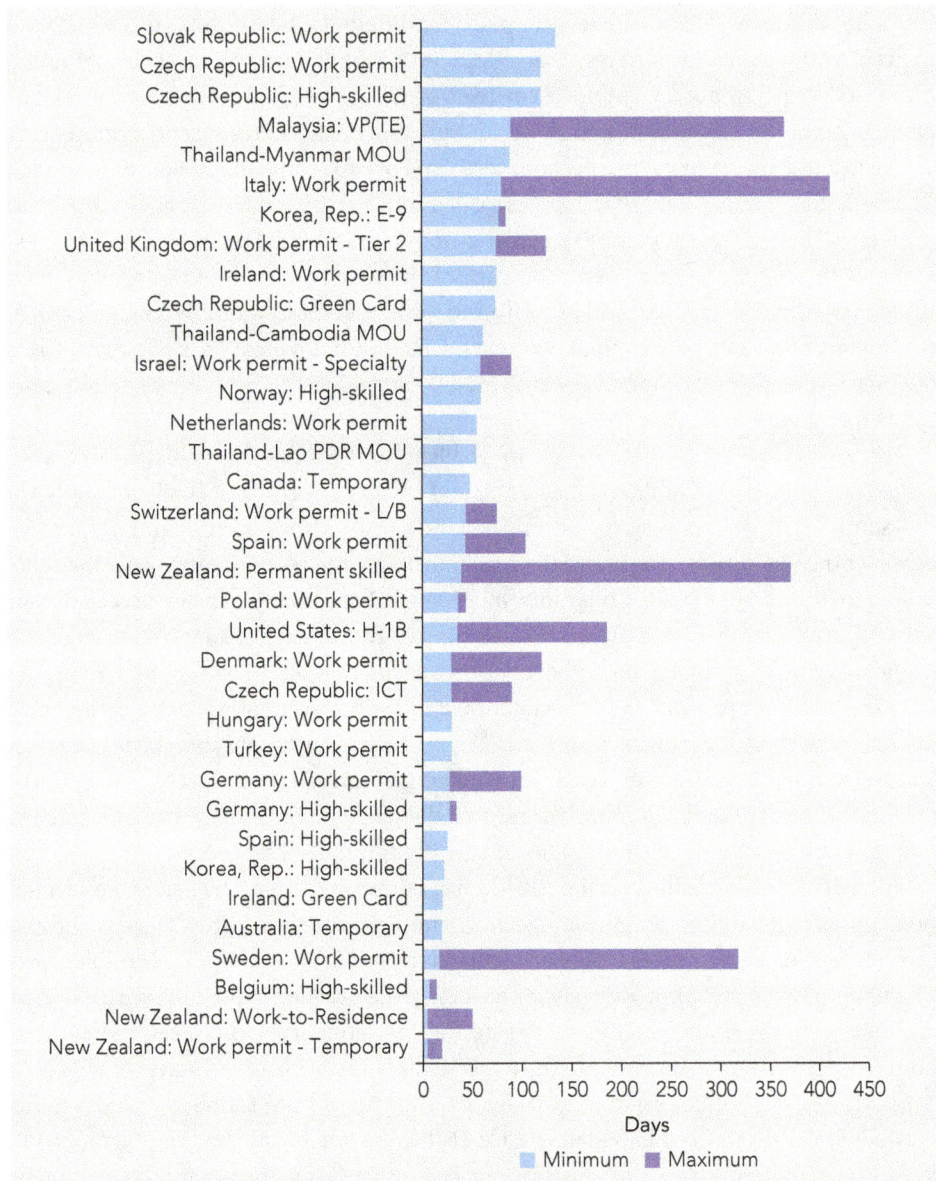

Sources: Abella and Martin 2016 for Malaysia; ILO 2015 for Thailand; and OECD 2014 for the OECD.

The entry of high-skilled migrants into Thailand is also complex, requiring high-skilled migrants to apply for separate work, stay, and reentry permits. Migrants must first apply for an entry visa at a Thai embassy or consulate. This allows them to enter the country for 90 days and apply for a work permit from within Thailand. After the work permit is issued, prospective migrants must apply in person to extend their visa up to one year. The migrant must apply for extensions of the work permit and the visa annually. A one-stop service center is available to expedite visa extension and work permit issuance for certain categories of skilled workers.

The entry process can also be time-consuming, involved, and opaque in Malaysia. Obtaining the VP(TE) for low-skilled workers involves approval from both the Ministry of Home Affairs and the Ministry of Human Resources, a medical examination in both the origin and destination country, two visas, and a labor market test that can involve advertising a post for as long as 30 days, twice as long as posting requirements in many OECD member countries (figure 6.3). In total, the approval process ranges from a minimum of three months to a maximum of one year, much longer than most OECD entry schemes (figure 6.2). A recent survey of employers undertaken by the Malaysian Employers Federation in conjunction with the International Labour Organization (ILO) showed that many employers find the application process to be lengthy and unclear (MEF 2014). In a recognition of the cumbersome process, improvements have been made in recent years to simplify the process, including the creation of a centralized system to handle applications and help employers comply with requirements.

Singapore and Malaysia both have special entry paths for particularly high-skilled workers that provide additional benefits, particularly additional flexibility. Singapore's Personalized Employment Pass allows current Employment Pass holders and foreign professionals to remain in Singapore for six months without a job to look for work and exempts them from applying for another pass if they change jobs. Current Employment Pass holders must earn at least S$12,000 a month to be eligible for the Personalized

FIGURE 6.3

Duration of labor market test in Malaysia and OECD countries

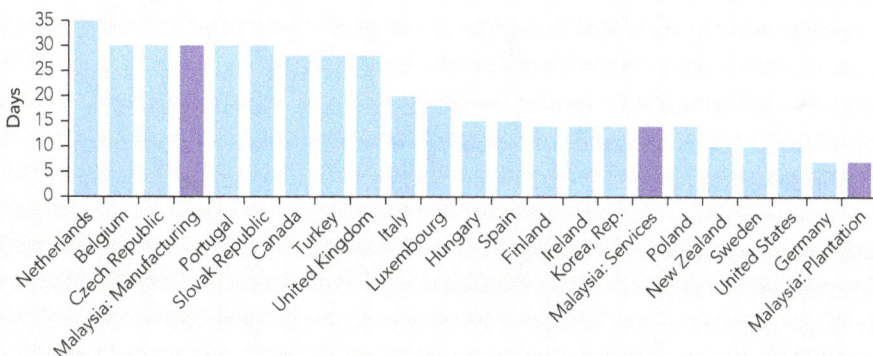

Sources: Abella and Martin (2016) for Malaysia and OECD (2014) for the OECD.
Note: OECD = Organisation for Economic Co-operation and Development.

Employment Pass; overseas foreign professionals must earn at least S$18,000 a month. In contrast, Malaysia's Resident Pass-Talent (RP-T) is for highly skilled expatriates who have worked in Malaysia for three years and already hold Malaysia's Employment Pass. RP-T requirements include a minimum of a diploma, five years of work experience, and an income of greater than RM180,000 per year. Benefits include the ability to live and work in Malaysia for 10 years, flexibility to change employers without renewing the pass, and passes for dependents. Singapore, Malaysia, and Thailand all offer entry to investors or entrepreneurs.

ASEAN's major migrant-sending countries offer differentiated entry paths for immigrants of different skill levels but are focused mainly on creating channels for high-skilled immigrants. The Philippines offers several paths for the entry of high-skilled migrants. Skilled migrants can enter the country on a temporary basis if they have an offer from an employer. The Philippines requires employers to comply with a relatively stringent labor market test by advertising the position for at least two weeks and checking whether the position is covered by the national understudy program (EU and DOLE 2011). If it is, employers are required to train two Philippine workers for the position filled by the foreign worker. The Philippines has also created a shortage list to exempt occupations from the labor market test (Jaymalin 2014). The Philippines offers various entry channels for intracompany transfers, investors, and specialists or professionals from countries with which the Philippines has reciprocal migration agreements. In Indonesia, labor migration is predominantly restricted to skilled professionals, though high-skilled sectors are at times also subject to restrictions to prioritize domestic employment. Employers must show that foreign workers hold appropriate qualifications for their position, or else have a minimum of five years of experience. Residence permits for work purposes are restricted to certain sectors and positions.

In Vietnam, immigration is generally quite restricted, though a new immigration law[8] that became effective in 2015 eased the restrictions somewhat. Immigration policy restricts entry primarily to the highly skilled, including managers, executive directors, specialists, and technical workers who must fulfill certain minimum requirements. The immigration systems of Cambodia and Lao PDR provide entry paths for migrant workers that preference skilled workers somewhat through more relaxed dependency ceilings for these workers. Cambodia's immigration system provides work permits to migrant workers who may enter the country without employment. The system makes hiring skilled migrants easier than hiring less-skilled migrants. Policies governing immigration to Myanmar can be confusing and change often. The visa regime for migrant workers in Myanmar is particularly challenging, as migrants are required to submit separate applications for work, stay, and at times reentry permits. The limited provisions for labor migration that are in place favor skilled migrants.

With a few exceptions, ASEAN countries are perceived as being less capable of attracting talent than migrant-receiving countries in the OECD. The World Economic Forum's Global Competitiveness Index includes a measure of a country's capability to attract talent (figure 6.4). Singapore ranks very high on the 7-point scale, scoring a 6 or about the same as the United Kingdom and the United States. Malaysia also scores

FIGURE 6.4

Capacity to attract talent in ASEAN and comparator countries, 2015–16

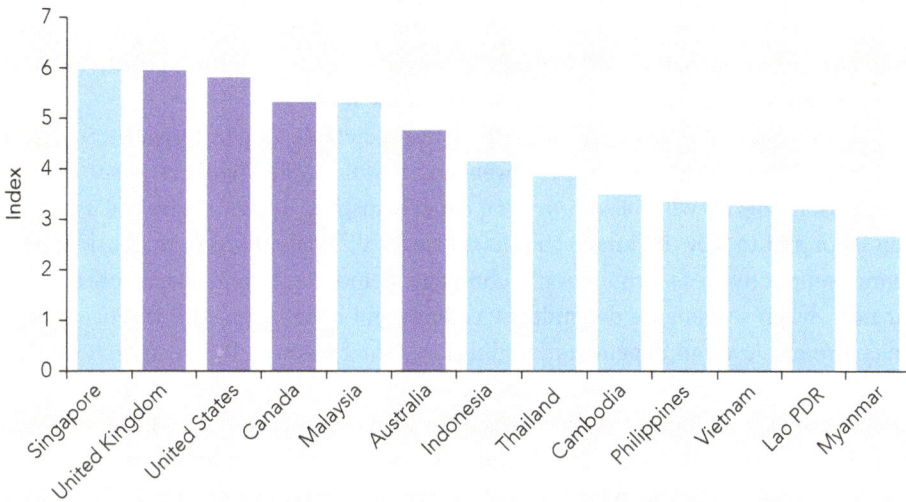

Source: Global Competitiveness Index, World Economic Forum.
Note: The index ranges from 1 to 7; 7 is the best score; ASEAN = Association of Southeast Asian Nations.

quite high, about the same as Canada. The other ASEAN countries, however, all score 4 or less, indicating that they are less well-placed to attract talent.

Quantity restrictions

Singapore uses a system of dependency ceilings and levies to regulate the number and type of migrant workers in the city-state. Singapore has publicly stated an intention to keep foreign workers at one-third of the workforce but also to improve these workers' skill level (Singapore, ESC 2010). Maintaining the ethnic balance of the city-state is also a concern, reflected in a preference for certain countries of origin that have historically provided migrants to Singapore. Singapore has used its system of dependency ceilings and levies to achieve these objectives. To this end, there are no quantity restrictions for the high-skilled workers hired under Employment Passes, Personalized Employment Passes, and the EntrePasses (for foreign entrepreneurs). Mid-skilled workers entering via S Passes and lower-skilled workers entering via work permits, however, do face such restrictions with these calibrated to incentivize the employment of more highly skilled foreign workers from certain source countries and the upskilling of existing foreign workers (Yue 2011). There is an overall dependency ceiling for each firm in a sector with levies that increase with the foreign worker share and decrease with the foreign work-er's skill level. For instance, the overall dependency ceiling for work permits in the man-ufacturing sector is set at 60 percent of a firm's workforce. Levies are set at S$370 for lower-skilled employees and S$250 for high-skilled employees in firms with a foreign worker share of less than 25 percent. Levies in firms with a foreign worker share of between 50 percent and the overall sectoral cap of 60 percent are significantly higher at S$650 and S$550 for lower- and higher-skilled workers, respectively. These higher-skilled foreign workers are identified by using indicators such as academic qualifications, skills evaluations, and minimum salary. The foreign worker levy cannot be passed on to migrant workers: the Ministry of Manpower monitors employer payments to foreign workers and can penalize firms that deduct the levy.

Singapore's quantity restrictions are flexible, predictable, and transparent. Singapore uses quantity restrictions to funnel lower- and middle-skilled workers to sectors with shortages. It does so while also providing a mechanism to disincentivize the use of foreign labor and to slow its intake should shortages dissipate. Singapore considers economic competitiveness, production technology, demography, and social cohesion and harmony when revising its dependency ceilings and levies (Teng 2014). For example, Singapore has lowered dependency ceilings in recent years in the manufacturing and services sectors with the aim of reducing reliance on foreign labor in these sectors. Similarly, Singapore increased levies in the construction sector in 2015 because of concerns about low productivity growth; in contrast, productivity improvements in the manufacturing sector meant levies in that sector remained the same (World Bank 2015). The use of levies instead of a hard numerical limit allows employers to continue to hire foreign workers in times of high demand, which would not be possible in a system of quotas. Changes to Singapore's quantity restrictions are announced well in advance. While Singapore's system for calculating dependency ceilings and levies is complex, the city-state provides online tools to assist employers who are trying to determine the number of foreign workers they can hire and the levies they will need to pay.[9] The government of Singapore also tries to collaborate with employer and labor representatives to understand the demand for labor and the needs of migrant workers. There is concern, however, that government deliberations on matters related to foreign labor are not transparent (Teng 2014).

Like Singapore, Malaysia has a system of both dependency ceilings and levies. Malaysia's dependency ceilings vary by sector and are set at the employer level according to firm characteristics such as exports, capital base, and types of projects. The ceilings put a cap on the foreign worker share of a firm's workforce. Malaysia's foreign worker levy was first introduced in 1991 with the objective of controlling the number of foreign workers, and it has been adjusted six times since. The levy varies by sector and geography with levies highest in the services and construction sectors in Peninsular Malaysia. Levies do not apply to mid- and high-skilled immigrants receiving employment passes.

Malaysia's system of quantity restrictions could benefit from additional transparency and predictability. The process of setting both dependency ceilings and foreign worker levies in Malaysia is unclear. Industry associations, however, do provide some input. Nonetheless, employers complain about a lack of transparency in setting the ceilings (MEF 2014). On the basis of conversations with officials and industry organizations, Abella and Martin (2016) describe the process of setting the ceilings as a "guesstimate." Indeed, employers frequently express surprise about announcements of levy changes and complain about their potential impacts, which have twice led to adjustments of those policies after their public announcement. Finally, there does not seem to be any formal coordination to ensure that levies, dependency ceilings, and other tools, like MOUs that include hiring targets, work together to meet Malaysia's stated goal of limiting foreign workers to 15 percent of the labor force.

Additionally, Malaysia's system of quantity restrictions is not attuned to labor market needs. Levies have been left unadjusted for significant periods of time, such as between 1999 and 2005, between 2005 and 2009, and between 2011 and 2016. This suggests a lack of responsiveness to economic and labor market needs. As described above, employer input about their needs is limited. The purpose of the foreign worker levy is also disputed. Responsibility for paying the levy has shifted from the foreign worker during the 1990s and 2000s to the employer in 2009, back to the foreign worker in 2013. This suggests a lack of consensus about the objective of the foreign worker levy that is alternatively described as a way of making foreign workers compensate Malaysia for their use of public goods and services and as a tool for rightsizing the employment of migrant workers according to the needs of the economy. Indeed, these shifts in responsibility seem to have had a greater impact than levy increases on the number of passes issued (figure 6.5 and figure 6.6).

Thailand's system of quantity restrictions for low-skilled migrants has never been implemented. In principle, the MOU channel for migration from Cambodia, Lao PDR, and Myanmar to Thailand should operate with a system of sector-specific levies and quotas with employers receiving a quota allotment from a Provincial Employment Office. In practice, levies have never been instituted and quotas are not binding because

FIGURE 6.5

Total VP(TE)s issued in Malaysia

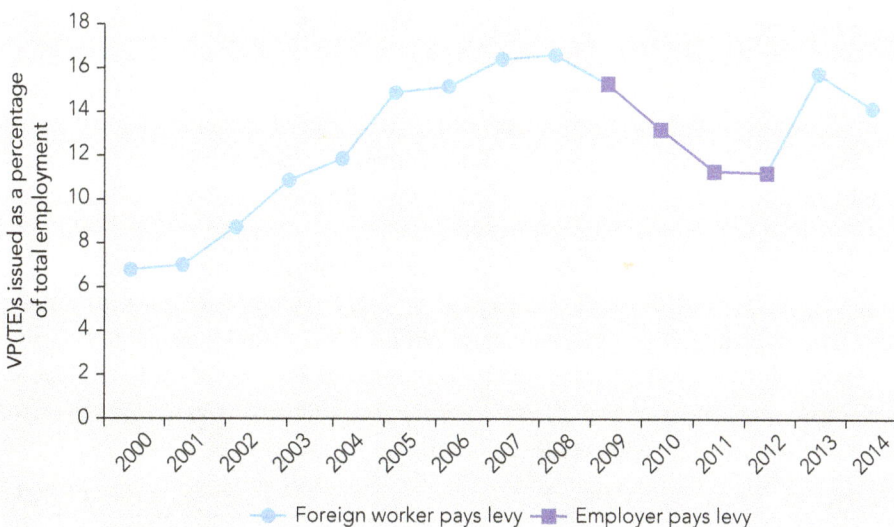

Source: World Bank 2015.
Note: VP(TE) = Visitors Pass (Temporary Employment).

FIGURE 6.6
VP(TE)s issued in the services sector in Malaysia

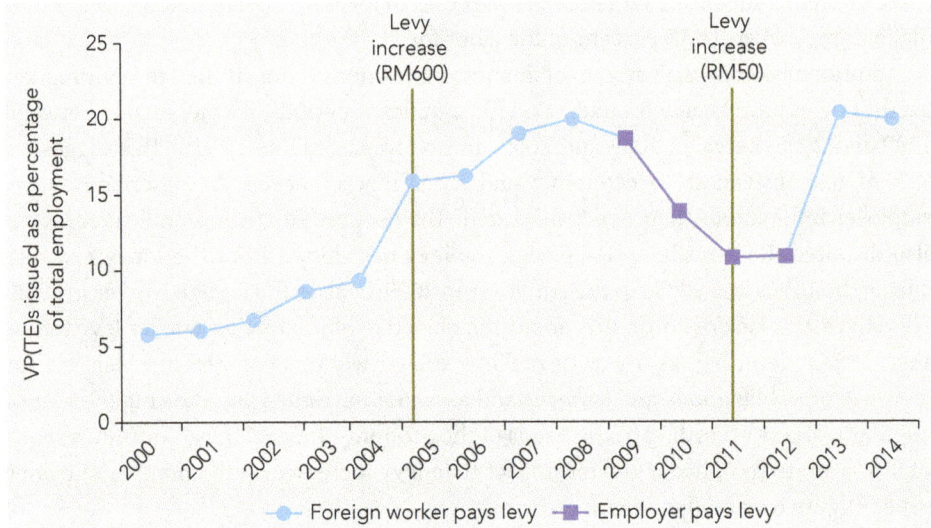

Source: World Bank 2015.
Note: VP(TE) = Visitors Pass (Temporary Employment).

too few workers are willing to migrate formally (ILO 2013, 2015).[10] Additionally, there is no quota or levy for migrant workers hired via the registration of informal migrants. The availability of a large population of irregular migrants makes the application of a quota or levy system challenging. There is no levy for high-skilled migrants, but there is a firm-specific dependency ceiling set at one foreign worker for every four local workers (with a cap of 10 intracompany transferees per company) along with restrictions based on paid-up registered capital and corporate income tax (Ruhs 2016). A maximum of 10 foreign workers applies in some cases with quotas eased in others.

Brunei Darussalam uses a unique system of geography- and sector-linked quotas and sectoral levies, though the extent of the implementation of this system is not known. The quotas are primarily used to limit the number of foreign workers in the country. As part of a suite of measures to limit the intake of foreign workers in 2014, Brunei Darussalam announced that foreign workers would not be permitted in rural areas, the share of the workforce in semiurban areas would be limited to 20 percent, and the share in municipalities would be limited to 30 percent (EIU 2014). Each sector is restricted by its own quota, and foreign employment in certain sectors can be prohibited outright. Quotas are issued to employers on the basis of sectoral assessments of foreign labor, a mechanism similar to a labor market test for the availability of local workers to fill jobs but operating at a more general level. Certain sectors may also be subject to a levy for the employment of each foreign worker. Finally, individual employers are each subject to a cap on the share of foreign workers that they can hire, typically about 50 percent.

Several ASEAN migrant-sending countries have quantity restrictions in place, though the extent to which these are implemented seems to be limited. To obtain a work permit, Indonesian employers must demonstrate a 10:1 ratio of domestic to foreign employees. Employers are also subject to a monthly tax of US$100 for each foreign hire. Cambodia and Lao PDR both have systems of dependency ceilings that are more relaxed for higher-skilled workers. In Cambodia, no more than 10 percent of a firm's employees can be foreign. Within this ceiling, unskilled workers are capped at 1 percent of the firm's workforce, foreign "office workers" at 3 percent, and "skilled" or "specialized" workers at 6 percent. Though these quotas are legally binding, enforcement is reportedly lax. In Lao PDR, employers hiring foreign labor must employ a minimum of 10 domestic employees. Dependency ceilings apply on the firm level with unskilled foreign labor restricted to 15 percent of the local workers in each firm and skilled foreign labor to 25 percent. These quotas have been increased from previous provisions that set them at 10 percent and 20 percent, respectively. Employers must contribute 15 percent of work permit registration fees to the Labor Fund, which is to be used for skills development and assistance for Laotian workers abroad and foreign workers in Lao PDR. However, this fund has not yet been created.

Recruitment

Singapore uses licensing, training, demerits, and public information to manage the recruitment process. Singapore's Foreign Manpower Management Division within the Ministry of Manpower licenses recruitment agencies and monitors compliance with regulations along with the Commission for Employment Agencies. Key recruitment agency personnel must register and obtain a Certificate of Employment Intermediaries that requires completion of a course on relevant legislation. Singapore's licensing system is based on the risk profile of the recruitment agencies[11]. The agencies are required to pay a security bond or deposit that varies depending on the type of license,[12] the number of Work Permit and S Pass holders placed, and whether the firm has been sanctioned in the past. This security bond is used to fund any liabilities the agency may incur and operates in conjunction with a demerit points system. As the number of demerits for recruitment violations increases, sanctions increase: first, the security deposit that must be paid increases; then, a portion of the security deposit is forfeited, the agency is placed under surveillance (this status is made public), and key personnel must retake the Certificate of Employment Intermediaries; and finally, the license is revoked. In 2015, 108 of 3,565 employment agencies were issued demerits and 7 had their licenses suspended or revoked. Most infringements related to misrepresentation of fees or costs or failing to sign a written agreement specifying these costs. In 2011, Singapore increased penalties, including fines and imprisonment, for unlicensed employment agencies and made the use of an unlicensed recruitment agency an offense. The Ministry also maintains a directory of recruitment agencies that allows employers to search for and compare potential agencies.[13]

Malaysian employers can hire workers directly or through a third-party recruiter, such as a private recruitment agency[14] or an outsourcing agency. In practice, most low-skilled migrants use third-party recruiters. A recent survey of Vietnamese immigrants to Malaysia found that 95 percent used a third-party recruiter, and only 2 percent were recruited directly by an employer (ILO and KNOMAD 2015). The outsourcing system has been a particular source of problems. In the outsourcing model, the agency rather than the employer is responsible for the foreign worker's contract upon entry into Malaysia. As such, the outsourcing company, rather than the employer, is responsible for the migrant's employment and legal status. The system has conflicted with the employer- and sector-specific VP(TE) because migrants could be shifted from employer to employer. Additionally, responsibility for oversight of recruitment was split between the Ministry of Human Resources for recruitment agencies and the Ministry of Home Affairs for outsourcing companies. Recognizing these problems, no new licenses for outsourcers have been granted and the outsourcing system is being phased out.

Although recruitment agencies or brokers are often involved in various aspects of the migration process in Thailand, no formal system of private recruitment oversight is in place for immigration. Recruitment agencies[15] have emerged to shepherd migrants and employers through the MOU migration channel's complicated procedures, though the MOUs themselves give no official role to recruitment agencies, envision a strong public role in recruitment, and do not cover the licensing or regulation of recruitment agencies (ILO 2013). At times, these agencies act as an outsourcing company contracting migrant workers to employers, creating confusion about whether the agencies are liable under labor laws (Natali, McDougall, and Stubbington 2014). The complicated national verification process, which involves periodic regularizations of informal migrants from Cambodia, Lao PDR, and Myanmar, has also led migrants and employers to seek out brokers to navigate them through the process. The Recruitment and Job Seeker Protection Act B.E. 2528 (1985), which regulates private employment agencies, has thus far not been used to regulate the recruitment of inbound migrants (as opposed to agencies recruiting Thai migrants to work abroad), though legal clarification that such labor agencies are subject to the Act has been issued.

Despite attempts to limit recruitment fees, the recruitment process in all three countries is costly in part because of high recruitment costs in countries of origin. In Singapore, the Ministry of Manpower has capped the fees charged by recruitment agencies to foreign workers at two months of salary; moreover, it has reiterated that costs such as overseas training, medical checkups, and airfare to Singapore cannot be charged to foreign workers (Singapore, MOM 2011). Additionally, foreign workers must be provided with receipts from agencies for monetary transactions. Still, Singapore's licensing approach means that the government does not engage closely with sending countries. This means that recruitment fees can still be high, driven by those charged by agencies in the sending countries (Teng 2014; Yue 2011).

In Malaysia, fees charged to foreign workers are frequently high, which can lead to indebtedness and, in turn, cause migrant workers to agree to poor living conditions, excessive work hours, and restrictions on their movement (Amnesty International 2010; United States, DOS 2015; Verité 2014). In Thailand, recruitment costs are particularly high for the formal MOU process with brokers necessary for migrants to navigate its complicated procedures. Recruitment costs are between US$560 and $620 for migrants from Cambodia; between US$470 and $650, from Lao PDR; and between

US$650 and $1,100, from Myanmar (ILO 2015). In contrast, for those migrants from Lao PDR using informal channels, costs are between US$80 and $90 (MMN and AMC 2013). Informal migrants must also pay fees to intermediaries who can help them with the national verification process, so that regularization costs can be almost three times the official level (Natali, McDougall, and Stubbington 2014). A royal ordinance that came into effect in August 2016 states that private recruitment agencies are not allowed to charge recruitment fees to migrant workers, though the impact of the ordinance is not known (ILO 2016a).

Employment

Employment Terms

Singapore uses employment terms in conjunction with entry paths to differentiate migrant workers by skill level with more preferable terms offered to higher-skilled workers. The initial work permit duration for low-skilled workers is up to two years, but it is up to three years for high-skilled workers with employment passes. Passes are renewable in all cases except for the Personalized Employment Pass. Work permits have maximum employment terms: 10 years for workers with basic skills and between 18 and 22 years, depending on the sector, for low-skilled workers with more advanced skills. Employment passes are employer- and occupation-specific in most cases. Thus, foreign workers unhappy with their current employment, whether because of pay and working conditions or mistreatment, are unable to change employers. Singapore has introduced some flexibility into its employment terms to help high-skilled migrants find suitable employment and employers to respond to economic needs. These include the Personalized Employment Pass that allows high-skilled foreigners to find employment in Singapore, cross-deployment in the construction and process sectors to improve the use of foreign workers during slow periods, and the Job Flexibility Scheme in the services sector to improve the use of foreign workers under lower dependency ceilings. Depending on salary, holders of Employment Passes and S Passes may migrate with certain dependents, who are permitted to work, while Work Permit holders may not migrate with dependents.

Malaysia also has a tiered system with more generous employment terms available to more highly skilled workers. The VP(TE) for low-skilled workers is valid for one year and renewable for 10 years; however, the pass can be extended longer for workers determined to be skilled (Abella and Martin 2016). The pass is employer- and job-specific. As in Singapore, foreign workers cannot seek out a different employer if they are treated poorly, their skills are not well suited to the job, or they identify a different job with a better salary. VP(TE) holders are not permitted to bring dependents to Malaysia, to marry, or to become pregnant. Renewing the VP(TE) annually can be time-consuming in Malaysia: employers are required to submit an application letter, pay another security bond, register for workplace insurance, and schedule another medical examination for a migrant worker. Additionally, the one-year duration of the initial pass may be too short for migrants to recoup the up-front costs of migrating.

In fact, a survey of Vietnamese foreign workers in Malaysia found that 79 percent of the foreign workers who had repaid their loans had been working in Malaysia for longer than a year and that 88 percent who had not repaid their loan had lived in Malaysia less than a year. Additionally, of the foreign workers whose employers had paid for them to come to Malaysia, 71 percent said deductions were made to repay these costs for longer than two years (ILO and KNOMAD 2015). The more highly skilled migrants receiving Employment Passes receive better employment terms. Holders of Categories I and II of the Employment Pass, who have the highest minimum salary requirements, are permitted to migrate with dependents, unlike the Category III holders. The RP-T for the most highly skilled expatriates offers the best employment terms including a 10-year pass, flexibility to change employers, and permission for spouses to work.

Thailand does not offer more generous employment terms to high-skilled migrants. For migrants from Cambodia, Lao PDR, and Myanmar using the MOU channel to migrate, employment terms were originally restricted to an initial two-year period that could be extended for another two years before a required three-year cooling-off period in the country of origin. Migrants regularized under the national verification process have been subject to the same conditions. This involved significant costs for migrants to travel home and wait three years before being able to return to Thailand. However, several actions in 2014 and 2016 have relaxed the cooling-off period requirement and permitted migrants to extend their existing work permits (IOM 2016). In particular, the newly signed MOUs, which are not yet operational, provide four-year terms of employment and a 30-day cooling-off period (ILO 2016b). Still, a cooling-off period requires migrants to return home. This is expensive and, in the case of migrants from Myanmar, may not be possible because of political and ethnic conflict. Irregular migrants who registered during registration campaigns have been issued work permits lasting one or two years. As in Singapore and Malaysia, migrants are generally not able to change employers. High-skilled migrants receive visas and work permits that are valid for a year and can be renewed annually. To change employers, they must file with the Immigration Bureau or leave Thailand and reapply for a new visa.

Protection

Malaysia, Singapore, and Thailand each have policies in place to protect migrant workers during employment. Protections for migrant employees tend to be similar to those of local employees, although coverage under social protection programs is more variable (table 6.2). Even when coverage is equal in law, the extent to which migrants can access mechanisms in place to protect them is often limited.

Workplace protections

In Singapore, local and foreign workers—except for executives and managers earning more than S\$4,500 a month, domestic workers, and several other occupations—are covered by the Employment Act, Singapore's main labor law. The Act provides the basic terms and conditions of work, including maximum working hours, overtime, rest days, annual and sick leave, and limits on salary deductions.[16] Additionally, the Employment

TABLE 6.2

Protections available to migrant workers in Malaysia, Singapore, and Thailand

	Malaysia	Singapore	Thailand
Workplace protections	Equal coverage with locals under labor legislation	Equal coverage with locals under labor legislation supplemented with additional legislation	Equal coverage with locals under labor legislation
Health insurance	Employers must purchase	Employers must purchase	Equal coverage with locals under social security with additional mandatory scheme for informal sector workers
Workplace injury	Inferior coverage under Amended Workmen's Compensation Act 1952 (amended 2006) with mandatory additional insurance	Equal coverage under Work Injury Compensation Act (1975) (amended 2011)	Equal coverage with locals under social security
Pension	Eligible but employer match inferior to that of locals	Not eligible	Equal coverage with locals under social security, but benefits are not portable
Labor unions	Can be members but not officers	Can be members but not officers	Can be members but not officers
Documents	Confiscation prohibited	Confiscation prohibited	Confiscation prohibited
Accommodations	Minimum standards in plantation and mining sectors	Safe working conditions; licenses for large foreign worker dormitories	—
Domestic workers	Not covered under main labor laws	Not covered under main labor laws but additional protections provided	Not covered under main labor laws

Note: — not available.

of Foreign Manpower Act and its amendments lay out additional responsibilities for employers of foreign workers, and provide protections for foreign domestic workers covered for other employees under the Employment Act. Malaysia's Workmen's Compensation Act 1952 (amended in 2006) covers workplace protections such as wages, rest days, and working hours and guarantees equal treatment of all workers. The Act excludes domestic workers. Foreign workers are covered by the minimum wage. Formal migrants entering Thailand via the MOU channel, informal migrants who have been regularized, and informal migrants who have registered with the Thai authorities during registration campaigns are covered by the 1998 Labor Protection Act (amended in 2008). Under this Act, these migrants are subject to the same protections as local workers related to work hours, overtime, leave, minimum wage, occupational safety, severance, and labor inspection (Paitoonpong 2011). However, the agriculture, domestic work, transport, and fishing sectors, in which many migrants work, are not subject to the Labor Protection Act. Brunei Darussalam's Employment Order 2009 establishes the minimum terms and conditions of employment for contract workers including foreign workers but excluding domestic workers, managers, and executives. The Order requires that foreign workers be provided with a written contract that specifies employment duration and salary, and establishes standards for hours of work, overtime, leave, and rest days. A different employment order provides some protections for domestic workers, including provisions related to employment contracts, prompt payment of salary, unauthorized deductions, and health and safety (UN Women 2013b).

Access to social protection

Employers in Singapore must provide medical insurance coverage for S Pass and Work Permit holders, including foreign domestic workers. Foreign workers are also covered by the Work Injury Compensation Act (1975) (amended 2011) that provides compensation in the case of injuries at work. Employers of domestic workers, who are not covered under the Act, must purchase at least S$40,000 of personal accident insurance payable to the domestic worker or the designated beneficiary. Foreigners are not eligible for contributions to the Central Provident Fund, Singapore's social security system.

Like those in Singapore, employers in Malaysia must purchase health insurance for foreign workers under the Hospitalization and Surgical Scheme for Foreign Workers, though domestic and plantation workers are exempt. The workplace injury insurance system is bifurcated between coverage that is inferior to that of locals under the Amended Workmen's Compensation Act of 1952 and coverage under the Foreign Workers Compensation Scheme, which makes up for the lack of coverage of migrant workers under the Employees' Social Security Act 1969, which offers additional protection to local workers for workplace injury. Foreign domestic workers have no workplace injury insurance. In Malaysia unlike in Singapore, foreign workers—again excluding domestic workers—are permitted to contribute to Malaysia's Employees Provident Fund, though their minimum contribution of 11 percent of wages need only be matched by an employer minimum of RM5. Employers match at 12 percent of wages for local workers.

Formal migrants entering Thailand via the MOU channel and informal migrants who have been regularized are eligible for social security benefits, which include health coverage and workers' compensation. Migrants and employers are each to contribute 3.5 percent of their wages for social security benefits (MMN and AMC 2013). These benefits are not portable; however, a lump sum payment of pension benefits is permitted regardless of the worker's contribution period but without any indication of how this should occur (ILO 2015; IOM 2015). Migrants in the agriculture, domestic work, transport, and fishing sectors are excluded from social security and worker compensation benefits, but are required to enroll in the Compulsory Migrant Health Insurance Scheme, a health insurance program for migrant workers. Informal workers who have registered with the Thai authorities are also required to enroll. Informal migrants may opt in to the Scheme for a fee, though health promotion and prevention services are available to all migrants regardless of status.

In Brunei Darussalam, foreign workers must be covered by medical insurance and workers' compensation insurance *(Insuran Pampasan Pekerja)*. Foreign female employees with more than 180 days of service are entitled to nine weeks of maternity leave with eight of them paid.

Several ASEAN migrant-sending countries make, or will soon make, social protection schemes available to immigrant workers. Foreign workers in the Philippines have access to health insurance via PhilHealth (the Philippine Health Insurance Corporation) as well as to social security. The government's universal health insurance scheme covers foreigners who have worked in Indonesia for more than six months (World Bank 2016). In 2018, foreign workers will be permitted to join Vietnam's compulsory social insurance scheme that covers sickness, retirement, and employment-related injury. How implementation will proceed is uncertain.

Accommodations

Employers in Singapore must provide workers with safe working conditions and acceptable housing, but the cost of food and housing can be deducted from a foreign worker's salary. In Malaysia, there are minimum standards for accommodations for foreign workers in the plantation and mining industries. The cost of accommodations may be deducted from foreign workers' salaries.

Association

In Brunei Darussalam, Malaysia, Singapore, and Thailand, foreign workers are permitted to take part in labor unions but are generally not allowed to be officers.

Documents

Confiscation of passports and other documents is prohibited in Brunei Darussalam, Malaysia, Singapore, and Thailand.

Domestic workers

After reports in the mid-2000s of abuses of foreign domestic workers, Singapore has taken action to improve conditions (HRW 2005; UN Women 2013a). Since 2013 employers of foreign domestic workers must provide one weekly rest day, but this requirement can be avoided if the domestic worker is compensated for working on the rest day. New foreign domestic workers must attend the Settling-In Program, an orientation course covering topics such as employment conditions and safety, while new employers of foreign domestic workers must attend the Employers' Orientation Program, a course covering the employer's roles and responsibilities. Some foreign domestic workers are interviewed by the Ministry of Manpower about their adjustment to employment and their working conditions, and a foreign domestic worker helpline is available. Penalties for employers who abuse foreign domestic workers have also been increased (Teng 2014). In Malaysia, employers must sign an employment agreement with domestic workers specifying the wages, the contract term, and the duties and responsibilities of each party including the provision of reasonable accommodations and amenities to the domestic worker. Non-Muslim employers must respect the religious sensitivities of Muslim domestic workers. Brunei Darussalam's Employment

Order (2009) excludes domestic workers, though a different employment order provided some protections for domestic workers, including provisions related to employment contracts, prompt payment of salary, unauthorized salary deductions, and health and safety (UN Women 2013b).

Protections in practice

There is evidence that protections available to migrant workers are not always enforced. In Malaysia, the application of the Employment Act 1955 and of the minimum wage is not always equal between locals and migrant workers. In a recent survey of Vietnamese migrants in Malaysia, 28 percent state that they were not entitled to the same wages as local workers (ILO and KNOMAD 2015). In Thailand, wage deductions are not permitted under Thai law, which the Supreme Court affirmed in 2015, though such deductions are the norm (United States, DOS 2016). In Singapore, frequent concerns include nonpayment of wages, poor accommodation, and lack of occupational safety (Yue 2011). In each country, there is evidence of excessive working hours and illegal wage deductions (see Devasahayam (2010) and Zweynert (2015) for Singapore; ILO (2015b), Holumyong and Punpuing (2014), and Vasuprasat (2008) for Thailand; and World Bank (2015) for Malaysia. Confiscation of passports is frequent despite being prohibited. Seventy-seven percent of the Vietnamese migrants surveyed in Malaysia stated that their travel documents were withheld by their employer (ILO and KNOMAD 2015).

In other cases, protections available to local workers are not available to migrants, are inferior to those of migrants, or are not accessible to migrants. In Singapore, migrant workers cannot contribute to the Central Provident Fund. In Malaysia, foreign workers are permitted to do so, but are not eligible for the same employer match as locals. The benefits available to foreign workers in Malaysia who experience injury or death at work are not as generous as those of local workers (Devadason and Meng 2014; World Bank 2013). In Thailand, access to social security benefits that, in theory, are available on par with locals is limited by the prevalence of informal migrants. Social security benefits are seldom available or taken in practice: employers (and migrants) may wish to avoid contributions; the process of obtaining benefits can be lengthy with language barriers and documentation creating additional barriers; and in some cases the nature of migration makes claiming benefits impossible (for example, old age pensions) (Harkins 2014). As of February 2016, only 40 percent of those having gone through Thailand's national verification process were covered under the Social Security Fund (IOM 2016). Although foreign workers are eligible to join unions, membership is rare in practice (ILO and KNOMAD 2014; MEF 2014; Paitoonpong 2011).

The treatment of foreign domestic workers is a frequent concern. Domestic workers are not covered by general employment legislation and are excluded from the social protection enjoyed by other migrant workers in Malaysia, Singapore, and Thailand. The treatment of foreign domestic workers is a particular concern in Singapore where, despite improvements in protections, concerns about lack of enforcement remain and there is evidence that abuses such as illegal deductions and long working hours continue (Devasahayam 2010; Zweynert 2015). A recent survey of 670 foreign domestic workers found that 40 percent did not have a weekly day off and 67 percent had their passport held by their employer (HOME 2015). There are frequent reports of mistreatment of foreign domestic workers in Malaysia (Harkins 2016).

Exit

Sanctions and incentives

Malaysia and Singapore put the onus on employers to ensure that migrant workers return to their country of origin, a responsibility enforced through punitive measures. Singapore requires employers to purchase a S$5,000 security bond for every non-Malaysian holder of a work permit. The bond is designed to incentivize the employer to oversee a work permit holder's return to their country of origin. Thus, the bond is repayable when the worker returns home or when the work permit is canceled. However, the bond is forfeited if the conditions of the work permit are violated, if a worker goes missing, or if the employer fails to pay the worker's salary on time. Employers are also required to pay repatriation costs. In Malaysia, the security bond differs by nationality. Additionally, foreign workers who do not depart Malaysia at the expiration of their employment term are blacklisted by the Department of Immigration. Neither Malaysia nor Singapore engages closely with source countries to facilitate the return of migrant workers. Brunei Darussalam requires employers to submit a security deposit or bank guarantee to the Department of Labor to cover the cost of return airfare, which varies by country.

Thailand's attempts to create a system that incentivizes return have not worked well thus far. Thailand's MOUs with Cambodia, Lao PDR, and Myanmar include a provision creating a repatriation fund through a contribution by the migrant of 15 percent of their monthly salary. The fund was to be used to defray the cost of deporting irregular migrants and to incentivize exit by returning contributions upon leaving Thailand. However, the fund was never implemented, and the policy has since been repealed (ILO 2015). Migrants who overstay their visa and work permits are banned from reentry for a period depending on the length of overstay and whether they have been arrested (IOM 2016). Perhaps the most significant hindrance to incentivizing return, however, has been Thailand's periodic registration and regularization programs for informal migrant workers. These programs have offered temporary work permits and full regular status to irregular migrants from Cambodia, Lao PDR, and Myanmar every several years. Given the high cost of formal recruitment, these campaigns incentivize migrants to travel cheaply and informally to Thailand where they can expect to be regularized within a few years.

Malaysia has also undertaken regularization campaigns. Malaysia offered amnesties in 1996, 1997, 1998, 2002, and 2004–05 that allowed irregular workers to depart Malaysia without legal charges (Kassim and Zin 2011). More recently, Malaysia's 6P regularization and deportation program allowed undocumented foreign workers to register with the Ministry of Human Resources, undergo legalization, and receive authorization to work in Malaysia. Those who did not register were sought out for arrest.

Enforcement

Coordination and targeting

Singapore has a robust system to enforce immigration policies. The enforcement system relies on licensing of recruitment agencies, reporting requirements for employers hiring foreign workers, and heavy penalties for violations of immigration rules including fines and imprisonment. In part because of advantageous geography and small size and in part because of the strict enforcement system that includes very stiff penalties for harboring and employing immigration offenders, Singapore has very few undocumented migrants. According to the Immigration and Checkpoints Authority, 1,901 immigration offenders were arrested in 2015, including 310 undocumented immigrants and 1,591 overstayers (Singapore, ICA 2016). There is more concern about foreign workers who are employed in occupations or sectors or by employers not specified in their work permit (Teng 2014).

Enforcement efforts in Singapore are coordinated by a single ministry, are primarily focused on employers, and incorporate risk-based assessments. The Employment Inspectorate Department and the Well-Being Department in the Foreign Manpower Management Division of the Ministry of Manpower are responsible for ensuring that employers follow regulations regarding employment protections for foreign workers. Employers are generally the target of enforcement efforts, with monetary and prison penalties directed at those employing foreign workers illegally. The Ministry of Manpower has reportedly increased inspections of housing accommodations provided to foreign workers by employers (Yue 2011). Laws are also in place to punish those harboring immigration offenders, including landlords who are required to check immigrants' documentation. The Ministry of Manpower and other government agencies pay particular attention to companies that have fewer Singaporeans in professional, executive, and management positions or that have been the subject of complaints about discriminatory hiring practices. In these cases, employers must provide the Ministry of Manpower with information about practices such as recruitment processes and grievance procedures. Penalties are in place for violations of levy payments, with employers in the construction sector open to closer scrutiny under the levy system.

Still, there are concerns about the enforcement of employment protections for foreign workers and particularly for foreign domestic workers in Singapore. The government has been suggested to have a pro-business bias that has led it to overlook illegalities in the employment of foreign workers, including the listing of fictitious local employees to circumvent the dependency ceiling (Ong 2014). Enforcement of protections for foreign domestic workers often relies on the workers themselves to submit complaints to the Ministry of Manpower, which the workers may be unwilling to do because of the possibility of retaliation (Teng 2014). Finally, the lack of coordination with source countries means that migration costs can remain high for migrants, circumventing the fee limit placed on recruitment agencies within Singapore.

Malaysia focuses its enforcement of migration policy on foreign workers rather than employers and on security and immigration violations rather than employment protections.

Immigration-related offenses are a crime in Malaysia with undocumented migrants subject to detention, prosecution, and deportation. Employers are less frequently subject to sanction, though employment of undocumented migrants is also an offense (Harkins 2016; Kaur 2008). Through September 2015, 625 employers and about 56,000 undocumented migrants were arrested (World Bank 2015). Only 143, or 22 percent, of the 625 employers were charged. Malaysia also focuses enforcement efforts more on security and immigration violations than on employment protections. The Ministry of Human Resources has only weak enforcement capacity with just 350 inspectors for more than 400,000 workplaces. The ILO recommends one labor inspector per 10,000 workers versus Malaysia's one per 40,000 (World Bank 2015). Given these constraints, inspectors tend to react to complaints rather than being proactive in investigating employers (Harkins 2016). The Ministry of Home Affairs, in charge of border security and immigration violations, has more significant resources with 3,000 officers and assistance from the army and other agencies. A citizen volunteer force was also created to identify undocumented migrants without training or eligibility requirements (World Bank 2013). Joint operations between the Ministry of Human Resources and the Ministry of Home Affairs are infrequent.

While legislation is in place to protect migrant workers, the enforcement regime in Thailand is weak. The large population of irregular migrants is evidence of the porousness of Thailand's borders. Private recruitment agencies are not regulated and operate under the guise of labor consulting agencies to facilitate admissions under the MOUs, which envision government-to-government recruitment. A cap on fees that could be charged by brokers facilitating the national verification process was never enforced (Natali, McDougall, and Stubbington 2014). Enforcement of labor protections are thought to be weak not only for migrant but also for Thai workers, with employers treated very leniently (Hall 2011; Natali, McDougall, and Stubbington 2014; Paitoonpong 2011; Vasuprasat 2008). Labor inspectors are not specialized and lack authority and data, while interdepartmental cooperation on enforcement of labor protections is limited (ILO 2015). The U.S. Department of State's 2016 *Trafficking in Persons* report does highlight several examples of increased enforcement including border enforcement and the creation of the Command Center for Combating Illegal Fishing. The Command Center has some oversight of particularly vulnerable workers in the fishing sector, but exploitation in the sector remains significant (United States, DOS 2016).

Complaint and dispute resolution mechanisms are available to migrants in Malaysia, Singapore, and Thailand, but are not always practical or accessible. In Singapore, the Ministry of Manpower provides assistance with resolving disputes and recovering money owed to foreign workers (Teng 2014). A foreign domestic worker helpline is also available. In Malaysia, the Department of Immigration has a mechanism that allows a foreign worker to remain in Malaysia while a complaint is being processed, but in practice this mechanism does not seem to function well. In Thailand, complaint mechanisms for migrant workers are lacking. No formal system is established in the MOUs, and most MOU workers lodge complaints about violations and abuse with the private recruitment agency that recruited them, likely an ineffective if necessary approach considering the divergent interests and frequent abusive practices of these agencies (ILO 2013). Migrant workers participating in the national verification process and registered migrants can only lodge complaints with nongovernmental organizations and diplomatic missions. The employer-specific nature of employment permits for low-skilled workers in Malaysia, Singapore, and Thailand can have a chilling effect on complaints by workers who may be concerned about employers retaliating by revoking the permit.

Notes

1. Information about migration in Brunei Darussalam is very limited. Consequently, the focus of this chapter is on Malaysia, Singapore, and Thailand. However, Brunei Darussalam's migration system is discussed where possible.
2. A comprehensive Foreign Workers Act has been discussed in the past.
3. The East Malaysian states of Labuan, Sabah, and Sarawak also have separate institutions governing migration.
4. As Teng (2014) notes, members of government are leaders of the National Trade Unions Congress.
5. Malaysia refers to these workers as "expatriates."
6. The agreements became active in 2006 in the case of Cambodia and Lao PDR and in 2009 in the case of Myanmar. Thailand signed new MOUs with Cambodia and Vietnam in 2015 and with Lao PDR and Myanmar in 2016. Although the new MOUs are not yet operational, they are more expansive, covering issues of skills development and reemployment (ILO 2016a; ILO 2016b). The MOU with Vietnam will provide a legal channel for Vietnamese migrants to Thailand in the construction and fishing sectors.
7. Candidates are reviewed on a case-by-case basis.
8. The Law of Entry, Exit, Transit, and Residence of Foreigners.
9. See the Ministry of Manpower's webpage, "Calculate Foreign Worker Quota," (accessed November 29, 2016), http://www.mom.gov.sg/passes-and-permits/work-permit-for-foreign-worker/foreign-worker-levy/calculate-foreign-worker-quota.
10. The Office of Foreign Workers Administration studied how a foreign worker levy would be set in Thailand. The following were proposed as potential criteria: the degree of labor shortage and the necessity of employing migrant workers, wage differences between migrant and Thai unskilled workers, employers' ability to pay the levy, differences among industries and working conditions, and the impact of migrant workers on Thailand (TDRI 2007).
11. These are called employment agencies in Singapore.
12. Different licenses are issued for the recruitment of local workers, all workers except foreign domestic workers, workers earning a salary of more than S$4,500, and workers of any type.
13. The Ministry of Manpower is also planning to launch the Trustmark program that grades recruitment agencies involved in placing foreign domestic workers on criteria such as contract completion and their processes for identifying a suitable domestic worker (Singapore, MOM 2016). These grades will be displayed in the recruitment agency directory. Customer feedback from employers of domestic workers who use recruitment agency services will be used to create the Employment Agency Customer Rating, which will also be posted on the directory website. See the Ministry of Manpower's webpage, "Employment Agencies and

Personnel Search (EA Directory)" (last accessed November 29, 2016), http://www.mom.gov
.sg/eservices/services/employment-agencies-and-personnel-search.

14. These are called private employment agencies in Malaysia.

15. These are often called labor consulting agencies in Thailand.

16. Singapore does not have a minimum wage.

References

Abella, Manolo, and Philip Martin. 2016. *Guide on Measuring Policy Impact in ASEAN*.
Geneva: International Labour Organization.

Amnesty International. 2010. *Trapped: The Exploitation of Migrant Workers in Malaysia*.
London: Amnesty International Publications.

Blomberg, Matt, and Kang Sothear. 2015. "Deal Ends Moratorium on Maids to Malaysia."
Cambodia Daily. December 11.

Devadason, Evelyn Shyamala, and Chan Wai Meng. 2014. "Policies and Laws Regulating
Migrant Workers in Malaysia: A Critical Appraisal." *Journal of Contemporary Asia*
44 (1): 19–35.

Devasahayam, Theresa W. 2010. "Placement and/or Protection? Singapore's Labour
Policies and Practices for Temporary Women Migrant Workers." *Journal of the Asia
Pacific Economy* 15 (1): 45–58.

EIU (Economist Intelligence Unit). 2014. "Restrictions on Foreign Labour are Tightened."
Economist Intelligence Unit. June 30.

EU (European Union) and DOLE (Philippines, Department of Labor and Employment).
2011. "A Cross Country Study of Labour Market Tests and Similar Regulatory
Measures: Implications for Labor Market Test Policy in the Philippines." EU and
DOLE, Manila.

Hall, Andy. 2011. "Migration and Thailand: Policy, Perspectives and Challenges." In
*Thailand Migration Report 2011: Migration for Development in Thailand: Overview
and Tools for Policymakers*, edited by Jerrold W. Huguet and Aphichat Chamratrithirong,
17–37. Bangkok: International Organization for Migration (IOM).

Harkins, Benjamin. 2014. "Social Protection for Migrant Workers in Thailand." In
Thailand Migration Report 2014, edited by Jerrold W. Huguet, 27–43. Bangkok:
United Nations Thematic Working Group on Migration in Thailand.

———. 2016. "Review of Labour Migration Policy in Malaysia." International Labour
Organization (ILO), Bangkok.

Holumyong, Charampor, and Sureeporn Punpuing. 2014. "A Cost-Benefit Analysis of
the Legal Status of Migrant Workers in Thailand." In *Managing International
Migration for Development in East Asia*, edited by Richard H. Adams and Ahmad
Ahsan, 263–82. Washington, DC: World Bank.

HOME (Humanitarian Organization for Migration Economics). 2015. *Home Sweet
Home? Work, Life and Well-Being of Foreign Domestic Workers in Singapore*.
Singapore: HOME.

HRW (Human Rights Watch). 2005. *Maid to Order: Ending Abuses against Migrant Domestic Workers in Singapore.* New York: Human Rights Watch.

ILO (International Labour Organization). 2013. "Regulating Recruitment of Migrant Workers: An Assessment of Complaint Mechanisms in Thailand," ILO, Bangkok.

———. 2015. "Review of the Effectiveness of the MOUs in Managing Labour Migration between Thailand and Neighbouring Countries." ILO, Bangkok.

———. 2016a. "Triangle II Quarterly Briefing Note: Thailand." (April-June). ILO, Bangkok.

———. 2016b. "Triangle II Quarterly Briefing Note: Thailand." (July–September). ILO, Bangkok.

ILO (International Labour Organization) and KNOMAD (Global Knowledge Partnership on Migration and Development). 2015. "Migration Cost Survey: Vietnamese Workers in Malaysia."

IOM (International Organization for Migration). 2015. "Migrant Information Note Issue 28," IOM, Bangkok.

———. 2016. "Migrant Information Note Issue 29," IOM, Bangkok.

Jaymalin, Mayen. 2014. "Phl Opens Hard-to-Fill Jobs to Foreign Workers." *Phil Star,* January 13.

Kassim, Azizah, and Ragayah Haji Mat Zin. 2011. "Policy on Irregular Migrants in Malaysia: An Analysis of Its Implementation and Effectiveness." Discussion Paper Series 2011–34, Philippine Institute for Development Studies, Makati City, Philippines.

Kaur, Amarjit. 2008. "International Migration and Governance in Malaysia: Policy and Governance." *UNEAC Asia Papers* 22: 4–18.

Koh, Chiu Yee, Charmian Goh, Kellynn Wee, and Brenda SA Yeoh. 2017. "Drivers of Migration Policy Reform: The Day Off Policy for Migrant Domestic Workers in Singapore." *Global Social Policy* 17(2):1–18.

MEF (Malaysian Employers Federation). 2014. *Practical Guidelines for Employers on the Recruitment, Placement, Employment, and Repatriation of Foreign Workers in Malaysia.*

MMN (Mekong Migration Network) and AMC (Asian Migrant Centre).2013. *Migration in the Greater Mekong Subregion Resource Book: In-depth Study: Border Economic Zones and Migration.* Chiang Mai: MMN and AMC.

Natali, Claudia, Euan McDougall, and Sally Stubbington. 2014. "International Migration Policy in Thailand." In *Thailand Migration Report 2014,* edited by Jerrold W. Huguet, 13–24. Bangkok: United Nations Thematic Working Group on Migration in Thailand.

OECD (Organisation for Economic Cooperation and Development). 2014. *International Migration Outlook 2014.* Paris: OECD.

Ong, Yanchun. 2014. "Singapore's Phantom Workers." *Journal of Contemporary Asia* 44 (3): 443–63.

Paitoonpong, Srawooth. 2011. "Different Stream, Different Needs, and Impact: Managing International Labor Migration in ASEAN: Thailand (Immigration)." Discussion Paper Series 2011-28, Makati City, Philippines, Philippine Institute for Development Studies.

Ruhs, Martin. 2016. "Preparing for Increased Labour Mobility in ASEAN: Labour Markets, Immigration Policies and Migrant Rights." International Organization for Migration, Bangkok.

Singapore, ESC (Economic Strategies Committee). 2010. *Report of the Economic Strategies Committee: High Skilled People, Innovative Economy, Distinctive Global City*

Singapore, ICA (Immigration and Checkpoints Authority). 2016. *Annual Statistics Report 2015*. Singapore.

Singapore, MOM (Ministry of Manpower). 2011. *Factsheet on New Employment Agency Regulatory Framework.*

TDRI (Thai Development Research Institute). 2007. "Projects on a Guideline for Setting Foreign Workers Levy Rates," Report submitted to Thailand, Office of Foreign Workers Administration, Department of Employment, Ministry of Labor.

Teng, Yap Mui. 2014. "Singapore's System for Managing Foreign Manpower," In *Managing International Migration for Development in East Asia*, edited by Richard H. Adams and Ahmad Ahsan, 220–240. Washington DC: World Bank.

United Nations (UN) Women. 2013a. *Contributions of Migrant Domestic Workers to Sustainable Development*. Bangkok: United Nations Entity for Gender Equality and the Empowerment of Women.

———. 2013b. "Managing Labour Migration in ASEAN: Concerns for Women Migrant Workers," UN Women, Bangkok.

United States, DOS (Department of State). 2015. *Trafficking in Persons Report 2015*. Washington, DC: DOS.

———. 2016. *Trafficking in Persons Report 2016*. Washington, DC: DOS.

Vasuprasat, Pracha. 2008. "Inter-state Cooperation on Labour Migration: Lessons Learned from MOUs between Thailand and Neighbouring Countries," ILO Asian Regional Programme on Governance of Labour Migration Working Paper 16, ILO, Bangkok.

Verité. 2014. *Forced Labor in the Production of Electronic Goods in Malaysia: A Comprehensive Study of Scope and Characteristics*Amherst, MA.

Wickramasekara, Piyasiri. 2015. "Bilateral Agreement and Memoranda of Understanding on Migration of Low Skilled Workers: A Review," International Labour Organization (ILO), Geneva.

———. 2016. "Review of the Government-to-Government Mechanism for the Employment of Bangladeshi Workers in the Malaysian Plantation Sector," International Labour Organization, Geneva.

World Bank. 2006. "Labor Migration in the Greater Mekong Sub-region: Synthesis Report: Phase I."

World Bank. 2013. "Immigration in Malaysia: Assessment of its Economic Effects, and a Review of the Policy and System," World Bank report for the Ministry of Human Resources Malaysia.

World Bank. 2015. *Malaysia Economic Monitor: Immigrant Labour*. Kuala Lumpur: World Bank.

World Bank. 2016. "Improving Migrant Workers' Protection: Review of the Indonesian Overseas Migrant Workers' Insurance (Asuransi TKI)."

Yue, Chia Siow. 2011. "Foreign Labor in Singapore: Trends, Policies, Impacts, and Challenges," Discussion Paper Series No. 2011–24, Philippine Institute for Development Studies, Philippines.

Zweynert, Astrid. 2015. "Singapore's Foreign Maids Exploited by Agents, Employers." *Reuters*, May 27, 2015.

CHAPTER 7

Migration Policy in Sending Countries

Introduction

Migrant-sending countries face different concerns from migrant-receiving countries. They worry about the recruitment of migrants in their own countries and the treatment of their migrants in host countries, including their protections under employment laws, their rights vis-à-vis host country citizens, and their access to services such as cost-effective channels to send remittances. Ensuring good treatment is particularly challenging because sending countries lack jurisdiction once migrants depart. Sending countries also worry about the loss of talented individuals to school and work opportunities abroad.

The migration system framework, presented in chapter 5, is also relevant for benchmarking the migration policies of migrant-sending countries (figure 7.1). Sending countries play an important role in regulating recruitment, providing protection and support services to migrant workers and facilitating their return. Sending countries generally must take the entry path, quantity restriction, and employment term subcomponents of the framework as given because they are determined by receiving countries. Still, sending countries can influence these components through bilateral agreements or memorandums of understanding (MOUs).

Using this framework, the rest of the chapter benchmarks the emigration systems of the main sending countries of the Association of Southeast Asian Nations (ASEAN). Most ASEAN sending countries view migration as a tool for economic development. For example, although migration policy in the Philippines formerly sought to promote migration for employment and remittances including through target deployment levels,

FIGURE 7.1
Framework of the migration system in sending countries

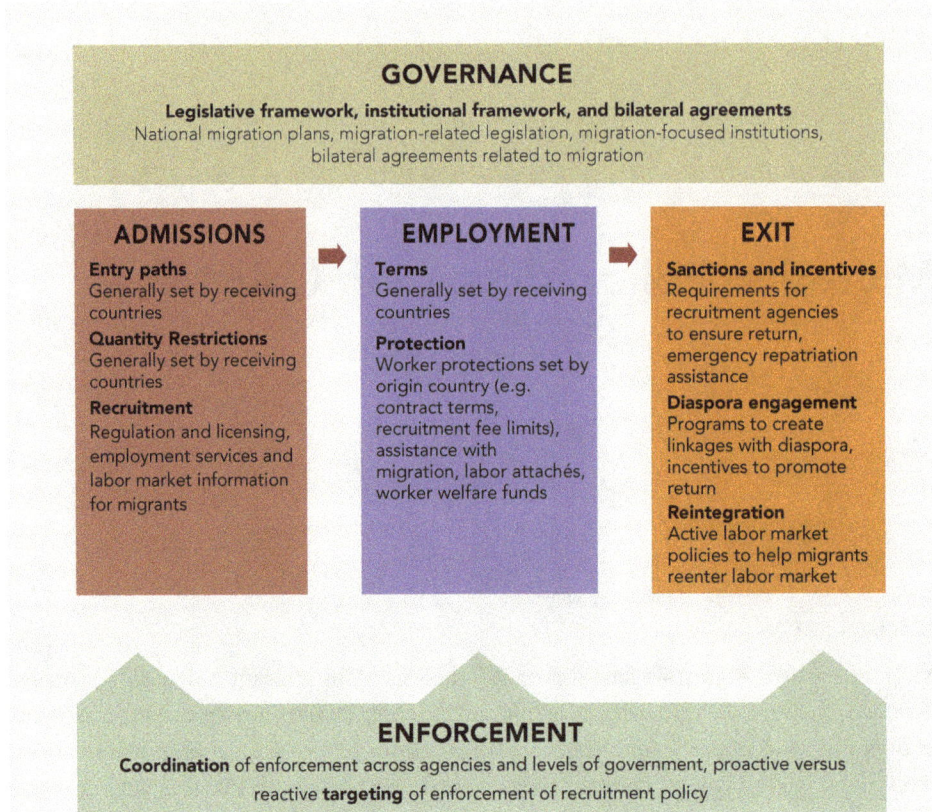

GOVERNANCE
Legislative framework, institutional framework, and bilateral agreements
National migration plans, migration-related legislation, migration-focused institutions, bilateral agreements related to migration

ADMISSIONS
Entry paths
Generally set by receiving countries
Quantity Restrictions
Generally set by receiving countries
Recruitment
Regulation and licensing, employment services and labor market information for migrants

EMPLOYMENT
Terms
Generally set by receiving countries
Protection
Worker protections set by origin country (e.g. contract terms, recruitment fee limits), assistance with migration, labor attachés, worker welfare funds

EXIT
Sanctions and incentives
Requirements for recruitment agencies to ensure return, emergency repatriation assistance
Diaspora engagement
Programs to create linkages with diaspora, incentives to promote return
Reintegration
Active labor market policies to help migrants reenter labor market

ENFORCEMENT
Coordination of enforcement across agencies and levels of government, proactive versus reactive **targeting** of enforcement of recruitment policy

current policy takes a more expansive view of the link between migration and development. The Philippines now aims to protect Philippine migrants who are abroad while also taking advantage of, and supporting, both returning migrants and the Philippine diaspora (IOM 2013). Similarly, Indonesia has generally focused on the promotion of out-migration, though attention has increasingly shifted to the protection of migrants with the promulgation of regulations and the creation of an agency designed to improve the experience of migrants. The Vietnamese government promotes migration as an economic development and poverty reduction strategy with annual goals for the number of migrant workers that were about 100,000 between 2010 and 2015 (Bowen and Huong 2012). Cambodia also promotes out-migration as a tool of social and economic development with a goal of establishing a migration system suited to this purpose. The Lao People's Democratic Republic and Myanmar have generally not promoted out-migration as a development tool.

The Philippines is a model in many respects, having achieved a migration system that works hard to reduce information asymmetries through information campaigns and job postings and seeks to work closely with receiving countries. Indonesia has much of the infrastructure necessary for an effective emigration system, but a complex legislative and institutional environment impedes coordination among stakeholders, including different government agencies, and a ban on the out-migration of domestic migrant workers threatens to disrupt the ability of Indonesian workers, especially female ones, to respond to economic needs. Although the Vietnamese government promotes out-migration as an economic development and poverty reduction strategy, no longer-term plans are in place to assist migrants when they return. Without a strong oversight system, recruitment agencies extract high fees from workers, including through a system of implicitly sanctioned security deposits that migrants claim are rarely returned. Cambodia, Lao PDR, and Myanmar have all made some progress in developing the basic legislative and institutional frameworks for migration. However, most migration from these countries remains informal. Weak processes for out-migration mean that recruitment agencies fill the gap, exploiting information asymmetries and earning rents without oversight. All of ASEAN's sending countries have much work to do to leverage the longer-term development impact of migration beyond the first-order effect of sending migrants abroad. Each is still struggling to achieve a model that channels remittances for productive uses, connects with its diaspora to spur investment and knowledge transfers, and reintegrates returned migrants into the labor force in a way that takes advantage of skills developed abroad.

Table 7.1 summarizes areas for improvement and indicates the countries in which they are a particular concern.

TABLE 7.1
Priority areas for improvement in the migration systems of ASEAN's main sending countries

	PHL	IDN	VNM	KHM	LAO	MMR
GOVERNANCE						
Legislation						
Weak legislative framework	O	X	O	X	X	X
Institutions						
No emigrant-focused institutions	O	O	O	X	X	O
Unclear institutional roles/coordination	X	X	O	O	O	O
Bilateral agreements						
MOUs lack coverage/transparency/input	X	X	X	O	O	O
MOUs are overly procedural	O	O	O	X	X	X
ADMISSIONS						
Entry paths						
No help with host country requirements	O	X	X	X	X	X
Quantity restrictions	n.a.	n.a.	n.a.	n.a.	n.a.	n.a.

table continues next page

TABLE 7.1
Priority areas for improvement in the migration systems of ASEAN's main sending countries *(continued)*

	PHL	IDN	VNM	KHM	LAO	MMR
Recruitment						
Informal/unlicensed brokers	X	X	X	X	X	X
Weak regulation	O	X	X	X	X	X
EMPLOYMENT						
Terms						
Rigid employment terms	O	X	O	O	O	O
Protection						
Host country/occupation/sector restrictions	X	X	O	X	X	X
No fee restrictions	O	O	O	X	O	O
Fee restrictions weak/ineffective	X	X	X	–	X	X
Contracts substituted/not provided to workers	X	X	X	X	X	X
No standard predeparture orientation curriculum	O	O	X	X	X	X
No postdeparture orientation	O	X	X	X	X	X
Reliance on informal remittance channels	O	O	X	X	X	X
Lengthy departure requirements	O	X	O	X	X	X
No/weak migrant worker welfare fund	O	X	X	X	X	X
No/limited/ineffective social protection for migrant workers	O	X	X	X	X	X
Assistance abroad limited by staff/resources	X	X	X	X	X	X
EXIT						
Sanctions and incentives						
Return policy absent	O	X	O	O	O	O
Return policy ineffective	O	O	X	X	X	X
Diaspora engagement						
Diaspora policy absent	O	X	O	X	X	X
Diaspora policy ineffective	–	O	–	O	O	O
Reintegration						
Reintegration policy absent	O	X	X	X	X	X
Reintegration policy ineffective	X	O	O	O	O	O
ENFORCEMENT						
Coordination						
Lack of coordination and clear institutional responsibilities	O	X	O	–	–	–
Targeting						
Reactive approach to enforcement of recruitment policy	O	X	X	O	–	–
Weak sanctions	O	X	X	–	–	–

Note: — = not available; n.a. = not applicable; X = problem area is a priority for a given country; O = problem area is not a priority; ASEAN = Association of Southeast Asian Nations; IDN = Indonesia; KHM = Cambodia; LAO = Lao PDR; MMR = Mynamar; MOU = memorandum of understanding; PHL = Philippines; VNM = Vietnam.

Governance

Legislative framework

Cambodia and Myanmar have developed or are developing strategic plans devoted to migration. The Cambodian government has two plans in place that set policy for labor migration. The Policy on Labor Migration for Cambodia 2010–15 sets three objectives for migration policy: formulating and implementing rights-based and gender-sensitive policy and legislation through social dialogue at all levels; protecting and empowering male and female migrant workers regardless of their status through all stages of the migration process; and harnessing labor migration and mobility to enhance social and economic development in Cambodia. The Labor Migration Policy for Cambodia 2015–18 builds on these objectives and outlines specific policy goals to achieve each objective. Responding to criticism that previous migration plans were not coordinated with other national strategies, the 2015–18 strategy is envisioned to work alongside the National Employment Policy, the National Strategic Development Plan 2014–18, and the Rectangular Strategy Phase III 2013–18 (Vutha, Pide, and Dalis 2011). Myanmar is currently working with the International Organization for Migration (IOM) to develop a national migration strategy modeled on Cambodia's plan (ILO 2013a; ILO 2015b). The plan covers several key policy areas: enhanced governance of labor migration, improved protection and empowerment of migrant workers, data collection and management, and labor migration and development (IOM 2016d).[1]

Indonesia, Lao PDR, the Philippines, and Vietnam all include migration-related provisions in strategic development plans.[2] The Philippines, for example, includes at least 60 migration-related provisions in its national development plan; it expands the focus from remittances and jobs to support for migrants working abroad, returning migrants, and the Philippine diaspora (IOM 2013).[3] Lao PDR includes mentions of migration several times in its 8th Five-Year National Socio-Economic Development Plan (2016–20).

The Philippines has a large suite of legislation and regulations covering all major aspects of migration, including engagement with overseas diaspora and special protections for migrant domestic workers. The Migrant Workers and Overseas Filipinos Act of 1995 (RA8042), which was amended in 2007 (RA9422) and in 2010 (RA10022), is the most significant legislation governing migrant workers in the Philippines. The Act and its amendments provide for the regulation of recruitment, the protection of Philippine migrants, and reintegration. Rules and regulations issued by the Philippines Overseas Employment Administration (POEA) provide more details on these functions. Among the most significant of these rules and regulations is the Household Service Workers Reform Package, adopted in 2006, that expanded protections for domestic workers.

Although Indonesia also has a comprehensive set of migration-related legislation and rules, the legislation does not define institutional responsibilities clearly. Labor migration from Indonesia is governed by the 2004 Law on the Placement and Protection of Indonesian Workers Abroad (Law No. 39/2004) that provides an overall framework for the emigration process. The law establishes procedures for placing workers in employment abroad, sets out the rights and obligations of migrant workers and their protections, and charges government agencies with the regulation and supervision of the recruitment process and with protection of workers while abroad. Presidential, government-wide, and ministerial regulations implement and build on Law No. 39/2004. Local governments have also enacted regulations (*perda*) to supervise the migration process, though these are superseded by national legislation (IOM 2010a; Bachtiar 2011; Farbenblum, Taylor-Nicholson, and Paoletti 2013). While Law No. 39/2004 covers most of the important elements of the migration system, its effectiveness is hindered by several flaws. Perhaps most importantly, the legislation clearly does not define responsibilities either among national government agencies or between national and local authorities. For instance, one section of the law assigns a supervisory role to all government agencies, including those at the local level, while another assigns it to the National Authority for the Placement and Protection of Indonesian Overseas Workers (BNP2TKI) (Bachtiar 2011). The lack of clearly defined responsibilities has resulted in duplication of tasks, competition among agencies, and weaker protections for migrant workers. The law is currently under review (ILO 2015c). Local regulations do not seem to make up for these shortcomings. A study of *perda* issued by local governments found that 81 percent of the 127 studied levied fees for the employment of Indonesians abroad and were primarily designed to raise local revenues (Bachtiar 2011).

Vietnam also has a relatively comprehensive set of laws and regulations covering migration, but the legal framework suffers from some weaknesses. The 2006 Law on Vietnamese Nationals Working Abroad under Contract (or, more commonly, the Law on Overseas Workers) became effective in 2007, consolidating a system of managing out-migration via commercial recruitment that had been evolving since the 1990s.[4] The Law sets out the rights and obligations of migrants, recruitment agencies,[5] and government agencies; establishes the framework for a recruitment system with agencies licensed by the government; and includes protections for migrants such as the regulation of recruitment fees and requirements to receive skills and other training. Subsequent regulations define the role of government agencies, clarify the responsibilities of recruitment agencies, establish sanctions for recruitment violations, improve protections for migrants, and set predeparture orientation requirements. Although the legislative framework for migration covers all the components of the migration system and creates relatively clear roles and responsibilities for the system's different actors, several criticisms have emerged. The Law on Overseas Workers does not include sufficient protections for migrant workers, excludes informal workers, and is not well known to workers (Anh et al. 2010; Le and Mont 2014).

Cambodia, Lao PDR, and Myanmar all have less comprehensive legislative frameworks governing migration. The 2011 Subdecree No. 190 on Management of Sending of Cambodian Workers Abroad through Private Recruitment Agencies provides the outline for a migration system based on private recruitment with protection mechanisms for migrant workers such as mandatory predeparture orientation and the availability of a complaint mechanism. Subsequent *prakas* (regulations), drafted in collaboration with the International Labour Organization (ILO) and with tripartite input, have built on this framework and clarified some of the vague aspects of Subdecree No. 190. Despite the progress represented by the *prakas*, Cambodia lacks legislation on migration. Neither subdecrees nor *prakas* are legally enforceable but instead are "practical implementation tools" (ILO 2015b, 7; LSCW 2013). Labor migration in Lao PDR is governed by the 2013 Labor Law (amended). The legislation provides the general outlines for an international labor migration system setting forth in general terms the minimum requirements for recruitment agencies and the protections for migrant workers that must be provided by recruitment agencies. Several regulations support this general framework by defining the requirements that Laotians must meet to work abroad and set out the rights and responsibilities of migrants, employers, and recruitment agencies. However, these regulations will likely need to be updated to reflect the new labor law (ILO 2015b; ILO 2016d). In Myanmar, the Law Relating to Overseas Employment, enacted in 1999, provides the legal framework for the migration system. The law seeks to facilitate employment abroad and lays out the responsibilities of government actors responsible for managing migration, the process for registering prospective migrants, and that for licensing recruitment agencies. The current legal framework does not form a comprehensive migration policy with important questions of oversight of recruitment agencies and protections for migrant workers left unaddressed (Hall 2012).

Institutional framework

Indonesia and the Philippines both have specialized agencies dealing with migration management and the protection of migrants. In the Philippines, different agencies are devoted to different stages of the migration process, and this clarity of objectives helps ensure that the system functions well. For instance, POEA is responsible primarily for migration management, including functions related to the licensing and regulation of private recruitment, the provision of public recruitment, and oversight of worker protection. POEA has overseas outposts referred to as Philippine Overseas Labor Offices (POLOs) that perform management tasks such as registering foreign employers and overseeing compliance with PEOA policies. Another set of institutions is then responsible for the protection of migrant workers, with the Overseas Workers Welfare Administration (OWWA) being the most important.

In Indonesia, two agencies with overlapping responsibilities are primarily responsible for managing out-migration at the national level. The Ministry of Manpower has responsibility for setting migration policies and supervising labor migration (Farbenblum, Taylor-Nicholson, and Paoletti 2013). This involves monitoring recruitment including licensing private recruitment agencies, establishing procedures for the placement process, and negotiating bilateral agreements. The Ministry of Manpower is responsible for enforcement of migration policy and has provincial and local offices that manage day-to-day interactions with prospective migrants (Farbenblum, Taylor-Nicholson, and Paoletti 2013). The National Authority for the Placement and

Protection of Indonesian Overseas Workers (BNP2TKI) is generally seen as the implementer of migration policy and the coordinator of migration processes with responsibility for providing services to migrants. BNP2TKI reports directly to the president, but the agency is subordinate to the Ministry of Manpower and lacks enforcement authority. Like the Ministry, BNP2TKI has provincial and local offices.

Despite robust institutional structures, both the Philippines and Indonesia face coordination challenges. In the Philippines, coordination is insufficient and at times leads to legal inconsistencies (Orbeta and Abrigo 2011). POLOs, which oversee the well-being of migrants in countries where they are present, may lack data about the workers present in their jurisdictions because POEA does not supply their lists of deployed workers (Orbeta, Abrigo, and Cabalfin 2009; Agunias 2007). Local governments are less involved in governance than is desirable (IOM 2013). There are also concerns that POLOs are understaffed and that POEA and POLOs lack sufficient resources (Agunias 2007). In Indonesia, lack of clarity in the responsibilities of the Ministry of Manpower and BNP2TKI, and of their provincial and local offices, has undermined the effectiveness of both agencies. Though BNP2TKI is technically subordinate to the Ministry, the vagueness of Law No. 39/2004, which views both as implementing agencies, and of subsequent regulations means that there are no clear lines of authority between the two agencies (Kuncoro, Damayanti, and Isfandiarni 2014). This has led to interagency conflict, uncertainty among migrants about which agency to seek out in case of need, inefficiency including agency shopping when recruitment agencies seek documentation from BNP2TKI in case of denial by the Ministry of Manpower (or vice versa), redundant documentation when recruitment agencies keep records such as identity cards from both agencies, and duplicative processes when provincial officials reapprove documents already verified by the Ministry of Manpower or require additional documentation (Farbenblum, Taylor-Nicholson, and Paoletti 2013; IOM 2010a; Kuncoro, Damayanti, and Isfandiarni 2014).

The institutions serving migrants in ASEAN's other main sending countries are less specialized than in the Philippines and Indonesia. Myanmar and Vietnam each have a specialized agency for out-migration, but the agency deals with issues of both migration management and migrant protection. In Vietnam, the Department of Overseas Labor within the Ministry of Labor, Invalids, and Social Affairs is the agency responsible for managing out-migration. The department oversees migration policy, regulates the recruitment industry, negotiates bilateral agreements, and provides information, training, dispute resolution, and other services to help protect migrants. In Myanmar, the Ministry of Labor, Immigration, and Population is the primary agency responsible for managing migration. Through the Overseas Employment Supervisory Committee, an inter-ministerial agency chaired by the Department of Labor within the Ministry, the Ministry is charged with facilitating overseas labor migration, regulating private recruitment agencies, and providing training to migrant workers. In both Cambodia and Lao PDR, the same agency is charged with overseeing both immigration and emigration. In Cambodia, the Ministry of Labor and Vocational Training is responsible for the management and protection of migrant labor through the Department of Employment and Manpower within its General Department of Labor. The Department performs functions such as issuing work permits, preparing regulations on migration, and overseeing recruitment agencies (Tunon and Rim 2013). In Lao PDR, the Ministry of Labor and Social Welfare is responsible for managing the labor migration system, including regulating recruitment agencies, along with labor and social welfare departments at the local level.[6]

Bilateral agreements and MOUs

The Philippines relies on a system of bilateral agreements to govern migration with many destination countries. The existence of a bilateral agreement is one of the factors considered by the Philippines in determining whether a country will protect the rights of its citizens while abroad and so should be a permitted destination country. The government views the agreements as part of an ongoing process to improve migration management (Lanto 2015). The Philippines has signed MOUs and Memorandums of Agreement (MOAs), neither of which are as binding as bilateral labor agreements, with 23 countries and 4 subnational governments regarding land-based migrants and with 6 countries regarding sea-based migrants.[7] The agreements range from facilitation of worker migration in very specific areas to broader frameworks covering required qualifications, worker welfare, and cooperation. The Philippines has been able to use bilateral agreements to engage in substantive dialogue with host countries about the important issues of hiring and migrant welfare that may otherwise have been ignored. In the best cases, particular concerns of host countries and migrant workers have been considered and the uncertainty and risk associated with migration have been limited (Rivera, Serrano, and Tullao 2013).

The Philippines has also pursued social security agreements with host counties. Social security agreements coordinate host country disability, retirement, and other pensions with those of the Philippines. The Philippines now has more than ten such agreements.[8] These social security agreements usually allow Filipinos to file claims with the host country or with the Philippines; provide equal coverage with host country nationals; allow Filipinos to receive their benefits on return to the Philippines; provide for the totalization of benefits so that employment in the host country and in the Philippines counts toward benefit accrual; and require benefits payment to be shared by the host country and the Philippines (Go 2012).

Although the Philippines has likely been more successful in negotiating bilateral agreements than any other sending country, weaknesses still remain. A recent report highlights several drawbacks in the Philippines' agreements, including insufficient coverage and agreements that are not binding; the lack of participation of civil society in negotiations and insufficient negotiating staff; a failure to account for the particular needs of female migrants; insufficient monitoring and oversight; and the lack of a central repository for bilateral labor agreement documents[9] (CMA 2010). Additionally, many agreements have been ratified by the Philippines but not by the host country or, otherwise, had a short lifespan and were not renewed (Battistella 2012). The agreements have also been criticized for being vague and limited in scope (Blank 2011).

Indonesia and Vietnam have many bilateral agreements with destination countries. Indonesia has negotiated bilateral agreements with 11 destinations. These include several in the Middle East such as with Saudi Arabia and the United Arab Emirates, two with ASEAN countries including another sending country (the Philippines), and several with East Asian countries outside of ASEAN. Most of the bilateral agreements are MOUs that provide for cooperation on recruitment and protection but do not include the binding elements of bilateral labor agreements. Indonesia and Malaysia have used the negotiation of MOUs as a forum to address concerns about the treatment of Indonesian domestic workers. Vietnam has signed bilateral agreements with 16 countries and territories including 3 ASEAN countries: Lao PDR, Malaysia, and Thailand.[10] These include both more formal MOUs, such as that with Malaysia, and agreements between agencies such as that between the Department of Overseas Labor and the Japan International Training and Cooperation Organization (JITCO) (Bowen and Huong 2012).

Although Indonesia and Vietnam have had some success with bilateral agreements, each country's agreements have weaknesses. In some cases in Indonesia, MOUs have not been negotiated transparently, and texts are generally not made available to the public (Farbenblum, Taylor-Nicholson, and Paoletti 2013; ILO 2015d). In other cases, bilateral agreements may not be functioning as designed. The additional protections included in the MOU with Malaysia seem to have incentivized the migration of domestic workers via irregular channels, perhaps to avoid the fixed recruitment fees included in the agreement (Harkins 2016). Finally, Indonesia has enacted moratoria on the deployment of domestic workers to several countries with which it has bilateral agreements, including Jordan, Kuwait, and Saudi Arabia. This suggests that these MOUs were not functioning well either to protect migrants or as channels to address concerns about migrant protections. Vietnam's bilateral agreements on migration are not published. The MOU with Malaysia includes a standard employment contract in the agreement, a good practice, but also allows employers to keep migrants' passports (ILO 2015d). Many popular destinations for Vietnamese migrant workers are not covered by bilateral agreements (ILO 2015e).

Cambodia, Lao PDR, and Myanmar have each signed an MOU with Thailand to manage labor migration and regularize undocumented migrants. Thailand signed MOUs with Lao PDR in 2002 and with Cambodia and Myanmar in 2003. The agreements became active in 2006 in the case of Lao PDR and Cambodia and in 2009 in the case of Myanmar. The MOUs established a formal migration process that had been lacking with the three countries before the 2000s. The agreements govern all aspects of the migration process from admissions to employment and exit, and pay particular attention to efforts to prevent irregular migration. Thailand is to provide information about employer demand, and the sending countries are to provide information about worker supply. Also, Thailand and the sending countries are to share data and coordinate on necessary documentation and employment protections, set terms of employment, and make efforts to prevent illegal migration (ILO 2015b). Finally, the MOUs helped facilitate a regularization and documentation process, known as the national verification process, for irregular migrants from Cambodia, Lao PDR, and Myanmar.

Despite the importance of the MOUs in establishing a formal migration process, the agreements are underutilized and have failed to replace irregular migration. The process of migrating to Thailand via the MOU is lengthy and complex, requiring several months to complete submissions to, and approvals from, government agencies in both Cambodia and Thailand (ILO 2015b). As a result, few migrants see a benefit in using the formal MOU channel, and uptake is limited (MMN and AMC 2013). For example, as of November 2014, only 90,757 Cambodian workers had work permits under the MOU, whereas 700,000 irregular Cambodian migrants registered with Thailand between July and October of that year (Cambodia, MOLVT and ILO 2014; ILO 2015b). Recruitment agencies are used by migrants in both Thailand and the sending countries to assist with the process despite the MOU channel being envisioned as a government-to-government process. The MOUs have also been criticized for focusing more on the procedural aspects of migration and on preventing irregular migration and less on filling labor market shortages. Additionally, they have been criticized for involving bilateral meetings that are not transparent, which creates confusion among migrants and employers, and for requiring only limited data collection and sharing and monitoring and evaluation (ILO 2015b). Thailand signed new MOUs with Cambodia and Vietnam in 2015 and with Lao PDR and Myanmar in 2016. Although these MOUs are not yet operational, they are more expansive, covering issues of skills development and reemployment (ILO 2016a; ILO 2016b).

Admissions

Entry paths and quantity restrictions

In general, sending countries take entry paths and quantity restrictions as given: host countries control who and how many migrants enter the country. However, sending countries can influence certain aspects of these components of the migration system through bilateral agreements. In extreme cases, a bilateral agreement is a precondition of entry. This is the case with the Republic of Korea's Employment Permit System in which all of ASEAN's main sending countries except Lao PDR participate. The Employment Permit System requires recruitment by a public agency in the sending country and close monitoring of several aspects of the migration process, particularly undocumented migration. Cambodia, Lao PDR, and Myanmar's MOUs with Thailand establish the admissions process for the entry of low-skilled formal migrants.[11] In other cases, bilateral agreements govern the entry of a more limited group of workers. For example, agreements between the Philippines and Bahrain, Germany, Japan, Norway, Spain, and the United Kingdom relate to the entry of Philippine health professionals.

Outside the scope of bilateral agreements, the Philippines provides assistance to migrants to help them comply with the entry requirements of host countries. Skills testing centers in the Philippines are accredited by the Technical Education and Skills Development Authority to allow out-migrants to comply with skills requirements. The Department of Health accredits medical clinics for migrant workers to comply with host country requirements for medical examinations. Recruitment agencies are responsible for overseeing both the skills and medical examinations.

Recruitment

In the Philippines, regulation of recruitment is designed to protect migrant workers from abuse and to help migrant workers comply with host country requirements. POEA regulates private recruitment through a two-step system of licensing private recruitment agencies and accrediting foreign employers. To be eligible for a license to recruit migrant workers, an agency must be owned by a Philippine citizen and meet minimum capital requirements. The agency must attend a prelicensing orientation seminar and a continuing agency education seminar for license renewal. The agency must agree to comply with rules designed to protect migrant workers and adhere to ethical standards. Finally, the recruiter is required to deposit ₱1 million into escrow to cover claims by workers for contract violations and penalties for illegal recruitment practices. POEA urges recruiters to specialize in certain occupations (Ahsan et al. 2014). The Philippines has the largest number of recruitment agencies of any ASEAN sending country, with about double those of Indonesia (figure 7.2).

FIGURE 7.2

Number of recruitment agencies in ASEAN's main sending countries

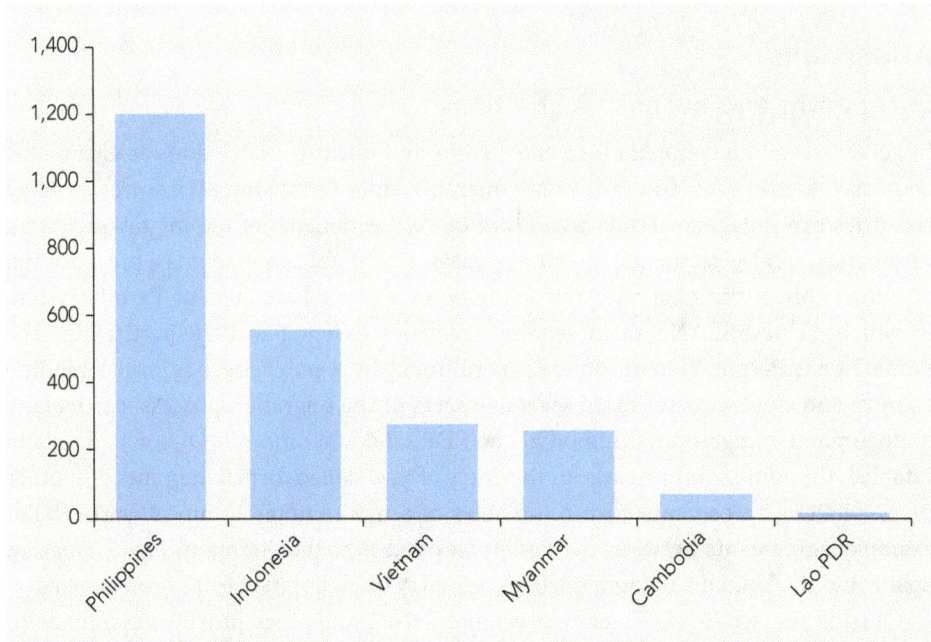

Source: Philippines, COA (2016a) for the Philippines; Farbenblum, Taylor-Nicholson, and Paoletti (2013) for Indonesia; the Department of Overseas Labor for Vietnam; the Ministry of Labor and Vocational Training for Cambodia; ILO (2016d) for Lao PDR; and the Ministry of Labor, Immigration, and Population for Myanmar.
Note: The year is 2013 for Indonesia, 2015 for the Philippines; 2016 for Cambodia, Lao PDR, and Myanmar; and 2017 for Vietnam. ASEAN = Association of Southeast Asian Nations.

The Philippines also requires employers of foreign workers to be accredited. To extend its oversight of recruitment and placement to host countries, the Philippines requires employers who wish to hire Philippine migrants to obtain accreditation with POEA or POLOs. The process of accreditation involves verification by officials from POLOs, a Philippines Embassy or consulate, or POEA that the rights and welfare of Philippine migrant workers will be protected and that employment contracts are consistent with laws in both the host country and the Philippines. To be accredited, employers, placement agencies, and staffing companies must work through a private recruitment agent and disclose the number of positions required, their salaries, and a master employment contract. Accreditation can be suspended for a variety of violations including contract violations and failure to assist or repatriate workers in distress. The employer is responsible for certain costs such as transportation costs and any skills or qualifications assessment fee. POEA has encouraged large foreign employers including multinational construction contractors, state authorities managing hospital systems, and hotel chains to employ Philippine workers (Ahsan et al. 2014).

Like the Philippines, Indonesia and Vietnam seek to regulate private recruitment of migrant workers through a licensing system (table 7.2). Also like the Philippines, Indonesia and Vietnam license recruitment agencies, have minimum capital and security deposit requirements, and have a process for reviewing employers of, or job orders for, migrant workers. In Indonesia, the Ministry of Manpower, BNP2TKI, and their local offices regulate recruitment agencies (PPTKIS) and labor brokers. Recruitment agencies must receive a license to recruit (SIPPTKIS), which requires minimum paid-up capital requirements, posting a bank deposit as collateral, and a three-year business plan.[12] To recruit migrant workers for a particular job order, recruitment agencies must also obtain a permit (SIP) that requires the recruitment agency to have a job order that has been reviewed by the Indonesian embassy or consulate in the destination country and a placement agreement with an Indonesian worker who has registered as a prospective migrant with the local Ministry of Manpower office. In Vietnam, the Department of Overseas Labor is responsible for issuing licenses to recruitment agencies, many of which are partially or wholly owned by the state, and for regulating the industry. Licensed recruitment agencies must have minimum capital and pay a deposit for the settlement of claims. Agencies sending more than 100 migrant workers to a destination

TABLE 7.2

Licensing requirements for recruitment agencies in ASEAN's main sending countries

Licensing requirement	PHL	IDN	VNM	KHM	LAO	MMR
Minimum capital	X	X	X	O	X	O
Security deposit	X	X	X	X	X	O
Orientation	X	O	O	O	O	O
Employer accreditation/job order review	X	X	X	O	O	O
Representative abroad	O	O	X	X	O	O

Note: X = the licensing requirement is present; O = the licensing requirement is not present; ASEAN = Association of Southeast Asian Nations; IDN = Indonesia; KHM = Cambodia; LAO = Lao PDR; MMR = Mynamar; PHL = Phillipines; VNM = Vietnam.

country must have a representative in that destination (Le and Mont 2014). Recruitment agencies must submit labor supply contracts to the department for review and supply reports on migrant workers sent abroad, with information on the situation of those who are employed abroad and those returning to Vietnam.[13]

The regulation of recruitment agencies is similar in Cambodia, Lao PDR, and Myanmar but less robust (table 7.2). Neither Cambodia nor Myanmar has minimum capital requirements, Lao PDR does not require recruitment agencies to have representatives abroad, and Myanmar does not require a security deposit. None of the three countries accredits employers of, or reviews job orders for, migrant workers. In Cambodia, the Ministry of Labor and Vocational Training oversees the licensing of private recruitment agencies. To receive a license, recruitment agencies must make a security deposit, provide regular reports on its activities, and have a permanent representative in any destination country with migrant workers. Recruitment agencies must also report a worker's arrival in the destination country to Cambodia's embassy or consulate (MMN and AMC 2013). In Lao PDR, the Ministry of Labor and Social Welfare, along with its local branches, approves and cancels recruitment agency licenses.[14] To obtain a license, agencies must be headed by someone with Lao citizenship, make a security deposit, and have minimum registered capital. In Myanmar, the Ministry of Labor, Immigration, and Population oversees recruitment with input from the Overseas Employment Supervisory Committee. The Department grants licenses to recruitment agencies that must inform the Department of Labor upon a migrant worker's departure.

Although the regulation of the recruitment process in the Philippines is regarded as a well-functioning model for source country governments, it has weaknesses. Recruitment costs are believed to be lower for Philippine migrants in the Middle East than those faced by migrants from India, Nepal, and Sri Lanka (Agunias 2010). The two-step recruitment process extends protection for migrant workers beyond the Philippines to host countries. Still, the difficulty of ensuring that host country and Philippine recruitment requirements are compatible, the difficulty of enforcing these requirements, and the involved process of migrating formally from the Philippines mean that migrants sometimes choose quasi-formal or informal migration channels. Agunias (2010) describes a three-tier migration system between the Philippines and the United Arab Emirates: a channel of informal agreements with less protection for workers and a wholly informal channel that circumvents the recruitment system exist alongside formal processes. Recruitment by unlicensed agencies and violations of recruitment rules are common, such as substituting contracts with lower wages and deployment to different or nonexistent jobs.

Regulation of the recruitment process is weak in Indonesia. Although Indonesia's Law No. 39/2004 and subsequent regulations require licensed recruitment agencies to carry out recruitment functions, in practice labor brokers (*calo*) that are not regulated often take on this role to identify and provide information about migration to potential migrants, often in rural areas. This is particularly the case for those migrants to the Middle East whom brokers connect to Jakarta-based recruitment agencies (Farbenblum, Taylor-Nicholson, and Paoletti 2013). The involvement of brokers can increase recruitment costs and subject migrants to abuse without redress because brokers are unregulated (IOM 2010a). Recruitment agencies at times recruit Indonesian workers directly, rather than from the pool of registered prospective migrant workers as required by law, and frequently house workers for predeparture training without first obtaining a job order (Farbenblum, Taylor-Nicholson, and Paoletti 2013). The lack of clear roles for the Ministry of Manpower and BNP2TKI means that recruitment agencies may obtain documentation from both agencies to demonstrate compliance with the same step of the recruitment or predeparture process or seek out the other agency if the first rejects a permit application (Kuncoro, Damayanti, and Isfandiarni 2014).

The recruitment environment is similarly weak in Cambodia, Lao PDR, Myanmar, and Vietnam. Despite the requirement that recruitment agencies deal directly with workers in Vietnam, informal brokers are a standard actor in the process. A report by the National Assembly Standing Committee found that 70 to 80 percent of workers were recruited by brokers. The involvement of brokers may cause migrants to pay fees twice, first to brokers and then to licensed recruitment agencies. Additionally, recruitment agencies and brokers charge migrants high fees despite the legal cap. This can take the form of charging higher fees to prospective migrants seeking higher-paying jobs, overcharging for taxes, or simply overcharging for fees (Phuong and Venkatesh 2016). Additionally, brokers may deceive migrants, skirt migration requirements, or provide migrants with fraudulent documents (Bowen and Huong 2012; CSAGA 2013; Le and Mont 2014). Finally, recruitment agencies do not follow reporting requirements, which makes maintaining records on migrant workers and protecting them in the case of need difficult (Vietnam, MFA 2012). In Cambodia, Lao PDR, and Myanmar, the high costs of using private recruiters leads most migrants to seek out unlicensed brokers.

Several countries have used self-enforcement and public ranking of recruitment agencies as a tactic to improve the recruitment process. The ILO has recently worked with the Vietnam Association of Manpower Supply, the association of recruitment agencies, to improve the recruitment process. Recruitment agencies have been encouraged to adopt a voluntary code of conduct to incentivize self-regulation (Ahsan et al. 2014). Each year since 2012, participating agencies have been ranked on their compliance with the code to provide more information about the quality of the agencies and to incentivize better behavior. More than one-quarter of all agencies now participate in the assessment, accounting for half of all contract-based overseas workers (ILO 2015a). The Vietnamese association has sought to increase the effectiveness of the ranking by encouraging participation through stakeholder engagement with recruitment agencies, central and local government agencies, and receiving countries (ILO 2013b; ILO 2015f). The Association of Cambodian Recruitment Agencies also adopted a voluntary code of conduct in 2009 to encourage recruitment agencies to self-regulate in coordination with the ILO. Members have reportedly been removed from the Cambodian association for not performing up to the code (Cambodia, MOLVT and ILO 2014). In Indonesia, BNP2TKI has rated recruitment agencies to increase competition among the agencies, provide information to prospective migrants, and increase supervision (World Bank 2016c). In Myanmar, the Overseas Employment Agencies Federation has created a code of conduct and a monitoring mechanism to improve recruitment practices through self-enforcement (ILO 2015a).

Finally, the Philippines has created an award system for high-performing recruitment agencies and employers. These awards exempt agencies and employers from certain administrative requirements such as document submissions and an easier approvals process. POEA publishes information about recruitment agencies that are delinquent (Orbeta, Abrigo, and Cabalfin 2009).

In addition to licensing private recruitment agencies, several of ASEAN's main sending countries have public recruitment programs, and most are used for recruitment to Korea's Employment Permit System. In the Philippines, the Government Placement Branch, a public recruitment agency within POEA, recruits workers for placement in Korea and Taiwan, China. In Indonesia, BNP2TKI recruits for deployment of migrants to Korea and Japan. In Cambodia, the Manpower Training and Overseas Sending Board within the Ministry of Labor and Vocational Training is responsible for recruitment and deployment to Korea. Vietnam's Center of Overseas Labor provides the public recruitment and training required for participation in the Employment Permit System. Concerns about high rates of Vietnamese workers overstaying their contracts in Korea led to the suspension of Vietnam's participation in 2012. These high rates of overstay seem in part caused by the persistence of informal brokerage, prohibited under both Vietnamese law and the MOU with Korea, which drove up migration costs to Korea incentivizing migrants to stay longer to earn back upfront costs (Ishizuka 2013; Le and Mont 2014). Public recruitment generally represents a small share of out-migration in the region. For example, in the Philippines in 2010 only 2 percent of newly hired migrants used public recruitment (POEA 2010).

Employment

Employment Terms

As with entry paths and quantity restrictions, sending countries generally take employment terms as given because host countries determine how long migrant workers can work, whether their work permits can be renewed, and other conditions such as whether migrant workers can bring dependents with them. Indonesia is an exception. Indonesia's Law No. 39/2004 states that employment contracts for migrant workers can only be made for a maximum period of two years with a maximum extension of two years subject to the approval of Indonesian authorities in the destination country. This provision is inconsistent with migration rules in countries such as Singapore where work permits can be renewed multiple times without exit.

Sending countries can also influence employment terms through bilateral agreements. The MOUs and MOAs that the Philippines has negotiated have included provisions related to employments terms, as in the case of the agreement with Qatar that includes a model employment contract and that with Iraq that had provisions regarding contract renewal. The MOUs signed between Thailand and Cambodia, Lao PDR, and Myanmar originally restricted employment terms to an initial two-year period that could be extended for another two years before a required three-year cooling off period.

Several actions in 2014 and 2016 relaxed the cooling-off period requirement and permitted migrants to extend their existing work permits (IOM 2016a).

Protection

Restrictions on host country, occupation, or sector

Several ASEAN sending countries restrict the countries to which workers can migrate or the occupations they can work in, or both. The Philippines only permits migrants to work in countries in which their rights will be protected. The Department of Foreign Affairs is responsible for compiling a list of compliant countries. In Indonesia, concerns about mistreatment and abuse of domestic workers led to a moratorium on Indonesian female domestic workers migrating to Malaysia in 2009, which was removed in 2011. However, similar concerns led to a moratorium on the deployment of domestic workers to Saudi Arabia in 2009 and then to 21 countries in the Middle East and North Africa in 2015.[15] Indonesia is now pursuing a policy to halt all deployment of domestic workers by 2017. This could impact as many as 4 million workers or 3.2 percent of Indonesia's 2015 workforce (World Bank 2016c). Responding to concerns about abuse and exploitation, Cambodia banned deployment of domestic workers to Malaysia in 2011. The ban was lifted in 2015 after the signing of an MOU, but no domestic workers were deployed there in 2016 (ILO 2016e). Though there is no formal ban on deploying workers into the fishing sector, the Cambodian government has pressured recruitment agencies not to do so. Migrant workers from Lao PDR are not permitted to work in the sex industry; in unskilled occupations such as domestic work and cleaning; and in dangerous occupations such as fishing (MMN and AMC 2013). Myanmar generally prohibits workers from migrating as domestic workers. Specific bans were put in place in September 2014 for Singapore and Hong Kong SAR, China and again in June of 2015 for Singapore. Responding to a political controversy, Myanmar prohibited all workers from migrating to Malaysia in late 2016.

Such restrictions tend to be ineffective or even have negative effects. Filipinos migrate to countries not included on the Department of Foreign Affairs' list of compliant countries. Despite Lao PDR's restrictions on unskilled work, many migrants work in these occupations. For instance, more than 62,000 irregular Laotian migrants registered as domestic workers in Thailand between 2009 and 2010 (MMN and AMC 2013). The same is true for Myanmar's ban on migrant domestic workers (HOME and MWRN 2015). A recent World Bank study shows that this seems to be true in the case of Indonesia's moratoria, as well (World Bank 2016c). The share of undocumented female domestic workers in Malaysia increased 31 percentage points during the moratorium and declined by 11 percentage points afterward. A more formal study of the moratorium on migration to Malaysia and Saudi Arabia has shown other negative effects (Makovec et al. 2016). The moratorium on migration to Saudi Arabia was found to have led to (1) a decline in household per capita consumption expenditure in districts with high migration to that country of between 3 and 4 percent per year in the four years after the moratorium; and (2) an increase in the poverty rate of between 2 and 3 percentage points per year in the three years after the ban. Additionally, the Malaysia and Saudi Arabia bans were found to have led to a decline in female employment and labor force participation of up to 4 percentage points.

Fee restrictions

Cambodia is the only ASEAN sending country that does not have legal restrictions on the fees that can be charged by recruitment agencies. In the Philippines, the fees that can be paid by migrant workers are limited to documentation costs such as passport and recruitment fees that can be up to one month of salary. Domestic workers and sea-based workers are exempt from recruitment fees. In Indonesia, the Ministry of Manpower regulates recruitment fees and decides which party should be responsible for which fees. Recruitment agencies can charge a placement fee and a range of other fees for processing documents, health and psychological examinations, job training, food and accommodation during training, transportation, and insurance (Bachtiar 2011). In Vietnam, regulations establish destination-specific ceilings on the fees, and migrants should only be charged recruitment fees (not for items such as vocational or foreign language training) (Bowen and Huong 2012; Le and Mont 2014). Lao PDR caps recruitment fees at 15 percent of a migrant's monthly wage during employment abroad (ILO 2015b; Lao PDR, DOS and NERI 2012). In Myanmar, the Overseas Employment Supervisory Committee determines the fees that can be charged to migrants by recruitment agencies. In Cambodia, in contrast, there is no legal restriction on the fees that can be charged by recruitment agencies to migrant workers (LSCW 2013; MMN and AMC 2013; Tunon and Rim 2013).

Fee restrictions seem to be difficult to implement and are generally ineffective. In the Philippines, evidence exists that recruitment agents charge a recruitment fee of more than the permitted one month's salary; they also employ deceptive practices when charging recruitment fees, at times inappropriately recouping costs for transportation and insurance via salary deductions once the migrant worker is employed (Agunias 2010; Jureidini 2014). Fees are sometimes charged to domestic workers, who are exempt. Migrants from Vietnam are often charged recruitment fees that are higher than the regulated ceiling (Bélanger et al. 2010; Bowen and Huong 2012). For instance, job placement in Taiwan, China can cost US$5,000 to $6,000, much more than the US$1,500 maximum (Ahsan et al. 2014). Fees for migrant domestic workers migrating from Myanmar to Singapore were reportedly capped at four months of salary, though the cap seems to have been weakly enforced (HOME and MWRN 2015). A 2013 survey of migrant workers by the World Bank in collaboration with Statistics Indonesia found that high fees are likely one explanation for significant undocumented migration from Indonesia. Undocumented migrant workers pay an average of Rp 4.9 million in fees compared to Rp 8.8 million for documented migrants (World Bank 2016c).

Contract requirements

The Philippines specifies certain provisions that must be included in the employment contract that must be provided to migrant workers. These include details about the employer, job site, position, duration, salary, hours, and leave. The salary must not be lower than the host country minimum wage or the prevailing minimum wage in the National Capital Region of the Philippines. The minimum wage for domestic workers is set at US$400. Food, accommodation, and transportation must be provided either in kind or a monetary equivalent. The recruitment agent must agree to negotiate for the best terms and conditions for migrant workers. Still, there is evidence that abuses of these requirements occur. Contracts with lower wages are sometimes substituted for those approved by POEA, at times with the migrant worker's knowledge. Other abuses include deployment to nonexistent jobs or different jobs from the original contract and dishonesty about job responsibilities and work conditions (Agunias 2010).

While Indonesia has similar contract requirements, they are less extensive, and migrant workers frequently do not receive required contract documents. A placement agreement is signed between the recruitment agency and the migrant and an employment agreement between the employer and the migrant. The placement agreement sets out the rights and responsibilities of the recruitment agency and the prospective migrant and provides some details about the job. The employment agreement, signed after the recruitment agency provides training to the prospective migrant, provides more job-specific details; these include the details of the employer, the hours of work and wages, and the rights and obligations of the employer and the prospective migrant. The employment agreement does not have to be written in a language the migrant understands (Farbenblum, Taylor-Nicholson, and Paoletti 2013). The survey of Indonesian migrant workers undertaken by the World Bank in collaboration with Statistics Indonesia found that only 42 percent of current and 58 percent of former migrant workers had signed the placement agreement, including 20 percent of documented workers (World Bank 2016c). Similarly, two-thirds of current migrant workers did not sign employment contracts and among those who did only about 60 percent signed them before departure. Only about half of all migrants are aware of their salary before departure. Undocumented migrants to Malaysia are the least likely to sign a job contract or know their salary before arrival in the destination country.

In Vietnam, contracts are frequently not provided to migrants or are later substituted, and contract requirements are less extensive than in the Philippines. Vietnamese employment contracts must contain information about the employment term, wages, working conditions, and fees; and migrants have a right to inquire about salary information. The contract must be provided to the migrant to be signed at least five days before departure. There is evidence, however, that contracts are not always given to migrants within this required time frame and that sufficient information about the contract is not always provided to migrants. For example, a survey of 357 returned migrants in the Ha Nam, Thai Binh, and Hung Yen provinces found that 24 percent were required to sign contracts that they did not understand (CSAGA 2013). A third of migrants did work that was not outlined in their contract, and one-fifth received lower salaries than that provided in the contract. Furthermore, in a recent survey of Vietnamese migrants to Malaysia, 6 percent reported not signing a contract, 26 percent reported working on a different contract than the one originally signed, and about 11 percent earned less than the salary promised (ILO and KNOMAD 2015).

Minimum contract provisions in Cambodia, Lao PDR, and Myanmar face similar problems. In Cambodia, migrant workers must sign a job placement service contract with the recruitment agency and an employment contract with the foreign employer that must specify working conditions, types of workers, and benefits and that must be written in Khmer, English, and the language of the receiving country. In contrast to requirements specified in previous regulations, the employment contract does not now have to include information about contract length, salary, working hours, and time off (LSCW 2013). There are also concerns that migrants are not required to sign employment contracts before deployment (LSCW 2013). Directive No. 2417/MLSW in Lao PDR requires the signing of contracts between (1) migrant workers and both the recruitment agency and the employer and (2) the recruitment agency and the employer. According to the Labor Law (Amended), the employment contract should include provisions regarding scope of work, salary, duration, working days, and benefits. A small survey of Laotian migrants in Thailand found that only half had signed contracts with their employers, and only 3 percent had the contract in their possession (ILO 2008). In Myanmar, recruitment agencies must submit job offers, including the employment contract and information about working conditions, salary, working hours, and leave for approval by the Committee of Health, Education and Human Resources Development. However, ensuring minimum standards in employment contracts remains a challenge (Oo 2016).

Orientation programs

The Philippines offers a series of orientation programs before and after departure to prepare migrants for employment abroad. The Pre-Employment Orientation Seminar (PEOS) is designed to help potential migrant workers navigate the job search and recruitment process and make informed decisions about going abroad. Previously, this orientation seminar was voluntary and offered in POEA and Department of Labor and Employment (DOLE) regional offices (IOM 2013). However, the PEOS is now mandatory and can be completed online at no cost (POEA 2016). Modules include general information about working overseas, job search information, details about illegal recruitment, information about allowable fees and the minimum provisions of the employment contract, and country-specific information. POEA also provides a listing of job opportunities available abroad through the job advertising site JobStreet.com. The Predeparture Orientation Seminar (PDOS) is a mandatory six-hour course for departing migrant workers; it is designed to help foreign workers adjust to work and living abroad, particularly during their first six months. The seminar includes seven modules on topics such as the employment contract, health and safety, financial literacy, and programs and services for migrant workers (Asis and Agunias 2012). Accredited recruitment agencies and industry associations must provide the course for free. More than 800,000 individuals participated in this predeparture orientation course in 2014 (PSA 2015). Finally, the Philippine Overseas Labor Offices offer postarrival orientation seminars in host countries to foreign workers who have recently arrived. These courses are not mandatory and are only available in countries that have POLOs. These courses are designed to inform workers about country-specific rights and responsibilities and information on assistance (ILO 2015g).

The Philippines is generally lauded for its commitment to increasing the knowledge of migrant workers. Some good practices identified with the Philippines' orientation programs are the involvement of local government partners, the inclusion of nongovernmental organizations (NGOs) to incorporate a rights perspective, creating the postarrival orientation seminars to ensure that learning does not stop at departure, developing orientation programs for recruiters, and providing migration information at the local level (Asis and Agunias 2012). At the same time, several weaknesses are apparent. A 2010 evaluation of the PDOS found that accredited providers diverged from prescribed content and methodology, provided certificates even when the orientation seminar was not attended, imposed fees, and held shortened sessions (Anchustegui 2010). Involvement of recruitment agencies, whose interest is facilitating employment and not protecting migrant workers, is criticized (Asis and Agunias 2012; Anchustegui 2010). There are complaints that the orientation sessions are used to promote remittance and insurance products (Ambito and Banzon 2011; Anchustegui 2010; Philippines, DOLE 2014). There is also concern that the sessions do not include skill- or country-specific information and are poorly timed with respect to a migrant's departure date (IOM 2013; Ambito and Banzon 2011). There is no clear link between the predeparture and post-arrival orientation seminars, which is a desirable feature of orientation programs (ILO 2015g).

Indonesia also offers a predeparture orientation program for migrant workers. In Indonesia, all migrants are required to undergo a predeparture orientation program that is overseen by the migrant-focused agency BNP2TKI and provided by BNP2TKI and its local offices in 16 provinces. The program is eight hours and covers subjects such as deployment terms, work contracts, details about the destination country, the rights and obligations of migrants and their employers, arrival and departure procedures, Indonesian embassies and missions abroad and accessing assistance through them, and remittance channels (Asis and Agunias 2012). The orientation program should be free for migrants, though responsibility for payment is unclear, and is to be given at least two days before departure (IOM 2010a). Indonesia does not offer an orientation program for migrants once they arrive at the destination.

There is some evidence that Indonesia's predeparture orientation program is effective in increasing the knowledge and awareness of migrants. The 2013 survey of migrant workers undertaken by the World Bank and Statistics Indonesia showed that migrants attending this orientation program were about 15 percentage points more likely to be aware of issues related to salary and working conditions. Knowledge of protection services such as contact numbers doubles for participating migrants. However, a significant portion of migrants still lack knowledge. Only about half of migrants are aware of the contact information of the Indonesian embassy or consulate, 40 percent are aware of the contacts of the recruitment agency, and 35 percent are aware of the contact of the nearest police station. Lack of attendance may be one reason for this continued lack of awareness. Despite being required for all migrants except those remigrating to the same job in the same destination country, about one-third of migrants do not receive the predeparture orientation program.

Orientation is required in Vietnam but is primarily the responsibility of recruitment agencies. Agencies must provide migrants with a 74-hour predeparture orientation program that includes information about the migrant's country of destination and details of the contract between the worker and the recruitment agency. The agencies are not permitted to charge migrants for the training. The Department of Overseas Labor has developed training content. Although recruitment agencies can team up with vocational training institutes, the agencies seem to use their own curriculum and do not always follow the 74-hour requirement (Bowen and Huong 2012). Despite the required orientation program, there are concerns about how well informed workers are about labor migration laws, the rights and duties of employers, and financial aspects of working abroad including costs and obtaining loans (Anh 2008; CSAGA 2013; Le and Mont 2014; Vietnam, MFA 2012). There is also evidence of significant levels of nonparticipation (Bélanger and Giang 2013; CSAGA 2013).

In Cambodia, Lao PDR, and Myanmar, orientation programs tend to be provided by recruitment agencies and tend to lack standardized curricula. In Cambodia, recruitment agencies are required to provide predeparture orientation training that includes key contact information for embassies or consulates and the Ministry of Labor and Vocational Training. The ministry issues certificates to migrants completing predeparture orientation as a precondition of exit. However, regulations do not specify the content of the predeparture orientation, and there have been concerns that training is not uniform (LSCW 2013).[16] Similarly, recruitment agencies in Lao PDR are required to provide information and training, including certificates of expertise, to migrant workers before departure. In practice, the provincial Department of Labor and Social Welfare works with the Federation of Trade Unions and the Lao Youth Union to provide the orientation (Lao PDR, MOLSW, MOFA, and MPS 2013). There are concerns about how often orientation programs are given and about orientation quality, with some evidence of migrants not undergoing predeparture training and others finding training to be broad and brief (ILO 2013a). In Myanmar, predeparture orientation is mandatory for migrants and should include information about the labor contract, remittance channels, important contacts, and the language and culture of the destination country (Naing 2014). The program lasts three days and for workers migrating to Thailand is conducted by employer representatives, labor department officials, and recruitment agencies (Oo 2016). The predeparture orientation program is not standardized, though standard materials are being created, and lacks certified trainers (ILO 2013a; ILO 2015a). Reports from one NGO suggest that orientation programs have delivered poor training in the past (HOME and MWRN 2015). The extent of training in all three countries is limited by the predominance of informal migration.

The impact of predeparture orientation programs has not been studied thoroughly. Some evidence suggests that these programs fail to motivate additional international labor migration. A recent impact evaluation of a package of interventions to improve information about, and access to, work overseas found no impact on the likelihood of international migration from Sorsogon Province in the Philippines (Beam, McKenzie, and Yang 2015). However, the impact on migrants once abroad is still an open question

(McKenzie and Yang 2015). A randomized control trial of different versions of the Philippines' Predeparture Orientation Seminar, a partnership between OWWA in the Philippines and the Asian Institute of Management, is ongoing (Barsbai et al. ongoing; Philippines, DOLE 2014).

Remittances

The Philippines has worked to increase access to formal remittance channels, increase financial literacy, and link remittances to development. Institutions responsible for remittance transactions in the Philippines include banks, nonbank financial intermediaries, pawnshops, and money transfer operators including mobile service providers. The institutions must register with the Philippines central bank (Bangko Sentral ng Pilipinas) which regulates them (Nejar 2012). Remittances can also be sent informally via friends, family, and other social networks. The central bank's efforts to increase transparency and competition and its establishment of the Philippine Payments and Settlements System (PhilPaSS), the expansion of ATMs and mobile technology, and the growth of grassroots financial institutions have helped to increase access to remittances and reduce remittance costs (Bagasao 2013). The Philippines has also enabled foreign workers to make social security payments, health insurance contributions, and other payments while abroad. Financial literacy is incorporated before departure in the PDOS, while abroad via the POLOs, and upon return through programs run by the National Reintegration Center for OFWs (overseas foreign workers). Consistent with the vision of the Philippine Development Plan 2011–16, programs also exist to funnel remittances to development purposes. The *Longkod sa Kapwa Pilipino* (LINKAPIL) program channels the resources of Filipinos overseas to support small projects, including livelihood programs, small-scale infrastructure projects, and scholarships. Commercial banks are urged by Bangko Sentral ng Pilipinas to provide specialized products to foreign workers (Bagasao 2013). Creating additional opportunities to invest remittances in productive activities and a better investment climate are viewed as key improvements (Ahsan et al. 2014).

Indonesia has undertaken several efforts to channel remittances through formal paths. These include requiring migrants to open a bank account, offering financial literacy classes before departure, and opening dialogues with destination countries (IOM 2010b). The use of formal channels seems high in most cases. A recent survey of migrants in three provinces found that 70 percent sent money through electronic bank transfers (World Bank 2010a). Those reporting problems in transferring money had mostly relied on relatives or friends. Informal channels are more common for Indonesian migrants in Malaysia who are frequently undocumented (World Bank 2010b). A pilot program providing financial literacy training to migrant workers in the Greater Malang area and the Blitar District of East Java had a positive impact on financial awareness and knowledge, budgeting, and savings, but did not increase the quantity or frequency of remittances (Doi, McKenzie, and Zia 2014). Notably, effects were most pronounced when both the migrant and family member received training, less pronounced when just the family member received training, and absent when only the migrant received training.

Sending remittances through informal channels is common in ASEAN's other sending countries. Vietnam has sought to facilitate remittances from migrant workers, but informal channels remain common with cooperation between Vietnam and destination countries insufficient (Anh et al. 2010; Vietnam, MFA 2012). Cambodia does not have a legal framework for remittances, and use of informal remittance channels is frequent (IOM 2010c). A survey of 526 households in six communities found that 85 percent of migrants working deep inside Thailand sent money through middlemen (Sophal 2012). Those living closer to the border in Thailand tended to use other migrant workers. However, with the assistance of the Ministry of Labor and Vocational Training recruitment agencies are required to help workers open personal bank accounts to facilitate the use of formal remittance channels. Use of informal channels for remittances is also common among Laotian migrants. An IOM survey of more than 1,000 Laotian migrants in Thailand found about half of respondents who sent remittances used bank transfers, whereas 26 percent used informal channels such as relatives or friends or carrying the remittances themselves (IOM 2016b). Respondents cited lack of mechanisms to receive remittances and remote destinations as the main challenges to sending remittances. Similarly, sending remittances informally is common among migrants from Myanmar. In an IOM survey of 5,027 Myanmar migrants in seven provinces of Thailand, 87 percent used unofficial channels with the lack of identity cards or bank accounts and the distance of urban centers cited as barriers to using formal channels (IOM 2016c).

Deployment requirements

The Philippines uses a strict system of deployment requirements to check that departing workers are fully covered by the migration system's protections (Orbeta and Abrigo 2011). To receive an overseas employment certificate, which allows a potential migrant to exit the Philippines for employment, the potential migrant must submit documentation. This includes a compliant contract, certificates verifying that predeparture orientations have been completed, and a certificate issued by the Philippine Technical Education and Skills Development Authority demonstrating skills qualification. The employment certificate exempts foreign workers from the travel tax that is imposed on all others who exit. This exemption acts, in part, as an incentive not to abuse other exit channels for informal migration.

The deployment process in Indonesia is very involved and lengthy, and likely leads migrants to seek out partially or fully irregular channels. Migrants themselves must perform more than twenty steps from registering as a job seeker to registering as a prospective migrant worker, attending training, undertaking health and psychological tests, obtaining insurance, and signing the placement and employment agreements (Makovec et al. 2016). This also includes obtaining permission from a husband, wife, parent, or guardian who is verified by the village head. The significant documentation required and the lengthy deployment process can make migrants vulnerable to exploitation or can lead migrants to seek out recruitment agencies that can expedite deployment by falsifying documents. A 2007 study of labor migrants in three provinces found that more than 40 percent of documents were falsified (IOM 2010a). Migrants to the Middle East often skirt portions of the lengthy process with brokers providing a link to Jakarta-based recruitment agencies (Farbenblum, Taylor-Nicholson, and Paoletti 2013). Indonesia has sought to ease the burden of deployment requirements in recent years through an online system to improve administrative services and a pilot one-stop deployment system (World Bank 2016c).

The deployment requirements for migrating from Cambodia, Lao PDR, and Myanmar to Thailand using the formal MOU channel are cumbersome.[17] In the case of migration from Cambodia, a prospective migrant worker contacts a recruitment agency who has received an employment request from an employer in Thailand, the prospective migrant selects a workplace, and the agency provides documentation to the Ministry of Foreign Affairs and International Cooperation (MOFAIC) and to the Thai Ministry of Labor. MOFAIC approves the list of visa applicants, and the Thai embassy in Cambodia issues visas. At the same time, the Ministry of Labor and Vocational Training issues a card to the prospective migrant and a list of migrant names to the Ministry of Interior for issuance of passports. This process takes at least 62 days. The procedures are similarly burdensome for migrant workers from Lao PDR and Myanmar, with the process lasting 55 days for Lao PDR and 89 days for Myanmar (ILO 2015b).

Migrant worker welfare funds

The Philippines offers substantial protection resources to migrant workers through membership in OWWA, the primary agency responsible for protecting the welfare of overseas Philippine workers and their dependents. OWWA is a membership organization funded by a mandatory US$25 contribution paid by a migrant worker's employer. The fee is paid at the time a migrant receives a contract to work abroad, and membership lasts for the duration of the contract and can be renewed when a new contract is signed (IOM 2013). OWWA is tasked with providing services, including insurance and legal assistance, to Philippine workers while abroad and after they return home. Benefits of membership include insurance in the case of disability and death, education and training assistance including predeparture orientation, legal and other assistance in the Philippines and abroad, and reintegration assistance. OWWA also provides repatriation assistance for all foreign workers, regardless of their membership.

Migrant welfare or support funds have struggled in other countries. Before migrating from Vietnam, workers pay a fee to the Overseas Employment Support Fund. The Fund is pooled from contributions from recruitment agencies, migrants, and the government and is used for labor market activities, such as identifying foreign labor market opportunities, supporting returned migrants in finding jobs, and assisting workers who repatriate because of emergencies (Vietnam, DOLAB and IOM 2014). The Fund's effectiveness has been questioned, however (Anh et al. 2010). For instance, efforts to support returned migrants to find jobs seem to be very limited. In Indonesia, migrants had been required to support monitoring and protection by paying a protection fee of US$15 per worker into a worker protection fund (DP3TKI). This requirement was abolished in 2013 after implementation problems, confusion about where funds should go once collected, and lack of use (World Bank 2016a). Lao PDR's 2013 Labor Law (amended) establishes a labor fund designed to promote skills development and assist workers from Lao PDR and foreign employees working in Lao PDR. The fund is to be financed by a contribution of 1 percent deducted from the income tax of domestic employees, 1 percent of the salary bill of domestic employers, 5 percent of one month's income of employees abroad, and 15 percent of registration fees for issuing work permits for one person for one month from employers importing foreign labor. The fund has not yet been created because of limited financial and staff resources, lack of clarity about management, and questions about how contributions would be collected (ILO 2015h; ILO 2015i; Vathanakoune 2015). However, the government is now undertaking a feasibility study along with the ILO.

Social protection for migrant workers

The Philippines has created an extensive social protection system for migrant workers. Recruitment agencies must provide life and personal accident insurance at no cost to the foreign worker. Migrant workers must obtain health insurance coverage via PhilHealth; migrants and their dependents can then be reimbursed for hospitalization and outpatient benefits in the Philippines and hospitalization outside of the Philippines. Irregular migrants are also able to obtain coverage. Overseas workers can contribute to the social security system on a voluntary basis, gaining access to retirement, death, disability, and other benefits and to a tax-free savings program. The system maintains 15 field offices in 11 countries and has participated in the PDOS to market participation to foreign workers (Bagasao 2013). The Philippines has also negotiated social security agreements, allowing Filipinos to file claims with the host country or with the Philippines (Go 2012). The Philippines now has more than ten such agreements.[18] Migrant workers are also required to become members of Pag-IBIG, the government-run mutual fund that provides savings options for migrant workers to purchase a home (Bagasao 2013; IOM 2013).

Indonesia also makes some social protection benefits available to migrant workers though the main program for migrants has significant flaws. All departing migrant workers are required to obtain Indonesian Overseas Migrant Workers' Insurance *(Asurans TKI)*. This insurance covers insurable risks such as illness, accident, disability, death, repatriation, and funeral expenses in addition to noninsurable risks such as early contract termination, unpaid salary, physical abuse, and sexual harassment (Farbenblum, Taylor-Nicholson, and Paoletti 2013; World Bank 2016a). Coverage begins a maximum of five months before departure, lasts for two years during employment with renewability for one- and two-year periods, and continues one month after return to Indonesia. Recruitment agencies obtain coverage on behalf of migrants from consortia of insurance companies overseen by the Ministry of Manpower, but can pass the cost along to migrants. In a recent report, significant problems were identified with the current structure of the insurance product (World Bank 2016a). Perhaps most important, this insurance bundles both insurable and noninsurable risks. Unlike illness or disability, risks such as abuse or contract termination are difficult to price and better-suited to a government-provided social protection scheme. Additionally, the claims process is complicated and documentation requirements are burdensome (World Bank 2016a). For example, claims must be filed within 12 months of the injury, making it very difficult for a worker on a two-year contract abroad to file a claim if harmed during the first 12 months of employment. Lack of uptake is also a challenge. The 2013 survey of Indonesian migrants undertaken by the World Bank in collaboration with Statistics Indonesia found that only 31 percent of all current migrant workers reported having health or work-related accident insurance, or both, despite the requirement that all be covered.

Host country social protection programs for migrants are very limited in all other sending countries. Vietnam's 62 poorest districts program, which seeks to facilitate overseas migration for the poor, includes an insurance policy for the poor and nonpoor for deaths, accidents, and contracts terminating outside the worker's control during the first year of the contract (Le and Mont 2014). Cambodia, Lao PDR, and Myanmar do not offer any special social protection coverage to migrant workers.

Special protections for migrant domestic workers

The Philippines has made additional efforts to protect migrant domestic workers. The Household Service Workers Reform Package is a group of rules instituted by POEA in 2006 setting out additional requirements with which domestic workers must comply before working abroad and additional rights for domestic workers during employment. Domestic workers must be 23 years old before they migrate and complete a training program resulting in the National Certificate for Household Service Workers. Domestic workers must attend the Comprehensive Predeparture Education Program in addition to the PEOS and the PDOS. The Education Program is a four- or six-day course in language, culture, and stress management. More than 200,000 individuals participated in the program's language training portion in 2014 (PSA 2015). Finally, as noted earlier, the reform package sets a minimum wage of US$400 and exempts domestic workers from placement fees.

The reform package's new minimum wage had a significant impact on the market for Philippine domestic workers abroad. Imposing the minimum wage led to an increase in their wages; however, it also reduced their employment by 55 percent in countries where the minimum wage was binding compared to countries where it was not (McKenzie, Theoharides, and Yang 2014). Although this decrease in employment is an important cost associated with the imposition of the minimum wage, that the Philippine policy had an impact in receiving countries has two important implications. First, the Philippines' system of regulating recruitment, and particularly contracts, seems to be effective, at least in the case of domestic workers. Second, the employment of Philippine foreign domestic workers did not fall to zero, suggesting that Filipinos are not perfectly substitutable with other nationalities. This is an indication that English language proficiency, migration-oriented training, or work ethic may be an advantage for migrant domestic workers from the Philippines. (McKenzie, Theoharides, and Yang 2014). Still, there are concerns that some of the main provisions of the reform package, including the minimum wage provision and the ban on placement fees, were ignored or skirted by reclassifying domestic workers as another worker type (Orbeta and Abrigo 2011; Battistella and Asis 2011).

Indonesia has relied mainly on bans on deployment to increase protections for domestic workers. In Indonesia, migrant domestic workers are required to be 21 years of age and to receive education and training provided by recruitment agencies. As noted earlier, concerns about mistreatment and abuse led Indonesia to implement moratoria on its female domestic workers migrating to Malaysia and countries in the Middle East. Despite removing the moratorium on migration to Malaysia in 2011, Indonesia is now pursuing a policy to halt all deployment of domestic workers by 2017. However, the ban does not seem to have been effective either in preventing domestic workers from migration to prohibited countries or in improving their well-being. As noted above, migrant domestic workers seem to have shifted to informal channels during the Malaysia ban. Additionally, it is not clear that the moratoria are responsible for an improvement in migrant experiences abroad. Although reports of unpleasant experiences have declined since the moratoria, these have occurred across all destination countries and occupational groups, suggesting the moratoria alone are not responsible (World Bank 2016c).

Cambodia, Lao PDR, Myanmar, and Vietnam either lack additional protections for migrant domestic workers or have banned deployment of such workers. Vietnam has no significant additional protections for migrant domestic workers. However, recent developments include passage of domestic legislation governing domestic workers that could be extended to cover migrants; an agreement by Taiwan, China to allow entry to Vietnamese domestic workers, thus lifting a 2005 ban; and an MOU on domestic workers with Saudi Arabia (ILO 2015j). Cambodia has banned domestic workers from migrating to Malaysia in the past, and Lao PDR and Myanmar have more general restrictions on the migration of domestic workers that create confusion about whether domestic workers can use the MOU channel for migration to Thailand (ILO 2016d).

Legal and other assistance while abroad

The Philippines has a significant network of overseas resources for migrant workers who are abroad. The Office of the Undersecretary for Migrant Workers Assistance is responsible for providing legal assistance to Filipinos abroad. There are 37 labor attachés to assist migrant workers in destination countries (ILO 2015f). OWWA provides legal assistance to foreign workers while they are abroad, and has 31 overseas posts. Additionally, the POEA has 16 POLOs in 29 countries that run information programs for migrants and oversee migrant welfare while abroad. The POLOs run Migrant Workers and Other Overseas Filipinos Resource Centers that provide temporary shelter for Filipinos abroad in distress. However, there are limitations to the assistance offered to migrants abroad. POLOs may lack data about the workers present in their jurisdictions because POEA does not supply them with their lists of deployed workers (Orbeta, Abrigo, and Cabalfin 2009; Agunias 2007). There are also concerns that POLOs are understaffed and that POEA and POLOs lack sufficient resources (Agunias 2007).

All of ASEAN's other main sending countries have representatives abroad who assist migrant workers, though this assistance is limited by staff resources and capacity. Legal assistance, temporary accommodation, and other support services are available to migrant workers while abroad from Indonesian embassies and consulates. However, the capacity and resources of these representatives are limited (IOM 2010a; ILO 2015c). Indonesia now has 13 labor representatives in consulates in its primary destinations:[19] of these, only 4 are labor attachés while the rest are technical staff (World Bank 2016b). Recruitment agencies are required to inform Indonesian embassies and consulates of the arrival of migrant workers in a destination country but often fail to do so (IOM 2010a; World Bank 2016c). Vietnam's embassies and consulates are tasked with aiding migrants while they are abroad. Vietnam has labor attachés in eight countries[20] (Bowen and Huong 2012). The extent to which Vietnam's representatives abroad can provide assistance is limited by insufficient resources and staff and the lack of information about the migrants present in destination countries. As in Indonesia, though recruitment agencies are required to inform Vietnam's overseas representatives about the arrival of migrants, they often do not do so (Vietnam, MFA 2012). Cambodia's embassies and consulates in destination countries are charged with aiding migrant workers. However, these offices often have inadequate staff, skills, and resources; and there are currently no labor attachés in any destination country (HRW 2011; ILO 2015b; United States, DOS 2016).[21] Recruitment agencies are responsible for having representatives in destination countries and for overseeing the working and living conditions of migrant workers while they are abroad. Lao PDR now has only one such labor attaché that is based in Thailand (ILO 2015a). Myanmar has labor attachés in Korea, Kuwait, Malaysia, Singapore, and Thailand, (ILO 2015f). Three additional labor attachés have been announced for Thailand, bringing the number there to five (ILO 2016c). There are concerns about the quality of the assistance provided by embassies and consulates, and procedures for obtaining official documents are said to be inefficient (Hall 2012).

Assistance to family members or dependents of migrant workers

The Philippines aids the family and dependents of foreign workers during and after their deployment. Dependents of PhilHealth members who are foreign workers are entitled to benefits. OWWA provides scholarships to dependents of members through the Education for Development Scholarship Program, the OFW Dependent Scholarship Program, the Congressional Migrant Workers Scholarship Program, and the Educational Livelihood Assistance Program (ELAP). The last also includes a grant for the spouse of a deceased migrant worker. OWWA's Information Technology Training Program provides computer literacy training to help foreign workers communicate with their families. OWWA also fields requests from families for assistance from OWWA offices abroad. Finally, OWWA, the Department of Education, the Department of Foreign Affairs, the Department of Labor and Employment, and the Commission on Filipinos Overseas run Philippine Schools Overseas in 10 countries, providing the Department of Education basic curriculum to the children of Filipinos abroad.

Assistance for the family members and dependents of foreign workers is limited in all other ASEAN sending countries. In Indonesia, family members of migrants are generally excluded from the protection system for migrant workers; however, recruitment agencies are required to provide information, and Indonesian representatives abroad are required to aid the family in case of a migrant's death (IOM 2010a). In Vietnam, the Overseas Employment Support Fund can be used to support the families of migrants who die oversees. Support was provided to the families of 72 workers in 2012, amounting to D 720 million (Thuy 2013). In Cambodia, recruitment agencies must notify family members in case of a migrant worker's death, while in Lao PDR recruitment agencies must help migrant workers and their family members access information, education, and social protection. However, it is unclear what responsibilities this requirement entails. Finally, in Myanmar there does not appear to be any aid provided to spouses or the dependents of foreign workers.

Exit

Sanctions and incentives

The Philippines makes employers and private recruitment agencies responsible for repatriating migrant workers upon contract completion, requiring them to pay for their return transportation. The Philippines also supports the repatriation of foreign workers in distress or in crisis (such as from war or natural disaster); they can be provided additional benefits, such as counseling and temporary shelter.

Indonesia has little infrastructure for migrants leaving work abroad and returning home. Recruitment agencies must report migrants' return, but do not seem to be responsible for ensuring return. In the case of death, disputes, or other difficulties, recruitment agencies and the Ministry of Foreign Affairs are responsible for the cost of repatriating workers (IOM 2010a; Kuncoro, Damayanti, and Isfandiarni 2014). Overseas Migrant Workers' Insurance is available to migrants for one month after their return. Until recently, migrants were required to return home via Terminal IV (BPK TKI Selapajang) at Soekarno-Hatta International Airport (World Bank 2016a). Although services, such as grievances reporting systems, were available at the terminal, migrants also faced challenges. These included corruption and the additional time and cost involved in being forced to return home via a single port of entry in Jakarta (IOM 2010a).

Vietnam also has weak exit and return policies for migrant workers. Recruitment agencies are required to report to the Department of Overseas Workers the return of migrants to Vietnam. The Overseas Employment Support Fund is available to assist workers who return because of emergencies. Recruitment agencies are also required to assist in cases in which a contract is terminated at no fault of the worker (Bowen and Huong 2012). In practice, the reporting requirements do not seem to function well (Anh et al. 2010; Ishizuka 2013; Vietnam, DOLAB and IOM 2014).

In the absence of a strong system of exit and return in Vietnam, recruitment agencies have instituted an informal, tacitly sanctioned security bond that has not improved the likelihood of return. To dissuade migrants from overstaying their work contracts abroad, recruitment agencies charge migrants a security deposit that is reimbursed only when migrants return to Vietnam. However, migrants have difficulty reclaiming the deposit (Bélanger 2014; CSAGA 2013; Phuong and Venkatesh 2016). A survey of 357 returned migrants in Ha Nam, Thai Binh, and Hung Yen provinces found that two-thirds did not have their full deposits returned to them (CSAGA 2013). This might occur because recruitment agencies claimed additional fees had to be paid, because migrants did not have the necessary documentation, or because the recruitment agency had disappeared. Perversely, by increasing the up-front costs of migration and causing migrants to borrow even more to migrate, the deposit can actually incentivize overstay (Ahsan et al. 2014).

A repatriation fund created in the MOUs between Thailand and Cambodia, Lao PDR, and Myanmar has never been instituted, and other exit programs are weak or nonexistent. The MOUs signed between Cambodia, Lao PDR, and Myanmar and Thailand include a provision creating a repatriation fund through the migrant's contribution of 15 percent of their monthly salary. The fund was to be used to defray the cost of deporting irregular migrants and to incentivize exit by returning contributions to migrants upon leaving Thailand. However, the fund was never implemented, and the policy has since been repealed in Thailand (ILO 2015b). In Cambodia and Lao PDR, recruitment agencies arrange the return of migrant workers. The Lao PDR government can use a recruitment agency's security deposit to assist with repatriation in the case of emergency.

Diaspora engagement

Several countries have programs to connect with their diaspora. The Philippines runs programs such as Diaspora to Development, which involves maintaining connections with Filipinos who are abroad permanently and incentivizing their return. The Overseas Absentee Voting Act (RA9189), amended by the Overseas Voting Act of 2013 (RA10590), and the Citizenship Retention and Re-acquisition Act of 2003 (RA9225) both aim to help overseas Filipinos remain connected with the Philippines by making voting easier in the first case and easing citizenship requirements in the second. Vietnam also tries to maintain connections with its diaspora (Anh et al. 2010; Vietnam, MFA 2012).

Malaysia and Singapore, two of ASEAN's main receiving countries, seek to connect with their diaspora abroad and, in some cases, promote return. Malaysia's Returning Expert Program aims to attract talented Malaysians living and working abroad to return to their country. Criteria for applications are tiered by education and salary. Expatriates are incentivized to return with a flat income tax and a tax exemption on car imports. A recent evaluation found that the program increases the probability that talented Malaysians return by 40 percent for applicants with a job offer in Malaysia, but found no effect for those without one. A cost-benefit analysis of the program estimates between a small negative and a small positive impact (Del Carpio et al. 2016). The emigration of high-skilled individuals is generally accepted in Singapore, but policies have been adopted to try to alleviate any negative consequences of this migration and to take advantage of its potential benefits (Ziguras and Gribble 2015). Investments in domestic education options and efforts to facilitate return have been introduced in reaction to concerns about Singaporean students studying abroad. The National Population and Talent Division in the Prime Minister's Office is charged with engaging Singaporeans overseas. The Overseas Singaporean Unit coordinates these efforts.

Reintegration

The Philippines provides reintegration services to migrants who have returned from working abroad (Tornea 2003). These services are generally provided by OWWA and the National Reintegration Center for OFWs. The latter handles two livelihood and self-employment programs that seek to create income-generating opportunities for former migrants. The *Balik-Pinay! Balik-Hanapbuhay!* (BPBH) noncash livelihood support program provides skills or entrepreneurial training, starter kits, and other services to returning migrant workers who were displaced from work abroad by conflict, policy change, illegal recruitment, or human trafficking. The Enterprise Development and Loan Program (EDLP), run in partnership with the Land Bank of the Philippines and the Development Bank of the Philippines, helps support enterprise development through entrepreneurial development and fixed interest loans. Other reintegration programs include the OFW-M3 program for financial literacy and entrepreneurship training, the Assist WELL program to train domestic workers to become teachers and other occupations, and the SMBT/FAS small business training program.

The success of these reintegration programs is limited. Based on interviews with a subset of beneficiaries, the Philippines Commission on Audit found that neither BPBH nor EDLP met its objective for 2015 (Philippines, COA 2016b). Fifteen of 36 BPBH interviewees said that the businesses started were no longer in existence. Interviews showed that most borrowers from the EDLP (known as the Reintegration Program when it was audited) were not able to sustain their income-generating activities. There were also violations of program rules, including defaults by some beneficiaries who had been granted larger loans than they applied for.

Reintegration programs in ASEAN's other main sending countries are very limited. In Indonesia, some reintegration programs are available at the local level (IOM 2010a; ILO 2015c). In Vietnam, local Department of Labor, Invalids, and Social Affairs offices are tasked with helping returning migrants find jobs and with encouraging firms to hire these workers (Le and Mont 2014). Assistance is also targeted to migrants in poor districts under the 62 poorest districts program. In practice, however, the reintegration policies do not seem to function well (Anh et al. 2010; Ishizuka 2013; Vietnam, DOLAB and IOM 2014). Cambodian recruitment agencies are responsible for assisting returning migrants with receiving a certificate from the Ministry of Labor and Vocational Training that recognizes their work experience abroad. Lao PDR and Thai officials agreed at a 2010 MOU meeting to issue certificates of employment to returning Lao PDR migrant workers upon completing their employment contract term, with a view toward assisting their reintegration into the labor market; how this has functioned, however, is not known (IOM 2011; ILO 2015a). Beyond those run by NGOs, labor market reintegration programs for returning migrants are absent in Cambodia, Lao PDR, and Myanmar (ILO 2013a; Naro 2009; Tunon and Rim 2013).

Enforcement

Coordination and targeting

The Philippines' enforcement strategy combines regular assessment of recruitment agencies with a unique liability requirement for recruitment agencies, a security deposit that can be drawn down for damages, and the dissemination of public information about high- and low-performing recruitment agencies. Licensed private recruitment agencies are assessed for compliance with regulations at various stages of the licensing process and every two years after renewal of a permanent license. In 2015, nearly all agencies had been subject to two or more inspections within the previous two years (Philippines, COA 2016a). Agencies, employers, and foreign workers who violate rules can be suspended or disqualified from the migration program. Agencies can also be fined. An interagency Taskforce Against Illegal Recruitment has also been created. One of the Philippines' most important efforts to extend the reach of its domestic regulations is the requirement that private recruitment agencies agree to joint and several liability with a foreign worker's employer: in other words, recruitment agencies are responsible for any claims or liabilities resulting from contract infringements, including unpaid wages, death and disability benefits, and repatriation costs. This requirement gives recruitment agencies an incentive to work with reliable employers and to oversee the treatment of foreign workers while they are abroad. The joint and several liability requirement does not apply in the case of rehiring, when foreign workers are less likely to use a recruitment agency (Orbeta and Abrigo 2011). The Philippines also requires private recruitment agencies to maintain an escrow account of P1 million against claims for violations of recruitment rules.[22] This is designed to ensure that foreign workers will be paid when violations occur (Philippines, COA 2016a). POEA requires aggrieved parties to attempt reconciliation before adjudication.

Despite these significant measures, weaknesses in enforcement in the Philippines show how difficult enforcing migration laws and regulations can be. At the end of 2013, 11 percent of all out-migration from the Philippines was estimated to be irregular (Philippines, CFO 2014). Although this represents a significant decline from 22 percent in 2001, the numerous steps involved in formal migration raise concerns that some migrants may seek to migrate informally to avoid the cost and duration of compliance.

Overseeing the implementation of the standard employment contract in host countries is challenging, with instances of contract substitution, inappropriate fees, and other illegal recruitment practices not uncommon (Agunias 2010). As noted earlier, some of the main provisions of a reform package to increase protection for domestic workers, including a minimum wage provision and a ban on placement fees, were ignored or skirted by reclassifying domestic workers as another worker type (Battistella and Asis 2011; Orbeta and Abrigo 2011). The Philippines Commission on Audit's review of POEA also shows some areas of weakness in enforcement (Philippines, COA 2016a). POEA undertook about 100 fewer enforcement cases than it targeted in 2015, and there is some evidence that POEA enforcement is not improving agency behavior. Eighteen percent of agencies with at least one complaint or breach had at least three or more breaches over the past three years, above the target of 10 percent. POEA is also having trouble ensuring that claims against private agencies are paid, despite the existence of the escrow account. In 2015, 123 cases against 116 recruitment agencies and involving 234 workers remained unpaid at the end of the year because the escrow accounts had insufficient funds. Another 337 payments were partial or delayed.

Enforcement of migration policies in Indonesia is hindered by lack of clear institutional responsibilities, passive oversight of recruitment, and weak sanctions and complaint mechanisms. Overlapping roles of the Ministry of Manpower and BNP2TKI lead to confusion or abuse by recruitment agencies. Additionally, the role of local governments in regulating the recruitment industry is unclear. Provincial governments may face difficulty in punishing recruitment violations by local branches: by law, the headquarters is ultimately responsible and most are in Jakarta (Bachtiar 2011). Though charged with oversight of the recruitment industry, the Ministry of Manpower's supervision is passive. It does not conduct inspections without first receiving a complaint, opening the door for recruitment agencies to pressure migrants not to report grievances (IOM 2010a). Sanctions for recruitment violations are limited mostly to suspension and revocation of licenses, are thought to be too small, and are not always available: for instance, recruitment agencies often fail to comply with many of the requirements to protect migrant workers but do not face sanctions for noncompliant placement and employment agreements (Farbenblum, Taylor-Nicholson, and Paoletti 2013). The 2013 survey of migrant workers undertaken by the World Bank in collaboration with Statistics Indonesia found that 19 percent of current migrants using a recruitment agency and signing a placement agreement did not receive training, and 8 percent did not undergo a medical examination (World Bank 2016c). Weak enforcement also contributes to significant flows of undocumented workers. Migrants often resort to informal complaint and dispute mechanisms. In a survey of migrants in three districts with significant out-migration, migrants often did not report problems experienced, and those who did often reported the problem to someone outside of government because of fear of the consequences of reporting, lack of knowledge or funds, or fear of embarrassment (IOM 2010a).

Vietnam suffers from similar problems of weak sanctions, insufficient oversight of recruitment, and ineffective complaint mechanisms. In Vietnam, the Department of

Overseas Labor enforces regulation of the recruitment industry and hears complaints from migrants. Sanctions and license suspensions and revocations are available as remedies for violations. Workers themselves can also be sanctioned for violation of contracts (Ahsan et al. 2014). However, oversight is not sufficiently strict, sanctions are too low, the inspection regime is inadequate, and capacity is limited (Anh et al. 2010; Ahsan et al. 2014; Bowen and Huong 2012; Vietnam, MFA 2012). Migrants face challenges in seeking redress, and public authorities are not always sought out when migrants are aggrieved (Anh et al. 2010; Phuong and Venkatesh 2016). For instance, migrants do not seem to seek out public authorities when attempting to recover security deposits made to recruitment agencies to guarantee return (CSAGA 2013). Some progress has been made to improve migrants' ability to seek redress. The Department of Overseas Labor has worked with the ILO to create migrant resource centers in Hanoi and five provinces to provide information and counseling to prospective, current, and future migrant workers and to improve complaint resolution (IOM 2014; ILO 2015a). However, even where policies are in place to assist migrants—for instance, policies to help returned migrants reintegrate into Vietnam's labor market—they are infrequently available in practice.

Cambodia, Lao PDR, and Myanmar have made some progress in enforcing migration legislation and regulations, in particular, in creating complaint mechanisms for migrant workers. All three countries have regimes for sanctioning licensed recruitment agencies for recruitment violations. In Cambodia, the Ministry of Labor and Vocational Training handles regular inspections of recruitment agencies, set by Prakas No. 251 at once every two years. The countries have also worked to develop complaint mechanisms for migrant workers. In Cambodia, Prakas No. 249 establishes a complaint mechanism at the ministry and provincial Departments of Labor and Vocational Training, and a migrant worker resource center was opened in 2014 in coordination with the ILO as the main center to receive complaints. A recent assessment of the complaint mechanism for migrant workers in Cambodia undertaken by the ILO found that the mechanism was generally effective, with 501 complaints resolved for 1,524 workers and more than US$200,000 recovered in compensation (ILO 2016f). Cases were generally handled efficiently, but gaps in implementation were also found. The Ministry of Labor and Social Welfare and its local offices are tasked with oversight of recruitment in Lao PDR. The ministry can impose sanctions for violations of recruitment practices that include warnings, fines, and temporary or permanent license revocations (Lao PDR, DOS and NERI 2012). A single-window complaint service is being planned along with provincial legal assistance offices in provinces to assist returning migrant workers (ILO 2015a). Three migrant resource centers have been created with the assistance of the ILO to assist with safe migration (ILO 2013a). Myanmar has developed several mechanisms to protect migrant workers (Oo 2016). The country has launched migrant resource centers in collaboration with the IOM and ILO in several locations to provide services to migrants before departure and upon return. Complaints from migrants are received at centers in Naypyitaw and Yangon. The centers received 327 complaints in 2014 and early 2015. The Migrant Workers' Reporting Counter at Yangon International

Airport provides information to migrants and collects information about those returning and departing.

Insufficient institutional capacity and resources—combined with long and porous
borders with Thailand and significant demand in destination countries—have made
enforcement of migration regulations in Cambodia, Lao PDR, and Myanmar challenging. Indeed, 58 percent of migrants from the three countries in Thailand in 2013
were irregular. Despite the progress made in improving the mechanisms available to
migrant workers, each country faces significant enforcement challenges. In Cambodia,
migrant workers still face difficulties in filing complaints because of lack of awareness,
concerns about traveling to Phnom Penh or provincial offices alone, or fear of retribu-
tion from recruitment agencies. In Lao PDR, lack of technical, human resources, and
financial capacity hinder enforcement, particularly inspections of recruitment agencies (Lao PDR, DoS and NERI 2012; MMN and AMC 2008). In Myanmar, cooperation
with destination countries is insufficient, contracts can lack minimum standards,
migrants do not always receive the necessary information, and inspections of recruitment agencies are insufficient (Naing 2014; Oo 2016).

Notes

1. A public version of the Plan is not available.

2. These are the *Philippine Development Plan (PDP) 2011–2016*, Indonesia's *National Medium
   Term Development Plan 2015–2019*, and Vietnam's *Socio-Economic Development Strategy
   2011–2020*.

3. Provinces in the Philippines have also included migration in their development plans
   (IOM 2013).

4. Prior to this system, Vietnam primarily negotiated with governments in the former Soviet
   Union to send workers abroad.

5. These are also referred to as sending agencies or sending enterprises.

6. Together, these agencies compose the Labor Administration Agency.

7. The land-based agreements are with Bahrain; Germany; Indonesia; Iraq; Japan; Jordan;
   Korea; Kuwait; Lao PDR; Lebanon; Libya; New Zealand; Northern Mariana Islands; Norway;
   Papua New Guinea; Qatar; Saudi Arabia; Spain; Switzerland; Taiwan, China; the United
   Arab Emirates; the United Kingdom; the United States and the territories of Alberta; British
   Colombia; Manitoba; and Saskatchewan in Canada. The sea-based agreements are with
   Cyprus; Denmark; Japan; Liberia; and the Netherlands.

8. These include agreements with Austria, Belgium, Canada and the Quebec province, France,
   Germany, Japan, the Netherlands, Spain, Sweden, Switzerland, and the United Kingdom.

9. POEA now publishes the text of the bilateral agreements on its website.

10. These are Bulgaria; the Czech Republic; Japan; Kazakhstan; Korea; Lao PDR; Malaysia;
    Oman; Qatar; the Russian Federation; Saskatchewan Province in Canada; Slovakia; Taiwan,
    China; Thailand; Ukraine; and the United Arab Emirates. See Vietnam, MFA (2012) for a
    description of the bilateral agreements.

11. The MOUs also establish a process for the registration and regularization of informal migrant
    workers in Thailand, which provides them with work permits.

12. In Malang District in East Java, recruitment agencies and their agents are required to complete a semiannual orientation course (IOM 2010b).

13. Vietnam Circular No. 21/2007/TT-LDTBXH.

14. Recruitment agencies, and even informal brokers, do not appear to be as dominant in Lao PDR as in other migrant-sending countries in the region. A recent survey of more than 1,000 Laotian migrants in Thailand undertaken by the International Organization for Migration (IOM) found that only 13 percent used brokers to migrate and only 22 percent migrated under the MOU, which normally requires the use of a broker or recruitment agency (IOM 2016b). This compares with 43 percent who migrated with friends or relatives and 21 percent who migrated on their own. These results are consistent with a study of 128 deported migrants undertaken by United Nations Action for Cooperation against Trafficking in Persons that found that a minority had used a broker to get to the Lao PDR border and then to their destination (Baker 2015).

15. These are Algeria; Bahrain; Egypt; Iran; Iraq; Jordan; Kuwait; Lebanon; Libya; Mauritania; Morocco; Oman; Pakistan; the Palestinian territories; Qatar; Saudi Arabia; South Sudan; the Syrian Arab Republic; Tunisia; the United Arab Emirates; and the Republic of Yemen.

16. The Ministry of Labor and Vocational Training has conducted trainings for providers of the orientation program and is developing standardized predeparture training materials for Malaysia and Thailand with information about host country laws, migrant worker rights and responsibilities, and how to remit money (ILO 2015b; ILO 2013a; Cambodia, MOLVT and ILO 2014).

17. See ILO (2015b) for a detailed flowchart of the MOU process on which this section is based.

18. These include agreements with Austria, Belgium, Canada and the Quebec province, France, Germany, Japan, the Netherlands, Spain, Sweden, Switzerland, and the United Kingdom.

19. The labor representatives are in Brunei Darussalam; Hong Kong SAR, China; Jordan; Korea; Kuwait; Qatar; Saudi Arabia (Riyadh and Jeddah); Singapore; Syria; Taiwan, China; and the United Arab Emirates.

20. These are the Czech Republic; Japan; Korea; Malaysia; Qatar; Saudi Arabia; Taiwan, China; and United Arab Emirates.

21. Cambodia is sending one to Korea (Cambodia, MOLVT and ILO 2014).

22. The Foreign Employer's Guarantee Fund is the equivalent for the government-to-government hiring process.

References

Agunias, Dovelyn Rannveig. 2007. "Protecting Overseas Workers: Lessons and Cautions from the Philippines." Migration Policy Institute, Washington, DC.

———. 2010. "Migration's Middlemen: Regulating Recruitment Agencies in the Philippines–United Arab Emirates Corridor." Migration Policy Institute, Washington, DC.

Ahsan, Ahmad, Manolo Abella, Andrew Beath, Yukon Huang, Manjula Luthria, and Trang Van Nguyen. 2014. *International Migration and Development in East Asia and the Pacific.* Washington, DC: World Bank.

Ambito, Julyn S., and Melissa Suzette L. Banzon. 2011. "Review of Philippine Migration Laws and Regulations: Gains, Gaps, Prospects." Discussion Paper Series 2011–37, Philippine Institute for Development Studies, Makati City.

Anchustegui, Iza M. 2010. "An Evaluation of the Implementation of the Pre-Departure Orientation Seminar (PDOS) by OWWA-Accredited PDOS Providers." ILS Discussion Paper Series 11-2010, Institute for Labor Studies (ILS), Manila.

Anh, Dang Nguyen. 2008. "Labour Migration from Viet Nam: Issues of Policy and Practice." ILO Asian Regional Programme on Governance of Labour Migration Working Paper 4, International Labour Organization, Bangkok.

Anh, Dang Nguyen, Tran Thi Bich, Nguyen Ngoc Quynh, and Dao The Son. 2010. "Development on the Move: Measuring and Optimising Migration's Economic and Social Impacts in Vietnam." Global Development Network (GDN) and Institute for Public Policy Research (IPPR), Delhi.

Asis, Maruja M.B., and Dovelyn Rannveig Agunias. 2012. "Strengthening Pre-Departure Orientation Programmes in Indonesia, Nepal and the Philippines," Migration Policy Institute, Washington, DC.

Bachtiar, Palmira Permata. 2011. "The Governance of Indonesian Overseas Employment in the Context of Decentralization." Discussion Paper Series No. 2011–25, Philippine Institute for Development Studies, Makati City.

Baker, Simon. 2015. "Migration Experiences of Lao Workers Deported from Thailand in 2013." United Nations Action for Cooperation against Trafficking in Persons (UN-ACT), Bangkok.

Bagasao, Ildefonso F. 2013. "Review of remittance-back products in the Philippines." International Labour Organization, Bangkok.

Barsbai, Toman, Andreas Steinmayr, Dean Yang, Erwin Tiongson, and Victoria Licuanan. Ongoing. "Harnessing the Development Benefits of International Migration: A Randomized Evaluation of Enhanced Pre-Departure Orientation Seminars for Migrants from the Philippines."

Battistella, Graziano. 2012. "Multi-Level Policy Approach in the Governance of Labour Migration: Considerations from the Philippine Experience." *Asian Journal of Social Science* 40: 419–446.

Battistella, Graziano, and Maruja M.B. Asis. 2011. "Protecting Filipino Transnational Domestic Workers: Government Regulations and Their Outcomes." Discussion Paper Series No. 2011–12, Philippine Institute for Development Studies, Makati City.

Bélanger, Danièle. 2014. "Labor Migration and Trafficking among Vietnamese Migrants in Asia." *The Annals of the American Academy of Political and Social Science* 653 (1): 87–106.

Bélanger, Danièle, and Linh Tran Giang. 2013. "Precarity, Gender and Work: Vietnamese Migrant Workers in Asia." *Diversities* 15 (1): 5–20.

Bélanger, Danièle, Le Bach Duong, Tran Giang Linh, Khuat Thu Hong, Nguyen Thi Van Anh, and Belinda Hammoud. 2010. "International Labour Migration from Vietnam to Asian Countries, 2000–2009: Process, Experiences and Impact." Report presented at the international workshop "Labour Migration from Vietnam to Asian Countries: Sharing Research findings and NGOs." Institute for Social Development Studies, Hanoi.

Beam, Emily A., David McKenzie, and Dean Yang. 2015. "Unilateral Facilitation Does Not Raise International Labor Migration from the Philippines." *Economic Development and Cultural Change* 64 (2): 323–368.

Blank, Nathan R. 2011. "Making Migration Policy: Reflections on the Philippines' Bilateral Labor Agreements." *Asian Politics & Policy* 3 (2): 185–205.

Bowen, Ruth, and Do Van Huong. 2012. "Women in International Labour Migration from Viet Nam: A Situation Analysis." UN Women (Viet Nam) and Viet Nam, Ministry of Labour, Invalids and Social Affairs, Department of Overseas Labor.

Cambodia, MOLVT (Ministry of Labor and Vocational Training) and ILO (International Labour Organization). 2014. *Policy on Labour Migration for Cambodia.*

CMA (Center for Migrant Advocacy). 2010. "Bilateral Labour Agreements and Social Security Agreements: Forging Partnership to Protect Filipino Migrant Workers' Rights." Center for Migrant Advocacy, Quezon City.

CSAGA (Center for Studies and Applied Sciences in Gender, Family, Women and Adolescents). 2013. "An Exploratory Research on the Experiences and Needs of Returned Vietnamese Overseas Migrant Workers." CSAGA, Hanoi.

Del Carpio, Ximena V., Caglar Ozden, Mauro Testaverde, and Mathis Wagner. 2016. "Global Migration of Talent and Tax Incentives: Evidence from Malaysia's Returning Expert Program." Policy Research Working Paper 7875, World Bank, Washington, DC.

Doi, Yoko, David McKenzie, and Bilal Zia. 2014. "Who You Train Matters: Identifying Combined Effects of Financial Education on Migrant Households." *Journal of Development Economics* 109: 39–55.

Farbenblum, Bassina, Eleanor Taylor-Nicholson, and Sarah Paoletti. 2013. *Migrant Workers' Access to Justice at Home: Indonesia.* New York: Open Society Foundations.

Go, Stella P. 2012. "The Philippines and Return Migration: Rapid Appraisal of the Return and Reintegration Policies and Service Delivery." International Labour Organization (ILO), Manila.

Hall, Andy. 2012. "Myanmar and Migrant Workers: Briefing and Recommendations." Mahidol Migration Center, Institute for Population and Social Research, Mahidol University, Thailand.

Harkins, Benjamin. 2016. "Review of Labour Migration Policy in Malaysia." International Labour Organization, Bangkok.

HOME (Humanitarian Organization for Migration Economics) and MWRN (Migrant Workers Rights Network). 2015. "Myanmar: A Submission by Humanitarian Organization for Migration Economics (HOME) and Migrant Workers Rights Network (MWRN) for the 23rd Session of the Universal Period Review." Singapore, HOME.

HRW (Human Rights Watch). 2011. "They Deceived Us at Every Step: Abuse of Cambodian Domestic Workers Migrating to Malaysia." Human Rights Watch.

ILO (International Labour Organization). 2008. "The Mekong Challenge: An Honest Broker—Improving Cross-Border Recruitment Practices for the Benefit of Government, Workers and Employers," ILO, Bangkok.

———. 2013a. "Background paper: Progress on the implementation of the recommendations adopted at the 3rd and 4th ASEAN Forum on Migrant Labour," Bangkok: ILO.

———. 2013b. "Monitoring and Evaluation of the Application of the VAMAS Code of Conduct: Phase I: 2012–2013," ILO.

———. 2015a. "Progress of the implementation of Recommendations adopted at the 3rd – 6th ASEAN Forum on Migrant Labour meetings: Background paper to the 7th AFML." ILO, Bangkok.

———. 2015b. "Review of the Effectiveness of the MOUs in Managing Labour Migration between Thailand and Neighbouring Countries." ILO, Bangkok.

———. 2015c. "Indonesia: Decent Work for Indonesian Migrant Workers." ILO, Jakarta.

———. 2015d. "Bilateral Agreements and Memoranda of Understanding on Migration of Low Skilled Workers: A Review." ILO, Geneva.

———. 2015e. "Regular and Irregular Migrant Workers in North Central Viet Nam: Findings from Household Surveys." ILO, Hanoi.

———. 2015f. "Coordination and Role of Key Stakeholders in Setting Up and Implementing Policies and Procedures to Facilitate Recruitment, Preparation, Production Abroad, and Return and Reintegration." Background paper to the 7th ASEAN Forum on Migrant Labour, ILO, Bangkok.

———. 2015g. "Strengthening Post-Arrival Orientation Programs for Migrant Workers in ASEAN." Policy Brief Issue 2, ILO, Bangkok.

———. 2015h. "Workshop Report: Sub-Regional Workshop to Validate the Findings of the Migrant Welfare Fund Feasibility Study Conducted in Myanmar, Cambodia and Laos." Vientiane, Lao PDR.

———. 2015i. "Establishing Migrant Welfare Funds in Cambodia, Lao PDR and Myanmar." Policy Brief Issue 3, ILO, Bangkok.

———. 2015j. "The Growing Trend of Vietnamese Migrant Domestic Workers." ILO, Hanoi.

———. 2016a. "Triangle II Quarterly Briefing Note: Thailand." (April-June). ILO, Bangkok.

———. 2016b. "Triangle II Quarterly Briefing Note: Thailand." (July–September). ILO, Bangkok.

———. 2016c. "Triangle II Quarterly Briefing Note: Myanmar." (October–December). ILO, Bangkok.

———. 2016d. "Triangle II Quarterly Briefing Note: Lao PDR (October–December)." ILO, Bangkok.

———. 2016e. "Triangle II Quarterly Briefing Note: Cambodia," (October–December). ILO, Bangkok.

———. 2016f. "Assessment of the Complaints Mechanism for Cambodian Migrant Workers," ILO, Phnom Penh.

ILO (International Labour Organization) and KNOMAD (Global Knowledge Partnership on Migration and Development). 2015. "Migration Cost Survey: Vietnamese Workers in Malaysia."

IOM (International Organization for Migration). 2010a. "Labour Migration from Indonesia: An Overview of Indonesian Migration to Selected Destinations in Asia and the Middle East," IOM, Jakarta.

———. 2010b. "International Migration and Migrant Workers' Remittances in Indonesia: Findings of Baseline Surveys of Migrant Remitters and Remittance Beneficiary Households," IOM, Makati City.

———. 2010c. "Analyzing the Impact of Remittances from Cambodian Migrant Workers in Thailand on Local Communities in Cambodia," IOM, Phnom Penh.

———. 2011. "Migrant Information Note Issue 9," IOM, Bangkok.

———. 2013. *Country Migration Report: The Philippines 2013*. Makati City: IOM.

———. 2014. "Viet Nam Migrant Resource Center Looks to Future," IOM, Ho Chi Minh.

———. 2016a. "Migrant Information Note Issue 29," IOM, Bangkok.

———. 2016b. "Assessing Potential Changes in the Migration Patterns of Laotian Migrants and Their Impacts on Thailand and Lao People's Democratic Republic," IOM, Bangkok.

———. 2016c. "Assessing Potential Changes in the Migration Patterns of Myanmar Migrants and the Impacts on Thailand: Supplementary Report," IOM, Bangkok.

———. 2016d. "IOM Myanmar: Labour Mobility," IOM, Yangon.

Ishizuka, Futaba. 2013. "International Labor Migration in Vietnam and the Impact of Receiving Countries' Policies." Institute of Developing Economies (IDE) Discussion Paper 414, IDE, Chiba, Japan.

Jureidini, Ray. 2014. "Migrant Labour Recruitment to Qatar." Report for the Qatar Foundation Migrant Worker Welfare Initiative. Doha, Qatar.

Kuncoro, Ari, Arie Damayanti, and Ifa Isfandiarni. 2014. "Indonesia's Regulatory, Institution and Governance Structure for International Labor Migration." In *Managing International Migration for Development in East Asia*, edited by Richard H. Adams and Ahmad Ahsan, 159–176. Washington, DC: World Bank.

Lanto, Nini A. 2015. "Negotiating Bilateral Labor Agreements for the Protection of Overseas Filipino Workers: The Philippine Experience." Presentation for the Senior Executive Seminar on ASEAN Economic Integration and Labour Migration: Challenges and Opportunities, December 7–11, Bali, Indonesia.

Lao PDR, DOS (Department of Statistics) and NERI (National Economic Research Institute). 2012. "Economic Costs and Benefits of Labour Migration: Case of Lao PDR." In *Costs and Benefits of Cross-Country Labour Migration in the GMS*, edited by Hossein Jalilian, 190–241. Singapore: ISEAS Publishing.

Lao PDR, MOLSW (Ministry of Labor and Social Welfare), MOFA (Ministry of Foreign Affairs), and MPS (Ministry of Public Security). 2013. *Operations Manual on the*

Protection and Management of Migrant Workers for three Ministries of Lao PDR. Bangkok: ILO Regional Office for Asia and the Pacific.

Le, Nguyen Huyen, and Daniel Mont. 2014. "Vietnam's Regulatory, Institutional and Governance Structure for International Labor Migration." In *Managing International Migration for Development in East Asia*, edited by Richard H. Adams and Ahmad Ahsan, 199–219. Washington, DC: World Bank.

LSCW (Legal Support for Children and Women). 2013. "Domestic Workers and Sub-Decree 190: Time to Protect Cambodia's Migrants," LSCW, Phnom Penh.

Makovec, Mattia, Ririn Purnamasari, Matteo Sandi, and Astrid Savitri. 2016. "Intended vs. Unintended Consequences of Migration Restriction Policies: Evidence from a Natural Experiment in Indonesia." Institute for Social and Economic Research (ISER) Working Paper Series 2016–03, ISER, Essex.

McKenzie, David, Caroline Theoharides, and Dean Yang. 2014. "Distortions in the International Labor Market: Evidence from Filipino Migration and Wage Responses to Destination Country Economic Shocks." *American Economic Journal: Applied Economics* 6 (2): 49–75.

McKenzie, David, and Dean Yang. 2015. "Evidence on Policies to Increase the Development Impacts of International Migration." *World Bank Research Observer* 30 (2): 155–92.

MMN (Mekong Migration Network) and AMC (Asian Migrant Centre). 2008. *Migration in the Greater Mekong Subregion Resource Book: In-depth Study: Arrest, Detention and Deportation.* Hong Kong SAR, China: MMN and AMC.

———. 2013. *Migration in the Greater Mekong Subregion Resource Book: In-depth Study: Border Economic Zones and Migration.* Chiang Mai: MMN and AMC.

Naing, Saw. 2014. "Policies and Programs on Migration Management System in Myanmar."

Naro, Neth. 2009. "Human Trafficking in Cambodia: Reintegration of the Cambodian Illegal Migrants from Vietnam and Thailand," S. Rajaratnam School of International Studies (RSIS) Working Paper 181, RSIS, Singapore.

Nejar, Eva Marie T. 2012. "Profile and Taxation of the Philippine Overseas Remittance Industry," *NTRC Tax Research Journal* 24 (3): 1–19.

Oo, Khin Nway. 2016. "Myanmar: Migration and Sustainable Development in the ASEAN and Korea Region." First International Experts' Meeting, First Step in Establishing the ASEAN-Korea Migration Network, April 26–27, Manila.

Orbeta, Aniceto C. Jr., and Michael R.M. Abrigo. 2011. "Managing International Labor Migration: The Philippine Experience." *Philippine Journal of Development* 70 (1&2): 57–83.

Orbeta, Aniceto C. Jr., Michael R.M. Abrigo, and Michael Cabalfin. 2009. "Institutions Serving Philippine International Labor Migrants." Discussion Paper Series 2009–31, Philippine Institute for Development Studies, Makati City.

Philippines, CFO (Commission on Filipinos Overseas). 2014. *CFO Compendium of Statistics on International Migration.*

Philippines, COA (Commission on Audit). 2016a. *Annual Audit Report on the Philippine Overseas Employment Administration.* Quezon City, Philippines.

———. 2016b. *Annual Audit Report on the Overseas Workers Welfare Administration.*

Philippines, DOLE (Department of Labor and Employment). 2014. "Baldoz Orders OWWA to Review the PDOS and Weed Out 'Undesirable' Providers." Department of Labor and Employment–News.

POEA (Philippines Overseas Employment Administration). 2010. *Overseas Employment Statistics 2010.*

———. 2016. *Governing Board Resolution No. 06 Series of 2016.*

PSA (Philippine Statistics Authority). 2015. *2015 Yearbook of Labor Statistics.*

Phuong, Nguyen Quynh, and Sundar Venkatesh. 2016. "Does 'Buyer Beware' Work in Migration? Contracting between Brokers and Migrants in Vietnam," *International Migration* 54 (6): 94–108.

Rivera, John Paolo R., Denise Jannah D. Serrano, and Tereso S. Tullao Jr. 2013. "Bilateral Labor Agreements and Trade in Services: The Experience of the Philippines," In *Let Workers Move: Using Bilateral Labor Agreements to Increase Trade in Services,* edited by Sebastián Sáez, 109–127. Washington, DC: World Bank.

Sophal, Chan. 2012. "Economic Costs and Benefits of Labour Migration: Case of Cambodia," In *Costs and Benefits of Cross-Country Labour Migration in the GMS,* ed. Hossein Jalilian, 190–241, Singapore: ISEAS Publishing.

Thuy, Ta Thi Thanh. 2013. "Overview of Overseas Employment Support Fund," Session 2: Vietnam MWF—Sub-regional Meeting to Validate Findings of the Migration Welfare Fund. Feasibility Study conducted in Cambodia, Laos and Myanmar, Vientiane, Lao PDR, 26–27 May 2015.

Tornea, Vivian F. 2003. "Reintegration Program for Migrant Workers," *Review of Women's Studies* 13 (2): 203–220.

Tunon, Max, and Khleang Rim. 2013. "Cross-border Labour Migration in Cambodia: Considerations for the National Employment Policy." Working Paper, International Labour Organization (ILO), Bangkok.

United States, DOS (Department of State). 2016. *Trafficking in Persons Report 2016.* Washington, DC: DOS.

Vathanakoune, Sanya. 2015. "Feasibility Study on the Establishment of Migrant Welfare Fund Programmes in Laos," presentation at workshop hosted by Lao PDR's Ministry of Labour, Employment and Social Security (MLSW), May 26–27, 2015, Vientiane, Lao PDR.

Vietnam, DOLAB (Vietnam, Department of Overseas Labour) and IOM (International Organization for Migration). 2014. "Returning Vietnamese Migrant Workers: Policy and Practice." DOLAB and IOM, Hanoi.

Vietnam, MFA (Ministry of Foreign Affairs). 2012. "Review of Vietnamese Migration Abroad," Consular Department in the MFA, Hanoi.

Vutha, Hing, Lun Pide, and Phann Dalis. 2011. "Irregular Migration from Cambodia: Characteristics, Challenges, and Regulatory Approach," Cambodia Development Research Institute (CDRI) Working Paper Series No. 58, CDRI, Phnom Penh.

World Bank. 2010a. "Enhancing Access to Finance for Indonesian Overseas Migrant Workers: Evidence from a Survey of Three Provinces," World Bank, Jakarta.

World Bank. 2010b. "Improving Access to Financial Services in Indonesia," World Bank, Jakarta.

World Bank. 2016a. "Improving Migrant Workers' Protection: Review of the Indonesian Overseas Migrant Workers' Insurance (Asuransi TKI)."

———. 2016b. "Indonesia's Global Workers: Juggling Opportunities and Risks."

World Bank. 2016c. "Policies on Enhancing Indonesian Migrant Workers' Protection." Background Paper 3. Washington, DC: World Bank.

Zigurias, Christopher, and Cate Gribble. 2015. "Policy Responses to Address Student 'Brain Drain': An Assessment of Measures Intended to Reduce the Emigration of Singaporean International Students," *Journal of Studies in International Education* 19 (3): 246–264.

CHAPTER 8

Regional Migration Policy

Introduction

Member countries of the Association of Southeast Asian Nations (ASEAN) have thus far proceeded conservatively in adopting regionwide policies on migration. As chapter 4 introduced briefly, most efforts have proceeded alongside attempts to facilitate trade and economic integration. In agreeing to liberalize trade in services, the 1995 ASEAN Framework Agreement on Services (AFAS) included an article related to the mutual recognition of education, experience, licenses, and certifications. Commitments under the ASEAN Framework Agreement have been made in line with World Trade Organization General Agreement on Trade in Services (WTO GATS) Mode 4 provisions, which relate to the cross-border provision of services by natural persons. These primarily provide for the temporary movement of skilled professionals across borders, and do not affect access to employment markets, residence, or citizenship on a permanent basis. ASEAN member countries collected these mobility-related commitments in a separate Agreement on Movement of Natural Persons in 2012, which sought to further liberalize cross-border movements but also clarified that the agreement related only to business visitors, intracorporate transferees, and contractual service suppliers. Again, the agreement included an article related to the mutual recognition of education, experience, licenses, and certifications. Still, the impact on mobility has been limited. Not all countries have ratified the agreement,[1] domestic migration law continues to apply, and most commitments for service provision across countries relate to business visitors or intracorporate transferees and not to contractual service suppliers (Jurje and Lavenex 2015).[2] The ASEAN Framework Agreement is binding, however: commitments under it are subject to ASEAN's dispute settlement mechanism (Nikomborirak and Jitdumrong 2013). The ASEAN Comprehensive Investment Agreement took effect in late 2012 and provides for the entry, temporary stay, and work authorization of employees of corporations investing in member countries (Papademetriou et al. 2015).

ASEAN's most ambitious effort on migration thus far has been including the mobility of skilled individuals as a core element of the ASEAN Economic Community (AEC), which envisions deeper economic integration among ASEAN member states. In laying out the vision for the AEC in the Declaration of ASEAN Concord II in 2003, ASEAN members pledged to "facilitate movement of business persons, skilled labor and talents" to promote economic integration. In 2007, the AEC Blueprint laid out specific actions to allow for the free flow of skilled labor including (1) facilitating the issuance of visas and employment passes for ASEAN professionals and skilled labor; and (2) working toward harmonization and standardization through cooperation among ASEAN University Network members, development of core competencies and qualifications for occupations, and strengthening of research capacity related to skills, job placement, and labor market information. Unlike the AFAS, the AEC Blueprint is nonbinding and member states' migration procedures remain paramount (Nikomborirak and Jitdumrong 2013). The AEC Blueprint 2025 envisions expanding and deepening commitments in the Agreement on Movement of Natural Persons, reducing or standardizing mobility-related documentation requirements, or both, and improving efforts for the mutual recognition of professional qualifications.

Regional efforts to address the mobility of low- and mid-skilled labor have been scant. Developments in this area have primarily related to dialogue and the creation of institutions for cooperation on migration-related issues. No agreements with binding provisions have been ratified. In the 2007 Declaration on the Protection and Promotion of the Rights of Migrant Workers, ASEAN member states agreed to promote the dignity of migrant workers, including those who are not documented. The declaration set forth the obligations of (1) receiving countries including promoting fair employment of migrants; (2) sending countries including regulating recruitment and preparing migrants for overseas employment; and (3) ASEAN itself including data sharing, capacity building, and developing an instrument for the protection and promotion of migrant workers' rights. The ASEAN Forum on Migrant Labor was created to promote implementation and has representatives from member states, employers, workers, and civil society (UN ESCAP 2016).

Although some progress on reducing barriers to labor mobility has been made at the regional level, significant challenges remain. Many ASEAN countries have made advancements in areas like recruitment, migrant orientation programs, and complaints mechanisms, drawing on lessons learned in regional forums and from other ASEAN member states. The International Labour Organization (ILO) has supported the ASEAN and GMS TRIANGLE projects to promote good recruitment practices and safer migration through increased cooperation and strengthening institutions. The ASEAN Trade Union Council and the ASEAN Confederation of Employers are both engaged on topics of migration. However, binding agreements about worker protections and social protection have not been formulated (ILO 2015). The Declaration on the Protection and Promotion of the Rights of Migrant Workers is nonbinding, and the instrument to protect migrant workers envisioned in it has not been adopted. (Martin and Abella 2014; UN ESCAP 2016).

This chapter discusses two areas where regional policy may have a role to play in ASEAN: the recognition of qualifications and the portability of social protection benefits. ASEAN member states have paid particular attention to the first, but implementation challenges remain significant. Much less progress has been made on the latter.

Skills and qualifications recognition

The difficulty of obtaining recognition for foreign qualifications abroad is one of the obstacles to the free movement of skilled labor in ASEAN and to realizing the benefits of high-skilled migrants. High-skilled individuals are often dissuaded from migrating because the process for skills recognition is too costly or complex, with recognition processes at times requiring professionals to repeat education or endure supervised work experience. Professionals who do choose to migrate may end up working in jobs for which they are overqualified because their qualifications are not recognized. Additionally, employers may not be familiar with qualifications earned abroad, and so may be reluctant to hire foreign workers who have been educated or received qualifications in other countries. Although the challenges posed by this so-called brain waste are widespread, they are most pressing in fields such as medicine, engineering, and accounting to which access is usually formally regulated and which require the certification of specific professional qualifications.

Skills underutilization, or brain waste, occurs when migrants work in occupations that do not tap into their skills. This can occur because of a lack of qualifications recognition, insufficient knowledge of labor market opportunities, or upskilling prior to migration to increase the chance for migration (Docquier and Rapoport 2012). Existing evidence suggests that the quality of education offered by source countries is an important determinant of skills underutilization (Gibson and McKenzie 2012). Studying highly educated immigrants in the United States, Mattoo, Neagu, and Özden (2008) find that differences in the likelihood of educated immigrants working in unskilled jobs varies by region. The variations seem to be explained by source country characteristics related to human capital, such as spending on tertiary education. This pattern is generally true for ASEAN migrants in Organisation for Economic Co-operation and Development (OECD) countries. Batalova, Shymonyak, and Sugiyarto (2017) estimate overqualification rates for skilled ASEAN migrants in the OECD area (figure 8.1). Skilled migrants from Malaysia and Singapore, which spend more than twice as much as ASEAN's other countries on tertiary education per student, have the region's lowest levels of overqualification for the jobs they hold, below those of even locals in OECD member countries.

In response to the challenges posed by brain waste, two complimentary approaches have been devised: mutual recognition arrangements (MRAs) and qualifications reference frameworks (QRFs). In an MRA, two or more countries agree to mutually recognize professional qualifications in certain occupations and to facilitate the

FIGURE 8.1
Overqualification rates of skilled ASEAN migrants in OECD countries

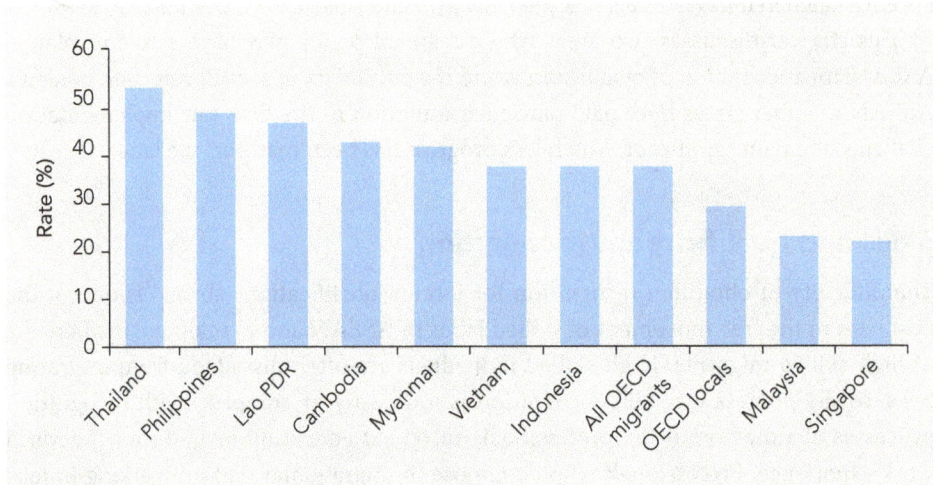

Source: Batalova, Shymonyak, and Sugiyarto 2017.
Note: ASEAN = Association of Southeast Asian Nations; OECD = Organisation for Economic Co-operation and Development.

mobility of professionals in those fields between or among the countries. Developing MRAs often requires aligning national legal systems to allow migrants' qualifications to be recognized, valued, and validated according to agreed terms of equivalence. This legal alignment is a necessary step in enabling migrants to work abroad in fields requiring regulated professional qualifications because partner countries' standards must be incorporated without compromising the quality of the qualification. MRAs can also establish transferable international standards in fields that are not formally regulated at the national level. Such MRAs effectively professionalize a field at the international level.

QRFs are generally less systematic than MRAs but broader in scope. Instead of bringing countries' systems of professional accreditation into alignment, QRFs determine terms of equivalence between foreign qualifications and those granted nationally. The main objective is to reduce uncertainty for both employers and migrants by providing information on the relative merits of specific foreign qualifications. Ideally, this information is arranged in a way that is indicative of likely labor market outcomes. With the information provided through QRFs, migrants and employers are better able to identify suitable job opportunities and skills or accreditation gaps. In contrast to MRAs, QRFs can be developed unilaterally by migrants' host countries. However, they can also be part of large multilateral initiatives such as the European Qualifications Framework.

The easier process of obtaining recognition and the certainty that professional qualifications will be recognized may facilitate the migration of skilled professionals (Papademetriou et al. 2015). Research on the issue is sparse, however. Using cross-country regressions to study the impact of policies designed to attract high-skilled migrants, Czaika and Parsons (2016) find that a bilateral agreement recognizing foreign qualifications increases the number of high-skilled migrants between 30 and 60 percent. However, the relationship between migration flows and the presence of the agreement might not be causal: the relationship might arise from the fact that the presence of an agreement indicates significant effort by the partner countries to facilitate skilled migration. Like other high-skilled migration policies, qualifications recognition must provide additional value to high-skilled migrants who seem to compare the costs and benefits of skilled migration entry paths to other (general) entry paths. Facchini and Lodigiani (2014) and Coppel, Dumont, and Visco (2001) both note the tendency for skilled migrants to select general channels of entry when skill-specific ones seem too onerous. Indeed, high-skilled migrants may even choose to work informally if the costs of formal migration are too high.

There is also tentative evidence that qualifications recognition moderates brain waste. Several case studies have identified benefits (IOM 2013). In Italy, for instance, participation in a qualifications recognition program improved employability and labor market participation, lowering the unemployment rate of migrants with tertiary education from 10 percent to 4 percent. In Australia, a reform of migrant selection that focused on qualifications recognition corresponded with a rise in the employment rate among migrants from 56 to 76 percent. However, the reform also involved a change in English language assessment, making the impact of both changes impossible to disentangle. In Denmark, migrants felt that the national qualifications assessment program had a positive effect on their ability to gain employment or continue education.

Recognition of professional qualifications involves several challenges. First, even where qualifications recognition programs are available, uptake among migrants might be low. This is the case in European Union (EU) and OECD member countries where migrants seem dissuaded by complex procedures and lack of information (Dumont and Aujean 2014). Second, again even if recognition frameworks are in place, employers might still be reluctant to hire migrants. This might happen if the assessments are not seen as informative, trustworthy, or reliable. Evidence from OECD countries suggests that many employers tend to attribute less value to qualifications obtained in non-OECD member countries even if these qualifications are supposedly of equivalent value (Chaloff and Lemaître 2009). Thus, to be useful, recognition frameworks must be developed in close collaboration with employers, focusing on what makes migrants valuable in the host country's labor market. Third, recognition schemes must be fairly granular in their description of the specific level of education, skill, and ability represented by a qualification. Large, multilateral frameworks risk becoming too abstract, outlining only broad areas of equivalency, and overlooking the particular requirements migrants need to adapt to specific labor markets. Indeed, the same profession may involve different capabilities or skills in different countries, which makes automatic recognition of qualifications difficult and partial recognition with compensatory training or education necessary (Papademetriou et al. 2015). Fourth, recognizing work experience is frequently necessary but can be more challenging than recognizing education, certificates, or licenses (Papademetriou et al. 2015).

Skills and qualifications recognition in ASEAN

Several ASEAN migrant destination countries have processes for recognizing the skills of foreign workers, whereas ASEAN as a region has used mutual recognition arrangements and a regional qualifications reference framework. In Malaysia, the Malaysia Qualifications Agency oversees recognition of the higher education qualifications of foreign workers, the National Vocational Training Council does the same for vocational competencies, and the Construction Industry Development Board offers a foreign personnel skills recognition certificate for construction workers. Singapore's National Skills Recognition System assesses the competencies of foreign workers. Thailand does not have a recognition system (Ducanes 2013). At the regional level, ASEAN has used MRAs and a regional qualifications framework as its primary strategies for realizing the AEC's vision for the free mobility of skilled labor. Initial efforts are underway to facilitate skills recognition for low-skilled workers.

Mutual recognition arrangements

Thus far, seven MRAs and one framework MRA agreement have been developed in ASEAN related to engineering, nursing, architecture, surveying (framework agreement), medical practitioners, dental practitioners, tourism, and accounting. The MRAs can be grouped into two types. The first group is accounting, architecture, dentistry, engineering, medicine, nursing, and surveying—normally regulated professions that require a license to practice legally. The MRA process varies by profession. For instance, the MRAs on architects and engineers require a three-step process for recognition in which these professionals obtain a license in their home country; are reviewed for regional registration by the ASEAN Chartered Professional Engineers Coordinating Committee or the ASEAN Architect Council, two industry bodies created for ASEAN-wide certification; and apply for host country registration as a registered foreign architect or a registered foreign professional engineer (Fukunaga 2015). The nursing MRA is a two-step process of registration in the home country and application for registration as a foreign nurse in the host country. There is no regional registration of nurses. The process for the other two health-related MRAs, on medical and dental practitioners, is similar. The second group consists of just one MRA that covers a profession that is not typically regulated. The tourism MRA, covering 32 job titles, grants ASEAN tourism workers recognition upon completing a common tourism curriculum and certification. Foreign tourism professionals are registered in a regional system. In all cases, the MRAs remain limited by national regulations such as immigration and occupation restrictions.

A recent report by the Economic Research Institute for ASEAN and East Asia provides an assessment of progress on the implementation of several of the MRAs (Fukunaga 2015). Progress on the MRAs is most advanced in architecture and engineering with regional registration systems available for both. For the architecture MRA, Brunei Darussalam, Malaysia, the Philippines, Singapore, and Thailand have completed preparatory work for implementation and have a system to admit registered foreign architects. Indonesia, Myanmar, and Vietnam are nearing completion. Cambodia and the Lao People's Democratic Republic, however, lag. Beyond implementation, national regulatory changes are also necessary.

Brunei Darussalam is alone in completing the regulatory changes necessary to permit foreign architects to work in the country, whereas all other countries are at various stages of reforming the relevant regulations. For the engineering MRA, Brunei Darussalam, Malaysia, the Philippines, Singapore, and Vietnam have completed preparatory work for implementation and have a system to admit registered foreign professional engineers, with all other countries nearing completion. Malaysia and Thailand have completed the necessary regulatory changes, and all countries except Indonesia, Lao PDR, and Myanmar seem to have made significant progress. For the nursing MRA, as no regional system is necessary, countries seem to have adjusted their regulatory environments according to the MRA. The legal text of the accounting MRA has been finalized, but the MRA has not yet been signed. Regional registration for the tourism MRA appears to have begun in 2015.

In the best cases, the ASEAN MRAs provide an indication of professional quality and competency. These MRAs also allow foreign professionals to work for longer periods of time in host countries than they would otherwise be able. However, the effectiveness of MRAs as a mobility tool in ASEAN is in doubt (Sugiyarto and Agunias 2014; Hickman and Irwin 2013). Progress on the labor mobility provisions of the AEC was the least among all services sector integration measures, with an average 20 percent completion rate compared to a 57 percent rate for liberalizing services restrictiveness and a 72 percent rate for liberalizing foreign direct investment (FDI) restrictions (Menon and Melendez 2017). Additionally, the MRAs cover a very small portion of ASEAN employment: Batalova, Shymonyak, and Sugiyarto (2017) estimate that the MRAs cover only 5 percent of all employment. Within this already small coverage, uptake of the MRAs is limited, as is knowledge about them. There are only 355 registered architects and 2,231 registered engineers in all of ASEAN, which does not mean they actually moved under the MRA. A recent survey of firms listed on the Thai stock exchange found that nearly 60 percent had no knowledge or understanding of the MRA on accounting, despite a positive attitude toward the free mobility of accounting professionals (Pichayasupakoon 2014). The tourism MRA also seems to suffer from a lack of awareness (Hickman and Irwin 2013).

The MRAs' effectiveness as a migration measure is also limited by host country immigration and regulatory restrictions that remain in place even where MRAs have been implemented, meaning that the MRAs have limited impact as facilitators of free mobility. This contrasts with the European Qualifications Framework that exists in the EU's setting of free mobility (Fukunaga 2015). Thailand, for example, bans migrants from working in 39 occupations including engineering, accounting, and architecture. Additionally, obtaining a license in nursing requires proficiency in the Thai language (Natali, McDougall, and Stubbington 2014). The Philippines has constitutional provisions barring migrant workers from receiving licenses in some occupations (Sugiyarto and Agunias 2014). These restrictions make the benefits of the MRAs uncertain. Indonesian professionals registered as ASEAN architects or ASEAN chartered professional engineers stated in interviews that they did not feel that there was a significant benefit to registration, and those not yet registered did not express much interest in becoming registered (Hirawan and Triwidodo 2012). Five-star hotels in Jakarta seem to have a negative perception of the MRA on tourism (Hidayat 2011). The benefits of

MRAs may also be limited by the cost of using them. For example, architects can be required to undertake additional assessments or a residency. Finally, MRAs may not alleviate employer concerns about the consistency of professional standards across countries because the education and testing capacity of ASEAN member states varies significantly (ILO and ADB 2014).

ASEAN Qualifications Reference Framework

ASEAN member states have also developed and in 2015 endorsed the ASEAN Qualifications Reference Framework (AQRF).[3] The AQRF is designed to permit translation of qualifications across ASEAN. To do this, member states have been creating national qualifications frameworks (NQFs) that can then be referenced to the common AQRF (Sugiyarto and Agunias 2014). These NQFs (1) specify levels of achievement in schooling, technical and vocational education, and higher education; and (2) describe domains of learning such as knowledge and skills. Referencing the NQFs to the AQRF involves performing quality assurance and linking the levels of the national frameworks to those in the AQRF. According to a recent assessment of progress, the AQRF is in the implementation phase that involves establishing infrastructure such as funding, management, and communications (SHARE 2016). Five countries have indicated that the AQRF would be implemented in 2017 or 2018, though this may be pushed to 2020 in some cases; two countries indicated implementation in 2016; and implementation in the remaining countries is uncertain or unknown.

One of the major challenges facing the implementation of the AQRF is that different ASEAN member states are at different stages of establishing their NQFs, which is an important (though not required) step in referencing to the AQRF (table 8.1).[4]

TABLE 8.1

Implementation stage of national qualifications frameworks in ASEAN

Country	Level of implementation	Stages = 1 through 8
Brunei Darussalam	Some structures and processes established and operational	6
Cambodia	Some structures and processes agreed and documented	5
Indonesia	Some structures and processes established and operational	6
Lao PDR	Background planning underway	3
Malaysia	Review of structures and processes proposed or underway	8
Myanmar	Background planning underway	3
Philippines	Some structures and processes agreed and documented	5
Singapore	Structures and processes established for five years	7
Thailand	Initial development and design completed	4
Vietnam	Background planning underway	3

Source: SHARE 2016.
Note: ASEAN = Association of Southeast Asian Nations.

Malaysia has made the most progress with NQF structures and processes in place and under review. Singapore is not far behind. Its NQF structures and process have been in place for five years, but review is not yet planned. Lao PDR and Vietnam, in contrast, lag with only background planning for the NQF underway.[5] The referencing process, which member countries have limited experience with and which depends on their willingness to participate, is an additional challenge. According to ASEAN member states, referencing requires more staff and financial resources, additional coordination across sectors, and more awareness among stakeholders (SHARE 2016). The process is made more difficult by the need for quality assurance to ensure that educational levels in one country's NQF are consistent with those in other countries' and by the lack of finalized governance and monitoring structures.

Skills recognition for low-skilled workers

Both the MRA and the AQRF are outgrowths of the AEC's vision for the free mobility of high-skilled labor and so benefit skilled workers. This ignores the much larger flow of unskilled workers in ASEAN. To fill this gap, the ILO is leading the Mutual Recognition of Skills initiative to recognize technical and vocational skills that can then be translated using the AQRF (Torres 2014). This recognition is to be done for key skills and occupations based on priorities identified by member states using a tool called the Regional Model Competency Standards that provides a regional benchmark for skill competencies.

Social protection for ASEAN migrants

Like all workers, international migrant workers face risks associated with employment, health, and the life cycle. The ability of social protection systems to assist migrants in managing these risks is complicated by the unique nature of international migration and by national legislation that treats migrants and locals differently. When social protection benefits are not portable, meaning that they cannot be transferred intact across national boundaries, returning home can mean that contributions in the host country are forfeited without any associated benefits. National legislation in migrant destinations can deny migrants access to social protection benefits by distinguishing between citizens or permanent residents and migrants and prohibiting access to the latter. Even when legislation does not explicitly deny access, eligibility and qualifying rules can make such access improbable, as when migrant workers have de jure access to benefits that require a lengthy contribution period and are only granted employment passes of limited duration.

The ability of migrant workers to access social protection is important not only to help migrants manage economic, life cycle, and other risks but also as a tool to improve the effectiveness of migration management. Where migrants contribute to social protection systems but their access is prohibited or restricted, an incentive exists for informality. Migrants may then migrate informally to avoid paying the cost of social protection contributions. Conversely, making pension and other benefits portable can create an incentive for migrants to return home, reducing the risk of overstay for host countries and increasing the probability of return (Avato, Koettle, and Sabates-Wheeler 2010). Although there is concern, on the one hand, that the benefits associated with social protection systems can attract additional migrants, the evidence is mixed and suggests a small impact compared to other pull factors (Giulietti and Wahba 2013; OECD 2016). On the other hand, access to social protection in sending countries can reduce the propensity to migrate in some cases (Hagen-Zanker and Himmelstine 2013; OECD 2016).

Access to benefits

This section describes the access of intra-ASEAN migrants to formal social protection, focusing on old age, invalidity, and survivors' benefits; workplace injury benefits; and health benefits. The section begins by laying out the benefits that are currently available to migrants in the region. As described by Avato, Koettle, and Sabates-Wheeler (2010), portable benefits require coordination between sending and receiving countries whereas benefits can be made exportable by the host country alone. The section then moves on to a discussion of the benefits and challenges of developing regional social security agreements in ASEAN.

Old age, invalidity, and survivors benefits in receiving countries

Migrants have limited access to old age, invalidity, and survivors benefits in ASEAN's main receiving countries (table 8.2). Brunei Darussalam and Singapore do not permit migrants to access their provident funds, and in Brunei Darussalam they are similarly excluded from the country's universal old age and invalidity scheme. In principle, migrants in Malaysia can contribute to the country's provident fund at a minimum rate of 11 percent of wages and are able to export these benefits upon completion of

TABLE 8.2
Migrant access to old age, invalidity, and survivors benefits in ASEAN receiving countries

Country	Type	Exportable	Qualifying benefits	Coverage Migrants	Coverage Migrant domestic workers	Coverage Informal migrants
Brunei Darussalam	PF	Yes	No	No	No	No
Brunei Darussalam	U[a]	No	Yes	No	No	No
Cambodia	n.a.	n.a.	n.a.	n.a.	n.a.	n.a.
Indonesia	PF	Yes	No	Yes	—	—
Lao PDR	SI	—	Yes	—	—	—
Malaysia	PF	Yes	No	Yes	Yes	No
Myanmar	n.a.	n.a.	n.a.	n.a.	n.a.	n.a.
Philippines	SI	Yes	Yes	Yes	—	—
Singapore	PF	Yes	No	No	No	No
Thailand	SI	Yes	Yes	Yes	No	No
Vietnam	SI	—	Y	—	—	—

Source: Updated based on Tamagno 2008.
Note: — = not available; n.a. = not applicable; ASEAN = Association of Southeast Asian Nations; PF = provident fund; SI = social insurance; U = universal scheme.
a. Brunei Darussalam's universal scheme does not provide survivors benefits.

their employment term. However, this contribution is matched by a RM 5 contribution from employers that contrasts with the compulsory employer match of 12 percent of wages for local workers. Legal migrants in Thailand can access the country's social security system, and benefits in theory are exportable. However, this system excludes the country's large population of irregular migrants, as well as regular migrants working in informal sectors such as agriculture and fishing. No framework for exporting benefits has been established. Perhaps most important, old age benefits involve a minimum qualifying period of 15 years while the new memorandum of understanding process for legal migration provides for only 4-year employment terms (Harkins 2014). Both Indonesia and the Philippines allow migrants access to old age, invalidity, and survivors benefits. Domestic and informal migrants do not have access to these benefits in any country with data available except Malaysia, where benefits are curtailed by the small employer contribution requirement.

Workplace injury benefits in receiving countries

Migrant workers in ASEAN tend to have access to workplace injury benefits of some type, though these benefits tend to be provided via a parallel system to those provided to locals (table 8.3). Access in Thailand is provided through the social security system, which means that access is limited to workers in formal sectors and to legal migrants. The process of obtaining benefits can be lengthy with language barriers and documentation creating additional barriers, which limits access (Harkins 2014). In Malaysia, employers

TABLE 8.3
Migrant access to workplace injury benefits in ASEAN receiving countries

Country	Type	Exportable	Qualifying benefits	Coverage		
				Migrants	Migrant domestic workers	Informal migrants
Brunei Darussalam	E	—	No	No	No	No
Cambodia	n.a.	n.a.	n.a.	n.a.	n.a.	n.a.
Indonesia	SI	—	No	—	—	—
Lao PDR	SI	—	No	—	—	—
Malaysia	SI	—	No	No	No	No
Malaysia	E	Yes	No	Yes	No	No
Myanmar	SI	—	No	—	—	—
Philippines	SI	—	No	Yes	—	—
Singapore	E	Yes	No	Yes	Yes[a]	No
Thailand	SI	No	No	Yes	No	No
Vietnam	SI	—	No	—	—	—

Source: Updated based on Tamagno 2008.
Note: — = not available; n.a. = not applicable; ASEAN = Association of Southeast Asian Nations; E = employer responsibility; SI = social insurance.
a. Employers must purchase personal accident insurance for domestic workers in Singapore.

are mandated to purchase insurance against the accidental death and temporary or permanent disablement of migrant workers. However, these benefits are not as generous as those available to local workers whose social security contributions allow them to access free treatment and obtain greater compensation (Devadason and Meng 2014; World Bank 2013). Migrant and local workers in Singapore are covered under the same Workmen's Compensation Act that makes employers liable for workplace injury. In Malaysia and Singapore unlike in Thailand, migrant workers can receive workplace compensation benefits if they exit the country. Brunei Darussalam is the only country with data available that does not provide migrant workers access to workplace injury benefits. Domestic workers only have access to workplace injury benefits in Singapore, where employers are required to purchase personal accident insurance. Informal workers lack access to these benefits in all ASEAN countries.

Health benefits in receiving countries

Similar to workplace injury benefits, migrants in ASEAN tend to have access to health benefits, but often through a parallel system to that of locals (table 8.4). In Malaysia, migrants can access medical benefits via the provident fund on a voluntary basis.

TABLE 8.4
Migrant access to health benefits in ASEAN receiving countries

| Country | Type | Exportable | Qualifying benefits | Coverage | | |
				Migrants	Migrant domestic workers	Informal migrants
Brunei Darussalam	U	—	No	—	—	No
Cambodia	n.a.	n.a.	n.a.	n.a.	n.a.	n.a.
Indonesia	SI	—	Yes	Yes	—	—
Lao PDR	SI	—	Yes	—	—	—
Malaysia	PF	—	No	Yes	Yes	No
Malaysia	SA	No	No	Yes	Yes	Yes
Malaysia	E	—	No	Yes	Yes	No
Myanmar	PF	—	Yes	—	—	—
Philippines	SI	Yes	—	Yes	—	No
Singapore	PF	—	No	No	No	No
Singapore	SA	—	No	No	No	No
Singapore	E	—	No	Yes	Yes	No
Thailand	SI	—	Yes	Yes	No	No
Thailand	U	—	No	Yes	Yes	Yes
Vietnam	SI	—	Yes	—	—	—

Source: Updated based on Tamagno 2008.
Note: — = not available; n.a. = not applicable; ASEAN = Association of Southeast Asian Nations; E = employer responsibility; PF = provident fund; SA = social assistance; SI = social insurance; U = universal scheme.

Similar to locals without access to another scheme, foreign workers are able to obtain medical care through a flat fee for primary and hospital care. However, migrants are charged a higher rate (Guinto et al. 2015). Access to benefits for informal migrants is limited by migration enforcement posts embedded at hospitals. Additionally, employers are required to obtain health insurance for their workers. Similarly, in Singapore employers are required to purchase health insurance on behalf of migrant workers. Both formal and informal migrants in Thailand have access to medical care. Formal migrants can participate via social security. Irregular migrants who have registered are required to obtain health insurance in the Compulsory Migrant Health Insurance Scheme. However, the scheme's financing is uncertain because of the sporadic nature of regularizations. Outpatient utilization rates are lower than for the other public health insurance schemes (IOM and WHO 2009). Irregular migrants can opt in to the Compulsory Migrant Health Insurance Scheme for a fee. Health promotion and prevention services are available to all migrants. Migrants in the Philippines may opt in to PhilHealth. Migrants who have worked six months can enroll in Indonesia's national health insurance program (Guinto et al. 2015).

Benefits provided to out-migrants by sending countries

Several ASEAN countries provide social protection benefits to their citizens while they are working abroad. The Philippines allows overseas workers to contribute to the social security system on a voluntary basis, giving them access to retirement, death, disability, and other benefits and to the tax-free savings program Flexi-Fund (Hall 2011). Private recruitment agencies must obtain life and personal accident insurance for migrant workers at no cost to the worker. The Overseas Workers Welfare Administration, which migrant workers must join, also provides access to disability, dismemberment, and death benefits. Migrant workers must obtain health insurance coverage via PhilHealth that allows migrants and their dependents to be reimbursed for hospitalization and outpatient benefits in the Philippines and for hospitalization outside of the Philippines. Philippine regulations also require host country employers to provide equivalent health insurance to local and migrant workers. The Philippines has negotiated more than 10 social security agreements, though none with ASEAN countries. In Indonesia, migrants receive health, accident, and death benefits through the mandatory Migrant Worker Insurance Program (Guinto et al. 2015). However, as the previous chapter described, implementation remains a challenge. Cambodia, Lao PDR, Myanmar, and Vietnam have also taken steps to increase social security protections for migrant workers (ILO and ADB 2014).

Challenges facing regional agreements on social protection

Following the 2007 Declaration on the Protection and Promotion of the Rights of Migrant Workers, ASEAN member states have paid increasing attention to the best ways to protect the rights of migrant workers, including through access to social protection. In the most recent meeting of the ASEAN Forum on Migrant Labor that is part of the strategy to implement the Declaration, participants recommended extending social protection for migrant workers through measures in each country to ensure equitable access and to remove discriminatory social protection laws. Participants also recommended working toward the portability of social protection by exploring the feasibility of bilateral and regional agreements on portability.

ASEAN lacks any bilateral or multilateral agreements on the portability of benefits. Portability refers to a migrant's ability to transfer and maintain access to social security rights in full without regard to nationality or residence (Holzmann, Koettle, and Chernetsky 2005). Bilateral agreements, which have traditionally covered long-term benefits rather than health benefits, typically provide for equal benefits for migrants and locals, help avoid double coverage in host and home countries, and outline cooperation between social security institutions on issues such as totalization of benefits (Taha, Siegmann, and Messkoub 2015). Totalization means that contributions in both receiving and sending countries are counted toward eligibility requirements, which also helps ensure that replacement rates are based on the entire period of contribution in both countries (Holzmann, Koettle, and Chernetsky 2005). Multilateral agreements then provide a framework for portability, and offer uniform treatment of workers and uniform administrative procedures across multiple countries (Tamagno 2008). There are about 1,500 bilateral portability agreements. Twenty-three percent of global migrants in 2000 had access to social services under a bilateral or multilateral social security arrangement (Avato, Koettle, and Sabates-Wheeler 2010). Although better practices have been identified for bilateral social security agreements based on their provision of fairness for individuals, fiscal fairness for countries, and bureaucratic effectiveness, evaluations are limited and at times agreements are not operative (Holzmann and Koettl 2015). Negotiations of both bilateral and multilateral agreements are time consuming and complex.

The EU, the Caribbean Community (CARICOM), MERCOSUR, and the Ibero-American Social Security Convention are all examples of multilateral social security arrangements. The EU's agreement allows full portability of social security benefits, and has set the stage for agreements with non-EU countries. The MERCOSUR agreements do not provide for totalization of benefits but facilitate administrative coordination to ensure portability (Pasadilla and Abella 2012). The CARICOM agreement does establish totalization in facilitating portability, but there are concerns about the agreement's design and take-up (Forteza 2008).

The promulgation of bilateral and multilateral social security agreements will be challenging for ASEAN member states for several reasons. First, unlike in the EU, the flow of intra-ASEAN migrants is predominantly unidirectional to Brunei Darussalam, Malaysia, Singapore, and Thailand and away from all other member states. These host countries, particularly Malaysia and Singapore, also have more developed social protection systems. These factors mean that the receiving countries bear the cost of administering social benefits for ASEAN migrants but do not have many migrants in the other member states benefiting from similar systems. This reduces their incentive for deal making (Pasadilla and Abella 2012). Second, the different structure of social protection schemes in the ASEAN member states creates difficulties for harmonizing benefits.

An agreement between a country such as Malaysia, which has a provident fund, and a country such as the Philippines, which has social insurance, is challenging because totalization could result in the country with social insurance incurring new obligations that it would not have had in the absence of totalization (Tamagno 2008). A solution is possible involving transfers between the provident fund and the social insurance scheme, but such an arrangement has never been undertaken. Third, ASEAN countries vary in the sophistication of their social protection systems and in their capacity. Bilateral and multilateral social security agreements are complex to negotiate and run. For some countries, particularly Cambodia, Lao PDR, and Myanmar, focusing attention on such agreements may not be possible or even desirable alongside ongoing efforts to strengthen their own social protection systems.

In reviewing the lessons from bilateral social security agreements between EU and non-EU member states, Holzmann (2016) suggests that such agreements are more likely to succeed in a migration corridor with significant flows, with similar schemes in the sending and receiving country, and with administrative arrangements that are computerized. A narrow approach that focuses on several benefits such as pensions, work injury, and health care is also advised. Holzmann and Koettl (2015) provide a more technical analysis of how social protection schemes may be reformed unilaterally, bilaterally, and multilaterally to improve portability.

Notes

1. Indonesia, Lao PDR, and the Philippines have not ratified the agreement.
2. Only Cambodia, the Philippines, and Vietnam have provisions related to contractual services providers (Fukunaga 2015).
3. The AQRF has been undertaken as a project of the ASEAN-Australia-New Zealand free trade area (AANZFTA) (ILO 2014).
4. The AQRF has been designed to allow countries to reference certain qualifications without having an NQF in place.
5. Additional details on the progress of each ASEAN country toward national qualifications frameworks are available in ILO (2014) and SHARE (2016).

References

Avato, Johanna, Johannes Koettl, and Rachel Sabates-Wheeler. 2010. "Social Security Regimes, Global Estimates, and Good Practices: The Status of Social Protection for International Migrants." *World Development* 38 (4): 455–466.

Batalova, Jeanne, Andriy Shymonyak, and Guntur Sugiyarto. 2017. "Firing Up Regional Brain Networks: The Promise of Brain Circulation in the ASEAN Economic Community." Asian Development Bank, Manila.

Chaloff, Jonathan, and Georges Lemaître. 2009. "Managing Highly-Skilled Labour Migration: A Comparative Analysis of Migration Policies and Challenges in OECD Countries." Social, Employment and Migration Working Papers 79, Organisation for Economic Cooperation and Development, Paris.

Coppel, Jonathan, Jean-Christophe Dumont, and Ignazio Visco. 2001. "Trends in Immigration and Economic Consequences." Working Paper No.284, Economics Department, Organization for Economic Co-operation and Development (OECD), Paris.

Czaika, Mathias, and Christopher R. Parsons. 2016. "The Gravity of High-Skilled Migration Policies." Working Paper 13, KNOMAD, Washington, DC.

Devadason, Evelyn Shyamala, and Chan Wai Meng. 2014. "Policies and Laws Regulating Migrant Workers in Malaysia: A Critical Appraisal." *Journal of Contemporary Asia* 44 (1): 19–35.

Docquier, Frédéric and Hillel Rapoport. 2012. "Globalization, Brain Drain, and Development," *Journal of Economic Literature* 50 (3): 681–730.

Ducanes, Geoffrey. 2013. "Labour Shortages, Foreign Migrant Recruitment and the Portability of Qualifications in East and South-East Asia." International Labour Organization Regional Office for Asia and the Pacific, Bangkok.

Dumont, Jean-Christophe, and Laurent Aujean. 2014. "Matching Economic Migration with Labour Market Needs in Europe." Policy Brief, Organisation for Economic Cooperation and Development/European Commission, Paris.

Facchini, Giovanni, and Elisabetta Lodigiani. 2014. "Attracting Skilled Immigrants: An Overview of Recent Policy Developments in Advanced Countries." *National Institute Economic Review* 229 (1): R3–21.

Forteza, Alvaro. 2008. "The Portability of Pension Rights: General Principles and the Caribbean Case." Social Protection Discussion Paper Series 0825, World Bank, Washington D.C.

Fukunaga, Yoshifumi. 2015. "Assessing the Progress of ASEAN MRAs on Professional Services." Economic Research Institute for ASEAN and East Asia (ERIA) Discussion Paper 21, ERIA, Jakarta.

Gibson, John, and David McKenzie. 2012. "The Economic Consequences of 'Brain Drain' of the Best and Brightest: Microeconomic Evidence from Five Countries." *The Economic Journal* 122 (May): 339–75.

Giulietti, Corrado, and Jackline Wahba. 2013. "Welfare Migration." In *International Handbook on the Economics of Migration*, edited by Amelie F. Constant and Klaus F. Zimmerman, 489–504. Cheltenham, U.K.: Edward Elgar Publishing.

Guinto, Ramon Lorenzo Luis R., Ufara Zuwasti Curran, Rapeepong Suphanchaimat, and Nicola S. Pocock. 2015. "Universal Health Coverage in 'One ASEAN': Are Migrants Included?" *Global Health Action* 8 (s3): 25749.

Hagen-Zanker, Jessica, and Carmen Leon Himmelstine. 2013. "What Do We Know about the Impact of Social Protection Programmes on the Decision to Migrate?" *Migration and Development* 2 (1): 117–31.

Hall, Andy. 2011. "Migrant Workers' Rights to Social Protection in ASEAN: Case studies of Indonesia, Philippines, Singapore, and Thailand." Mahidol Migration Centre, Salaya, Thailand.

Harkins, Benjamin. 2014. "Social Protection for Migrant Workers in Thailand." In *Thailand Migration Report 2014*, edited by Jerrold W. Huguet, 27–43. Bangkok: United Nations Thematic Working Group on Migration in Thailand.

Hickman, Alan, and Jim Irwin. 2013. "Gap Analysis on Implementation of MRA on Tourism Professionals." ASEAN Australia Development Cooperation Program Phase II (AADCP) Final Report.

Hidayat, Nila Krisnawati. 2011. "Analysis of the Adoption of ASEAN MRA on Tourism Professional at Jakarta Five Star Hotel Towards the Human Resources Global Competitiveness."

Hirawan, Fajar B., and Wahyu Triwidodo. 2012. "Examining the ASEAN Mutual Recognition Arrangement (MRA) Implementation Process on Engineering and Architectural Services and Its Impact to the Professionals: Indonesian Perspective." Economic Research Institute for ASEAN and East Asia (ERIA), Jakarta.

Holzmann, Robert. 2016. "Do Bilateral Social Security Agreements Deliver on the Portability of Pensions and Health Care Benefits? A Summary Policy Paper on Four Migration Corridors Between EU and Non-EU Member States." Policy Paper 111, Institute for the Study of Labor (IZA), Bonn.

Holzmann, Robert, and Johannes Koettl. 2015. "Portablity of Pension, Health, and Other Social Benefits: Facts, Concepts, and Issues." *CESifo Economic Studies* 61 (2): 377–415.

Holzmann, Robert, Johannes Koettl, and Taras Chernetsky. 2005. "Portability Regimes of Pension and Health Care Benefits for International Migrants: An Analysis of Issues and Good Practices." Social Protection Discussion Paper Series 0519, World Bank, Washington, DC.

ILO (International Labour Organization). 2014. "Assessment of the Readiness of ASEAN Member States for Implementation of the Commitment to the Free Flow of Skilled Labour within the ASEAN Economic Community from 2015." ILO, Bangkok.

———. 2015. "Progress of the Implementation of Recommendations Adopted at the 3rd–6th ASEAN Forum on Migrant Labour Meetings: Background Paper to the 7th AFML." ILO, Bangkok.

ILO (International Labour Organization) and ADB (Asian Development Bank. 2014. *ASEAN Community 2015: Managing Integration for Better Jobs and Shared Prosperity.* Bangkok: ILO and ADB.

IOM (International Organization for Migration). 2013. "Recognition of Qualifications and Competencies of Migrants," IOM, Brussels.

IOM (International Organization for Migration) and WHO (World Health Organization). 2009. "Financing Healthcare for Migrants: A Case Study from Thailand," IOM, Bangkok.

Jurje, Flavia, and Sandra Lavenex. 2015. "ASEAN Economic Community: What Model for Labour Mobility?" Working Paper 105/02, Swiss National Centre of Competence in Research, Bern.

Martin, Philip, and Manolo Abella. 2014. "Reaping the Economic and Social Benefits of Labour Mobility: ASEAN 2015." Asia-Pacific Working Paper Series, International Labour Organization (ILO), Bangkok.

Mattoo, Aaditya, Ileana Cristina Neagu, and Çağlar Özden. 2008. "Brain Waste? Educated Immigrants in the U.S. Labor Market." *Journal of Development Economics* 87 (2): 255–69.

Menon, Jayant, and Anna Cassandra Melendez. 2017. "Realizing an ASEAN Economic Community: Progress and Remaining Challenge." *The Singapore Economic Review* 63 (1): 681–702.

Natali, Claudia, Euan McDougall, and Sally Stubbington. 2014. "International Migration Policy in Thailand." In *Thailand Migration Report 2014*, edited by Jerrold W. Huguet, 13–24. Bangkok: United Nations Thematic Working Group on Migration in Thailand.

Nikomborirak, Deunden, and Supunnavadee Jitdumrong. 2013. "ASEAN Trade in Services." In *The ASEAN Economic Community: A Work in Progress*, edited by Sanchita Basu Das, Jayant Menon, Rodolfo Severino, and Omkar Lal Shrestha, 95–140. Singapore: ISEAS Publishing.

OECD (Organisation for Economic Cooperation and Development). 2016. *Perspectives on Global Development 2017: International Migration in a Shifting World*. OECD: Paris.

Papademetriou, Demetrios G., Guntar Sugiyarto, Dovelyn Rannveig Mendoza, and Brian Salant. 2015. "Achieving Skill Mobility in the ASEAN Economic Community: Challenges, Opportunities, and Policy Implications." Asian Development Bank, Manila.

Pasadilla, Gloria, and Manolo Abella. 2012. "Social Protection for Migrant Workers in ASEAN," Working Paper 3914, CESifo, Venice.

Pichayasupakoon, Tiyadah. 2014. "The Impact of the ASEAN Economic Community (AEC) on the Recruitment of Accountants: A Case Study of Listed Firms on the Stock Exchange of Thailand," *Silpakorn University Journal of Social Sciences, Humanities, and Arts* 14 (2): 1–24.

SHARE (European Union Support to Higher Education in the ASEAN Region). 2016. "ASEAN Qualifications Reference Framework and National Qualifications Frameworks State of Play Report." SHARE, Jakarta.

Sugiyarto, Guntur, and Dovelyn Rannveig Agunias. 2014. "A 'Freer' Flow of Skilled Labour within ASEAN: Aspirations, Opportunities and Challenges in 2015 and Beyond," International Organization for Migration (IOM) and Migration Policy Institute (MPI), Bangkok and Washington D.C.

Tamagno, Edward. 2008. "Strengthening Social Protection for ASEAN Migrant Workers through Social Security Agreements," Asian Regional Programme on Governance of Labour Migration Working Paper No. 10, International Labour Organization (ILO), Bangkok.

Taha, Nurulsyahirah, Karin Astrid Siegmann, and Mahmood Messkoub. 2015. "How Portable is Social Security for Migrant Workers? A Review of the Literature," *International Social Security Review* 68 (1): 95–118.

Torres, Carmela I. 2014. "AEC, AQRF and Development: Commitments of ASEAN Member States on MRS and RMCS," presentation to the National Consultation Workshop: Implementation of MRS, Yangon, Myanmar.

UN ESCAP (United Nations, Economic and Social Commission for Asia and the Pacific). 2016. *Asia-Pacific Migration Report 2015: Migrants' Contribution to Development.* Report prepared by Asia-Pacific RCM Thematic Working Group on International Migration including Human Trafficking. Bangkok: United Nations.

World Bank. 2013. "Immigration in Malaysia: Assessment of its Economic Effects, and a Review of the Policy and System," World Bank report for the Ministry of Human Resources Malaysia.

CHAPTER 9

Policies to Reduce Migration Costs in ASEAN

Introduction

The previous part II chapters discussed breakdowns in the migration systems of migrant-sending and migrant-receiving countries in the Association of Southeast Asian Nations (ASEAN) that can drive up migration costs. This chapter presents policies that can help reduce these costs, which in turn could help ASEAN countries maximize the benefits of trade integration discussed in chapter 4. This chapter uses the framework for migration systems to structure the policy recommendations and highlight how interventions in different parts of the migration system could lead to reductions in labor mobility costs. Potential interventions can also be grouped into five key solution areas:

- *Solution area A: Improve the governance of the migration system.* This solution area responds to the lack of coordination that characterizes the governance of many migration systems in ASEAN countries, from coordination with local government to collaborative enforcement actions. It also highlights the need to simplify the engagement of migrants with government agencies in sending countries during the migration process.

- *Solution area B: Deepen and widen collaboration among all stakeholders.* This solution area highlights the importance of involving the labor demand side in the immigration process of receiving countries, which is now overlooked particularly in Malaysia and Thailand. This area also highlights the importance of collaboration and coordination between sending and receiving countries, particularly through memorandums of understanding (MOUs) and bilateral agreements. Additionally, this solution area refers to the need for sending countries to create programs to engage their diasporas to encourage investment and knowledge transfer.

- *Solution area C: Use data, information, and transparency to guide decision making.* This solution area highlights the importance of using data to inform decisions about economic needs in receiving countries, information to limit information asymmetries for migrant workers in sending countries, and transparency to develop trust in the migration system in both sending and receiving countries. This area is based on the potential for sending and receiving countries to use both new data and old data in new ways to improve the efficiency of overseas employment search, regulating recruitment, and the migration process.

- *Solution area D: Balance protection and economic development in the migration process.* This solution area refers to the need for receiving countries to navigate the trade-off between formal migration and protections for migrant and local workers and the need for sending countries to navigate the trade-off between protecting migrant workers and promoting migration as a means of economic development.

- *Solution area E: Reform domestic policies.* As emphasized in chapters 3 and 4, domestic policies can make an impact on the ability of local workers to adjust to the presence of immigrants. Additionally, local workers may seek work abroad if domestic labor mobility costs are too high. This solution area highlights the need to reform domestic policies to ensure that local workers can adjust and take advantage of new opportunities created by migrants and can take advantage of opportunities both at home and abroad.

To make clear the connections between the individual policy actions described in the chapter, table 9.1 groups them into the five key solution areas and the party—the sending or receiving country or ASEAN as a region—best placed to implement the policy action. These solution areas are cross-cutting and address different aspects of the problem areas summarized in chapter 5 (see figure 5.2) and detailed in chapters 6, 7, and 8. For instance, improving the governance of the migration system (solution area A) is closely related to coordination among stakeholders (problem area 3), to a country's strategic approach to migration (problem area 5), and to how responsive a migration system is to economic needs (problem area 1). Given the different country contexts and country priorities described throughout the book, the policy actions that are likely to reduce migration costs differ in each ASEAN country.

Destination countries should work to develop migration systems that are responsive to economic needs and consistent with domestic policies.

- With very low levels of informal migration and a sophisticated system of productivity-linked entry paths, **Singapore** will need to continue working to build public trust in the migration system and to improve protections for migrant workers.

TABLE 9.1

Solution areas and policy recommendations for improving migration management in ASEAN

Solution areas and policy recommendations	Implementation		
	Sending	Receiving	ASEAN
A) Improve governance			
R1: Develop a national migration strategy	X	X	
R2: Update legislative framework to reflect migration objectives	X	X	
R3: Rationalize institutional roles and responsibilities	X	X	
R14: Introduce stricter licensing requirements for recruitment agencies	X	X	
R39: Consider introducing joint and several liability for recruiters	X		
R40: Ensure that workers have access to complaint mechanisms	X	X	
B) Deepen and widen collaboration			
R4: Engage stakeholders to inform policy discussions	X	X	
R5: Use MOUs and bilateral agreements	X	X	
R6: Create a clearinghouse for MOUs and bilateral agreements			X
R9: Encourage student migration	X	X	X
R13: Align MOUs and bilateral agreements with quantity restrictions	X	X	
R17: Improve coordination between senders and receivers on recruitment	X	X	X
R22: Involve civil society in ensuring migrant workers have access to protection	X	X	
R26: Work toward the portability of social protection benefits	X	X	X
R30: Install labor attachés in destination countries		X	
R31: Use MOUs, bilateral agreements, and regional forums to set protection standards	X	X	X
R33: Use MOUs and bilateral agreements to facilitate exit	X	X	
R34: Create diaspora engagement and return programs	X		
R36: Balance border security and interior enforcement		X	
C) Use data, information, and transparency to guide decisions			
R7: Make application process transparent, trackable, and streamlined		X	
R8: Use shortage lists		X	
R10: Use price- rather than quantity-oriented restrictions		X	
R11: Adjust quantity restrictions regularly according to economic needs		X	

table continues next page

TABLE 9.1

Solution areas and policy recommendations for improving migration management in ASEAN *(continued)*

Solution areas and policy recommendations	Implementation		
	Sending	Receiving	ASEAN
R15: Reduce information asymmetries between employers and migrants	X	X	
R16: Improve oversight through dissemination of information about recruitment agencies	X	X	
R27: Use orientation programs to increase migrant workers' knowledge	X	X	
R37: Leverage data to improve enforcement	X	X	
R41: Ensure that regularization programs balance inclusiveness and fairness		X	
D) Balance protection and economic development			
R18: Use employment terms to differentiate migrants		X	
R19: Allow migrant workers to change employers		X	
R20: Expedite the renewal process for employment passes		X	
R21: Provide comparable protection to migrant and local workers		X	
R23: Ensure deployment requirements are not overly burdensome	X		
R24: Consider predeparture migration loans	X		
R25: Control remittance costs, and expand access to formal remittance channels	X	X	
R28: Promote skills upgrading and recognition	X	X	X
R29: Consider migrant welfare funds to protect migrants	X		
R32: Use sanctions and exit incentives to encourage voluntary return		X	
R35: Conduct more research on helping migrants reintegrate into the labor market		X	
R38: Increase enforcement efforts on employers		X	
E) Reform domestic policies			
R12: Use levy revenues to compensate those who lose out from migration		X	
R42: Reduce rigidities in domestic labor market	X	X	

Note: ASEAN = Association of Southeast Asian Nations; MOU = memorandum of understanding.

- With high levels of informal migration but a less sophisticated admissions system than Singapore, **Malaysia** will need to work to make its immigration system more responsive to economic needs and to collaborate more closely with both employers and sending countries.

- With high levels of informal migration, **Thailand** will need to work to formalize its large population of undocumented migrants, rationalize entry procedures that are costly and time-consuming, and rethink immigration policies, such as levies and a repatriation fund, which exist in law but not in practice, undermining the credibility of the migration system.

- As the country seeks to encourage private sector employment among locals, **Brunei Darussalam** will need to ensure that a relatively complex system of quotas and levies based on geography, sector, and employer supports this goal, while also meeting economic needs.

Sending countries should work to balance protections for migrant workers with the needs of economic development.

- **The Philippines** has a highly developed support system for migrant workers that is a model for other sending countries. To build on this status, the country should continue to evaluate and improve its migration management system, including oversight of recruitment agencies, programs for returned migrants, and data sharing and interoperability.

- **Indonesia** should work to improve coordination among the agencies responsible for managing labor migration, and to streamline exit procedures for migrants to encourage documented migration.

- **Vietnam** will need to evaluate its current policies for incentivizing out-migration to determine whether they are meeting the country's needs. While the intention of these policies is laudable, other reforms are also necessary, including review of recruitment agencies' frequent and at least tacitly sanctioned practice of requiring migrant workers to pay a security deposit to guarantee their return, which is frequently not repaid. A national migration strategy could help to guide reforms.

- Lower-capacity **Cambodia**, **Lao People's Democratic Republic** and **Myanmar** should continue considering how migration can fit into their economic development strategies, shaping programs to make out-migration less costly and more formal, and creating connections with diaspora to facilitate the transfer of knowledge and capital accordingly. These countries can look to the experience of the Philippines in their efforts to develop institutions serving migrants and services such as predeparture orientation programs.

Governance
Legislative framework

Recommendation 1: Develop a national migration strategy. Explicit national migration strategies can be useful, even in those countries in which migration-related priorities are included in national development strategies. A national migration plan should set both short- and long-term objectives for migration. In primarily receiving countries, a migration strategy can provide clarity to employers and other labor market stakeholders about how policy makers view immigrant workers and how they plan to adjust their numbers and skill level to meet longer-term economic objectives.

The plan could also acknowledge the potential negative impacts of immigration on some workers, particularly low-skilled ones, and highlight efforts to assist them. In East Asia, immigration systems were first established assuming that immigration would be a temporary phenomenon. However, the increasing evidence that migration is a structural feature of the region's economy means that longer-term plans are needed to coordinate migration and other labor supply policies. A long-term vision for immigration can provide some clarity to employers and workers about the potential path of policy, so that they are informed about the implications for production and employment. In primarily sending countries, a migration strategy could describe how policy makers view the role of out-migration and lay out strategies for protecting migrants while they are abroad. Such a document should also consider longer-term objectives, such as using emigration as a strategy for economic development, which would involve setting out policies for diaspora engagement and reintegration of returning migrants as priorities.

A national migration strategy should be comprehensive in covering all aspects of migration and coordinating migration policy with employment, education, and skill strategies. Although primarily sending and primarily receiving countries have different priorities, every country in ASEAN both sends and receives migrants. In ASEAN's primarily sending countries, high-skilled immigration is critical for filling skills gaps, and the recognition of the importance of using skilled foreign labor should be addressed in a national migration strategy. In ASEAN's primarily receiving countries, high-skilled emigration is increasingly prevalent, and strategies for diaspora engagement should be addressed by a national migration strategy.

The migration strategy should also consider all types of migration, including non-employment channels such as students, tourists, and noncitizen family members. These different streams affect each other, and should be evaluated holistically when considering how to use migration to fill shortages. A now-defunct version of Australia's shortage occupation list, which had granted permanent residency to migrants in shortage occupations, suffered from a lack of coordination with other immigration streams. Foreign nationals could use student visas to obtain low-cost technical/vocational education and training (TVET) qualifications in occupations for which there were shortages, essentially purchasing permanent residency (Birrel, Healy, and Kinnaird 2007; Birrel and Perry 2009). Finally, the national migration strategy should seek to be consistent with, and to complement, existing human resource strategies. Like immigration, training and education and activation policies are used to fill labor market shortages. Similarly, promotion of emigration for employment should be thought of alongside, not separate from, domestic employment promotion.

National migration strategies can also help coordinate institutional roles and responsibilities. Once objectives are set, the national migration plan can contemplate which agencies are best placed to implement changes and deliver results. The strategy can provide clarity to different government stakeholders involved in the migration process and provide a common action plan for the management of the migration system. This can help prevent duplication of tasks, which would introduce additional costs into the migration process.

The Republic of Korea's national migration plan and Cambodia's experience in developing a national migration strategy provide models. Korea introduced a national migration strategy in 2008. The First Basic Plan for Immigration Policy (2008–12) sought to improve cooperation among government agencies and lay out a longer-term, consistent immigration policy (Korea, Ministry of Justice 2009). The plan clearly states objectives, identifies priorities, lays out the roles and responsibilities of different agencies, and identifies areas for collaboration. The Second Plan (2013–17) included an assessment of the First Basic Plan against several targets (Korea, Ministry of Justice 2012). Cambodia has developed two national migration plans: the Policy on Labor Migration for Cambodia 2010–15 establishes the main objectives for labor migration policy, whereas the 2015–18 policy introduces specific actions and the agencies responsible for implementing them.

Recommendation 2: Update the legislative framework to reflect migration objectives. The legislative framework for migration should be sufficiently flexible to permit adjustment to changing economic conditions but should empower public and private sector actors by providing clarity. Several ASEAN countries rely on outdated or incomplete laws and regulations to govern the management of migration. These regulations often respond to a particular problem and may be issued without preparing important stakeholders. Additionally, legislation and regulations have not kept pace with the increasing engagement of local governments with migration issues. Where possible, legislative frameworks should be updated with emphasis on clarifying institutional roles and coordination. This should include establishing an interface between private recruiters and their regulators, setting out the framework for the admissions and departure processes, establishing the parameters of protections for migrant workers, and establishing enforcement mechanisms. However, policy makers should be careful that legislation and regulations are not overly rigid. This has occurred in the United States, where the number of permanent visas for skilled workers was set by legislation in 1990 and has not been updated since (OECD 2014). Korea, which shifted its migration management system for low-skilled workers from a trainee scheme to a work permit scheme, provides an example of how immigration policy can evolve to reflect new economic needs. Box 9.1 provides a brief description of the evolution of Korea's immigration system.

Institutional framework

Recommendation 3: Rationalize agency roles and responsibilities to avoid duplications and gaps. Labor ministries are likely best suited to oversee international labor migration. In all countries in ASEAN, labor ministries are either in charge of, or significantly involved with, managing international labor migration. This is likely a good model for handling overseas workers because these agencies often specialize in worker protections; as such, they have the information and staff necessary to make informed decisions about the labor market. Home ministries and border authorities can then focus on border control and enforcement of immigration (as opposed to employment) law. However, in ASEAN, agencies within labor ministries often conflict

BOX 9.1
The evolution of Korea's immigration system

Korea's immigration system has evolved significantly over time to meet economic needs. Korea's old migration management model, the Industrial Trainee Scheme (ITS), brought in low-skilled labor as trainees who were not subject to labor laws. Thus, migrants received wages below the minimum wage and no employment protection for doing jobs that would otherwise have been subject to both. Several factors led to a shift to a new migration management model. First, under the ITS as many as 80 percent of all trainees were reported to be undocumented. The causes for this high rate were both financial and social: (1) ITS trainees incurred significant debt to finance their migration to Korea (with anecdotes that workers paid $10,000 to private recruiters); (2) undocumented trainees, at times, earned more than documented ITS trainees; and (3) trainees lacked a mechanism to file complaints about abusive behaviors or exploitation by employers. Second, civil society championed the improvement of labor rights in Korea and proactively called for equal treatment of ITS trainees and local workers in terms of labor rights and protection. Finally, the Korean government in place at the time was supportive of additional labor protection. Recognizing the drawbacks of the ITS system, the government evaluated various migration regimes in other countries. This led to the creation of the Employment Permit System (EPS) in 2004. To generate buy-in from all stakeholders, the government did not shift the system suddenly; instead, it introduced an interim period during which both ITS and EPS were in place. This permitted business associations that profited under the ITS system to continue to provide for a limited period fee-based services to firms, such as application for an EPS permit or transportation of EPS workers after their arrival.

with each other, with agencies in other ministries, and with local governments. This is most notably the case in Indonesia, where two migration-related agencies, one inside and one outside of the Ministry of Manpower, compete for authority and where the divisions of responsibility for implementing migration policy between local and national authorities are unclear. Inter-ministerial input on migration is important for a migration management system to run well. However, a single agency like the labor ministry should have ultimate responsibility for managing labor migration to avoid duplication of roles and gaps in implementation. The national migration plan and a clear legislative framework can help ensure clear lines of responsibility.

Korea, the Philippines, and Singapore are good examples of countries with migration systems in which a single agency is the key actor in the oversight of employment-based migration. In Singapore, the Ministry of Manpower develops and implements foreign labor policies. Divisions and departments within the Ministry oversee issues related to the welfare of foreign labor, work permits, and enforcement of regulations regarding foreign manpower. In Korea, the Ministry of Employment and Labor develops foreign labor policies and is responsible for the EPS. The Korean national migration strategy defines the responsibilities of different agencies to ensure that roles do not overlap (table 9.2). In the sending country context, the Philippines' several migrant-focused

TABLE 9.2

Korea's first basic plan for immigration (2008–12): division of oversight roles regarding low-skilled migration

Responsibility	Department
1. Supporting efficient corporate use of unskilled labor	
A. Attract workers needed by corporations	Ministry of Employment and Labor
B. Simplify employment procedures, and improve the environment for stable employment	Ministry of Justice and Ministry of Employment and Labor
C. Rationalize labor cost	Ministry of Employment and Labor
2. Improving quota system for unskilled labor	
A. Reinforce links between Immigration Policy Commission and committee on foreign workers	Ministry of Justic and Ministry of Employment and Labor
B. Consider number of illegal aliens when allocating nonskilled worker quotas	Ministry of Employment and Labor
3. Improving working environments and reinforcing safety and health training	
A. Reinforce management of work sites with foreign workers	Ministry of Employment and Labor
B. Reinforce foreign workers' health protection	Ministry of Employment and Labor
C. Improve working environment with dangerous processes	Ministry of Employment and Labor
4. Supporting foreign workers' life in Korea	
A. Reinforce complaint counselling for foreign workers and provide legal assistance	Ministry of Justice and Ministry of Employment and Labor
B. Transfer operation of foreign worker support centers to local governments	Ministry of Employment and Labor and Ministry of Public Administration and Safety

Source: Adapted from Korea, Ministry of Justice 2009.

agencies are mainly housed within the Department of Labor and Employment. The roles and responsibilities of the two main agencies are well defined, with the Philippine Overseas Employment Administration responsible mainly for migration management and the Overseas Workers Welfare Administration responsible mainly for migrant protection. Sri Lanka is another example of a sending country with a comprehensive institutional framework for managing migration, with the additional good practice of undertaking training programs for staff in the ministry responsible for managing migration (see box 9.2).

Recommendation 4: Engage all relevant stakeholders to inform policy discussions through structured consultations. Consultations with employers should inform migration policy making. Employers can supplement labor market data with context, provide information about human resource and staffing plans, and generate private sector buy-in. As the demanders of foreign workers, employers are key stakeholders, and their buy-in for decisions about quantity restrictions and other migration policy instruments are important to ensure that the system functions as envisioned. Involving employers in the decision-making process builds trust and confidence

BOX 9.2

Sri Lanka's institutional framework for managing migration

Like the Philippines, Sri Lanka has a relatively advanced legislative and institutional framework governing labor migration. With the support of the International Labour Organization, Sri Lanka adopted the 2009 National Labor Migration Policy that articulated a long-term vision for labor migration. This vision included enhancing the positive impact of migration on both migrant workers and Sri Lanka, as a whole, and protecting migrant workers. Three main agencies oversee labor migration in Sri Lanka. The Ministry of Foreign Employment (MOFE) is responsible for not only migrant worker protection but also facilitating migrants' ability to contribute to the economy. Under this ministry, the Bureau of Foreign Employment regulates private recruitment agencies, works to connect Sri Lankans with employment opportunities abroad, and provides predeparture training to migrants. The Foreign Employment Agency is Sri Lanka's public recruitment agency. Additionally, the Ministry of Youth Affairs and Skills Development provides vocational training programs and oversees skills certification and accreditation for potential migrants. Sri Lanka helps ensure that officials responsible for assisting migrants are prepared to do so through training programs for new officers in the MOFE and continuing education. These agencies have considerable reach inside the country, with 892 posts of the Bureau of Foreign Employment in 25 districts. Sri Lanka also extends its efforts to manage migration abroad by posting labor officials to its missions.

Sources: ADBI, ILO, and OECD 2016; Thimothy et al. 2016.

that the playing field is level. In Organisation for Economic Co-operation and Development (OECD) member countries that receive significant immigrant inflows, such as the United Kingdom and Australia, structured consultations with employers are an important part of decision making on migration. These conversations are used both to inform policy makers about economic needs such as where skills gaps are and to engage employers in the policy-making process so that they are not surprised by migration decisions. The U.K. Migration Advisory Committee (MAC) holds in-person consultations to gather intelligence from employers about many different types of immigration decisions from labor market shortages to quantity restrictions. The MAC has undertaken these consultations regularly and has been able to develop enough credibility so that employers submit detailed reports about labor market issues they are confronting. This is also true in Australia, where submissions inform the creation of the Skilled Occupation List.[1] The process of consulting stakeholders serves not only to solicit information but also to raise awareness about government efforts to understand labor market needs, which can generate trust in migration policy.

Malaysia has recently begun to undertake stakeholder consultations for its Critical Occupations List. TalentCorp, responsible for a variety of human resource development tasks in Malaysia, including administering a program for high-skilled expatriates, has used structured consultations with employers, regulators, and industry associations to supplement and validate quantitative data analyzed for the creation of a Critical Occupations List. The List, developed in consultation with the World Bank, includes occupations that are sought after and hard to fill.[2]

Tripartite commissions are a useful tool to bring policy makers together with employers and workers. Many countries employ tripartite structures for setting minimum wages. In Malaysia, this is done by the National Wage Consultative Council (NWCC), which makes recommendations to the government about wages and includes both representatives from the government and equal representation from employers and employees. In the context of migration policy, a tripartite commission of policy makers, workers, and employers or recruitment agencies could be useful in both sending and receiving countries. In sending countries, such committees could give voice to migrant workers' concerns about the recruitment process and government protections during that process while also considering the perspective of the recruitment agencies that connect workers to employers abroad. Such commissions could help find a balance between a recruitment system that protects migrants and one that incentivizes private sector actors to connect potential migrant workers with jobs. In the Philippines, the Governing Board of the Philippine Overseas Employment Administration includes both migrant and private sector representatives. In receiving countries, such committees could bring both domestic and migrant workers into consultation with employers and policy makers to weigh concerns about protecting local employees and migrant workers and employers' demand for labor. In both sending and receiving countries, such commissions are no guarantee that the right balance between the interest of all parties will be reached. However, engaging each of these stakeholders can generate confidence in the policy-making process and in the migration management system.

MOUs and bilateral agreements

Recommendation 5: Use bilateral agreements for better coordination between sending and receiving countries. Bilateral agreements can help reconcile the objectives of sending and receiving countries by providing a venue for cooperation. Sending and receiving countries have overlapping but different objectives from migration that often result in inefficiencies in the migration process. Efforts to reduce these inefficiencies are constrained by the limited reach of domestic laws and regulations. MOUs and bilateral agreements provide the basis for sending and receiving countries to reconcile their interests and align their legislative and institutional frameworks. When they work best, these agreements are the formalization of an ongoing process of negotiations related to the management and protection of migrant workers. Stakeholder engagement, transparency, and monitoring and evaluation are important components of good MOUs and bilateral agreements. The success of an agreement depends on its ability to adjust to emerging labor market needs, continued engagement between sending and receiving country representatives, and the complementarity of national migration and employment frameworks (KNOMAD 2014). Box 9.3 provides an example of a successful collaboration between sending and receiving countries.

The Recognized Seasonal Employer Scheme and the Pacific Seasonal Worker Programme

Given the geography, size, and changing demographics of the Pacific Islands, labor mobility offers an important means to reduce poverty and boost shared prosperity. The Pacific Island countries face a triple burden of economic geography owing to their small size, remoteness, and internal dispersion. These structural characteristics, coupled with a high exposure to natural disasters, have limited the region's ability to generate economic growth and jobs. Moreover, many Pacific Island countries are witnessing rapidly growing populations and a youth bulge—the fertility rates across the Pacific are almost twice the average of the East Asia and Pacific region at large. Many parts of the region have seen employment decline at a time when working age populations are increasing (figure B9.3.1). Employment rates are estimated to be less than 50 percent of the working-age population across most Pacific Island countries. Where these countries are unable to bring jobs to the people, it becomes necessary to bring the people to where jobs are located.

Over the past decade, there has been a renewed push for greater mobility between the Pacific and the neighboring metropolitan countries. The misalignment between labor-sending and labor-receiving country objectives in the region has long proved a barrier to international mobility. The Pacific Island countries are largely reluctant to see their most skilled workers migrate, while they are typically open to opportunities for low-skilled workers. Meanwhile, Australia and New Zealand have in place points-based immigration systems geared toward skilled workers, with limited pathways for low-skilled migrants. This changed following a prolonged push by Pacific Island countries and acute labor shortages in Australia and New Zealand with the rollout of the Recognized Seasonal Employer (RSE)

FIGURE B9.3.1
Employment and population growth in the Pacific

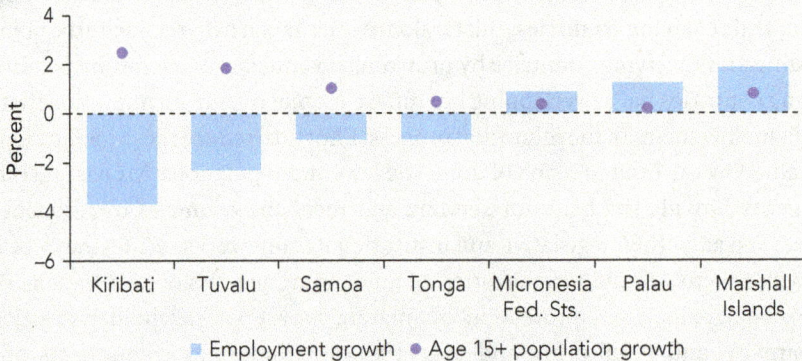

Source: World Bank 2016b.

box continues next page

BOX 9.3

The Recognized Seasonal Employer Scheme and the Pacific Seasonal Worker Programme (continued)

Scheme in New Zealand. Introduced in 2007, the RSE Scheme is a low-skilled temporary preferential scheme for Pacific Islanders. Australia followed suit in 2008 with the introduction of a similar program modelled on the RSE Scheme, the Pacific Seasonal Worker Pilot Scheme (PSWPS).

A strong effort to evaluate the impacts of these schemes and to project the gains of greater mobility has allowed policy makers to improve outcomes for existing migrants and to make the case for new migration pathways. The World Bank conducted separate impact evaluations of the RSE Scheme and the PSWPS from 2008–12, determining the net income gains from each. These evaluations helped strengthen the case for turning the PSWPS into a full-fledged Seasonal Worker Programme in 2012 and increasing the cap on workers in the case of the RSE Scheme. The World Bank also carried out a large-scale survey of horticultural employers in Australia to determine the demand-side constraints for the Seasonal Worker Programme. This has helped inform the Australian government's policy on the cost-sharing arrangements and minimum length of stay, and ultimately led to a decision to uncap the scheme. More recently, the World Bank has produced a vision piece in collaboration with the Australian National University titled *Pacific Possible*. This report examines where the region could be on labor mobility in 2040 if both sending and receiving countries were to significantly alter their existing policies and practices on labor migration and quantify the gains. Key proposed reforms include expanding access through existing migration pathways; opening up access to new labor markets, such as Korea via its Employment Permit System; providing access to new sectors, like elder care, through programs tailored to the Pacific; and expanding opportunities for permanent migration, especially for low-mobility countries and the atoll countries most affected by climate change. The significant gains in income and government revenue projected through this exercise are expected to help governments in the Pacific make the case for allocating domestic resources toward facilitating labor migration. Moreover, as the labor-receiving countries in the region are beginning to explore ways to minimize the impacts of an aging domestic workforce, the proposals set out in *Pacific Possible* will support them in opening up new migration pathways in sectors that are expected to experience labor shortages (elder care and construction, for example).

Source: Curtain et. al. 2016.

MOUs and bilateral agreements can address challenges throughout the migration system. Korea's EPS relies on a public recruitment model and has been able to keep recruitment costs relatively low (Kim 2015). Malaysia's recent government-to-government agreement with Bangladesh reduced migration costs significantly, in part by using public recruitment in both Malaysia and Bangladesh. However, caps on the number of Bangladeshi migrant workers who could be hired limited the impact of the agreement, and a subsequent bilateral arrangement has reportedly incorporated private recruiters. Public recruitment is often not possible due to resource constraints or not desirable because of the availability of private sector actors with better access to information about foreign labor markets. However, given high recruitment costs and frequent reports of abuse of migrants in the recruitment process, Malaysia's and Korea's experiences using MOUs to structure public recruitment suggest that it is a model worth continuing to test, though the design and implementation of the model are particularly important.

Several good practices have been identified that relate to MOUs and bilateral agreements. Model employment contracts, wage protection measures such as mechanisms for automatic deposit of wages into migrants' bank accounts, transparency about the contents of MOUs, involvement of public employment services in sending and receiving countries, inclusion of gender-specific issues, and concrete implementation and evaluation measures are all suggested as important for success (Wickramasekara 2016). These practices can lower migration costs by improving the information available to migrant workers, particularly about their contracts, working conditions, and rights. MOUs and bilateral agreements can provide guidelines about information that must be provided to migrants and can be used to inform the types of training that migrants should receive before departure and after entry. Korea's EPS and Canada's Seasonal Agricultural Workers Programs both use MOUs to promote exit at the end of a migrant's contract. The EPS provides trainings to foreign workers that are tailored to their source country and even provides job matching services in the source country in conjunction with local counterparts (Kim 2015). Canada's system requires compulsory contributions to a savings scheme that is available to migrant workers only upon their departure from the country. Social security agreements that provide for the portability and totalization of benefits can incentivize exit by ensuring that migrants continue to have access to these benefits upon exit.

Sending countries face challenges to negotiating bilateral agreements, but they continue to be a useful channel to pursue. In most cases, sending countries lack leverage when negotiating with receiving countries: the supply of potential migrant workers is much larger than the demand, and any sending country negotiating stronger terms for its migrant workers risks being undercut by another country. Additionally, weak enforcement mechanisms can mean that migrant workers avoid formal channels established by MOUs and bilateral agreements and migrate informally. Despite these challenges, sending countries have been able to use agreements as forums both to discuss concerns and to limit the uncertainty and risk associated with migration (Rivera, Serrano, and Tullao 2013). Even Thailand's MOUs with Cambodia, Lao PDR, and Myanmar, though they do not capture most migration, have provided an important venue for the countries to discuss and to take action on the large population of irregular migrants in Thailand. The Philippines has been particularly successful in negotiating MOUs with receiving countries, including social security agreements. The government of the Philippines views the agreements in incremental terms as part of an ongoing process of improving migration management, a view that is reflected in a gradual shift to agreements that are narrower in scope (CMA 2010; Lanto 2015). The Philippines has several guiding principles for negotiations, including ensuring safe and orderly migration; safeguarding the rights and welfare of migrants; recognizing mutual benefits and shared responsibilities; sustaining a good relationship with the host country; and developing human resources (Lanto 2015).

Recommendation 6: Create a clearinghouse for MOUs and bilateral agreements at the regional level. ASEAN countries can learn from each other to improve existing and create new MOUs and bilateral agreements. The ASEAN Secretariat could provide a resource center for both sending and receiving countries that would collect MOUs and bilateral agreements from around the world, provide information on best practices, and provide technical assistance with the development of agreements and their key components. The secretariat could act as a clearinghouse to review proposed agreements and provide advice about potential changes. It may even consider creating a common, but flexible framework, for the agreements. Such a framework could provide sending countries with expertise in negotiating agreements with receiving countries both inside and outside the region. In some cases, sending countries might even find working together on agreements with receiving countries beneficial. A common framework would also benefit ASEAN's receiving countries, which could work toward common standards for recruitment and other practices.

Admissions

Entry paths

Recommendation 7: Make the application process transparent, trackable, and streamlined. Entry paths for migrants should be clear and transparent, and admission should be trackable. Application processes that are confusing and opaque create inefficiencies, increase migration costs, and lead to doubts about the integrity of the admissions process. Increasing transparency and ensuring that both employers and migrants are aware of the eligibility requirements and the selection criteria for entry are critical. Systems that allow employers and migrant workers to track their progress toward entry can increase confidence in the system and help officials make changes when bottlenecks are discovered. New Zealand has used an "Expression of Interest" system that involves selecting qualified migrants from a pool of migrants who have registered their interest in migrating and meet an initial set of requirements. The system has helped eliminate backlogs of applicants through the initial screening and periodic expirations of registrations (Bedford and Spoonley 2014).

Entry paths should be as streamlined as possible, with clear criteria to differentiate different paths. Application processes that provide clear guidance, limit the number of steps, and limit the number of approvals by government agencies can reduce processing times and migration costs. In turn, such efficient systems improve the migration system's attractiveness to high-skilled migrants and reduce the likelihood that low-skilled ones will seek out cheaper informal channels. Clear criteria to differentiate entry paths can target different types of workers for different streams. Singapore has three well-defined entry streams for lower-, middle-, and higher-skilled workers that rely on salary and education requirements to distinguish workers of different skill levels. These entry streams work in conjunction with employment terms, with the more stringent entry requirements also affording more beneficial employment terms. The combination of salary with other requirements to differentiate entry paths is desirable because it reduces the incentives for employers to misreport salaries for their migrant workers. Evidence from Malaysia shows that some employers reported higher salaries for their foreign workers in order to take advantage of more convenient entry paths.

Recommendation 8: Use shortage lists to expedite entry, reduce uncertainty, and increase confidence. Shortage lists can be used to improve the entry process. Shortage lists address the question of which potential immigrants should be allowed entry. The lists are data-driven approaches to identifying labor market shortages that draw on quantitative and qualitative evidence, including labor force surveys, administrative data about immigration admissions, productivity data, vacancy data, employer surveys, and stakeholder consultations. Using data to identify labor market shortages creates a feedback loop between the immigration system and the labor market to target migrant workers to the occupations in which they are most needed. Shortage lists can ensure that employers are able to fill gaps in both their high- and low-skilled workforces that cannot be filled by local workers. The lists also reassure the public that policy makers are closely monitoring the labor market and immigration. Constant monitoring of indicators of shortage allows policy makers to adjust quickly to changing labor market conditions. Many countries now use labor market tests to identify where foreign workers are needed. Shortage lists formalize the process of determining the sectors, occupations, and skills that are in demand by relying on data, incorporating the on-the-ground experience of stakeholders, and publishing the findings.

Shortage lists offer several benefits related to the entry process. First, shortage lists can expedite the entry process. Shortage lists circumvent the need for employers to advertise jobs in a labor market test, which is frequently seen as an unnecessary obligation rather than a real indication of the lack of domestic workers available to fill a job. This means that applications to hire foreign workers can be processed more quickly and that both migrants and their employers have more certainty about how the needs of the migration system are determined. Additionally, shortage lists can formalize often opaque requirements for employers to hire foreign workers only if local workers are unavailable. The lists create a clear, transparent standard for judging this availability, and create common ground for officials tasked with reviewing applications for entry. The lists could even allow for automation of aspects of the application process, with details provided by employers about the vacant position checked against the skills and requirements normally associated with occupations on the shortage list.

Australia, Malaysia, New Zealand, and the United Kingdom are prominent examples of countries using shortage-type lists. Australia's Consolidated Sponsored Occupation List includes occupations that require skilled migration to meet the medium- to long-term needs of the Australian economy. Its Skilled Occupation List identifies occupations that are eligible for permanent and some temporary points-based skilled migration. Though not technically shortage lists, the lists do attempt to identify labor market needs in the medium and long term. New Zealand's Immediate Skills Shortage List exempts employers from a labor market test. The United Kingdom's Shortage Occupations List uses a combination of top-down analysis of labor market data and bottom-up consultations with stakeholders to identify occupations and job titles in shortage that would sensibly be filled by workers from outside of the European Economic Area. The list exempts employers from a labor market test and grants priority access to occupations on the shortage list under certain conditions. Finally, Malaysia's Critical Occupations List, developed in coordination with the World Bank, uses an approach similar to the United Kingdom's Migration Advisory Committee to identify sought-after, hard-to-fill, and strategic occupations by sector. The Critical Occupations List is used to inform both immigration and human resource development policies (box 9.4).

BOX 9.4
Malaysia's Critical Occupations List

Malaysia's Critical Skills Monitoring Committee was created as part of the Eleventh Malaysia Plan to monitor skills mismatches in high-skilled occupations. It is chaired by the Institute for Labour Market Information and Analysis under the Ministry of Human Resources and TalentCorp, an agency that is devoted to improving human capital in Malaysia and engages closely with the private sector. This structure allows the Committee to have access to both labor market analysis and employers.

One of the Committee's main objectives is to develop an inventory of high-skilled occupations that are sought after and hard to fill: the Critical Occupations List. The first two versions of this list, for 2015/2016 and 2016/2017, were developed in partnership with the World Bank. This Critical Occupations List combines a top-down analysis of labor market data with bottom-up consultations with employers to develop a product that is both objective and reflective of current labor market needs. The list is currently being developed for high-skilled occupations, defined as the first three major occupational groupings in the Malaysia Standard Classification of Occupations (roughly equivalent to the International Standard Classification of Occupations classification scheme), for occupations that are strategic, sought after, and hard to fill. Occupations often associated with sectors important to Malaysia's growth are considered to be strategic.

Top-down and bottom-up analyses are combined to determine those occupations that are sought after and hard to fill. The top-down analysis uses indicators of labor market shortage, such as employment and wage growth, to provide an indication of whether skilled occupations are having shortages. The bottom-up process involves a Call for Evidence Survey from employers, which solicits information from employers about occupations that have been hard to fill, and consultations with employers, regulators, and other stakeholders that provide additional information about hard-to-fill occupations and the labor market context. The two approaches are then merged to create a final list, which is used to help guide immigration policies, workforce upskilling policies, TVET and higher education programming, and other decisions.

Skills shortage lists do have weaknesses, though most are common to any migration instrument and can be minimized if the lists are updated and monitored regularly. These weaknesses include difficulties identifying shortages and ensuring migrants work in the shortage occupations for which they were admitted (IOM 2012). Shortage lists, though relatively widespread in the OECD, are not a common immigration channel in many of the OECD countries that use them (Chaloff 2014). Other concerns include the concentration of migrants in certain occupations, the persistence of certain occupations on the list, and the potential for stakeholder influence (Birrel, Healy, and Kinnaird 2007; Australia, DEEWR and DIC 2009a, 2009b; OECD 2014). Solutions to help counteract these weaknesses include sunset clauses for occupations on the shortage list, reliance on quantitative indicators to counteract stakeholder influence, and constant monitoring of immigration channels.

Recommendation 9: Encourage student migration. Whereas qualifications recognition can be a costly and complex process, encouraging student migration with a pathway for former students to work can create a supply of skilled workers. As discussed in chapter 3, ASEAN countries are becoming increasingly important as destinations for international students. The ASEAN University Network, the Southeast Asian Ministers of Education Organization, and the ASEAN Qualifications Recognition Framework (AQRF) are seen as important factors behind this increase (Batalova, Shymonyak, and Sugiyarto 2017). The ASEAN University Network, for example, has helped lead to the establishment of intraregional networks among universities in certain areas of study. Destination countries can further promote this trend by adjusting migration policies to make it easier for international students to work during their education and after graduation.

Quantity restrictions

Recommendation 10: Use price-oriented rather than quantity-oriented restrictions. Countries use a variety of instruments to control migration flows. Quantity restrictions are a common reality in migration systems throughout the world. Restrictions on migrant workers are often introduced to protect domestic labor markets from competition from abroad. In doing so, they raise the possibility of disrupting employers who need workers and of informal migration as legally restricted migrants enter through informal channels. Quantity restrictions include levies, quotas, and dependency ceilings. Levies are "price-oriented" mechanisms that charge a fee for the employment of foreign workers. Quotas and dependency ceilings, in contrast, are "quantity-oriented" mechanisms that place caps on the number or proportion of foreign workers from a certain country or in a certain sector, occupation, or firm. Both price-oriented and quantity-oriented mechanisms seek to control the number of migrant workers used by firms, but price-oriented mechanisms do this by increasing the cost of hiring foreign workers and quantity-oriented ones do so by limiting the number. This choice between price- and quantity-oriented measures also arises in international trade policy when choosing between quotas and tariffs.

Price-oriented mechanisms have several advantages over quantity-oriented ones, though their use is limited around the world. First, levies are a source of revenue that is not generated by quotas or dependency ceilings. Second, levies tend to be more transparent. Once quotas are set, allocating foreign workers to individual firms under the quota is subject to lobbying and pressure by interest groups. Levies allow any employer to continue hiring migrant workers as long as the employer is willing to pay the levy. Similarly, levies allow employers to continue hiring foreign workers—for a price—even if economic conditions change suddenly because of an unexpected shock. Quotas, in contrast, may negatively affect firms that need to adapt to sudden economic changes or may lead them to hire informal migrant workers if they are not able to hire more migrant workers legally. Korea's EPS, an otherwise good model for migration management, is less effective in responding to economic needs in part because of its reliance on quotas. In Korea, the first-come-first-served allocation of quotas can result in many employers being unable to hire the desired number of migrants, creating incentives for informal hiring. Despite the advantages of price-oriented mechanisms, very few countries outside of Singapore and Malaysia have implemented such a system. The United Kingdom recently considered adopting a charge for skilled migration to disincentivize the hiring of immigrants, incentivize investments in the local workforce, and raise revenue for skills development (United Kingdom, MAC 2016).

In migration systems that use price-oriented tools, efforts to ensure that employers bear the cost of levies are important. The objective of levies is to make hiring foreign workers more expensive. To do so, employers, not their foreign workers, must pay levies so that their hiring decisions are affected by the higher cost of using foreign as opposed to local labor, all else equal. The importance of employers bearing the cost of the levy to disincentivize hiring immigrants was emphasized in a recent report by the U.K. Migration Advisory Committee that considered the possibility of imposing a levy on skilled foreign workers (United Kingdom, MAC 2016).[3] Singapore has a system of strict oversight that attempts to ensure that the cost of levies is not passed on to foreign workers.

Recommendation 11: Adjust quantity restrictions regularly according to economic needs. Setting and revising quantity restrictions should rely on an evidence-based approach. Quantity restrictions should reflect economic needs and be able to adapt as these needs change. Setting the restrictions should rely on measurable indicators that come from survey data, administrative data including programmatic and budgetary data, and innovative sources such as real-time labor market information. Examples of measurable indicators include vacancies, wages, the unemployment rate, job creation, total factor productivity, the producer price index, and immigration statistics. A shortage list, ideally based on both quantitative and qualitative data, can be an important indicator of labor market demand. Thus, it is useful for decisions about quantity restrictions. Such a list can be a first step in determining whether immigrant workers should work in a given sector or occupation. But additional analysis and input are needed to determine a price for or a cap on immigrant labor. Analysis of indicators over time, with a particular focus on how foreign labor affects key labor market variables and how quantity restrictions may affect other labor market policies, can inform the setting and revision of quantity restrictions. An independent research body could be charged with analysis of technical inputs and gathering stakeholder input.

Quantity restrictions should also reflect the concerns of different stakeholders. These stakeholders have different concerns about migrant workers that should be reflected in the process for setting and adjusting quantity restrictions. Governments are concerned about factors such as unmet demand, productivity, competitiveness, informality, and unemployment; employers about prices, labor costs, labor shortages, and training costs; and workers about wages, employment opportunities, and the cost of living. Structured consultations with these stakeholders are important both to inform the setting and revision of quantity restrictions and to create buy-in from these stakeholders so that the restrictions are sustainable. A tripartite body could review inputs from the independent research body and provide recommendations to policy makers (box 9.5). New Zealand's Recognized Seasonal Employers scheme and Canada's Seasonal Agricultural Workers Program both involve consultations with employers to assess labor market needs (World Bank 2015a).

Countries that are seeking to encourage the immigration of more skilled foreign workers could consider eliminating quantity restrictions. Many of ASEAN's primarily sending countries also face shortages for skilled labor that could be filled by foreign workers. Imposing quantity restrictions including levies on this type of migrant worker would be inconsistent with economic needs.

Korea's process for setting quantity restrictions incorporates both analysis of labor market needs and input from a tripartite committee. Korea uses an industry- and country-specific quota to regulate the entry of low-skilled workers. The annual quota results from cross-sector and multiparty negotiations that draw on economic and labor force analyses. The Foreign Workforce Policy Committees, which decides the quota, is chaired by the prime minister, and it incorporates stakeholders representing the perspectives of government, industry, worker welfare, small and medium-sized enterprises (SMEs), and gender. A tripartite Foreign Workforce Employment Committee chaired by the Ministry of Employment and Labor provides analytical and technical input to the decisions. Quotas reflect assessments of labor demand and needs expressed by SMEs as well as assessments of the implementation of the EPS that provide information about employer preferences, overstays by origin, and undocumented workers by origin. Before a new sending country is permitted to send workers under the EPS, the government assesses its capacity to manage the EPS, the transparency in the country's deployment process, and the country's relationship with Korea.

Singapore has used levies dynamically in recent years to adjust to economic developments. Singapore uses price- and quantity-oriented mechanisms to differentiate foreign workers by skill level. Firm-specific dependency ceilings and sector- and skill-specific levies seek to discourage overreliance on low-skilled migrant workers. Singapore analyzes economic competitiveness and demographic factors when revising its quantity restrictions. In recent years, dependency ceilings in manufacturing and services have been lowered to limit reliance on foreign workers in these sectors. Similarly, when a slowdown in

BOX 9.5
Why not use tripartite bodies to set quantity restrictions?

In Korea's EPS, a quota for low-skilled workers is set annually for each sending country and for each industry. The quota is the outcome of extensive deliberations within
the Foreign Workforce Policy Committee under the prime minister. However, these
deliberations incorporate input from the Foreign Workforce Employment Committee,
a tripartite body made up of representatives from government, employers, workers,
civil society, and other ministries. The deliberations are based on forecasts of labor
demand and supply; the number of EPS workers departing within a year; the number of overstays by country; EPS workers demanded by firms; and reports on foreign
worker counseling services. Figure B9.5.1 shows the quota by industry over time
since 2004 and demonstrates how the quota has been adjusted frequently in accor-
dance with changing needs.

In Malaysia, deliberations on quantity restrictions are informal, and engagement
with stakeholders is not structured. However, Malaysia employs a tripartite structure
for setting the minimum wage. The National Wage Consultative Council makes recommendations to the government on minimum wages and includes representatives
from the government as well as equal representation from employers and employees.
The minimum wage is recommended by the Consultative Council to the government
and is based on a voting process. Four council meetings are required each year. The
minimum wage has clear parallels with quantity restrictions for migrant workers: in
both cases, employer and worker interests and even those of the government are at
odds and in both cases a decision must be made by policy makers on the basis of
both data and political considerations.

FIGURE B9.5.1
Change in the EPS quota over time

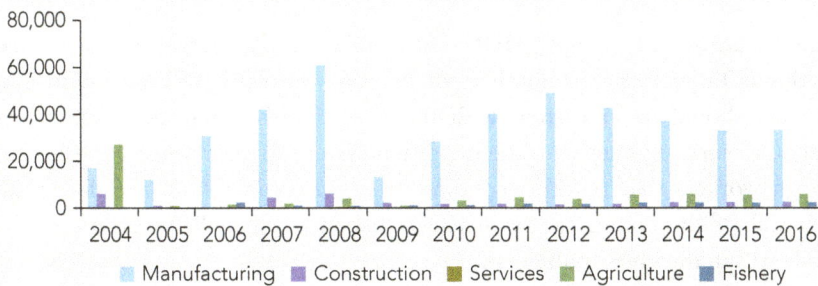

Source: Korea, Employment Permit System (EPS).

productivity was detected in the construction sector in 2015, Singapore increased levies
to disincentivize the hiring of foreign workers whereas levies in the manufacturing sector
were not changed (World Bank 2015a). Singapore encourages negotiations among government, employers, and labor to develop intelligence on employers' needs, how to limit
immigration during economic downturns, and how to protect migrant workers.

Levies and dependency ceilings require constant review to maintain their relevance to economic needs. Because of the difficulty of predicting long-term economic outcomes, quantity restrictions should be revised regularly to ensure that the levels still correspond to economic conditions. Korea and Singapore revisit their quantity restrictions annually. The outcome of the process need not be an adjustment, but repeating the exercise ensures continued relevance and increases confidence in the migration system.

Stakeholders should be informed about the process for setting and updating quantity restrictions. To ensure that stakeholders understand and trust the process of setting these restrictions, the methodology for setting the restrictions should be published. Providing employers and the public with details about this process can give employers confidence that all firms are being treated equally and reassure the public that the admission of foreign labor is tied to verifiable economic needs. Singapore announces its levy adjustment well in advance, creating certainty for employers. For example, the levy rate for July 2017 had already been published in the summer of 2016. Singapore also provides an online tool that allows employers (and the interested public) to calculate how many foreign workers the firms are eligible to hire and the amount of levy the firms owe.[4]

Recommendation 12: Use levy revenues to compensate those who lose out from migration. Although the overall impact of immigration is quite small and generally positive, some groups, particularly the less-skilled and less-educated, may lose out. The revenues generated by a foreign worker levy can be used to compensate those who lose out through retraining, skills upgrading, and other programs. In the United States, for example, a tax on certain categories of immigrants is used to train locals in shortage occupations (Holzmann and Pouget 2011).

Recommendation 13: Align MOUs and bilateral agreements with quantity restrictions. Targets on the numbers of migrants covered by MOUs and bilateral agreements should be consistent with those set for the migration system overall. They should work together with the migration system to permit entry to the quantity of foreign workers that reflects economic needs. Korea's EPS accomplishes this by requiring all sending countries to sign MOUs that ensure that all immigration decisions are made within the same framework.

Recruitment

Recommendation 14: Introduce stricter licensing requirements for recruitment agencies. Though dependent on available capacity and resources for implementation and enforcement, additional licensing requirements can help ensure that recruitment agencies provide good services to migrant workers. In Singapore, recruitment agencies are required to undertake a training program before being licensed and must retake it if the agency commits a certain number of violations. In the Philippines, recruitment agencies must attend a prelicensing orientation seminar before receiving a license and a continuing agency education seminar for renewing it. Additional requirements might also include minimum qualifications, prohibitions on conflict-of-interest provisions, and security deposit requirements that are explicitly held against liabilities to migrants and potential migrants. Sending countries may consider requiring licensed agencies to agree to joint and several liability for claims made by migrants against employers, as occurs in the Philippines. Still, any stricter licensing requirements must be balanced against the capacity for enforcement and the deterrence of private sector involvement. Overly stringent rules may encourage informal brokers.

Recommendation 15: Reduce information asymmetries between employers and migrants. The provision of public information is particularly important because informal brokers remain the norm in many ASEAN sending countries. Informal brokers perform an important function in many ASEAN countries where they connect migrants, at times from rural villages with limited outside information, to recruitment agencies and employers abroad. However, these informal brokers are not regulated, and so are not subject to the fee restrictions and other protections in place to protect migrant workers. As a result, the involvement of informal brokers can significantly increase migration costs.

Providing information to migrants has the potential to reduce recruitment fees, protect migrants from exploitation during the recruitment process, and improve the quality of matches with employers. Information asymmetries arise between foreign employers and migrant workers because the former know about the jobs that are available and their requirements, whereas the latter know about their skills. Recruiters and brokers arise to eliminate the gap in information between the two, which involves a cost to both employers and migrants for this service. As the intermediary, recruiters and brokers are often able to exploit particularly low-skilled migrants who are unfamiliar with migration rules. Providing migrants with access to employment-related information can empower them. It may even improve matches with employers when migrants have information about available employment abroad. In the best cases, providing information about job opportunities directly to migrants may reduce the role of informal brokers. Strategies to improve migrants' access to information include the use of public employment services to provide potential migrants with job opportunities abroad and training courses that provide detailed information about migration procedures. Korea's EPS has a user-friendly website with information available to foreign workers in their native language. The Philippines provides a listing of jobs abroad through the job advertising site JobStreet.com.[5] The Philippines' Pre-Employment Orientation Seminar includes modules on working overseas, job search, illegal recruitment, allowable fees and the minimum provisions of the employment contract, and country-specific information. The orientation seminar is mandatory for potential migrants, but the course can be completed online at no cost (POEA 2016). The Moroccan agency ANAPEC promotes the employment of skilled individuals and registers foreign employers and Moroccan youth for job matching.

Recommendation 16: Improve oversight through dissemination of information about recruitment agencies. Both sending and receiving country governments can use public information to improve oversight of recruitment agencies. All sending countries in ASEAN and all receiving countries except Thailand have a system to license and regulate private recruitment agencies. However, public agencies charged with oversight often lack the staff and resources to conduct regular inspections of recruitment agencies. A low-cost complement to this approach is to make information about recruitment agencies publicly available. This information can include violations, the worker retention rate, and worker placement, as occurs in Singapore.[6] Singapore has announced a system to allow employers of foreign domestic workers to rate employment agencies on their performance in explaining the application process, providing advice, and selecting a worker. A more comprehensive system would also permit the worker to rate the agency. Recruitment agencies can even be scored for their compliance with regulations, and these scores be made public. Associations of recruitment agencies can be encouraged to adopt codes of conduct, rate the performance of individual agencies, and publish these ratings. The International Labour Organization has worked with recruitment agencies in several ASEAN countries to do so. Good performers can be awarded publicly for their effectiveness, as in the Philippines, or even receive expedited processing of licenses or waiver of license renewal obligations. An evaluation of the impact of providing information about the quality of recruitment agencies to potential migrants is in process in Indonesia.[7]

Recommendation 17: Improve coordination between sending and receiving countries on recruitment. Coordination between sending and receiving countries could fill a significant gap in oversight of the recruitment process. Oversight of this process generally stops at a country's borders. This can leave a large gap in regulating recruitment practices because (1) fees can be duplicated by agencies in sending and receiving countries and (2) strict requirements can be undermined as responsibility for migrant workers is transferred from one jurisdiction to another. However, there is scope for cross-country collaboration to improve recruitment practices. Labor attachés posted overseas can help oversee recruitment practices in both sending and receiving countries, though the scope for action is limited and labor attachés from ASEAN countries often lack resources and expertise. Receiving countries can require recruitment agencies recruiting in sending countries to register in both countries, as occurs in the United Kingdom (IOM 2015). Sending and receiving countries can seek to use MOUs and bilateral agreements to improve oversight of the recruitment process, which has been left relatively unexplored in past agreements. Requirements for recruitment could include informing host and destination country officials about the arrival and departure of migrant workers, establishment of branches in both sending and receiving countries, and a common set of recruitment violations in both countries. Improved oversight of recruitment would be beneficial both to receiving countries, which face undocumented migration that is often linked to high recruitment costs, and to sending countries, which are concerned about the exploitative practices of recruitment agencies.

Coordination could extend to the regional level. A regional authority at the ASEAN level could even be established to monitor recruitment agencies (IOM 2015). This authority could provide best practices on recruitment and work on mainstreaming them, create an inventory of recruitment agencies and publish information on agency performance, and even extend the code of conduct approach to the regional level. Additionally, this regional authority could also provide some basic labor market services to potential migrant workers, including gathering and publishing job openings in typical destinations for ASEAN migrants, as the Philippines does for its migrants, and providing information about the types of skills needed, salaries to be expected, and working conditions in these countries.

Employment

Employment terms

Recommendation 18: Use employment terms in conjunction with entry paths to differentiate migrants. Employment terms can be used in conjunction with entry paths to differentiate migrants according to skills and productivity. Receiving countries can offer more generous terms to more highly skilled migrants, including lengthier employment passes and the ability to bring dependents. This is the model Singapore follows, with employment terms dictated by different skill levels. More generous employment terms can also be used to reward productivity improvements. Chung, Choi, and Lee (2015) use firm surveys to show that in Korea's EPS the productivity of migrant workers tends to be about 50 percent of their local counterparts' in the first year of employment, 80 percent in the second year, and 100 percent in the third. The longer migrants are employed in a receiving country, their findings suggest, the more productive they become as they learn language and technical skills and become accustomed to the work culture. Consistent with these findings, Korea allows EPS workers to upgrade their employment permit to an E-7 visa for semiskilled foreign workers, which is not subject to a limitation on the employment period. ASEAN countries could consider lengthier employment terms for workers receiving additional training or for workers renewing employment passes.

Recommendation 19: Allow migrant workers to change employers. Flexibility in employment terms can improve matches between employers and foreign workers. In most ASEAN receiving countries, foreign migrants are tied to a single employer. This means that migrant workers can be sent home if their employer no longer needs them, regardless of the larger economic need and the fact that these workers cannot change employers if offered another job at a higher wage or if mistreated. This rigidity in the labor market for foreign workers likely limits productivity by preventing better matches between employers and workers; it also makes foreign workers vulnerable to mistreatment by employers who can, in essence, revoke their employment pass. In Korea's EPS, foreign workers can change jobs up to three times. This provision reflects lessons learned from the country's previous training scheme for migrant workers in which trainees often changed job sites and so became undocumented. Both Singapore and Malaysia have a type of employment pass that is not employer-specific, but in both countries the pass is only available to very highly skilled migrants.

Recommendation 20: Expedite the renewal process for employment passes. The renewal process for employment passes should be easy for both employers and foreign workers. The renewal of passes for foreign workers is a signal from employers that foreign labor is still needed and that a particular foreign worker meets the needs of the employer. Renewal procedures should then be limited with requirements such as additional medical examinations subject to rigorous cost-benefit analysis. To expedite renewal of employment passes, a trusted employer scheme could be created to limit renewal steps for previously compliant firms or for those whose profile makes them unlikely to violate employment or recruitment procedures.

Protection

Recommendation 21: Provide comparable protection to migrant and local workers. Differences in employment protections between migrant and local workers can create unfair competition and leave migrant workers exposed to abuses. Migrant and local workers have different needs for protection. For instance, migrant workers may need insurance to cover emergency repatriation but may wish to avoid contributing to pensions that they are not eligible to recover. However, these differing needs should not mean less protection or cheaper labor. Employers will hire more migrant workers when they are eligible for fewer benefits and so impose less of a cost, all else equal. This is the case in Malaysia, where employers must contribute 12 percent of a local worker's salary to the Employees Provident Fund compared to just RM 5 for a foreign worker. Bi- and multilateral social security agreements can help ensure migrants' equitable participation in social protection schemes and equitable access to benefits and remove discriminatory social protection laws. Such agreements are more likely to succeed in a migration corridor with significant flows, with similar schemes in the home and host countries, and with administrative arrangements that are computerized (Holzmann 2016). Enforcement of protections that are in place is also critical. Lack of enforcement of protections for foreign workers—such as minimum wages, hours worked, and payment of wages—can make migrants cheaper to employ despite de jure protections. Ensuring that foreign workers are not cheaper either by design or in practice can discourage overreliance on migrant workers and enhance protections for them.

Recommendation 22: Involve civil society in ensuring that migrant workers have access to protection. Particularly in countries with limited capacity and resources, civil society partners are important to hold policy makers and employers accountable for protecting local and migrant workers. Civil society organizations exist in all ASEAN countries and can help provide training to migrant workers, connect migrant workers with government resources, and monitor the performance of recruitment agencies in both sending and receiving countries and employers in receiving countries. Engagement with civil society groups can extend government resources and provide input to both policy makers about conditions on the ground and additional actors who can assist in implementing government policy.

Recommendation 23: Ensure that deployment requirements protect migrant workers without being overly burdensome. Sending countries should balance protections for migrant workers with the need to provide an efficient deployment process. The departure process for migrants in several ASEAN sending countries is very involved, requiring significant documentation and interaction with several different public agencies. This increases the time costs of out-migration and can lead migrants to seek out informal channels. Providing model employment contracts with protections that should be included for recruitment agencies to follow is one potential method for protecting migrants while also limiting the need for bureaucratic oversight. One-stop centers to process migrant documents and the establishment of local offices to process migrants for departure could also speed up the deployment process. Governments of Pacific Island countries assist with documentation for migrant workers' visa applications to work in Australia and New Zealand.

Recommendation 24: Consider predeparture loans to help migrants finance migration costs. Sending countries could consider providing loans to migrant workers. Potential migrant workers, particularly poorer and low-skilled ones, may not migrate because of high migration costs (McKenzie and Rapoport 2010). Source-country actions to facilitate migration—including removing information, job search, and documentation barriers—do not seem to increase international migration (Beam, McKenzie, and Yang 2015). However, there is some indirect evidence that easing financial constraints may be an effective way for sending countries to incentivize additional migration. Recent research from Mexico shows that poor households receiving cash transfers from the government program *Oportunidades* increased their out-migration by about 50 percent after receiving their first transfers (Angelucci 2015). Other evidence comes from internal migration in Bangladesh. When households in a famine-prone region were offered an incentive to send a seasonal migrant internally to an urban area, there was a significant increase in the number of seasonal migrants, and households that received the incentive were more likely to migrate subsequently (Bryan, Chowdhury, and Mobarak 2014). The authors argue that the incentive helped households overcome a poverty trap in which the risk of failed migration prevents households from migrating. Providing loans may then allow more, poorer potential migrants to migrate, opening up more job opportunities to the poorest households.

Bangladesh and several other sending countries have or are starting predeparture loan programs for migrants. The nongovernmental development organization BRAC has developed a migration loan program in Bangladesh. The loan program, begun in 2011, provides loans of between US$300 and US$3,700 to migrants with a one-month grace period and a maximum two-year payback. The loans are provided to migrants only after work contracts and travel documents are verified. Predeparture orientation services are made available to recipients. The loan is designed both to finance migration and to provide a bridge for remaining household members until the migrant begins work abroad. A total of 194,000 migrant workers had received these loans as of June 2016. Loans based on remittances are also available. The loans enable households to make more significant lump sum investments on the basis of remittance flows. Forty thousand households received these loans between June 2014 and June 2016. While the loan program has not yet been evaluated, recent research shows that many would-be migrants fail to leave the country because of financial constraints or abuse by recruitment agents (Das et al. 2014). This suggests that a loan program may be an effective response. In ASEAN, the government of Vietnam permits migrants to borrow from the Vietnam Bank for Agriculture and Rural Development at more favorable conditions such as no collateral requirements (Ishizuka 2013; Le and Mont 2014). The 62 poorest districts program covers travel-related expenses and provides preferential credit to poor workers; moreover, a pilot program in the 28 poorest of these districts pays the entire cost of migrating. In Sri Lanka, the Sri Lanka Bureau of Foreign Employment has provided subsidized predeparture loans since 2002 to cover the costs of expenses such as plane tickets, but experiences have been mixed, with reports of repayment problems (Martin 2009). A similar problem plagued a loan program in the Philippines that was eventually terminated because of a lack of repayment. Nepal is planning to offer subsidized predeparture loans to potential migrants through a Labor Bank (Nepal, MOLE 2013).

Recommendation 25: Control remittance costs and expand access to formal remittance channels. Reducing remittance costs can increase the amount of remittances sent home. Several impact evaluations and other nonexperimental research have found that reducing remittance costs has a large positive impact on the amount of remittances sent (McKenzie and Yang 2015). For example, Aycinena, Martinez, and Yang (2010) find that remittance fee reductions of US$1 for Salvadoran migrants in Washington, DC, led to fee savings of US$0.47 per month but an increase in average remittances sent of US$25. Increasing access to formal remittance channels in sending countries—including through expanding access to and use of mobile money transfers, and removing domestic regulations that are anticompetitive or lack clarity—can reduce remittance costs. Efforts to target remittances to uses with more significant development impacts, such as toward education or community infrastructure projects, have had mixed success (McKenzie and Yang 2015).

Recommendation 26: Work toward the portability of social protection benefits. Making social protection benefits portable is an important part of providing comparable protection. Even where local and migrant workers have equal access to social protection benefits, migrant workers are often limited in the extent to which they can access these benefits when back in their home country. This may incentivize migrants to seek out informal employment if they are required to contribute to social protection schemes but are unable to benefit from them. Making benefits portable can eliminate an incentive for informality while also increasing protection for migrants. Portability can even be an incentive for exit, as foreign workers maintain access to social protection benefits even upon repatriation.

Recommendation 27: Use orientation programs to increase migrant workers' knowledge. Orientation programs have the potential to improve migrant workers' experience abroad. Orientation programs are provided by most ASEAN countries before a migrant's departure for employment abroad. These programs seek to improve protection for migrant workers by expanding their knowledge of their rights, of the destination country, and of available complaint mechanisms. Evidence on the impact of these trainings is limited (McKenzie and Yang 2015). The Philippines is generally lauded for its commitment to increasing the knowledge of migrant workers. Some good practices identified with its approach are involving local governmental and nongovernmental partners to incorporate a rights perspective; creating the Post-Arrival Orientation Seminar to ensure that learning does not stop at departure; developing orientation programs for recruiters; and providing migration information at the local level (Asis and Agunias 2012). Use of a standardized curriculum and oversight of implementation to ensure that all migrants undertake orientation seem to be key elements of success. Offering orientation programs to migrant workers after their arrival in the destination, as the Philippines does in some cases, may help reinforce knowledge gained during predeparture training. BRAC's migration program in Bangladesh has focused significant attention on providing information to migrants to facilitate safe migration, and has supplemented information provision with community-driven programs to enforce accountability among labor brokers (box 9.6). The Pacific Islands involve destination country representatives in their predeparture orientations through audiovisual material and training of local officials.

BOX 9.6
BRAC's migration program

The nongovernmental development organization BRAC has developed a suite of migration programs to assist Bangladeshi migrants. BRAC's migration program, which began in 2006 and now covers 124 of 490 subdistricts (*upazilas*), provides services to migrants before their migration decision, before and during migration, and upon return with the objective of promoting safe migration and successful reintegration. Much of the program's services are information provision and involve facilitating access to skills and language training, but extend beyond these in some cases to involve aiding migrants abroad.

Migration Community Volunteers provide help to migrants with documentation. Migration forums have been created at the community level to help migrants access arbitration in case of wrongdoing by brokers. Safe Migration Facilitation Centers provide support services, including legal aid and predecision orientations with information on the social and economic costs of migrating and referral services for skills and language training. The Safe Migration for Bangladeshi Workers program, undertaken in collaboration with the World Bank, has worked to strengthen community-based organizations to provide information and life skills to potential migrants during the migration decision process and to assist with remittance management. Reintegration services have also been developed in collaboration with UN Women, particularly for returning women migrants. Migration loans are also available to potential migrants through the BRAC's Migration Loan Program.

Financial literacy programs can improve financial knowledge, though the design of these programs and their targeted beneficiaries are particularly important. A pilot program providing financial literacy training to migrant domestic workers in the Greater Malang area and the Blitar District of East Java in Indonesia had a positive impact on financial awareness and knowledge, budgeting, and savings but no impact on the quantity or frequency of remittances (Doi, McKenzie, and Zia 2014). Notably, effects were most pronounced when both the migrant and a family member received training, less pronounced when just the family member received training, and absent when only the migrant received training. Awareness of mandatory migrant insurance increased significantly (26 percentage points) in households receiving the training program in cases in which both the migrant and the migrant's family member received the training. Impacts were smaller when just the migrant or just the family member received the training. Overall, several impact evaluations have shown that financial literacy programs can be positive, but have different impacts depending on the type of intervention (McKenzie and Yang 2015).

Recommendation 28: Promote skills upgrading and recognition. Promoting economic integration in destination countries through skills recognition and skills upgrading can leverage the skills of migrants and improve their ability to contribute productively to destination countries. Policies that facilitate migrant workers' integration into destination country labor markets can help ensure that migrant skills match the occupations in which migrants work. For instance, skill and qualification recognition schemes can avoid the problems of brain waste when more highly skilled migrants are overqualified for their jobs. Additionally, providing language and other training to migrant workers can increase their productivity, reduce costs for employers by reducing turnover, and promote social cohesion. Singapore offers training to migrants to improve their skills while in Singapore, and it offers preferential levies to employers who hire more skilled migrants, including those who have gained experience working in Singapore. The involvement of employers in the design of training programs for migrants is critical. MOUs and bilateral agreements may offer a good opportunity to establish training and certification programs, as has been done between Ecuador and Spain and with the Migration Information and Management Center in Mali for migration from Africa to the European Union.

Sending countries can also increase the capacity of their migrants to benefit from migration through skills recognition and skills upgrading. Migrants may be employed in lower-skilled occupations that do not suit their skills if host country qualifications are not recognized in destination countries. The ASEAN Economic Community's use of mutual recognition arrangements to recognize professional qualifications across borders is an attempt to overcome this problem. However, there is room for human capital development organizations in sending countries to assist even less-skilled migrants to have their skills recognized. The Technical Education and Skills Development Authority in the Philippines helps migrants obtain the skills necessary for jobs available abroad. Sri Lanka's Ministry of Youth Affairs and Skill Development and its technical education and vocational training institutions provide technical support for training for migrants of different skill levels (Thimothy et al. 2016).

Recommendation 29: Consider migrant welfare funds to protect migrants. Migrant worker welfare funds are a devoted source of funds to assist migrants throughout the migration process. These funds require migrants to make a deposit, at times mandatory, to a fund that is then used to provide services such as predeparture training in skills necessary for employment abroad; support for repatriation in the case of abusive employment, illness, emergency at home, or other hardship; access to social protection, such as health, life, accident, or disability insurance; and help for returning migrants to reintegrate into the labor force (IOM 2015).

The implementation and management of migrant welfare funds is particularly important to ensure that the benefits provided are those that migrants need and use. The funds require start-up capital from the government; identification of a reliable financial administrator; an office devoted to running the fund in the source country and labor attachés in destination countries; a board of directors with representatives from government, recruitment agencies, trade unions, and civil society; and program offerings that are targeted to the needs of migrants (ILO 2015).

The Philippines provides a useful model of a migrant welfare fund. The Overseas Workers Welfare Administration is funded by a mandatory US$25 contribution paid by a migrant worker's employer. The fee is paid at the time a migrant receives a contract to work abroad, and membership lasts for the duration of the contract and can be renewed when a new contract is signed (IOM 2013). The administration is tasked with providing services including insurance and legal aid to Philippine workers when abroad and after repatriation. Membership benefits include insurance in the case of disability and death, education and training assistance including predeparture orientation, legal and other assistance in the Philippines and abroad, and reintegration assistance. The administration also provides repatriation assistance for all foreign workers, regardless of their membership. The Board of Trustees is composed of the secretary and undersecretary of the Department of Labor and Employment; representatives from other government agencies; and representatives from the land- and sea-based migrant worker sectors, the sea-based sector, women, labor, and management. The Overseas Workers Welfare Administration has 31 posts abroad and 17 offices in the Philippines with 377 permanent staff.

Several other Asian sending countries use migrant welfare funds. Pakistan's Overseas Pakistani Foundation manages a welfare fund that takes out insurance for accidental death and disability for registered migrant workers who pay a US$6 premium (World Bank 2016a). Plans are also under way to create a pension for migrant workers. In Nepal, migrants must pay a US$10 fee to a welfare fund that also receives funds from recruitment agencies' security deposits and licensing fees (IOM 2015). The fund provides training, employment programming for return migrants, medical treatment, and child care for the dependents of migrants. Sri Lanka's welfare fund includes an insurance scheme to which migrant workers must pay US$25 plus a US$2 facilitation fee for natural and accidental death and disability coverage (del Rosario 2008). Bangladesh, India, and Thailand also have migrant welfare funds.

Recommendation 30: Install labor attachés in destination countries. Sending countries can use labor attachés to improve the access of migrant workers to protection while abroad. Labor attachés can be particularly useful for sending countries because they provide an in-country source of assistance to migrant workers. Although the destination country controls whether such attachés can be located in the embassy, the source country is able to define the types of services offered, and can offer legal and other assistance that may not otherwise be available. Resources for and training of labor attachés are a challenge for many ASEAN countries. However, having a representative in a destination country provides migrant workers a vital resource that understands the challenges they face. India presents an interesting model. The Indian Community Welfare Fund, which operates in 43 countries with a large Indian population, is administered by diplomats overseas and provides support to migrant workers in distressed situations (Thimothy et al. 2016).

Recommendation 31: Use MOUs, bilateral agreements, and regional forums to set protection standards. Sending countries can use MOUs and bilateral agreements to establish protection standards. These agreements have often been used to clarify protections available to migrant workers; they have even included model employment contracts that specify conditions such as wages, hours worked, and rest days. While these agreements often do not supersede domestic labor law, they can be a forum for source countries to discuss and reinforce migrant workers' equal access to labor protections. Allowing employers and workers to participate in the negotiation of these agreements and making them public can help establish expectations and provide civil society a role in helping oversee their implementation.

The ASEAN Secretariat can play a key role in migrant worker protection. The secretariat could establish a suggested list of minimum protection standards for migrant workers and even a model employment contract that sending and receiving countries could use in developing their own model contracts. It could draw from both international conventions and regional best practices when developing these standards, and encourage ASEAN member states to ratify relevant conventions. Information about the laws on migrant workers' access to different forms of protection could be published on the secretariat's website for the use of migrant workers, recruitment agencies, and government officials in sending countries. ASEAN could assist with developing best practices to control remittance costs and provide public information on these costs.

Exit

Sanctions and incentives

Recommendation 32: Use both sanctions and exit incentives in destination countries to encourage voluntary return. Sanctions and exit incentives can work together in destination countries to encourage voluntary repatriation at the end of a migrant's employment term, but lower migration costs are also important. A recent model of return migration suggests that lower migration costs reduce both the likelihood of overstay and the length of overstay when it occurs (Djajić and Vinogradova 2015). In addition to negative incentives for employers to encourage on-time return, as in Singapore and Malaysia, wages might also be withheld from migrants or deposited in a compulsory savings scheme until they return to their source country. In Korea, employers are required to enroll in Departure Guarantee Insurance and workers in Return Cost Insurance. The employer's monthly contribution of 8.3 percent of wages is available to workers when they depart Korea or change employers, while the Return Cost Insurance, covering the return cost for workers leaving Korea, is available only when workers complete their employment term. Similarly, Canada's Seasonal Agricultural Workers Program requires workers to contribute to a compulsory savings scheme that is only available upon a worker's return to the source country. However, withholding funds increases the risk for migrant workers who are vulnerable to unscrupulous employers who allow their work status to expire (OECD 2013). The design of these policies is critical. Though sanctions on employers should decrease both the probability and length of overstay, if salary withholding or exit penalties are insufficient to eliminate overstay, they will actually increase its length (Djajić and Vinogradova 2015).

Positive incentives for return also exist. This type of incentive includes tax rebates; guarantees of future employment; and assistance with transportation, medical examinations, and document preparation (OECD 2013). EPS workers in Korea can receive free vocational training and job counseling during employment; job matching services with Korean employers in their home countries; and access to returnee networks that Korea has created to expand job opportunities.

Recommendation 33: Use MOUs and bilateral agreements to facilitate exit. Collaboration between sending and receiving countries, particularly through MOUs and bilateral agreements, can facilitate exit. Sending and receiving countries often share an interest in ensuring that migrants return home safely, creating room for collaboration on systems of sanctions for overstay that work together with inducements for return. Such agreements can contemplate how costs can be shared for repatriation of foreign workers between destination and source countries. Additionally, MOUs and bilateral agreements can govern the portability of savings and other social security rights between sending and receiving countries, allowing migrant workers to retain benefits they have earned in the destination and thereby incentivizing return. These agreements are most likely to succeed in migration corridors with significant flows, similar schemes, and computerized administrative arrangements and when they begin with a focus on a few benefits such as pensions, work-related injury, or health care (Holzmann 2016; Holzmann and Koettl 2015).

Diaspora engagement

Recommendation 34: Create diaspora engagement and return programs. Sending country policies to engage with and incentivize the return of their diaspora can generate numerous benefits for home countries. Return migrants bring both financial and human capital resources with them. Members of the diaspora who remain abroad can be sources of learning for local experts and of financial connections to destination countries. Diaspora engagement policies help construct diaspora networks that circulate ideas, technology, and even capital (Dickerson and Özden 2017). Programs such as Argentina's Research and Scientists Abroad (RAICES), Thailand's Reverse Brain Drain project, and Ethiopia's Diaspora Volunteer Program seek to create linkages with talented members of the diaspora to assist in the host country. Jamaica has a database of migrants now working abroad that employers can use to identify potential workers (McKenzie and Yang 2015). In India, the Overseas Indian Facilitation Centre (OIFC) engages in investment facilitation and in creating knowledge networks, and the Financial Services Division in the Ministry of Overseas Indian Affairs provides advice on investing in India (Thimothy et al. 2016). Return migration policies seek to break down policy barriers to return and help incentivize it through recognition of professional qualifications and through tax, citizenship, and residency benefits for repatriated migrants, their spouses, and their dependents (Dickerson and Özden 2017). There is limited evidence of the effectiveness of these programs, and their coverage is limited (McKenzie and Yang 2015). But in Malaysia, a recent impact analysis of TalentCorp Malaysia's Returning Expert Programme found positive results. The program, which provides incentives for high-skilled Malaysians abroad to repatriate, was found to increase the probability of return by 40 percent for applicants with an existing job offer while having only a modest impact on government finances (Del Carpio et al. 2016). Good practices for effective diaspora engagement and return migration include clear objectives, a targeted diaspora group, a defined budget, and clear program terms (Dickerson and Özden 2017).

Reintegration

Recommendation 35: Conduct more research on helping migrants reintegrate into the labor market. More research is necessary into how sending countries can help reintegrate repatriating workers into their labor markets. Source countries can offer reintegration benefits to returning migrants. These can include active labor market policies to help migrants find jobs or start businesses upon return. This type of intervention may be necessary to help reintegrate migrants into a labor force in which they have lost the networks to find jobs. However, there is little research on the effectiveness of reintegration programs. Audits of programs offered in the Philippines have found significant challenges and little evidence of success (Philippines, COA 2016a; Philippines, COA 2016b).

Enforcement

Coordination of enforcement

Recommendation 36: Balance border security and interior enforcement. The impact of the enforcement of entry policies is not always straightforward. Evidence from the United States suggests that significantly increased resources spent on border enforcement have not deterred irregular immigrants (Gathmann 2008; Hanson 2006) and that more deportations and tighter border controls can actually increase the unemployment of low-skilled locals. (Chassamboulli and Peri 2015). In fact, increased enforcement at the border can decrease the outflow of irregular migrants from host countries and so result in a higher population of undocumented immigrants (Massey and Pren 2012). Interior enforcement can be effective in reducing the benefits of undocumented migration with some evidence that the deterrent effect is more cost-effective than that of border enforcement, though this area is less well studied (Roberts, Alden, and Whitley 2013; Orrenius 2014; Bohn and Lofstrom 2012; Orrenius and Zavodny 2014; Wein, Liu, and Motskin 2009). However, interior enforcement involves its own unintended consequences including informality and increased use of fraudulent documents (Orrenius and Zavodny 2015; Bohn and Lofstrom 2012). Indeed, migration flows depend on more than border enforcement alone. Economic conditions are generally a more important determinant of undocumented migration than border enforcement (Orrenius and Zavodny 2015). Migrants adapt even where border security is effective. One study in the United States found that increased border enforcement shifted undocumented migration to more remote, more time-intensive, and more dangerous border crossings (Gathmann 2008).

Effective enforcement of immigration laws requires coordination among agencies to develop the right balance of border security and interior enforcement. Ensuring that immigrants do not enter and work without proper documentation requires more than border control, which while effective in some cases is also costly, particularly along long borders like Thailand's borders with Lao PDR and Myanmar. Interior enforcement measures that target employers to ensure that they are using documented labor and that they are treating immigrant workers appropriately can be effective.

Recommendation 37: Leverage data to improve enforcement in both sending and receiving countries. Good recordkeeping is a critical component of enforcement for both sending and receiving countries. Studies of minimum wage enforcement suggest that accurate recordkeeping increases the ability of enforcement agencies to monitor compliance (Del Carpio and Pabon 2014). This likely extends to monitoring of emigration and immigration, as well-kept and standardized recruitment and employment records allow enforcement officers to assess compliance with recruitment practices, migration rules, and employment protections.

The ability to share data on migrants across agencies increases the power of existing data in enforcement efforts. Migrants are in contact with several agencies in both sending and receiving countries before, during, and after migration. Information technology systems and databases that are interoperable and allow different agencies to upload and exchange information would lead to increases in efficiency and improve enforcement targeting. The United States recently adopted such a coordinated approach in its Person Centric Query Service that compiles data from several different agencies at the federal and state level while also seeking to address concerns about privacy and agency authority by aggregating data and displaying it only temporarily (Rockwell 2016). In Korea, public agencies are encouraged to use a standardized database with identity information that can then be used to analyze data across agencies (Korea, Ministry of Justice 2009). Sharing data could be particularly useful between public agencies in sending countries and their labor attachés and other representatives abroad. The ability to share information on migrants, employers, and recruitment agencies could improve oversight of good and bad recruitment agencies and employers and help target assistance to migrant workers in case of emergency.

A shared and interoperable data platform for agencies involved in immigration enforcement can better leverage existing border control and employment inspection resources. The United States Department of Homeland Security has studied how border surveillance technology, the number of border patrol agents, available places in detention centers, worksite inspectors, and targeted versus random worksite inspections impact the number of undocumented immigrants (Chang, Reilly, and Judson 2012). Risk-based approaches to employer and recruitment agency verification, which use past behavior or certain characteristics to determine the risk of violations, can help to streamline and hasten approval processes or target inspections. Data can also be used to predict the types of employers that are likely to hire undocumented migrants, which can help target limited enforcement resources. Similar approaches can be applied to recruitment agencies. Most of these data are already collected by different agencies in ASEAN countries, and could be used together to study the best mix of immigration enforcement measures and to target enforcement resources.

Targeting of enforcement

Recommendation 38: Increase enforcement efforts on employers. Enforcement of migration laws on employers, and not just migrant workers, can improve compliance with immigration laws. Migrant workers are often at greater risk of sanction for immigration violations than their employers. Korea and Singapore have worked to strengthen enforcement of violations by employers. In Korea, the Ministry of Justice undertakes raids at job sites with warrants, and fines employers that have hired undocumented migrants. Those found violating labor laws or EPS-related rules are subject to fines and are no longer eligible to participate in the EPS. Inspectors also seek to resolve conflicts between workers and employers proactively. Singapore imposes significant fines on employers with jail terms possible for repeat offenders.

Efforts to increase compliance with migration regulations among employers should also involve policies to positively incentivize compliance. In some OECD countries, accreditation or sponsorship schemes are used to engage employers and reward them for compliance. These systems evaluate compliance with relevant employment and immigration laws, employer history of approved applications, their recruitment of workers, their resources and training systems, and their recruitment and training of local workers (OECD 2013). Benefits of taking part in the schemes vary. In the United Kingdom, lower-rated firms must submit action plans for how they will improve their ratings. In New Zealand, accredited employers are exempt from the labor market test of whether a local can fill a job opening. Australia offers priority processing. Such systems may work better for larger employers that employ migrant workers consistently, but could also be used to help SMEs that do not have the recruitment networks of larger firms.

Recommendation 39: Consider introducing joint and several liability for recruiters. Sending countries could consider introducing joint and several liability for recruiters as has been done in the Philippines. One of this country's most important efforts in extending the reach of its domestic regulations is the requirement that private recruitment agencies agree to joint and several liability with a foreign worker's employer. This means that recruitment agencies handle any claims or liabilities resulting from contract infringements, including unpaid wages, death and disability benefits, and repatriation costs. This requirement gives recruitment agencies an incentive to work with reliable employers and to oversee the treatment of foreign workers while they are abroad. Such a requirement could also work alongside improved complaint mechanisms to ensure that migrant worker grievances are heard and addressed.

Recommendation 40: Ensure that workers have access to complaint mechanisms. Improving access to complaint mechanisms would allow migrants better access to redress when recruitment terms are violated or when they are overcharged for recruitment fees. In much of ASEAN, formal procedures for migrants to register complaints are underdeveloped. This lack of access is compounded because, lacking resources, enforcement agencies typically rely on complaints to investigate firms for recruitment violations. Migrant Resource Centers, which combine access to migration information with complaint mechanisms, have opened in several ASEAN countries with the assistance of the ILO. These are important first steps in providing migrants with access to grievance mechanisms. However, formal procedures for resolving disputes between migrants and recruitment agencies must be improved. An assessment of complaint mechanisms in Bangladesh, Cambodia, Sri Lanka, and Thailand finds that, to be effective, these mechanisms must be gender responsive and have well-trained staff and a unified approach (ADBI, ILO, and OECD 2016).

Recommendation 41: Ensure that regularization programs balance inclusiveness and fairness. Regularization campaigns are widely used to regularize undocumented migrants, but attention should be paid to objectives and design. For the host country, regularization campaigns have both benefits, including additional tax revenue, and costs, such as additional transfers to newly regular immigrants (Orrenius and Zavodny 2012). Host countries must also consider how regularization campaigns will affect current and future flows of irregular migrants, including by stimulating increased undocumented migration during the amnesty campaign as migrants seek to be included or after as migrants expect future amnesties (Orrenius and Zavodny 2003). In launching a regularization campaign, policy makers must balance inclusiveness, the reach of the campaign, and fairness, as perceived by the public, while also considering cost-effectiveness and the likelihood of eligible migrants complying with regularization requirements (Rosenblum 2010).

Policy recommendations for domestic labor mobility

Recommendation 42: Reduce rigidities in the domestic labor market. Reforms of domestic labor market policy work alongside migration policies. Domestic labor market policies can reduce internal mobility costs by making it easier for local workers to switch sectors, occupations, or locations at home rather than abroad. Box 9.7 discusses China's efforts to reduce domestic labor mobility costs and improve internal mobility through the Rural Migrant Skills Development and Employment Project. Domestic labor market policies can also complement labor-receiving strategies. Evidence from Europe suggests

---

BOX 9.7

The Rural Migrant Skills Development and Employment Project in China

Internal labor mobility has been a characteristic feature of the Chinese economy over the past 30 years. Wage differentials, labor surpluses in rural areas due to increased agricultural productivity, and labor shortages in urban areas have all been contributing factors to the large flows of migrants from rural to urban areas. According to the Chinese Rural Household Survey, approximately one in every three workers in urban areas is a migrant.

Rural migrants in China tend to be employed in low-skilled occupations characterized by a high risk of work-related injuries, but were rarely covered by social insurance programs or any form of worker protection. In addition, workers coming from rural areas mainly used informal channels to obtain information on job openings and working conditions in urban centers. Finally, rural migrants had limited access to training opportunities to build the skills required in the urban labor market before departure and, even after arrival, were very unlikely to benefit from training provided by employers. To address these issues, the Chinese government introduced various programs and initiatives aimed at relaxing and removing some of the constraints faced by workers migrating from rural to urban areas.

The Rural Migrant Skills Development and Employment Project was introduced by the government of China to improve the earnings and working conditions of rural workers moving to urban areas. Financed by the World Bank, this project aimed to achieve its objectives by (1) increasing access to skills training; (2) improving the provision of public employment services; and (3) improving labor protections including by providing legal services and labor mediation and arbitration.

Implemented in three provinces or autonomous regions (Anhui, Nigxia, and Shandong) between 2008 and 2015, the project helped ease the transition of rural migrants to urban centers, thereby helping to reduce domestic labor mobility costs. In particular the following targets were achieved: (1) an increase in the total number of trainees from rural areas in project schools; (2) an increase in the number of graduates finding employment in the occupation for which they were trained within six months; (3) an increase in the use of local public employment services for counselling, job referral, and career guidance; (4) an increase in the level of wages of the students who graduated from long-term training in project training institutions; and (5) an increase in the number of rural migrants who received legal assistance for addressing labor disputes.

Source: Based on World Bank 2015b.

that flexible labor markets reduce the negative effects of immigrants on locals (Angrist and Kugler 2003; D'Amuri and Peri 2014). Such reforms include reducing rigidities in labor markets, such as dismissal costs, and requirements and restrictions on using temporary workers. A detailed discussion of domestic labor market policy reforms is beyond the scope of this work but is available in *East Asia Pacific at Work: Employment, Enterprise, and Well-Being* (see World Bank 2014).

Notes

1. See the Australian Government, Department of Education and Training submissions webpage "2016-17 Skilled Occupations List Review" (accessed February 9, 2017), https://submissions.education.gov.au/forms/archive/2015_16_sol/pages/index.

2. See TalentCorp's webpage "Critical Occupations List" (accessed July 22, 2017), https://www.talentcorp.com.my/facts-and-figures/critical-occupations-list.

3. The actual, rather than de jure, incidence of the levy on employers versus foreign workers is a concern. According to economic theory, if employers are more sensitive to changes in wages than foreign workers are, the burden of paying the levy may fall on foreign workers in the form of lower wages.

4. See the Singapore Government, Ministry of Manpower's webpage "Calculate Foreign Worker Quota" (accessed July 22, 2017), http://www.mom.gov.sg/passes-and-permits/work-permit-for-foreign-worker/foreign-worker-levy/calculate-foreign-worker-quota.

5. See "Jobstreet.com – Overseas Jobs" (accessed December 9, 2016), http://poea.jobstreet.com.ph/.

6. See the Singapore Government, Ministry of Manpower's webpage "Employment Agencies and Personnel Search (EA Directory)," (accessed November 29, 2016), http://www.mom.gov.sg/eservices/services/employment-agencies-and-personnel-search.

7. See "Empowering Female Migrant Workers to Access Quality Overseas Placement Services in Indonesia" (accessed July 20, 2017), https://www.povertyactionlab.org/es/evaluation/empowering-female-migrant-workers-access-quality-overseas-placement-services-indonesia.

References

Angelucci, Manuela. 2015. "Note: Migration and Financial Constraints: Evidence from Mexico." *Review of Economics and Statistics* 97 (1): 224–28.

Angrist, Joshua D., and Adriana D. Kugler. 2003. "Protective or Counter-Productive? Labour Market Institutions and the Effect of Immigration on EU Natives." *Economic Journal* 113 (488): F302–F331.

ADBI (Asia Development Bank Institute), ILO (International Labor Organization), and OECD (Organisation for Economic Co-operation and Development). 2016. "Labor Migration in Asia: Building Effective Institutions." ADBI, ILO, and OECD, Tokyo.

Asis, Maruja M. B., and Dovelyn Rannveig Agunias. 2012. "Strengthening Pre-Departure Orientation Programmes in Indonesia, Nepal and the Philippines." Migration Policy Institute, Washington, DC.

Australia, DEEWR (Department of Education, Employment and Workplace Relations) and DIC (Department of Immigration and Citizenship). 2009a. "Select Skills: Principles for a New Migration Occupations in Demand List." Review of the Migration Occupations in Demand List Issue Paper 1. Australia Department of Education, Employment and Workplace Relations and Department of Immigration and Citizenship.

———. 2009b. "Future Skills Targeting High Value Skills through the General Skilled Migration Program." Review of the Migration Occupations in Demand List Issue Paper 2. Australia Department of Education, Employment and Workplace Relations and Department of Immigration and Citizenship.

Aycinena, Diego, Claudia Martinez, and Dean Yang. 2010. "The Impact of Transaction Fees on Migrant Remittances: Evidence from a Field Experiment Among Migrants from El Salvador." Working paper, University of Michigan, Ann Arbor.

Batalova, Jeanne, Andriy Shymonyak, and Guntur Sugiyarto. 2017. "Firing Up Regional Brain Networks: The Promise of Brain Circulation in the ASEAN Economic Community." Asian Development Bank, Manila.

Beam, Emily A., David McKenzie, and Dean Yang. 2015. "Unilateral Facilitation Does Not Raise International Labor Migration from the Philippines." *Economic Development and Cultural Change* 64 (2): 323–68.

Bedford, Richard, and Paul Spoonley. 2014. "Competing for Talent: Diffusion of an Innovation in New Zealand's Immigration Policy." *International Migration Review* 48 (3): 891–911.

Birrel, Bob, and Bronwen Perry. 2009. "Immigration Policy Change and the International Student Industry." *People and Place* 17 (2): 64–80.

Birrel, Bob, Ernest Healy, and Bob Kinnaird. 2007. "Cooks Galore and Hairdressers Aplenty." *People and Place* 15 (1): 30–44.

Bohn, Sarah, and Magnus Lofstrom. 2012. "Employment Effects of State Legislation against the Hiring of Unauthorized Immigrant Workers." IZA Discussion Paper 6598, Institute for the Study of Labor (IZA), Bonn.

Bryan, Gharad, Shyamal Chowdhury, and Adhmed Mushfiq Mobarak. 2014. "Underinvestment in a Profitable Technology: The Case of Seasonal Migration in Bangladesh." *Econometrica* 82 (5): 1671–748.

CMA (Center for Migrant Advocacy). 2010. "Bilateral Labour Agreements and Social Security Agreements: Forging Partnership to Protect Filipino Migrant Workers' Rights." Center for Migrant Advocacy, Quezon City.

Chaloff, Jonathan. 2014. "Evidence-Based Regulation of Labour Migration in OECD Countries: Setting Quotas, Selection Criteria, and Shortage Lists." *Migration Letters* 11 (1): 11–22.

Chang, Joseph, Allison Reilly, and Dean Judson. 2012. "A Unified Model of the Illegal Immigration System." Presented at the 2012 American Economic Association Annual Meeting, Chicago.

Chassamboulli, Andri, and Giovanni Peri. 2015. "The Labor Market Effects of Reducing the Number of Illegal Migrants." *Review of Economic Dynamics* 18 (4): 792–821.

Chung, Kiseon, Seori Choi, and Chang Won Lee. 2015. "Analysis on Employment and Work Life of Skilled Migrant Workers Transited from EPS Visa." IOM MRTC Policy Report 2015-01, IOM Migration Research and Training Centre, Goyang, Republic of Korea.

Curtain, Richard, Matthew Dornan, Jesse Doyle, and Stephen Howes. 2016. *Pacific Possible: Labour Mobility—The Ten Billion Dollar Prize.* Australia National University and World Bank.

D'Amuri, Francesco, and Giovanni Peri. 2014. "Immigration, Jobs, and Employment Protection: Evidence from Europe before and during the Great Recession." *Journal of the European Economic Association* 12 (2): 432–64.

Das, Narayan, Alain de Janvry, Sakib Mahmood, and Elisabeth Sadoulet. 2014. "Migration as a Risky Enterprise: A Diagnostic for Bangladesh." Working Paper. University of California, Berkeley.

Del Carpio, Ximena, and Laura Pabon. 2014. *Minimum Wage Policy: Lessons with a Focus on the ASEAN Region.* Washington, DC: World Bank.

Del Carpio, Ximena V., Çağlar Özden, Mauro Testaverde, and Mathis Wagner. 2016. "Global Migration of Talent and Tax Incentives: Evidence from Malaysia's Returning Expert Program." Policy Research Working Paper 7875, World Bank, Washington, DC.

del Rosario, Teresita. 2008. "Best Practices in Social Insurance for Migrant Workers: The Case of Sri Lanka." Asian Regional Programme on Governance of Labour Migration Working Paper 12, International Labor Organization (ILO), Bangkok.

Dickerson, Sarah, and Çağlar Özden. 2017. "Return Migration and Diaspora Engagement." In *Handbook on Migration and Globalization,* edited by Anna Triandafyllidou. Cheltenham, U.K.: Edward Elgar Publishing.

Djajić, Slobodan, and Alexandra Vinogradova. 2015. "Overstaying Guest Workers and the Incentives for Return." *CESifo Economic Studies* 61 (3): 764–96.

Doi, Yoko, David McKenzie, and Bilal Zia. 2014. "Who You Train Matters: Identifying Combined Effects of Financial Education on Migrant Households." *Journal of Development Economics* 109: 39–55.

Gathmann, Christina. 2008. "Effects of Enforcement on Illegal Markets: Evidence from Migrant Smuggling along the Southwestern Border." *Journal of Public Economics* 92: 1926–41.

Hanson, Gordon H. 2006. "Illegal Migration from Mexico to the United States." *Journal of Economic Literature* 44 (4): 869–924.

Holzmann, Robert. 2016. "Do Bilateral Social Security Agreements Deliver on the Portability of Pensions and Health Care Benefits? A Summary Policy Paper on Four

Migration Corridors Between EU and Non-EU Member States." Policy Paper 111, Institute for the Study of Labor (IZA), Bonn.

Holzmann, Robert, and Johannes Koettl. 2015. "Portablity of Pension, Health, and Other Social Benefits: Facts, Concepts, and Issues." *CESifo Economic Studies* 61 (2): 377–415.

Holzmann, Robert, and Yann Pouget. 2011. "Admission Schemes for Foreign Workers: A Labor Market Tool for National Economic Development." World Bank, Washington, DC.

ILO (International Labour Organization). 2015. "Establishing Migrant Welfare Funds in Cambodia, Lao PDR and Myanmar." Policy Brief Issue 3, ILO, Bangkok.

IOM (International Organization for Migration). 2012. *Labour Shortages and Migration Policy*. Brussels: IOM.

———. 2013. *Country Migration Report: The Philippines 2013*. Makati City: IOM.

———. 2015. "Recruitment Monitoring & Migrant Welfare Assistance: What Works?" IOM, Dhaka.

Ishizuka, Futaba. 2013. "International Labor Migration in Vietnam and the Impact of Receiving Countries' Policies." Institute of Developing Economies (IDE) Discussion Paper 414, IDE, Chiba, Japan.

Kim, Min Ji. 2015. "The Republic of Korea's Employment Permit System (EPS): Background and Rapid Assessment." International Migration Papers 199, International Labour Organization, Geneva.

KNOMAD (Global Knowledge Partnership on Migration and Development). 2014. "Technical Workshop on Review of Bilateral Agreements Low-Skilled Labor Migration: Summary," held in Kathmandu, December 1–2.

Korea, Republic of, Ministry of Justice, Korea Immigration Service. 2009. *The First Basic Plan for Immigration Policy: 2008–2012*. Gwacheon-si, Kyunggi-do, Korea: Ministry of Justice.

———. 2012. *The Second Basic Plan for Immigration Policy 2013–2017*. Gwacheon-si, Kyunggi-do, Korea: Ministry of Justice.

Lanto, Nini A. 2015. "Negotiating Bilateral Labor Agreements for the Protection of Overseas Filipino Workers: The Philippine Experience." Presentation for the Senior Executive Seminar on ASEAN Economic Integration and Labour Migration: Challenges and Opportunities, December 7–11, Bali, Indonesia.

Le, Nguyen Huyen, and Daniel Mont. 2014. "Vietnam's Regulatory, Institutional and Governance Structure for International Labor Migration." In *Managing International Migration for Development in East Asia*, edited by Richard H. Adams and Ahmad Ahsan, 199–219. Washington, DC: World Bank.

Martin, Philip. 2009. "Reducing the Cost Burden for Migrant Workers: A Market-based Approach." Paper presented at the Third Meeting of the Global Forum on Migration and Development, November 2–5, Athens.

Massey, Douglas S., and Karen A. Pren. 2012. "Unintended Consequences of US Immigration Policy: Explaining the Post–1965 Surge from Latin America." *Population and Development Review* 38 (1): 1–29.

McKenzie, David, and Hillel Rapoport. 2010. "Self-Selection Patterns in Mexico-U.S. Migration: The Role of Migration Networks." *Review of Economics and Statistics* 92 (4): 811–21.

McKenzie, David, and Dean Yang. 2015. "Evidence on Policies to Increase the Development Impacts of International Migration." *World Bank Research Observer* 30 (2): 155–92.

Nepal, MOLE (Ministry of Labour and Employment). 2013. *Labour Migration for Employment: A Status Report for Nepal: 2013/2014.* Kathmandu: MOLE.

OECD (Organisation for Economic Co-operation and Development). 2013. *Economic Outlook for Southeast Asia, China and India 2014: Beyond the Middle-Income Trap.* Paris: OECD.

———. 2014. *International Migration Outlook 2014.* Paris: OECD.

Orrenius, Pia. 2014. "Enforcement and Illegal Immigration: Enforcement Deters Immigration with Many Unintended Consequences." *IZA World of Labor* 81: 1–10.

Orrenius, Pia, and Madeline Zavodny. 2003. "Do Amnesty Programs Reduce Undocumented Immigration? Evidence from IRCA." *Demography* 40 (3): 437–50.

———. 2012. "The Economic Consequences of Amnesty for Unauthorized Immigrants." *Cato Journal* 32 (1): 85–106.

———. 2014. "How Do E-Verify Mandates Affect Unauthorized Immigrant Workers?" IZA Discussion Paper 7992, Institute for the Study of Labor, Bonn.

———. 2015. "Undocumented Immigration and Human Trafficking." In *Handbook of the Economics of International Migration Volume 1A*, edited by Barry Chiswick and Paul Miller, 659–716. Oxford, U.K.: Elsevier.

Philippines, COA (Commission on Audit). 2016a. "Annual Audit Report on the Philippine Overseas Employment Administration." Quezon City, Philippines.

———. 2016b. "Annual Audit Report on the Overseas Workers Welfare Administration." Quezon City, Philippines.

POEA (Philippine Overseas Employment Administration). 2016. "Governing Board Resolution No. 06 Series of 2016." POEA, Mandaluyong City.

Rivera, John Paolo R., Denise Jannah D. Serrano, and Tereso S. Tullao, Jr. 2013. "Bilateral Labor Agreements and Trade in Services: The Experience of the Philippines." In *Let Workers Move: Using Bilateral Labor Agreements to Increase Trade in Services*, edited by Sebastián Sáez, 109–27. Washington, DC: World Bank.

Roberts, Bryan, Edward Alden, and John Whitley. 2013. *Managing Illegal Immigration to the United States: How Effective Is Enforcement?* New York: Council on Foreign Relations.

Rockwell, Mark. 2016. "How USCIS Consolidates Immigration Data." *Federal Computer Week,* March 11.

Rosenblum, Marc R. 2010. "Immigration Legalization in the United States and European Union: Policy Goals and Program Design." Policy Brief, Migration Policy Institute, Washington, DC.

Thimothy, Rakkee, S. K. Sasikumar, Padmini Ratnayake, and Alvin P. Ang. 2016. "Labour Migration Structure and Financing in Asia." International Labor Organization (ILO), Bangkok.

United Kingdom, MAC (Migration Advisory Committee). 2016. *Review of Tier 2: Balancing Migrant Selectivity, Investment in Skills and Impacts on UK Productivity and Competitiveness.* London: United Kingdom Migration Advisory Committee.

Wein, Lawrence M., Yifan Liu, and Arik Motskin. 2009. "Analyzing the Homeland Security of the U.S.–Mexico Border." *Risk Analysis* 29 (5): 699–713.

Wickramasekara, Piyasiri. 2016. *Review of the Government-to-Government Mechanism for the Employment of Bangladeshi Workers in the Malaysian Plantation Sector.* Geneva: International Labour Organization.

World Bank. 2014. *East Asia Pacific at Work: Employment, Enterprise, and Well-Being.* Washington DC: World Bank.

———. 2015a. *Malaysia Economic Monitor: Immigrant Labour.* Kuala Lumpur: World Bank.

———. 2015b. *China: Rural Migrant Skills Development and Employment Project.* Washington, DC: World Bank.

———. 2016a. "Improving Migrant Workers' Protection: Review of the Indonesian Overseas Migrant Workers' Insurance (Asuransi TKI)." World Bank, Washington, DC.

———. 2016b. *Systematic Country Diagnostic for Eight Small Pacific Island Countries: Priorities for Ending Poverty and Boosting Shared Prosperity.* Washington, DC: World Bank.

www.ingramcontent.com/pod-product-compliance
Lightning Source LLC
Chambersburg PA
CBHW081428270326
41932CB00019B/3129